A Georgian at Princeton

Other books by Robert Manson Myers

HANDEL'S MESSIAH: A TOUCHSTONE OF TASTE (1948)

FROM BEOWULF TO VIRGINIA WOOLF (1952)

HANDEL, DRYDEN, AND MILTON (1956)

RESTORATION COMEDY (1961)

THE CHILDREN OF PRIDE (1972)

A Georgian at Princeton

ROBERT MANSON MYERS

NEW YORK AND LONDON

Harcourt Brace Jovanovich

Printed in the United States of America

Library of Congress Cataloging in Publication Data
Main entry under title:

A Georgian at Princeton.

Letters drawn from the family papers of C. C. Jones.
1. Jones, Charles Colcock, 1804–1863. I. Myers,
Robert Manson, 1921–   II. Jones, Charles Colcock,
1804–1863.
BX9225.J69G46   301.45′19′6073024 [B]   75-33772
ISBN 0-15-135105-8

First edition
B C D E

IN MEMORIAM C. C. J.
OBIIT MDCCCLXIII

THE following story is told exclusively in letters drawn from the voluminous family papers of the Rev. Dr. Charles Colcock Jones (1804–1863), a Presbyterian clergyman of Liberty County, Georgia. The source of each letter is indicated at the end of its title line by the appropriate superior character: *g* (University of Georgia, Athens); *t* (Tulane University, New Orleans). An asterisk (*) terminating a dateline indicates that the date has been supplied or corrected.

The Jones Family

At Maybank, Montevideo, and Arcadia

Rev. Dr. Charles Colcock Jones, *a Presbyterian clergyman*
Mary (Jones) Jones, *his wife*
Charles Colcock Jones, Jr.
Joseph Jones } *their children*
Mary Sharpe Jones

At Social Bluff (Point Maxwell)

Susan Mary (Jones) (Maxwell) Cumming, *twice-widowed sister of the Rev. Dr. C. C. Jones*
Laura Elizabeth Maxwell
Charles Edward Maxwell } *her children*

In Sunbury

Colonel William Maxwell, *a planter*
Elizabeth (Jones) Maxwell, *his wife, half-sister of the Rev. Dr. C. C. Jones*

At Lodebar

Henry Hart Jones, Esq., *a planter, half-brother of Mrs. Mary Jones*
Abigail Sturges (Dowse) Jones, *his wife*

At the Retreat

James Newton Jones, Esq., *a planter, half-brother of Mrs. Mary Jones*
Sarah Jane (Norman) Jones, *his wife*

In Walthourville

Charles Berrien Jones, Esq., *a planter, half-brother of Mrs. Mary Jones*
Marion Susan (Anderson) Jones, *his wife*

In Marietta

Rev. John Jones, *a Presbyterian clergyman, brother of Mrs. Mary Jones*
Jane Adaline (Dunwody) Jones, *his wife*
James Dunwody Jones
Mary Elizabeth Jones } *their children*

Eliza Greene (Low) (Walker) (Robarts) Robarts, *thrice-widowed half-aunt of the Rev. Dr. C. C. Jones*

Mary Eliza Robarts ⎱ *her daughters*
Louisa Jane Robarts ⎰

Joseph William Robarts, *her son, a widower*

Mary Sophia Robarts ⎫
Elizabeth Walton Robarts ⎪ *children of Joseph William Robarts*
Ellen Douglas Robarts ⎬
Joseph Jones Robarts ⎭

A Georgian at Princeton

I

Rev. C. C. Jones *to* Col. *and* Mrs. William Maxwell[t]

Columbia, South Carolina, *Wednesday,* April 17th, 1850

My dear Brother and Sister,

We have had and are now having a good deal of sickness in Columbia in the form of colds and pleurisy and *pneumonia.* Charles, as we wrote you, had an attack of the last which confined him to his bed about a week. He is up again, though he has a cold. Joe is complaining, but about his duties. Mary is pretty well. But our dear daughter has been above a week in bed with a touch of pneumonia, and the fever still continues. Dr. Trezevant was taken sick, and Dr. Fair attends her, and they consult together. Dr. Fair does not consider her dangerously sick, but is anxious to remove the cause of the fever; and we hope the medicines now used may be blessed to her restoration. Her state of mind has been very calm and pleasant. Her mother has conversed particularly with her, and her hope is in the Lord Jesus, and I trust it is a good one.

Cousin Louisa arrived last night from Marietta: well, but looking thin. We were rejoiced to see her. Left Aunt recovering and Cousin Mary and children well.

But we have been called to pass through trials and afflictions within the last ten days; and as I know you wish to know all, will begin at the beginning.

Last week the junior class, numbering some seventy—*Charles's class,* refused to attend Professor Brumby's recitation, which he had fixed at an hour which belonged to another professor, who was absent—the class taking the ground that he had no right to do it without consulting the class, or having an order from the faculty to that effect. Charles, while he was in *doubt* about the point, acted with his class, and did not go to the *first* recitation; but he told his class if the faculty ordered the class to go, he would go if no other went, as the authority of the college and its order must be preserved. He came home, and finding nothing in the constitution of the college on the point, he drew up a brief note to the faculty stating the question at issue between them and Professor Brumby, and requesting the faculty to decide and the class would yield to their decision. This was exactly the course to be pursued; but he could not get a man in his class to unite with him.

Saturday morning last, when the next recitation came on, the president of the college announced the decision of the faculty (they had had a meeting about it), and stated it was both *the law* and *custom* of college, and always had been, and the class *must go to recitation.* Charles came out of the chapel,

3

and in the face of his whole class walked into Professor Brumby's recitation room! After he had been there *two* others came in. The *monitor* and Professor B.'s *assistant* and the professor's *own son,* who were obliged to be there, *were there.* The class thus openly *rebelled.* I felt grateful that my son had the moral courage and decision to do right in the face of his whole class. He said it was harder to go than to stay, but he went, believing it to be his duty. The trial and his being enabled to bear it will, I trust, fit him for other trials which may come upon him of a like kind. We and all his friends and professors have been satisfied with his conduct. We have endeavored to bring up our children *to do right.* If friends will go *with* them, then be glad of their good company and support; but if they will not, then *go alone.* There is no other way. The question is not *who approves* and *who will go* but *what is right and proper to be done.* Everyone must keep his own conscience.

Well, what is the upshot of the whole? Why, the faculty had a meeting on Saturday and suspended *all the rebels,* and added a recommendation to the trustees that they be *expelled.* (This last was, I believe, mitigated.) Did the students submit? No. That night they collected all their class books and burnt them in the campus before Professor Brumby's house, had a funeral sermon or oration, a prayer and doxology, and paraded around the campus with drums and horns and shoutings, dashed in some windows and doors, tore off some palings, and so on! All the members of the class not in the rebellion have taken *dismissions,* and the class is blotted out of college. Not a man remains. Charles at the president's request took a leave of absence for an unlimited time, but will get a dismission, as there is no probability of forming another class.

Here is an affair! What am I to do with my son? He is thrown out of the college by the improper conduct of his class. God has some design in all this which we cannot see into yet.

Nor have we had time to do anything about it so far, for we were when all this happened in deep affliction. Our faithful old friend and servant *Jack* was taken with the prevailing cold two weeks ago. Got nearly well of it, and coming out into the cold damp weather one morning before breakfast, *took a relapse.* A dreadful ague came on in the night. Dr. Trezevant came a little after daylight, bled and relieved him; and for forty-eight hours everything went well with him. And then he took a turn for the worse. On Sunday hope began to give way, and on Monday all was gone; and last night—or rather this morning, half-past two o'clock—*he passed away from us;* and we have now nothing of the good, faithful old man but his cold body sleeping placidly in death, his countenance wearing that smile of life which you remember was so natural and constant with him. I was with him night and day, and am worn down with anxiety and watching. Almost every dose of medicine he took and every spoonful of nourishment he took from my hands. It is a heavy stroke to Mary and myself and the children. It is the loss not only of one of the most faithful and excellent, long-tried servants, but of a devoted, long

4

tried and affectionate friend—to us and to all our family. Jack was one of the family. I know you will sympathize with us and shed a tear for the old man.

But oh, how happy was his deathbed! Not a murmur; a smile for everybody; and his mind clear and stayed on the Saviour to the last! His exercises were very remarkable. No doubt; no distress. He expressed himself ready to depart. Told his mistress "he was in God's sight but a filthy rag," but "his hope was in Jesus"; that "his Saviour was shedding unnumbered mercies all around him." He told me "it was a blessed thing to have a good master and mistress"; that "he could not begin to speak of God's mercies to him."

Seeing that he was failing on Monday morning, I told Marcia (who had been attacked with the same disease, pneumonia, and was lying ill on a cot in the same room) that Jack was not to be with us long, and if she wished to see and converse with him she had better do so now. She, poor thing, could not believe it; said it could not be death; that it was *the turn* in the sickness, and I had better send for the doctor. I helped her on her feet, and she staggered to him and put her hand on his forehead and cheek and said: "Jack, you know me?" "Oh yes, Marcia child," and then gave her his parting counsel in a most clear and touching manner, and begged her no longer to put off her soul's salvation.

I had all the family called, white and black; and as each one came up, he took them one by one by the hand and charged them in the Lord and commended them to God. His reception of Charles was affecting. He was very fond of him, and when I said: "Jack, here is Charles," he reached his hand and said: "Oh, my young master, this is my whole heart." He was very affectionate to his mistress; said to her: "I am so sorry to leave you; I know how you will miss me." He would catch her voice sooner than that of any other person; frequently told her "it was peace with him." We then prayed with him. Whenever religion was mentioned, a smile would come over his countenance. Indeed, it seemed as if the sun shone on his dying bed all the time, and suffered no cloud to rest there. When he was not able to speak above a whisper, I asked him: "Jack, is your mind at rest? Is Christ still precious to you?" And he smiled and raised his hand toward heaven.

He gradually grew weaker from Monday morning till Wednesday morning (17th), when, as I before observed, he died between two and three o'clock. Dr. Fair had insisted that I should not sit up, and so Mary and myself arranged everything. Mr. Rogers kindly with Charles took charge of the medicine, and sent it out at the proper time to faithful men whom we had got to attend upon him; and when he died they carefully laid him out; and he looks like one asleep and that has a pleasant dream.

It is a sad loss to us—not only of a servant but of a friend; and then there were so many thousand associations with Jack. He was a link that connected us with the past—with many of the beloved ones now dead, and with all the living. My dear wife feels it deeply. As I went down to dinner today, and he was not in his place by the table, but was lying dead in the servants' house in

5

the yard, the tears came full and fast and fell down on the tablecloth; and I could not see the knife I held carving in my hand, and gave my seat to Charles and begged Mr. Rogers to ask a blessing! We expect, God willing, to bury him tomorrow at 10 A.M.

But this is not all. Poor Marcia Mary gave up to nurse him; and the day after Jack had his severe relapse she was taken violently ill, and has continued so, with a short intermission of twelve or fifteen hours, when she seemed much better. Yesterday she was so ill Dr. Fair said she might die before Jack. Her case was nearly hopeless. Today she may be a shade better; but you may know how ill she is when Jack died on a bed near her cot, was removed to another room and laid out, and this morning all his clothing and bedding were removed and the bedstead turned up, and she has noticed nothing nor asked for him but once. Her case is peculiarly distressing, for she has no hope that we know of beyond the grave! Has uniformly put off religion, and now she cannot possibly attend to it! Alas, our infatuation and sin! If she dies, it will add sorrow upon sorrow.

The hand of the Lord is heavy upon us. But we would remember His mercies still. We derived much consolation from reading last night at family worship the first two chapters of Job. How hard it is for us to bring ourselves to believe in our own approaching end, and to resolutely prepare for it! I feel that I must look to God and depend upon Him alone to sanctify my afflictions to me; otherwise all will be in vain. Pray for us, and for our dear children, that we may be all sanctified and saved in Christ Jesus our Lord. How much we think and long for you both, and for my dear sister and her children in Savannah! It is useless to wish, but it would be an unspeakable happiness to me and mine if we could all live where we could see each other from day to day. But even then earth is not our home. We shall soon be called away; and therefore let us gird up our loins and seek a better—that is, an heavenly—country, where we shall meet to love and part no more!

Dr. Trezevant told Dr. Fair that "when he first saw Jack he knew him to be an old family servant—a gentleman of the old school; and as old as he was, were he well, and his servant, he would take no man's thousand dollars for him." He has made a great impression on all in Columbia, white and black, who have known him. He was universally respected. For two years the old man has been very punctual in all his duties, and very attentive to religion, and has been ripening for his end. The Sermon on the Mount and the 3rd Chapter of John were favorite portions of his Testament which he used most frequently to read—though he was not a fluent reader.

As this letter will lie over a day or two in Savannah, I shall enclose it to Sister Susan to read and forward to you by Monday's mail. I know she will be glad to read it; and I would write her separately, but then one letter would be the same as the other; and I am so pressed and have to be watching the sick, etc., that I thought I would not wait, but send at once, and so that you both might hear from us now. Mary and Louisa and Mary Sharpe and the

6

boys send love to Aunty and Uncle and to Sister and Laura and Charles. Please write us soon.

Do be kind enough to let Patience know of her uncle's death, who loved her as his own child; also Madison at Henry's. I will write Cato a special letter about his death, which he can have read to all his children. I remain, my dear brother and sister, as ever,

Your affectionate brother,
C. C. Jones.

Rev. C. C. Jones *to* Mrs. Susan M. Cumming[t]

Columbia, Wednesday, April 17th, 1850

My dear Sister,

Please read this letter and envelope it to Brother and Sister for me by Monday's mail. We long to see you. Death makes us long for those we love. Our love to yourself and dear Laura and Charles.

Your affectionate brother,
C. C. J.

Rev. C. C. Jones *to* Col. *and* Mrs. William Maxwell[t]

Columbia, Tuesday, April 23rd, 1850

My dear Brother and Sisters,

I closed my last letter to you on the afternoon of the 17th inst., and sent it to the post office. I walked out into the yard in the dusk of the evening. The heavens were overcast, the yard wet from the recent rain; and the atmosphere about the lot was oppressive. Whether it was the effect of my melancholy state of mind on the death of Jack, the extreme illness of Marcia, and the continued sickness of our dear child and little change for the better, or the reality of things, I cannot tell; but there appeared to be a peculiar gloom hanging over the house and lot, and a mysterious calm that portended some further development in providence, the purport of which it was not given me to understand. A solemn stillness pervaded everything.

The coffin came, and we put our faithful old friend into it. We had all taken our leave of him, and his wife knew not that he was dead. She was herself almost in the article of death. To save the anxiety of watching, and to avoid *rats,* which abounded in the house, I had the coffin lid firmly screwed down. It was a handsome coffin: every respect was shown him in his burial.

The night shut in. The doctor came and prescribed for Marcia; and I engaged a most excellent woman by the name of Isabella (belonging to Mrs. Ewart) to sit up with Marcia and give her medicine while I endeavored to get some rest; for I was much worn down with watching and grief and anxiety. Mrs. Howe's woman Rachel came over to watch with Bella; and John slept in the room, to be ready for any call. The Negroes have a habit in

7

this town of gathering in houses where the dead lie and spending the night in singing, praying, and exhorting; and too frequently it is a scene of excitement, and partakes more of a religious revel than a solemn service. Such a gathering I objected to—first on principle, believing it wrong in the manner carried out by the Negroes; and second on account of the extreme illness of Marcia, and Mary Sharpe's sickness, and all requiring rest. Consequently no Negroes came but one or two, who went away near twelve midnight.

We all lingered around the fire in the sitting room, somehow hard to get to bed. Mr. Rogers wished to sit up to attend to Marcia's medicine, but there being no necessity, he went away about eleven o'clock. The fire in the hearth had burnt down to a few coals—so few Mary could not heat a little water which she needed for Mary Sharpe. Louisa went to bed. I did not, as was the custom with me, go up into my study, but went immediately into our chamber and shortly after to bed, leaving Mary and Charles in the parlor. Joe had gone up to bed. Mary came to bed before I was fairly asleep; and Charles after fixing the fire went up to bed also. It was so late we would not let Phillis and Jane lay the breakfast table, which was always done; and after we went to bed, they soon locked up the back doors and came to bed in a little room between ours and the room Louisa slept in. We were all soon sound asleep.

About half-past one in the morning of the 18th we were aroused by the dreadful cry of "Fire! Fire! The house is all on fire! Come out! Come out! Fire! Fire! Wake them! You'll all be burnt up! Come out! Come out!"

I sprang up, and Mary also, from the bed on the floor where we were sleeping. The room was full of smoke. Mary Sharpe, lying sick on the bedstead, had been awake some time, and smelt the smoke, but supposed it was from the fire in the open stove in the room. Mary's first exclamation was: "Are the boys awake upstairs?" I opened the room door leading into the entry, and she ran upstairs and burst in their door and woke them up. In the meantime in my nightdress I went out of the front door and ran around to the wing of the house to see where and how the fire was. It had caught all the end, and was running up in flames on the sides and windows of the common parlor, and was rushing along the under part of the floor of the house in a roaring sheet of fire.

No time was to be lost. I hurried back, and met Mary coming downstairs. The smoke in the entry and room was suffocating. Louisa had meantime come into our room, and passing through the little room stumbled on Phillis and Jane, and opening the door told them to run for their lives. They ran out of the back entry and down the back steps, now all afire, and so escaped. Mary threw on part of her dress; I a part of mine. Our dear child was perfectly calm. Said she: "Mother, if I am not removed I shall suffocate." I answered: "My dear child, Father will take you in one second." My boots were on—right on left foot and left on right. I took up my child; Mary threw a blanket over her. The flames were running into the blinds of the window at the foot of the bed and popping the glass. As we started to

8

leave the room the light of the fire shined on Mary's watch and mine; they caught her eye; she threw them into her pocket. She caught up her little box containing the family likenesses; and as we were moving, Mary Sharpe said: "Oh, Mother, save my Bible!" But it was too late. We were gasping for air, and hurried to the front door. The boys had come down, and we all went out together. As I came to the door a man met me who I knew not and said: "You cannot come out this way." I was startled for a second. I knew it was the only way. I told him to stand aside, and thrusting him aside, we hastened down the front steps. I was so overcome with the suffocation that I could not hold up my child, but let her fall on her feet. At that instant John was there and said: "Master, give her to me." And he took up his young mistress, and Mary and Louisa went over across the street to Mr. Thompson's.

As soon as they were safe, and the boys, I hastened to the back part of the house to save *the living and the dead* in the servants' house. Joe looked back as we went out the front gate, and the flames were bursting through the entry floor! Mr. Thompson and Mr. Shelton met Mary going over, and hurried past to the house. Mr. Shelton could not get up the front steps. He went to the end of the piazza to a flight of steps leading into the garden. He went up and advanced to the front door to see if anything could be saved. He was driven back by fire and smoke! All entrance was closed by the devouring element!

Persons had now begun to collect. I got some people, and part went in and took up poor Jack in his coffin, and bore him out of the servants' house and carried him across the street and laid him down on the sidewalk. Others took up poor Marcia (almost in a dying state) and put her, cot and all, through the window farthest from the fire; and she was covered with blankets and carried over to Mr. Thompson's also. All now were safe but *Jane*. I had not seen her, and was much distressed, but soon found her and Phillis standing by Jack's coffin, and having under their charge some few things saved out of the servants' house.

Meanwhile Charles and Joseph broke into the loft over the kitchen and set to work with John saving the corn. Mr. Talley went up to help them. Said he in the dark: "Here's a bag broken!"

"Never mind, *Old Daddy*," says Joe. "Pull away! Save it! Better get it out any way than let it burn up here."

Mr. Talley, who lives very near, had come over; and about the time Phillis and Jane made their escape he went into the back entry and pushed open a door and cried "Fire!" but fled out in haste, as fire was all under him. He thought we were still in. We had then just escaped out of the front door.

Seeing all safe at the house, I went over to Mr. Thompson's and found my dear wife and child and Lou in the parlor, surrounded with kind friends, and Mr. and Mrs. Thompson and their family doing all in their power to make them comfortable. I embraced them all, and then went back for the boys. They had saved the corn. Mr. Thompson loaned me a cap. Charles and Joe were in the back yard getting out the horses and carriage. The cow and the calf Mr. Thompson had turned out, and they scampered away in great affright. Charles was without hat, stockings, or shoes, but with pantaloons, coat, and vest. Joe was without hat, stockings, and shoes, and in his night clothes, excepting a pair of thin pantaloons which he jerked on. He heard his Cousin Louisa calling for someone to open the front gate, and he rushed down to her help, and could no more go upstairs to his room. He was away behind the crowd. You know how modest he is. I put my arm around him and carried him over to Mr. Thompson's, and he soon dressed him in a suit of his clothes.

We gathered in Mr. Thompson's parlor. Brother Howe and some other friends were there. I thanked God for our salvation from the devouring fire, and said to Brother Howe: "We must now give thanks to God," and begged him to pray with us, which he did in a most earnest and affecting manner; and our hearts were relieved at a throne of grace!

We looked out. There was the dwelling sinking down in fire—every individual thing in it consuming! We saved nothing but what we stood in, except the few articles named.

But my mind has been and was calm. It was the hand of the Lord! It was mine *to use,* not *to hold* nor *keep.* He took but what He gave—but what was His own. It all resolved itself into a *question of time only.* The time was coming when *I* must be taken from all that was consumed. It pleased God to take all from me and leave me alive. Who were we, then, that we should complain? In all this we would not speak unadvisedly with our lips, nor charge God foolishly. And when we remembered how miraculously He had saved us from the devouring fire (for had Bella discovered the fire a few moments later, some if not all of us must have perished), and how much He had preserved to us, we had nothing to do but to bless His holy name. When we remember our sins, and how that God could justly cast us into everlasting burnings, what afflictions or distresses can possibly come upon us that we ought not to submit to with a quiet and thankful spirit?

The house took fire, as we believe, from the fire in the hearth getting between the bricks and coming in contact with the wood foundation of the hearth and the wooden piece set into the chimney under the hearth. It was from no carelessness; nor was it the work of any incendiary, as some supposed. If I have enemies in Columbia, white or black, I do not know them. If Mrs. Ewart has any, I scarcely think they would burn me up for her sake. If a man wanted plunder, he would not set fire to a private dwelling off by itself, but to some house near to others, or to some store or stores. If anyone set fire to the building, it was a most wanton piece of wickedness imaginable. But I have no idea that it took place in any other way than from the hearth, as I before said. There were *rat holes* in the chimney opposite, and by their burrowing they perhaps loosened the bricks and let in the fire. The place where the fire originated—right under the hearth—would go to show this. From that place it spread out in all directions. It is not the first instance of a house taking fire from such a cause.

You never saw a house burn down as rapidly. It was an *old house,* built of *fat* pine, somewhat *decayed,* the under part dry as punk; and a strong *north-east wind* that drove the fire across the under part of the house. The flames seemed to rise up on all sides from under the house and eat it up. It was impossible to save anything.

I cannot begin to tell you of the kindness and sympathy extended towards us by our friends and the good people of Columbia. Mr. and Mrs. Thompson gave up their bedroom to us, and we stayed with them from the 18th to the 22nd; and had we been their own relations in distress they could not have done more for us. Almost everybody whom we knew called to express their sympathy, and some six or eight families offered us rooms and welcome in their dwellings. Some persons sent baskets of things to eat; others baskets and rolls of clothing and things to make up for Mary and Mary Sharpe. The students in the seminary rigged out Joe from head to foot, and Charles as far as he needed, and took them to room and board with them, where they now are. One gentleman called and tendered me $100, which I thanked him kindly for but declined taking. All my clerical brethren called to see me, and expressed their sorrow, and condoled with me particularly on the *loss of all my library and papers, lectures, and sermons, etc., of every kind—the accumulation of some twenty years or so. A great loss indeed! Can never be restored.* I am in respect to *ministerial stores* burnt out!

But our sad tale is not ended. Our faithful servant *Marcia* did not seem to suffer by her removal, but gradually grew worse and weaker and more insensible, until Saturday morning the 20th, when about eleven o'clock *she breathed her last!* Thus has God taken away our two old and chief stays in the household! Her death is a melancholy one, since she was not pious; and from the time of her being taken to her final insensibility and death she had no time to attend to her soul's concerns, although she told her mistress that she prayed all the time! Alas, the folly of putting off religion to a dying hour, or even of procrastinating it a single day! Her death added to our sorrow.

The day of the fire at ten o'clock (the 18th) I buried Jack in the public graveyard. Charles, Joseph, Mr. Rogers, and Don Fraser and a few Negroes attended him with me to his grave. There I prayed. The early hour of his funeral and the confusion incident on the fire made the attendance small. On Sunday—just *three* days after—I buried his wife by his side! Her funeral was attended at Mr. Thompson's yard, and we had a respectable attendance. The Methodist Negroes conducted the funeral for me; and while they were filling up the grave they sang two hymns. I never saw it so done before, but it was exceedingly solemn and affecting.

On Monday we left our kind friends Mr. and Mrs. Thompson and came to Brother Howe's, where we—that is, Mary and Mary Sharpe and myself—are. Cousin Louisa came to Brother H.'s on the day of the fire. I say day of the fire: the fire took place between *half-past one and three o'clock in the morning of the 18th—before day.*

Louisa, as she came down the steps escaping with us, in some way turned and sprained her foot very badly. She has not walked a step since; dresses and lies on the bed, and will be some time confined to her chamber. This is in addition to her misfortunes, for she saved only a part of her dress. Her trunk, about $150 worth of jewelry of one kind and another, her watch, bonnet—yea, everything—all went. We were so sorry on her account. We have shared with her in making up our losses. But she is cheerful; and we have all been wonderfully sustained—I hope by the Lord.

But it does not look any better after the lapse of time. We are like them who have encountered fearful things, and have not yet fully realized the fact! It was a dreadful night: then you see a house suddenly in flames, the family escaping, bearing in darkness and now by the light of the fire their languishing child to some place of safety; then you see a coffin borne out, and another in a dying state to escape the awful death! And not an article saved! Seldom is such a providence witnessed! We hardly seem yet to know all that has happened. We shall only find out all our losses by time. We have received good above measure from the Lord; and now that He sends evil, we must say: "It is the Lord; let Him do what seemeth good unto Him. All our desire is that these afflictions may be sanctified to the spiritual good of our dear children, and to our own souls, and the souls of our servants. If God shall so sanctify them, then will they be great gain to us."

Our present plan is, so soon as our dear child gets able to travel, Mary and she and Charles and the servants will go home to Liberty; and perhaps Joseph and myself. I may stay longer. But it is all in the future. We can only say: "If the Lord will, we shall live and do this or that."

Charles in consequence of the breaking up of his class and other considerations has taken a dismission from college—at least for the present. The president gave him a dismission couched in the most honorable terms. The college is in a very uncomfortable state at present.

Our kind friends Dr. and Mrs. Howe presented us with a handsome family Bible, and other friends gave us books. Two of my ministerial brethren gave me a few books by way of sympathy and encouragement. It was kind.

One thing I feel grateful for: the calmness and self-possession of my dear wife and of Mary Sharpe and the boys and Lou under the sudden and alarming state we were in when the fire occurred. All were quiet, prompt, energetic; no noise, no confusion. Everything is as distinct before my mind as the paper I write on, and my mind was clear and calm and decided. Had we made a false move even in the slightest particular, the consequences might have been fatal.

I have thus given you a detail of all the circumstances of God's late dealings with us. Pray for us, that we may be sanctified and directed aright. Mary Sharpe is not so well today (24th), but hope it is only the change in the weather from warm to cold. Brother and Mrs. Howe load us with kindness. They with Louisa unite with us in love to you all. We long, long to see you. When Sister Susan has read this letter, she must send it out to Brother and Sister by *the first* mail afterwards. Please write soon. Let the people on the places as you may have opportunity know how it has been with us. Howdy for them all by name.

Your ever affectionate brother,
C. C. Jones.

P.S. Please keep this letter.

THE PRESBYTERIAN BOARD OF MISSIONS *to* REV. C. C. JONES[t]

Philadelphia, Pennsylvania, *Wednesday*, May 8th, 1850

Dear Brother,

The undersigned were this day appointed a committee to inform you that you were chosen by the Board of Missions their corresponding secretary in the place of the Rev. William A. McDowell, D.D., who, after having for many years faithfully and successfully served them in that office, has resigned his station. They take pleasure in announcing to you your election to fill his place; and they can assure you that it was *unanimous*.

The great importance of the office to which you are invited you know, and how very extensive the field of labor that is spread before the Board of Missions. Their labors during the past year have been in advance of any preceding year, and their funds much increased. God has graciously smiled upon them, and greatly encouraged our hearts.

Now, dear sir, we earnestly urge you to undertake the very important duties of the office to which the board have elected you. It will furnish ample scope to that zeal for your Master's honor and the best interest of your fellow men which you have manifested. While we deplore the calamity to which it has pleased your Heavenly Father to subject you, you will permit us to suggest to you the consideration whether you may not find in it an indication that it is His will that you serve Him in the new station to which you are invited by your brethren.

We do not wish you to give an early reply unless you soon feel disposed to announce your acceptance of the appointment; but desire you to look at the subject in all its bearings, to survey the large field of usefulness spread before you, and to consider how much you may be enabled, with the blessing of God, to do in advancing the interests of our church and the cause and honor of our Divine Lord and Master, who bought us with his precious Blood. This may profitably occupy your thoughts for a fortnight, and may overcome any reluctance that may perhaps arise at first in your mind.

May God be pleased to guide your thoughts and incline your heart, if it be for His glory, to accept the office, and bring you to our Mission House, where you will receive a cordial welcome, and a number of your brethren to aid you in the labors that will fill your hands and delight your heart.

Very sincerely and affectionately your brethren in Christ,
J. J. Janeway, president
John McDowell
William A. McDowell.

Rev. William A. McDowell *to* Rev. C. C. Jones[t]

Philadelphia, *Friday,* May 10th, 1850

My dear Brother,

I send you enclosed a letter from a committee of our Board of Missions announcing to you your election as secretary of the board. I have many things I wish to say to you on that subject, but have no time to say them now. I will write you more fully in a few days.

All I can say now is: Do not decide hastily to decline this appointment; keep your mind open to conviction. What the board ask of you *now* is what they asked of me when I was elected: Look at the subject *carefully* and *prayerfully,* and after one or two weeks of careful and prayerful thought, then decide. The post is one of unspeakable importance, and my firm conviction is, there is no situation in our church which opens to a suitable man a prospect of such extensive usefulness. We think you are *the man* for the place. I believe I can say this is the honest belief of every member of our board here. The appointment was not only *unanimous* but with deep interest.

The Lord, my brother, has indeed called you to a severe trial in the burning scene. We have felt a tender sympathy with you. The allusion to that event in the letter is not exactly what I would have said had I written it. Our good president wrote it, and left it for my brother and myself to sign; he had left the city. I trust God will direct you right in this important matter. As I have resigned my place, I can now write you freely on the subject without being suspected of any personal bias. I confess I am deeply anxious you should accept. More in a few days.

Affectionately your brother,
William A. McDowell.

Rev. William A. McDowell *to* Rev. C. C. Jones[t]

Philadelphia, *Friday,* May 17th, 1850

My dear Brother,

In my brief note to you which accompanied the letter from a committee of our Board of Missions I intimated that I would write you more fully on the subject of your appointment as corresponding secretary of the Board of Missions. My time since has been so completely occupied in the business of the office that I have been unable until now to fulfill my promise, and now I am compelled to be brief.

I need hardly say to you, my brother, that I feel a deep interest in the decision you may make in regard to the important question before you. *Personally* I have no longer the interest I once had; my *official* connection with the board and the office has terminated. But my interest in the cause has not at all lessened; and after seventeen years of arduous service, and in the healthful and prosperous state in which, through favor of God, I am now permitted to leave this great and important concern, I confess I do feel deeply anxious to leave it in good and *safe* hands. My decided impression is, you are the man for this place; and this is the place where you can do most for the cause of Jesus Christ.

Of the importance of domestic missions in such a country as ours, and at such a time as the present, I need not speak. You know well how important this work is, and especially at this time. I have no hesitation in giving it as my deliberate opinion that there is no cause in which our church is engaged at the present moment in importance to be compared with domestic missions. I do not mean by this to undervalue any other cause; far, far from it. Each is important in its place. But such is the peculiar state of things in this great country, and such will be the influence of the country on the destinies of the world, that the evangelization of this country is an object in its magnitude and importance perfectly overwhelming. And *the man* who is placed at the head of our house operations, and is competent to direct and manage them wisely, will certainly have an opportunity, with God's blessing, of doing more for the extension of Christ's Kingdom than in any other situation in which he could possibly be placed. This, my valued brother, is my calm, deliberate opinion; and in saying all this you will not *now* charge me with unduly magnifying my office. It is no longer *my office,* and therefore I speak more freely.

But I am compelled to close. May the Lord direct you in this important matter! I will be glad to hear from you. I am still kept here, hard at work; my love to the cause will not suffer me to leave until I can place the concern in good hands.

Affectionately your brother,
William A. McDowell.

REV. C. C. JONES *to* MRS. MARY JONES[t]

Columbia, *Thursday,* May 30th, 1850

My dear Mary,

Through God's blessing I had a prosperous ride to Savannah after parting with you at Riceboro; saw our dear child, Sister, and Laura; took a cup of tea; and went on board the slowest steamer on the line—the *Jasper.*

We did not reach Charleston until 12 M. Saturday. A little seasick on the passage. Stayed with our kind friends in Guignard Street. They inquired most particularly after you, and requested to be remembered to you. . . . Preached for Brother Adger's colored charge on Sabbath afternoon; and the ladies went with me in the evening to the dedication sermon of his new colored church. It was preached by Dr. Thornwell to a very full house. I took the part of the dedication prayer. An interesting occasion. Next Sabbath the church is formally opened for the Negroes.

Reached Columbia Monday evening at five. Found our dear boy well, and anxious for my return. Dr. and Mrs. Howe and Lou and all the children well also. The children thank you for the candy and sugar babies. Gave Joe his two shirts, which he needed. Students welcomed me back most heartily.

Wednesday 29th (yesterday) moved from Dr. Howe's (much against their will) to our old boarding house: *Clarke's,* now Boatwright & Janney. Room on Main Street; third story, handsome prospect *west;* warm in evening.

Now let us turn to other matters. You recollect when we were burnt out and lost our poor servants I told you I felt like a man suddenly arrested in his work, and while it was dark above and all around, was set in a place and commanded to remain there until he should receive further directions. When I got to Dr. Howe's on Monday afternoon, the Misses Leland were there; and they said they had heard from the doctor (who you know has been elected *moderator* of the General Assembly), and that he had used all his influence to prevent *my election to fill Dr. William A. McDowell's place in Philadelphia as secretary of the assembly's Board of Domestic Missions,* fearing it would take me away from the seminary; *but that I had been elected!* This affected me with profound astonishment. Told them I knew not a word of it, and that there must be some mistake. They assured me it was true. At tea Joe came in and brought a parcel of letters which he had from time to time taken from the office. I opened them and found my official appointment, notified by a subcommittee of the board, dated the very day we left Columbia for Liberty; and also a note and letter from Dr. McDowell. So the fact was evident. These letters I have enclosed to you for your careful perusal; and when you have done with them return them to me.

And now, my dear wife, what does this mean? Here is—to say the least of it—a most remarkable conjunction of God's providences towards us, one series of events seeming to lay the foundation for and open the way for another. The appointment has filled the friends here who know of it with surprise. Mr. Snowden says he was "astonished." He called to see me soon after he heard it, and said "of all the men he knew in the church I was the man for the office," and that my appointment was "wonderful in the circumstances of it." Mrs. Howe says "she cannot say anything; she and Dr. H. did all they could to get us here, and Providence seemed to be against it, or moving to take us away." Dr. H. says "if I go, the seminary is done—that it is now enlarging its influence; its students and funds are increasing; confidence is restored; and if I go, things will go backward. There is no man to fill my place, and in the circle of my acquaintance in Columbia there is no man more respected and loved," etc.

I thought it my duty to write immediately to you; and I exceedingly regret we are separated just now. But it may all be precisely the hand of Providence that in separate places, under separate influences, and where we may take separate views, we may contribute more to a right decision than if we were together. I wish you, my dear wife, to give this call to Philadelphia a conscientious and candid and prayerful consideration, as I know you will, and then give me your views and conclusions. I will endeavor to do the same. I wrote Dr. McDowell yesterday telling him you were in Georgia and that I must have the time for a decision extended beyond that intimated in the letter of the committee. You will receive this letter on Monday, June 3rd; you can

16

reply in part or in full by Friday, June 7th, and again on Monday the 10th and Friday the 14th.

You know that the appointment in Philadelphia is one of importance—one of the most important and useful in the church; falls much in the line of my helping on the religious instruction of the Negroes. The secretary is required to *reside* in Philadelphia, where the principal office is, though he may make some excursions in the way of agency. The salary, I presume, is sufficient. The city is but two or three hours by railroad from Princeton. You have been in Philadelphia and know what it is. One may either board or keep house. It is a long way from home. We are burnt out and have no fixtures in Columbia and nothing to move.

If I know my own mind and heart, I have no objections to remaining in Columbia, no objections to going to Philadelphia, no objections to returning to Liberty County and my old work; for to me it is work everywhere, and my only desire is to know what is agreeable to God's will. That I desire to be my guide. It is vain to endeavor to look anywhere for rest and heaven on earth; we shall meet with sin and its consequences both within and without, go where we may. To go anywhere against God is folly and unhappiness. The true peace of the soul lies in loving God supremely and living to Him. His service must be our delight.

You have always cheerfully made sacrifices and gone with me where it appeared to be our duty to go, and have been my helper and friend. But I feel, my dear wife, that in removals it is not unlawful to look at their influence upon domestic comfort; and I do not wish that at our time of life you should be burdened and relinquish what Providence has put within your power to enjoy. This is not an unlawful consideration but a just and necessary one, and which I hope you will give due weight to. Our boys are so far advanced in their education, and I trust have now such knowledge of college life, and are of such principles, that we might venture, with God's blessing, to send them from us. I have said only a few things about Philadelphia that might be useful to you in your reflections, and nothing of Columbia; for you know all about it—the field as to my work and labor in it, our sickness and trials in it, etc.; and you know all about its advantages and disadvantages; and you know how we feel in view of our late afflictions. The determination, I suppose, must lie between Columbia and Philadelphia—unless we take up the question of our return home to Liberty.

Until this call to Philadelphia came, I was turning over in my mind our continuance in Columbia. Houses may be had. Mr. Duncan's next Rev. Mr. Martin's (he leaves in July); rent: $350; the only one I have as yet heard of. Rooms may be taken in the hotel where I now board—*four* (*two large* to accommodate *two persons each,* and *one* for *one* person, and one for a study), contiguous to each other, everything furnished *except washing*—at $5.50 each per week for thirty days during session time, then $1.60 per day or $11.20 per week. During session time the family would eat at the table of *the members;* this lasts only a month or so. The whole expense for nine months would then be $1,120! No charge for *one servant* to wash and wait in rooms, nor for servant's *small child* if there be one, nor for her husband, who may be at home at night to sleep but not board. If we should return and bring up Lucy and Charles, Charles could work at the railroad and Lucy do the washing and her little child be a little waiting maid. We should then have left of the salary for expenses of the family, clothing, education, traveling to and from home $880, which would perhaps be enough. Yet it is a question if we could not rent and furnish a house in a plain, genteel way and keep house as economically as we could board out; and then for comfort and convenience it would be far better. So, should *Philadelphia* be the place, we might board for the present (three of us), and the boys be at Princeton. Their being at Princeton would not much (if any) increase the expense. We could board *lower* than here, which is probable. A Mrs. Brown from Philadelphia in the hotel tells me a family can be boarded in Philadelphia for what it can here—in excellent houses, with more comforts; and in more *retired* parts of the city for less, she thinks. I send you these items that you may have them before your mind; and they may be of some assistance to you.

Took tea with Professor Brumby last evening. Tell my dear son that his class is to be received back on examination and *acknowledgments*. Those who fail on examination and will not make acknowledgments cannot come in. All right. Dr. Thornwell expressed his desire that Charles should return, that such was the wish of the faculty and of many of the students in college, with whom he had conversed. This he told me in Charleston—from which, upon a nearer view of the case, it will be seen that he has receded from the opinion he at first expressed to Dr. Howe. Dr. Laborde expressed his warmest desires to me last evening that he should return, saying that he was one of their *standbys* in college. The faculty are all unanimous in the wish; and my good friend Mr. Robert W. Barnwell, when attending the meeting of the trustees, met Dr. Howe and sent a special message to me begging me to see that my son came back. He was particularly desirous of it. I told Dr. Laborde last evening that we were just now in a state of uncertainty and could come to no positive decision, but that Charles was not averse to returning, and that I felt grateful for the kind feelings of the faculty towards him, and that his conduct and scholarship had met their approbation. Chalmers and Goodman, who were so loud, have come back, and have been living in the upstairs of the male academy, and set up a mark and amuse themselves firing pistols at it; and they *have applied to be received into college again.* And it is supposed— or certain (I cannot tell which)—that they will get in. This is fine on their part, and promises well for the future! I trust they may learn wisdom for time to come. Joe told me all this, with amusement.

Do write us something every mail if you can. Your friends in Columbia all send much love to you. Joe's love and mine to Brother and Sister. Hope Brother is restored. Also to Charles and all our relatives and friends. Howdy for all the people. Enclosed is something for chickens and so forth. Do let me know if you want anything. Have the articles come from Savannah? You had

better have a good supply of lambs brought down from Arcadia. Try and live upon the text: "Be careful for nothing." Take your leisure, rest, take your exercise, see your friends, and try and build up your health and strength again, by God's blessing. I remain, my dear Mary,

Your ever affectionate husband,
C. C. Jones.

Rev. W. W. Hill *to* Rev. C. C. Jones[t]

Louisville, Kentucky, *Thursday,* May 30th, 1850

Reverend and dear Sir,

Permit me, though a stranger to you personally (though I have long known you by reputation), to address you a few lines on a subject that lies near to my heart. I learn that you have been appointed corresponding secretary of our Board of Missions, and my object in addressing you is to assure you that it is the earnest and ardent desire of the Western Executive Committee, of which I have been the corresponding secretary ever since its organization, that you will accept the appointment.

All the members that I have seen—and I have seen nearly all—say that your appointment is the best that has yet been made; and they wish me in their name to assure you of their most hearty cooperation and support in carrying out any great measures you may devise for spreading the gospel in the field more immediately assigned to them. There has not been the slightest collision between the board and our committee located in the West within the last four years. We thought the board did try to hamper us the first year a little, as they were then opposed to our appointment and continuance; but Dr. McDowell himself soon became convinced that upon the whole it was the best arrangement that in the existing state of public sentiment could be adopted, and we have worked very harmoniously together ever since. The work is growing rapidly in our hands, and there is preeminent necessity that some wise, prudent, sagacious man should immediately take the helm and push it forward with great energy and force. We all feel that you can do much more than any other man for two millions of our countrymen whose peculiar condition claims our sympathies and efforts. In no position can you exert so widespread an influence for good to that race as at the head of the board. You will have the confidence of all the South. You understand their peculiarities and the difficulties they have to encounter, and can adapt your measures to them. The North and the West too have heard of your philanthropic efforts in their behalf, and are ready to hail any measures you may devise with approbation. In short, all parties will give you a welcome in your new position, except it may be a few ambitious men who have had their own ends to compass by placing others in that position.

I sincerely hope and fervently pray that you may be induced speedily to devote your head and heart to this noble work of giving the gospel to our whole country—emphatically *the great work* of the Presbyterian Church in the United States at this particular juncture. May we hope soon to hear from you that you have accepted the office and entered upon its duties! Should you do so, we greatly desire that you will at an early period pay us a visit and let us have full consultation over the whole subject.

Respectfully your brother,
W. W. Hill.

REV. WILLIAM A. MCDOWELL *to* REV. C. C. JONES[t]

Philadelphia, Tuesday, June 4th, 1850

My dear Brother,

Your letter of the 29th of May arrived yesterday. We were much gratified to hear from you, *and* the more so as your letter seemed to give some hope that your decision would be in favor of accepting the appointment. We all here, so far as I know, would welcome that decision; and I have understood from one of our delegates to the General Assembly that there was a general and strong feeling at Cincinnati in approbation of your appointment. All that is as it should be, and I trust will not be without its influence in deciding you as to what is duty.

You ask me for information on several points, and put a number of questions which you wish me to answer to assist you in your decision. I feel the propriety and necessity of your having the information asked, and will cheerfully do what I can to present it. I am quite unwell this morning, and my nerves in such a state that I write with difficulty, and would gladly defer to another the duty of giving you the necessary information. But it has been devolved on me; and my warm personal attachment to yourself, and the deep interest I feel in a favorable decision of the important question before you, will not suffer me to decline. I will take your questions in the order stated and give to each the best answer I can.

You ask: "What are the central duties of the office?" I would state in reply to this what have been the duties I have performed, remarking at the same time that the board, I presume, will deem it necessary to appoint an assistant or associate to aid the secretary, as I doubt whether any man can perform without assistance the present and prospective duties of this office. But to the question, what are its duties? To understand this matter fully I would remark there are now *three* departments; and for the business of each the secretary is answerable: the missionary department, the Christian extension department, the editing the monthly periodical. The whole business of each of these departments devolves on the secretary except the single item of funds (receiving and paying money), which devolves on the treasurer. But to be more particular: (1) The correspondence, which is necessarily very extensive and very laborious, devolves on the secretary. (2) It belongs to him to prepare all business for the board and the executive committee, which meets weekly; to write all documents, whether for the board or the public; to suggest places for carrying forward the work; and when plans are adopted by the board, it devolves on him to carry them into effect. (3) The secretary has hitherto been the editor of our monthly periodical, and all the matter for it is furnished by him. (4) As general agent the secretary in the office has hitherto had the oversight of all the agencies, giving no small amount of correspondence, and as he has had time and strength has himself performed the work of an agent. In a word, he is the responsible man for the *whole work,* a large portion of which he must do himself; and for what is done by others in the office the public are very much disposed to hold him responsible for having it well done. The work to be done is constant and arduous, requiring care and much labor.

"Are you confined to Philadelphia for the most part?" As I have had no assistant, and had to do the work and bear the responsibility myself, I have necessarily been much confined to the city and the office. With an associate the confinement would be less. Still the duties of the office are such that the secretary—the responsible man—cannot be much or long absent without loss to the cause.

"Do you preach much?" A secretary able and willing to preach will not lack opportunities for holding forth. And it is desirable he should preach frequently. As general agent it is deemed important he should plead the cause in as many churches as can be reached by going on Saturday and returning on Monday. He is expected to do this in Philadelphia, Baltimore, New York, and adjacent places in New Jersey, Pennsylvania, and Delaware. This will occupy a considerable portion of his Sabbaths, and for the balance he will not want opportunities for preaching.

"What time is there for study?" Not much for study apart from your special work of promoting the great cause of domestic missions. That will necessarily so absorb the mind and occupy the time that but little time is left for other study.

"What is your salary?" This should have been mentioned by the committee of the board in their letter to you. It seems, however, it was overlooked. My salary has been $2,000 per annum. This was the salary fixed when I was called here, and it has remained the same since I have been here. The board have, however, fixed the salary of the secretary hereafter at $1,800 per annum. This was done some two or three months since, before the election of Dr. Backus. That is the salary as now fixed by the board. I presume whatever may be found necessary the board will be willing to give. I speak, however, in this matter without knowing the mind of the board. The reason assigned by the board when the change was made was that this was the salary received by the secretaries of the other boards.

"Is this sufficient for the support of a family?" In reply I would say with economy I have been able to live comfortably on what I have received. The expense of living here is about the same as I found it in Charleston. From that you can judge for yourself what it would cost you to sustain your family here.

"Can you find time to compose sermons, essays, etc., etc.?" The secretary here will not find much time for writing sermons, etc., if he does the business of this office. He will have some time, and to a disciplined mind much can be done in a little time; but he will require a good control of his mind, and to use his time very diligently, if he writes many sermons or essays except on the subject of domestic missions.

"Do you think my owning servants would interfere with my usefulness should I accept the office?" I hardly know whether I am competent to answer fully this question. My own impression is, *it would not.* In this city I am well persuaded it would not; and so far as I know, I think it would not elsewhere. *I* was called here from the heart of slavery; I have uniformly been known as warmly Southern in my feeling; and from my own experience I do not anticipate the slightest difficulty on that subject. I think you need not apprehend any difficulty on that score.

"Is the winter in Philadelphia severe?" The weather here is sometimes cold, but I consider this a good winter climate—much milder than New York, equally removed from the sea and mountain air. It is on the whole a pleasant and healthy winter climate.

"What makes you think I am the man for the place?" It would be a long story, my brother, to tell you all I think and know on that subject. I do think you are well qualified to fill this office. You have good business talents, good preaching powers, can think clearly and so express your thoughts that others can understand you; you know men and things, and with your easy and pleasant manners will be an acceptable companion or guest in any society. You have, I believe, the entire confidence of the churches. For these and other reasons I think you are well qualified to fill this important and responsible office.

"If I accept, will it be necessary for me to remove to Philadelphia immediately, or could I remain winding up my matters until autumn?" In reply I would say should you accept, as we fondly hope you may, it will be of importance to the cause and to yourself as secretary that you should be in the office at as early a day as is practicable. Everything now is in a sound, healthful state; to keep it in this state and urge the work forward as the present exigency requires will demand immediate, constant, untiring effort. A single month without a secretary here will throw things back and be attended with serious loss. I have remained here and kept hard at work much longer than I anticipated when I resigned. The deep interest I feel in the cause would not suffer me to leave until I saw a prospect of having the office well filled; but I must now leave in two or three weeks, and it is all-important the office should be filled with as little delay as possible.

I have thus, my valued brother, endeavored to answer your questions fully and with great frankness. Perhaps I have been even too frank; but I suppose you are anxious to know matters just as they are, and I have written to you just as I would desire and expect my brother Jones to write to me under a change of circumstances. The post is one of great responsibility, of arduous

22

and unceasing labors, and, I may add, furnishing the opportunity for great and extensive usefulness. It will require for the faithful discharge of its important duties the head and the heart, the absorbing interest and devoted labors of any man who may fill it. But with God's blessing you can fill it—and fill it, I believe, with comfort to yourself and great usefulness to the church.

Your present situation I know is important—very important. I feel a deep interest in the prosperity of that seminary. You know I was there at its birth, and for years while it was in its infancy assisted in nurturing it. I should most deeply regret any check to its present prosperity; and I know, too, you are of no small importance to that institution. I would not venture any comparison between the importance of the place you now hold and that to which you are called; both are important—very important. I may, however, be permitted to say it is my firm conviction: in the present state of our country there is no post at this moment of such unspeakable importance as that which places a man at the head of our domestic missionary operation. This is my honest, deliberate conviction.

And now, my valued brother, my heart's desire and prayer to God is that He would so direct you in this important matter that His name may be honored, His cause advanced, and your comfort and usefulness be greatly increased. Write me soon in reply, so that I may receive it before leaving the city. I will be anxious to hear from you.

Affectionately your brother,
William A. McDowell.

Mrs. Mary Jones *to* Rev. C. C. Jones[t]

Maybank Plantation, Liberty County, Georgia
Wednesday, June 5th, 1850

My dear Husband,

Your welcome letter was received yesterday. It fills my mind with wonder and astonishment! What can all this mean? The chain of circumstances, the working together of events, overwhelms me. I know not what to do or say, and have felt like one treading an unknown path at midnight, surrounded by awful gulfs: the right direction would lead to safety; a false step to utter ruin. O Thou who hast led us all our life long, desert us not now, but in Thine infinite sovereignty and wisdom incline and *make us* to go on that way which is best for us, and which shall most honor and glorify Thy great name through Jesus Christ our Lord and Saviour!

I have no doubt but the office of secretary to the Board of Domestic Missions to which you have been called by the unanimous election of the General Assembly is one of vital importance to our whole country—West and South especially. The wants of the people and the young and growing interests of our church call for its occupancy by a devoted and efficient man; and I feel that a great honor has been conferred upon you by your election to the secretaryship. The location would be in one of the most delightful cities of the Union. Of all places north of Virginia I have always felt that Philadelphia would be the most desirable as a place of residence. I have formed a high estimate of its religious, intellectual, social, and *domestic* advantages. Charles laughed and said immediately: "Father can now have his *calf's head* and *peck of asparagus* as often as he pleases."

The advantages of education to Mary would certainly be greater than any she has enjoyed; and Princeton of all colleges you know has long had the preference for our dear boys. I asked C. if he thought his brother and himself could now withstand the temptations which surround youths at college, away from the watch and care of their parents. He replied: "Mother, I could have gone astray at *first* if there was not principle to restrain." How true! God alone must write His law upon their hearts and keep them from the snares of the wicked and convert them from the depravity of their own evil hearts. I feel this every day more and more, and my only comfort and support is in commending them to the grace of God. I cannot rely upon the performance of any past duty in their education or early training. I can only say that I sincerely tried to do what I knew to be duty. But I am conscious of many failures, imperfections, and neglects. One only feeling I can say has never wavered in my heart: the desire that God would convert and use them for His own honor and glory. And my constant prayer is that He would deny them *anything, everything* but salvation through His dear Son.

But I have been led into a long digression from the main point of which I was writing. As regards Columbia as a place of residence for our family, God's dealings with us have been most remarkable. We decided to go *there* from the united voice of the synod and Christian friends after much prayer and honest deliberation, as we thought. Our removal and welcome to the place was as auspicious as we could desire. We have been favored with the kind attentions and confidence of many friends; and the beloved institution you came to serve by common acknowledgment has been greatly blessed and aided by your presence and labors. Many even have volunteered the remark that it was rescued from ruin, and through your instrumentality has been restored to the confidence of the church. Herein the removal has been surely owned and blessed by the Great Head of the Church, whilst His severe providences in other respects seem to be teaching us that Columbia shall not be our home: your own indisposition from protracted sore throat, the sickness (oft-repeated) of the children, my own ill health for eight months, Charles's situation in college, the disappointment of our plans and expectations touching the education of our children, and then the final awful close—the entire destruction of all your private papers, writings, books, etc., of our household furniture and nameless domestic comforts and many precious memorials of our children and of departed friends and other years; and the death of our valued old servant Jack and his wife, those whom we depended upon as the guardians of the establishment—all, all consumed and swept away in awful and rapid succession.

When I think and allow myself to take in the full scope of the *affliction alone,* my heart and head are well-nigh to bursting; and although it seems so sad in a moment to break us all into pieces as a family and scatter us so widely, yet I bless God for my present quiet resting place, although I seldom close my eyes at night before the little clock below numbers one for the coming day. Memory is the reigning faculty, and I know usurps too much of time and feeling for happiness or usefulness; and yet I hope in all this I do not murmur or arraign the divine goodness and wisdom. It is the Lord; let Him do what seemeth Him good. If it be His will to remove us to another sphere, He has surely first taken away every earthly encumbrance so far as Columbia is concerned. And how mysterious! Whilst chastened and afflicted in one place, provision was making for you in another.

And yet in all this I cannot pretend to interpret the divine will. It may be only sent to try and prove your faithfulness in your present situation and your determination to persevere unto the end in labors for the seminary, whose existence we feel is identified with the prosperity of the Southern church. The thought of doing anything adverse to the best interests of this institution is very painful to me. Individually I could sacrifice any selfish feeling to promote its good, and for its sake would tomorrow return cheerfully to Columbia. I *love it* in its every interest. My dear friend Mrs. Howe I am warmly attached to, and to the doctor and their children, and Dr. and Mrs. Leland and their family; and for each of the students I feel a strong personal regard, and very strong attachments to numerous friends endeared in joy and sorrow.

But the point is: What is the divine will? Where shall you do most good? Where best glorify God? Where most advance the growing interests of our dear children in their education and the formation of their characters? We must ask from on high the decision of this doubtful case.

Another point for serious consideration would be your health, and the nature of the duties required of you. Can you—can any of us—stand the severe cold of that climate? And would not the confinement and close application necessary for the performance of the business of the station be more than your constitution would endure at your time of life? When the harness was buckled on, would there be any respite? *Now* you have nine months' labor, *three of rest.* I presume the office would not require as much mental exertion in the way of study and composition as the professorship; it would consist mainly of preparing reports and conducting correspondence, locating missionaries and supplying church destitutions.

Not a word is said of the salary; I presume it would be equal to your present situation.

There is a view of affairs which perhaps ought not to enter my mind when I remember that "God is over all, ruling in the army of heaven and amongst the inhabitants of earth"; and yet in seeking a Northern home it does obtrude itself. I am Southern born and Southern reared; my hopes, my desires, my sympathies, and my interests are with the land of my nativity. I wish my children free from the prejudice of sectional feeling when carried to animosity; yet I want them to love the South and to support and defend her honest rights; and in the event of any national division (which I trust in the goodness of Providence will never take place) I hope they would be found true to the land of their birth. The liberalizing effect of a Northern education is desirable, but not alienation, leading to dishonorable and traitorous conduct.

As my mind runs hastily over the whole aspect of affairs connected with this removal, it rests painfully upon one point: the condition of our poor servants! What will become of them when no master, no mistress, comes at least once a year to inquire into their temporal wants and to provide for their spiritual necessities? It cannot be duty to leave them to live and die like the heathen. You would have been so much pleased if you could have looked in upon us on Sabbath and seen their attentive countenances as Charles read to them, assembled in Patience's house, or have heard their correct answers as I catechized them in the afternoon. I never really feel more profitably employed than when thus engaged. The interests of our plantations will necessarily decline if we are removed from them for a series of years.

Brother William speaks of buying the old house in Sunbury, but my sincere wish if they could be contented to do so would be for them to remove to Maybank and make that their permanent home. There is land and accommodations for all his people. *Now* they are in a very unsettled condition. The day after your letter was received I rode into Sunbury and laid the subject before them, knowing that we would receive their prayers and their sympathy. Sister Betsy says I must tell you that ever since the fire she has made you more than ever the special object of her prayers. She has asked of her Heavenly Father to reveal His will to you; and if He has seen fit to afflict you on account of any secret sin or improper spirit or unworthiness in your office as a minister of the gospel, that He would reveal the cause to you and sanctify your chastisement to your eternal good; and if you are not in the line of your duty, that He would put you into it, and if it be His will restore more than you have lost. Neither she nor Brother William appear to think it your duty to return to Liberty. The latter favors your going to Philadelphia; says it is the hand of God and no one can doubt it. Sister B. says she knows not what to say, but prays the Lord to direct aright.

On Communion Sabbath I met at Midway our humble friend Old Maria. She met me with tears, and seemed greatly moved; said she never forgot to pray for us, and I must tell you God had sent these afflictions to try your faith and patience and see if you would humble yourself and trust in Him and go on with your duty, said you must remember Job how God took away his children and oxen and *plantation* all at one time, and even his wife wanted to make him curse God; but he only said: "The Lord gave, and the Lord hath taken away; blessed be the name of the Lord." She said that like Job she felt the Lord would in the latter end restore more than He had taken away.

And now, my dear husband, what shall I say in conclusion? I confess myself in deep perplexity to know the path of duty; but this much I can sincerely say: I am willing to go either to Philadelphia or to return to Columbia, where I feel that we have many warm friends. Wherever the Lord inclines you to decide is for the best. I have felt repeatedly that I am a poor wife, and little or no account *to you;* but I never have and wish never to stand in the way of your occupying any field of usefulness to which you seem in providence called. You should consult your brethren capable of advising. I mean to write Brother John by this mail. I am very much gratified at the expression of kind feeling from the professors of the college. If Colonel Preston leaves, the institution will probably be in an unsettled state the coming year. When would you be required to enter upon the duties of secretary? And what is the salary? These are important inquiries.

On last Friday we had a severe hailstorm at Arcadia that did much injury to the crops. Our recent rains have been very refreshing, and it has been so cool I have slept several nights under blankets. Everything at Maybank is delightful, and Joe and yourself will enjoy your home when you come. We are thinking of all the good things we can treat you to when you come.

Today we spent with Julia in company with Brother William and Sister Betsy. Miss Brooks is with her during Mr. K.'s absence. As of old she is my kind friend and good neighbor, and desires sincere regards to yourself and Joseph. Sister Betsy and Brother W. send much love to you both, and all the servants desire to be remembered. Present my best love to Mrs. Howe and to Louisa and to Dr. H. and the children. And make my kindest remembrance to all friends as though named. Do not forget to call and see old *Mrs. Beckett* and *Mrs. John Taylor* on the hill; for all the kindness rendered me please do this. Kiss my dear son for me. Charles unites with me in best love to you both. Oh, that the hour had come for your return! Kind regards to Mr. Rogers. May the Lord bless, preserve, and direct you aright, ever prays

Your affectionate wife,
Mary Jones.

Rev. Benjamin Gildersleeve *to* Rev. C. C. Jones[t]

Richmond, Virginia, *Thursday,* June 6th, 1850

Dear Brother Jones,

Without any delay I hasten to lay before you my first impressions upon the subject on which you ask my judgment.

Someone—I think it was Brother Lanneau—told me that you were very much troubled with something like the impression that you had abandoned, or possibly may have abandoned, your appropriate work in resuming your professorship; and that the afflictive providences of God to which you have alluded were but tokens of your Heavenly Father's displeasure. Now, all this may have been only the temptation of the enemy, who delights to worry those of God's people whom He is disciplining for a work that they could not otherwise so well perform. In connection with this call may you not look upon these providences as indicating the will of your Heavenly Father? He has stripped you of the fruits of your anxious mental toil—of your memoranda, your notes, your lectures, your sermons, your books—all of which you prized. And for what? It may be to teach you more and more your dependence upon Him. It may be to throw you upon the resources which you have left. It may be for the purpose of reviving all the ardor of your first love, and for calling into requisition all your energies, tempered with observation and experience and wisdom. And it may be—and in this point of light I am inclined to look upon it—to make you willing to accept of a station in the Church of Christ where these memoranda and notes and lectures and papers are not required, and where you can dispense with them with the least possible loss to yourself or to the cause of Christ's Kingdom.

But, my brother, you are invited to take the charge of a great work—the most important and the most responsible of any of the enterprises in which our church is embarked. It demands qualifications which very few possess. And it behooves anyone who shall enter upon it to do so with fear and trembling. It may be called the primacy or the archbishopric of our church. And were it not that the powers of him who enters upon it are curbed and restrained and held in check by the intelligent and wise action of the lower judicatories, it might in time and under a bad administration become dangerous to the peace and purity of the church. But with the blessing of Zion's King it may be made instrumental of achieving victories in every section of this immense country, and be made to bear with great energy upon your own beloved work, the religious instruction of the blacks. It is the lever of Archimedes, the *pou sto* and all.

But you may ask: "Am I the man?" You may be afraid that you are not. You may feel that there is involved in it more of responsibility than you are willing to assume. But as the board has called you, is there no responsibility in saying that you are *not* the man—that you cannot undertake it? And let me also say that I have full confidence that the church in all its branches will concur most heartily in what the board has done. You have a countinghouse training, a business habit, a methodical habit which are too rare among our ministers. And though I wish to do nothing to the injury of the seminary, and nothing to your own injury, my candid impression is that you can serve the Church of Christ in no way more effectually than by accepting this appointment.

Present my most affectionate regards to Mrs. J. and family. We are all well.

Your very affectionate brother,

B. Gildersleeve.

P.S. I have written *currente calamo;* yet I do not see on reading it anything to retract, but much on which I could amplify, and much that might be added had I time. But *verbum sat.*

28

Rev. Archibald Alexander *to* Rev. C. C. Jones[t]
Princeton, New Jersey, *Thursday,* June 6th, 1850

Reverend and dear Sir,

I have this day received your letter asking advice in relation to the proposal to become corresponding secretary of the Board of Missions of the Presbyterian Church. While I am not sufficiently acquainted with all the circumstances by which you are surrounded to venture an advice as to your duty, I am free to express an opinion on two points: (1) that there is at present no station in the church more important and affording an opportunity of more extensive usefulness; (2) that as far as I have had opportunity of knowing your talents and course of life, the station is one which you would fill as well as anyone that has been thought of. And it would open a wide door of usefulness to that part of our population among which your labors have been hitherto bestowed.

How important your services may be to the seminary at Columbia I am incapable of judging; but I presume that that office can be filled much more easily than the one to which you are invited. Still I would not be understood as expressing a positive opinion respecting your duty. I feel myself to be incompetent to form such an opinion for want of a full knowledge of the whole grounds on which it should rest. I am
Very truly yours, etc.,
A. Alexander.

Rev. John Leyburn *to* Rev. C. C. Jones[t]
Philadelphia, *Friday,* June 7th, 1850

Reverend and dear Sir,

As I am writing to your seminary, I cannot refrain from enclosing a note to you to say how much in common with all concerned here I desire your acceptance of the secretaryship of the Board of Missions. Dr. A. W. Mitchell and Mr. Symington, two of our most valued laymen, members of that board, have just been in my room, and wished me to say to you that they believe your acceptance of the office is of great importance to the harmonious operations of that institution. The appointment was spoken of in the West as probably the most popular which could have been made, and I am sure would be received with general favor throughout the church.

Dr. Robert Breckinridge and Dr. Plumer have both said they considered the secretaryship of the Board of Missions as the most important position in the Presbyterian Church. I have no doubt the former would have been glad to have had it.

I sincerely trust you may see your way clear to come and cast in your lot amongst us. Philadelphia is a delightful place of residence after you get a little used to it.
Very truly and respectfully yours in the best of bonds,
John Leyburn.

REV. C. C. JONES *to* MRS. MARY JONES[t]

Columbia, *Saturday,* June 8th, 1850

My dear Wife,

I received a letter last evening from Dr. McDowell in answer to one I wrote him last week, and as he has set down the questions I propounded to him, his letter will speak for itself. You will be interested in it. You will find another from Rev. W. W. Hill from Louisville, Kentucky, where the seat of the Western Committee is, which is certainly very kind and flattering in its nature. The idea that the appointment is acceptable to *the church* is an important one; and so is the idea that one in the office may accomplish much for the religious instruction of the Negroes in our country.

I am much exercised on the point of duty. It would give me the greatest relief and pleasure in the world to see you and interchange feelings and ideas with you in relation to it. We have had so much of moving of late, and such afflictions and changes, that I feel as if it would be a relief for us to turn aside and "rest awhile"—if God would suffer us so to do. And I know, my dear wife, how much you have been burdened with my removal to this place, and I do not feel inclined to add the weight of a hair more. If you are happy in your own home in Liberty and are content to remain there, then we can send our children to school, and I can return to my old vocation, and carry on my studies, and bring to completion some things which I should like to do and publish; and I see no prospect of it without some retirement of the kind—if life be spared. I suppose some suitable person could soon be had to fill my place here. It is a strange thing to me that my brethren should set me forward in places of so much responsibility; and I wonder how I entertain their views.

Mr. Snowden said in conversation this morning that he thought I ought to go to Philadelphia, though he regretted our loss from the seminary and the society of the town. This is his present view; whether upon further consideration he would continue to hold it I cannot tell. My friend Dr. Howe is grievously put out with the idea of my leaving the seminary. He can see duty in no other line, nor room nor place for consideration of any other field of labor; thinks our recent afflictions are not other intimations of the divine will than ordinary dispensations, and we ought to view them in that light—and that only—and remain where we are.

I hope you have informed my dear brother and sister of the call and shown them the letters. Please do it, and get their views for me. I have written to John; hope to hear from him in a few days. Also to Mary Sharpe, and let Sister Susan know through her letter.

Took tea last evening at Father Law's. Mrs. Ellison is remarkably well and cheerful. Spent a most agreeable time with them, and came home before nine. Mrs. Law and Mr. Law and Mrs. Ellison and their mother Mrs. Adger sent the kindest remembrance to you, and express the hope that we may not leave the place.

The students do not express their opinions beyond their fears I may go. They seem to apprehend the importance of the call. They are all well. Our conferences closed this week. The professors will begin to review for examination very shortly. The examination commences on the 10th of July, and will last two days. My review will be with the middle class only, and that on so much of the first part of church history as we went over before the fire.

Expect, God willing, to preach at Barhamville tomorrow. Their term closes on the 20th of June. A number of their scholars have left already for the summer.

Mr. Latta's family leave next week for the summer. Am engaged to take tea with them on Monday evening, D.V.

Dr. and Mrs. Howe gave a party last evening to Lou; I was invited, but was previously engaged at Mr. Law's. Was glad of it; not that I do not wish to see my friends, but do not feel inclined to be much in such assemblages. Fewer suit me better.

Joe begs Charles to answer his letter or he will be too late. He was out parading for the last time this term. Captain Wharton delivered his valedictory on the campus. He is going to Cambridge, and will not return next term.

The boys in college wrapped a hank of twine around a pound of powder on the campus and touched it off, and the twine was blown on the top of Major Williams' house and set it on fire. The fire was speedily extinguished; but the boys said Dr. Laborde was so scared he could not find his clothes, or was unable to dress himself—I forget which. Either bad enough. After the fire was all out, they ran down to the town house and set the bellman ringing and alarmed the whole town. Engines were running, and people in all directions, hunting for the fire.

The transient boarders in my entry were much moved. A brother Georgian appeared at his room door in the strangest nightdress imaginable: a tight-fitting pair of drawers and a tight-fitting flannel up to his neck—for all the world looking as if he had no clothes on at all. He would run to the door of his sister's room across the entry crying: "Sister! Sister! There's no fire. They can't find it." And hearing someone come, he would skip back and parade himself at his room door to ask the passerby: "Where's the fire?" A countryman threw open his door, his face red, his hair standing out in all directions; holding his pantaloons, he would take sight for the legs with his foot and miss every kick. Said he: "Mister, *where's* the fire? I thought it might be in *this* house." Self-possession is a great blessing, and in many cases the greatest mercy, as it is the means of securing priceless blessings. I have given rather a florid account of the movements in our entry to amuse you a little.

We have all our troubles. A Mrs. Brown who boards here has two children at school in Philadelphia, and heard last night that they had *scarlet fever*. Mr. Brown is upon the railroad at his business. I went with her to the telegraph office, and she dispatched a message to her mother. We saw it sent as far as Raleigh, North Carolina. But at dinner she had received no answer. I told her that God was with them, and through Him she was nigh to them.

The remains of Colonel Elmore are expected up from Charleston this

31

evening. The train is not in yet: $7\frac{1}{2}$ P.M. Two hours behind the time. So we shall have no mail opened tonight. I hoped to hear from you, but must wait now until Monday morning. Love to Brother and Sister, and to my dear boy. Joe sends much love. He is at his society. Howdy for all the servants. The Lord be with you and bless you, my dear wife!

Your affectionate husband,
C. C. Jones.

Mr. CHARLES C. JONES, JR., *to* REV. C. C. JONES[t]

Maybank, Saturday, June 8th, 1850

My dear Father,

It is about time that I was writing you, and it is accordingly with pleasure that I undertake this agreeable duty. Your long and interesting letters have kept us duly apprised of your operations, so that although absent in person, still you have been often present in mind. We also hear from Sister, so that despite our scattered condition, we are not altogether divided. Still there are pleasures and profits connected with the actual and personal intercourse of friends which cannot be derived from a mere interchange of feelings and affections in an epistolary correspondence.

Your letter conveying an announcement of your call to the secretaryship of the Board of Domestic Missions was as unlooked for as it was astonishing. The circumstances under which it occurred all conspire to render it remarkable. I well remember a remark of yours immediately subsequent to the fire that you felt like one who had been suddenly checked in his present duties, placed in the dark as regards his future course, with the command to remain for further light. And it does really seem as if a light from on high has shone upon you, perchance pointing to a more important and enlarged field.

The question of a removal is one of serious moment, involving many considerations of the most interesting and important nature. If you accept this call, it does really seem that Providence has been paving the way, by sundering whatever ties may have existed to attach us to Columbia. You can now move *sine impedimentis,* as Caesar would express it: free from everything in the way of baggage. Had this offer presented itself before the breakup in college, the burning of the house, and the death of our valued servants, when everything was fair and promising, then it appears to me the question of removal would have been one of a far different nature. As regards the leaving of our relations, friends, people, dissolving your connection with the seminary, and other considerations of like importance, these have, I am persuaded, been so fully urged and duly weighed by Mother and yourself that nothing which I could say would be of any account. Suffice it to say that as regards myself, to return to Columbia would be very pleasant in many respects, and I would by no means object to a move to the North; or in other words that any decision which you may make in this matter would meet with my hearty concurrence. The situation offered in Philadelphia, so far as I know anything concerning it, is one which when viewed abstractly presents many advantages, affording perchance advantages *superior* (in some respects, at least) to those of Columbia—viz., Sister's education, your own extended influence, the health of the place, polished society, the proximity to Princeton, etc. Excuse these remarks, for although they may be superficial and uncalled for, still I am persuaded that it is duty for me to make known to you my own feelings on a subject which so nearly concerns us all.

Mother has been pretty well, although not, I fear, sufficiently observing your injunction: "Be careful for nothing." Uncle William has entirely recovered, and appears to enjoy his usual health, and to be possessed of his accustomed flow of spirits. . . . We have had but little rain lately, the weather being very warm and sultry, and the ground getting very dusty. On Friday last (May 31st) we had a little hail, but not enough to hurt anything. At Arcadia, however, the fall was quite heavy, injuring the cotton considerably—to what extent, however, I am uncertain, as I have not been there for some time. It is my intention, however, to visit that place in the early part of next week, and I can then inform you more particularly. The crop here seems to be improving. Corn good; so with the potatoes and peas; and the cotton is doing very well. Have heard of no blossoms yet in the county. Uncle William has the finest cotton crop in this part of the country, and with common seasons can calculate upon a fine yield. Andrew is just finishing his corn, and will then go over his cotton again.

I am now reading aloud to Mother Bancroft's *History of the United States,* which we find at once interesting and improving. I was so much interested in the expedition of De Soto that I am at Mother's request preparing a short essay on that subject. Have not accomplished much as yet in way of study, as there have been many little odd jobs occupying my attention and time.

Cousin Charlie has returned from his Troup tour; and stopping a while in Marietta, he saw our relatives in that place. Says that Aunt Eliza does not appear to be very well, and also little Dunwody somewhat indisposed; the rest, however, were enjoying fine health.

I am now breaking my little pony, and hope that he will make a fine riding horse. Ring is about either to go mad or to depart this life. He is very thin, eats nothing but meat, and has as bad a distemper as ever you have seen in a sheep. One or two dogs on the place are affected in a like manner, and will, I am persuaded from present appearances, share a similar fate. 'Tis hard to see a dumb beast thus perishing; but what cannot be helped must, I presume, be endured.

The death of Senator Elmore is a very unusual one, occurring as it did just upon his succession to Mr. Calhoun. Doubtless his funeral offices will be performed with honor, though with less pomp than those of his predecessor.

Mother says that she has nothing special to say—only a great deal of love to yourself and Brother. I received his letter, and will reply to it shortly. Would be glad if he could obtain four or five copies of *The Temperance Advocate* when my speech is published. We wish to see you both very much, and will try to have everything ready for your reception in July. Mother unites with me in kind remembrances to Dr. and Mrs. Howe, Cousin Lou (if she has not left), Mr. Rogers, and all other friends—Messrs. Peace, Witherspoon, Foster, etc. With feelings of high regard and sincere attachment, I remain, as ever,

Your son,

Charles C. Jones, Jr.

P.S. Mother returns her thanks for your letter, as well as the chicken money, which came safe to hand.

C. C. Jones, Jr.

Miss MARY SHARPE JONES *to* REV. C. C. JONES[t]

Savannah, Georgia, *Monday,* June 10th, 1850

My dear Father,

I received your long-expected letter yesterday. I had heard through Aunt Lou's letter of your safe arrival in Columbia, and am glad to hear of your escape from seasickness. . . . We had heard nothing of your appointment until I received a letter from Aunt Lou. I do not think that it has been published in the newspapers. What can it mean?

There are some strange reports in Charleston about yourself. Cousin Mary Nisbet wrote Cousin Laura that she had heard that you had had misgivings before the fire, and considered this fire as a providential intimation that Columbia is not the place for you, and that you had determined to return to Liberty County and devote yourself again to the Negroes. I cannot see from what source some people derive their information. Cousin Laura wrote her that at the time of your remove to Columbia you considered that you were doing your duty, and that you had no misgivings about that—not even since the fire. She also told her that when you left Savannah you had formed no plans at all, and the report was all new to us.

I think this appointment seems to favor Brother Charlie's going to Princeton. Aunt Susan says that you have had the *labors* and *toil* of domestic missions for a long time, and now it is time for you to enjoy the *honors* and *profits*. She thinks that the climate of Philadelphia can hardly be more trying than that of Columbia; the changes will not be so sudden and great. She says that Mr. Ingersoll's health has decidedly improved since his remove to Springfield, Massachusetts. We built quite an air castle when the report reached us —Cousin Charlie to go to Philadelphia to attend the medical lectures, Brother Charlie and Brother Joe to go to Princeton, and the rest of us to live in Philadelphia. But it strikes me that this is easier talked of than done. Cousin Laura says that she will be your private secretary. Aunt Susan says she told you to wait; now the church has given you a call, and if you can consistently with other claims accept, *do so*. She says that with so much *sage counsel* you will not be at a loss how to decide.

Much to my surprise, I saw Dr. McWhir at church yesterday week. He has since been to Montgomery, which is about eight or ten miles from this place.

34

When I went to see him, I did not think that he would ever be able to get out again.

The weather here has been very warm, and we have had some very severe thunderstorms. One young woman was struck by lightning as she was crossing her room and killed immediately. A man who was in the same house was struck also, and his life was despaired of; I have not heard whether he recovered or not. An Irishman was knocked across his house, and the same stroke killed a calf in the yard, and knocked down several persons in an adjoining house who were playing cards.

Uncle Roswell left with Willie and Fred about two weeks ago for New Haven. Willie was suffering with an attack of rheumatism, and I did not see him. There were forty passengers on board of the boat, most of them ladies. Uncle said that he would as leave be in an "ant's nest" as in the cabin with all of those ladies.

I am very glad to hear that Brother Joe is eating with Mrs. Young; I know that she will do all that she can for him. Please give my love to her and to Miss Amanda. Do give my best love to Aunt Lou, Dr. and Aunt Howe, also to Dr. Leland's family. Have you seen Mrs. Thompson since your return? Do give love to her. Give my respects to Mr. Rogers. Aunt Susan, Cousins Charlie and Laura unite with me in sincere love to yourself and Brother Joe. I remain, dear Father,

Your affectionate daughter,
Mary S. Jones.

Mrs. Mary Jones *to* Miss Mary Sharpe Jones[t]

Maybank, *Wednesday,* June 12th, 1850

Did you remember, my darling daughter, that this is your fifteenth birthday? It was the first thought which entered my mind at sunrise this morning; and my heart went up to "the Father of every good and perfect gift" for blessings on my dear child. May you first of all things know what it is to have Christ formed in your soul the hope of glory; through the influences of the Holy Spirit be taught your nothingness and the infinite fullness and preciousness of salvation through His atoning Blood and righteousness; and have the spirit of adoption, whereby you can look up unto God and cry: "Thou art my Father, and the Guide of my youth." Then and then only will you possess that peace which the world can neither give nor take away. I desire for you next an increase in all true wisdom and knowledge; a warm heart with well-regulated and well-directed affections; a temper amiable, cheerful, generous, and free from selfishness; with manners polite, unaffected, and refined; with habits of industry and economy; feelings of benevolence and kindness to everyone, especially the poor ("Blessed is he that considereth the poor"); and your mind stored, strengthened, and enlarged by sound study and the acquisition of useful knowledge, not only in the departments of science and literature but also in the essential everyday duties of life. If you attain these

35

things, your life will be one of usefulness and happiness—a blessing to yourself and others, especially to your dear parents, whom I know you love, and to whom you have ever been an affectionate and obedient child.

I am sorry the little sealed *package* which you were to have opened on this day was brought out in the box of likenesses. It shall remain until you come.

I long to have you once more with me, but feel grateful to your kind aunt and cousin for all they have done for you, and know that your opportunities for improvement have been very great. Your little room is all ready to receive its mistress, and I am going to send up this week for the old cat and kittens. The old plague hid them away the morning we were leaving Montevideo, so they could not be found; but as it is for their better education, she must be made to produce them. Your brother's pony (Firefly) is so docile in spirit and easily managed, I think by the time you come he will be able to accompany you on horseback.

Your uncle is entirely restored; he and your aunt came early and spent the day with us yesterday. We had some fine boiled and fried fish, which they enjoyed very much. This afternoon your Aunt Julia, Miss Brooks, and the little folks are to be with us to tea. Bayard and Clarence have both been sick, but not very seriously. Last Friday your Aunt Augusta and Uncle Troup spent the day and night with us; also Audley and Mr. Randolph; so you see I have not been entirely alone. On Friday we are going in to Sunbury.

Your brother reads every day to me that we are not interrupted Bancroft's *History of the United States.* He has not yet done much study.

You must excuse your dear father for not writing you; he says he is employed from eight to ten hours every day with his pen, trying to recover his *lost lectures;* and his mind is very deeply exercised at this time to know what is duty in this call to the Board of Missions. You must pray for him; God alone can direct us aright. It would be the most important move of our lives. . . . Did your father leave money with you to pay his bill? If not, I will send it to you.

When you bring your brother's shirts, do not forget his cloak. He very carelessly left it—I think in the little room. One would suppose from the state of his wardrobe he would learn to be more precious of his things. But it is apt to be the reverse: when we have little to lose, we are apt to be careless of that little—particularly when sure of a supply from others.

I am happy to hear that Mrs. Vanyeverine improves, and think Mrs. Porter ought to go North with so many good friends to take care of her aunt. Please remember me affectionately to them.

Your brother went this morning to Arcadia, to return this afternoon.

Give my best love to your aunt and cousins, and respects to the gentlemen. The servants all send howdies for you, and long to see you. Phoebe and Patience have a merry crew; sometimes I am stunned by their voices in the yard in full concert screaming "Dearest Mag" and "Susannah." I call them my "Ethiopian band," and they are quite delighted at it. We have formally changed little Edmund's name to *Jack* in honor of our faithful departed friend and servant. The little fellow seems to appreciate the honor; and if one of the children makes a mistake and calls him Edmund, he comes in and informs on them as if they had committed a heinous offense. Your last letter has been received, and I have been very much pleased to hear from you every week. May the blessing of God rest upon you, my dear daughter, on this and all the days of your life, ever prays

Your own affectionate mother,
Mary Jones.

Mrs. Mary Jones *to* Rev. C. C. Jones[t]

Maybank, *Wednesday,* June 12th, 1850

Did you remember, my dearest husband, that this was the anniversary of our dear daughter's birth? And a precious child has she been to us—affectionate and obedient in all things. My first thoughts at awakening were of her, and my heart was lifted up in prayer to God to bless her, to be her Father and the Guide of her youth. I have written her a long letter today. She has written me every week since you left. In her last she says: "I cannot think why my dear father does not write me, and Brother Joe too. I have written both of them, but suppose they are both too busy."

You must be in possession of my long letter ere this. We have written once every week since you left.

Your last affectionate favor reached me on Monday. If you only knew how much happiness your letters confer upon me in your absence, it would be some compensation for the trouble of writing—especially now. Although my friends may not see or think so, yet I feel that the awful events of April have written their impress in deep gashes on my heart; and yet I bless God for the comfort and strength mercifully imparted. But there is at times a feeling I have no power to explain or express. And then I was so suddenly hurried away from Columbia, separated from you and two of my dear children all at once. I often go to the end of the piazza, where I used to sit and strain my eyes to catch a glimpse of you returning from your missionary labors, weary in body but refreshed in spirit, and wish that I could recall those days, or sit alone in my rocking chair and silently muse on the past, when our dear children like a little flock were gathered around us—our pleasant friends and neighbors, our domestic school, our little social Bible class. Then the images of our valued servants in every nook and corner come flitting before my vision. I have to close my eyes and bless God for all the enjoyments that are past, and trust Him for all that is to come. But I must stop. It has been the effort of my life to *repress,* not to *express,* my feelings; and yet the heart yearns at times with an intense longing for kindred sympathy.

And now what shall I say of the *call?* Oh, that I could be directed to say what is proper! I strive to make it a subject for constant prayer. When I think of all the kindness received in Columbia, the many kind friends already known there, the interest of the seminary, the nearness to our home, *with the privilege of being three months with our people,* the comfortable support, and many other considerations, my heart draws back from the change. And then comes the tremendous impression: Hath not God spoken to you with a voice of fire, and in almost every way hedged up your path? And will you persist? The thought of willful disobedience is awful. I think if we mistake not we are willing to do God's will. Oh, if we could only know what it is!

One thing is certain: if we leave, our people must be provided for religiously. If you determine to do so, let me urge you to write and offer Maybank as a home to Brother William. It would be to his and our interest too. *I mean if you think it best to do so.*

Charles says he would prefer to finish his college course at Columbia, as he knows all the professors and feels much attached to them. At the same time he feels that his advantages would be increased by going to Princeton. Who is likely to succeed Colonel Preston? And will not his leaving necessarily distract the affairs of college for the coming winter? Please write us all about this. . . . I think C. would be placed in better college influences in Princeton than Columbia. Now that we are alone I can see the effect of erroneous opinions upon him, and I fear he has not that feeling and regard for sacred things—I mean the worship of God, reading the Bible, and prayer—that even a child religiously educated should have. Oh, that the Lord would be pleased to convert him! Let us not forget the spiritual condition of our dear children.

Dr. Wells writes Mrs. King that his son William, recently converted, is going to study theology.

13th. Your letter mailed the 9th, my dear husband, containing Dr. McDowell's and Dr. Hill's have just been received; also one from my dear son and from dear Lou. It is so strange that you have not yet received my long letter. We have written every week since you left.

From Dr. McDowell's letter I fear the situation would require more labor than you can undergo. You could let me help you in the use of the pen. As I have said before, I am perfectly willing to go to Philadelphia if you decide it to be best, or to remain in Columbia. Suppose you ask Dr. Trezevant's opinion of the change to us old folks. Brother William says if he decided as his love for you dictates, he would say remain in Columbia, but if according to what seems to be the will of Providence, he would say go to Philadelphia. The salary there would be less, and our removal very expensive, but so far as the family is concerned, advantages increased. I ask the question: What will the children do there after they are educated? And then comes the feeling: Who has taken care of and directed you? *Trust God for all these things.* I know your leaving the seminary would injure it; but if you are called by your Father in Heaven, as our poor Jack said of dying, you "must go with a cheerful, willing spirit." I hope, my dear husband, you will not let these matters press upon your mind to the injury of your health. Is there no one else to advise with you? Have you spoken to Dr. Trezevant and Mr. Palmer? But they have no sympathy with boards, foreign or domestic. Suppose you write *Dr. Talmage;* I think he would answer as a Christian brother. In your *decision* keep in view our poor servants. It is true we may aid them there as well as here. Dr. Howe, Lou writes me, feels very deeply upon the prospect of your removal.

And now for a word about home. Everything is delightful here—if my dear husband and children were only here to enjoy all the pleasant things. This afternoon Charles went to the second bluff about an hour and a half before sunset and returned with over a dozen of the finest sort of fish—young drum, bass, whiting, croaker, all of which we are going to take early in the morning to Sister Betsy.

The servants all inquire constantly after you, and long for your return. I have changed the name of Edmund Burke and call him in honor of our departed servant Jack. All the servants seem pleased at it, and the little fellow very much impressed. If any of the children forget and call him by the old name, he comes and reports it as a heinous offense.

My good neighbor Julia is as kind as ever. Miss Brooks is staying with her in Mr. King's absence; and they desire best regards to you. They spent last afternoon with me, and Brother and Sister the day before. Dr. Maxwell and Augusta have also spent a day and night with us. So you see we have not been alone. Also Mr. Randolph and Audley.

Have you, my dear, written to Mr. Adger? Perhaps *his views* would aid you.

I feel deeply for Mrs. Taylor and her daughter in the death of Colonel Elmore. *Do go and see them;* they have been so kind to me in my troubles.

Remember me to all friends in Columbia as though named, especially to Dr. and Mrs. Howe; and best love to Lou. I want to write them both soon. This afternoon I took a nap after dinner, and a *long* walk—the second since I came down; felt that I was *obeying* you, and am quite bright tonight. Kiss my dear Joseph for me, and ask him to bring me some rose cuttings of the cloth-of-gold and any other he can obtain; and beg him to thank my good friends Mrs. Young and Miss Grazier for all their care of him. The servants all send howdy for you, and Charles unites with me in warmest love to you and his brother, and to Mr. Rogers.

Ever your affectionate wife,
Mary Jones.

You did not say I must return the letters. Shall I do so?

Rev. C. C. Jones *to* Mrs. Mary Jones[t]

Columbia, *Thursday,* June 13th, 1850

My dearest Wife,

Your letter received on Monday was a great comfort to me; and I am looking out for another from you tonight in answer to several that I have written you—and all very much on the subject which now so much absorbs my mind.

I do not in the consideration which it demands desire to forget the chastisement of God in our afflictions and losses. No. Let the lessons of those sad events be deeply engraven on my heart, and produce the peaceable fruits of righteousness. Have been twice down to see the graves of Jack and Marcia. They are undisturbed, and have no more a share in anything that is done under the sun! It is difficult to realize that they are gone. Those sickrooms; those dark days and nights; that constant anxiety of mind; the awful fire; the escape, by its glare, of the living, the sick, the dying, and the dead; the complete annihilation of our domestic establishment—all, all have a voice teaching us that neither we nor anything we have can we call our own. God owns all. There is emptiness in the creature, and no durable home here; and our own life is but a vapor. Oh, for grace to improve it all! I thank my dear sister for her prayers; they are more to me than fine gold. May God answer them to my good and to His glory! I never desired more to know what is duty, nor endeavored to pray with a greater freedom from all unholy and improper motives. The dealings of God towards us are wonderful.

The considerations you suggest are very judicious. Our people weigh much with me, and the opportunity of being at home three months in the year with our dear relatives is a great privilege and advantage to our interests. But in deciding upon a field of labor may we not throw them in with the mass (as it were) of those upon whom we operate? May not a field of wider influence call us to a separation from them? I do not mean that we shall cease to do for them, both temporally and spiritually, to the extent of our ability. They are left now for three-fourths of the year. The contingency of a dissolution of the Union I pray may never occur. It is not my impression that the present disputes in Congress will end in division. I am willing to abide *in* and *by* my country, but hope we may have never any country beside the republic as it now stands. On this point I say: "Sufficient unto the day is the evil thereof." In respect to the climate, you will see what Dr. McDowell says about it in his late letter enclosed to you. It will be a matter to be tested—though I feel that if Providence calls me there, He will give me constitution for the place. The change may be beneficial to us all.

I feel very anxious on your own account, and would be glad to see you in a healthy climate, and free from so many domestic cares, which are no greater than are borne by the great majority of ladies, but to which you devote yourself with a care and solicitude and unremitting constancy which are corroding to mind and heart. I do not think we are in the path of duty when we do so. Surely it is not displeasing to God, who makes the flowers gay in their exquisite colors, and puts the most joyful and the sweetest songs into the hearts of the little birds, and who casts over the green and beautiful earth and the deep blue heavens the brilliant light, and seems to form all things that they may have delight—surely it is not displeasing to Him that His own chosen ones should take some rest, and be glad too before Him, and be happy in His boundless and unmerited favors towards them. For this cause, should we be directed to Philadelphia, a quiet private place of boarding will be better —at least for a year, if we live so long—than housekeeping.

Brother's decision was very quick. He may be right. I do wish they could be content to live at Maybank. The great objection to Sister would be the distance from friends and church; and a great objection it would be. A couple of good families on the Island would change the face of things materially.

Greatly disappointed! No letter from you this evening! I have written you *four* and received *one*. This is my *fifth*. I thought surely you would write and help me out in the decision, but suppose you have not matured your views yet. Tell Charles I thank him very much for his interesting and handsome letter. It was very gratifying to me to receive it, and will answer it shortly. I enclose you three letters received lately which you will be pleased to see. You *need not return any* sent you.

It will be necessary for me to come to some decision in a short time about the call to Philadelphia; and as writing seems to be a slow mode of communication, I propose to return home with Joe and spend a few days with you, and talk over the matter and pray over it and try to come to some conclusion, so that I may answer the committee in Philadelphia, who are waiting upon me, and so also that we may make arrangements either for going to Philadelphia or returning to Columbia. Joe will be through with his examination on the *24th;* we will leave the 25th, be in Savannah Wednesday the 26th, and take the stage *Thursday the 27th for Liberty*. The carriage can meet us *at Midway*. Gilbert can bring the trunk straps. If Mary Sharpe does not leave Savannah *before,* she can come along with us. Will write her to that effect. But do not wish her to remain on our account. Will preach *in Sunbury Sunday the 30th*. All this if *God will*. Stay with you till Friday the 5th of July, then leave in stage for Columbia again to attend the examination, and return home immediately after. Give notice about the preaching. So pray and meditate and let me know your conclusions when we meet.

Love to my dear boy. Joe sends much love to you both. Our love to my dear brother and sister and all around you. Howdy for all the servants. The Lord bless you, my dear wife, with every blessing!

Your ever affectionate husband,
C. C. Jones.

Rev. C. C. Jones *to* Rev. William A. McDowell[t]

Columbia, *Monday,* June 17th, 1850

Reverend and dear Brother,

Your kind reply reached me last week, and let me thank you for it. It shed light on my way, but the conclusion is not reached yet.

I am very much perplexed, but not in despair; and writing is a slow mode of communication in the decision of a question like the one now before me, involving as it does so many considerations both of a public and a private nature. I am consequently under the necessity of going home to confer personally with my dear wife, who, I wrote you, was in Liberty County, Georgia. She has written twice, and in a prudent, judicious manner. Her desire is to do that which is the will of God—if we can know what that will is. We do not wish to leave our present field and go to Philadelphia from *worldly motives,* for we cannot then expect God's blessing. Yet His dealings with us *here* have been so peculiar we must give this call consideration.

It seems in some points of view almost like a voice from heaven. My family has had no continued health since we were here; my own indifferent. For near three weeks sickness and illness in the house, ending in the death of our head servant and friend. And then the awful fire consuming everything, from which *the living, the ill, the dying,* and *the dead* barely escaped! Then the call to go away to a field congenial to my tastes, feelings, previous life—bringing me once more directly in contact with my favorite labor of life: the evangelization of the Negroes, a field in which I could best of all others do without my sermons, lectures, and manuscripts, etc., etc.; and where my family might also be benefited; and in which the prospect of usefulness in the church seems as great as where I now am. And then the general approbation in the church of the appointment, etc. All these things put together make out a very strong case.

Then, on the other hand, the prospect (and, as some think, the certainty) of injury to the seminary, the consequent diminution of students, the difficulty of filling the place; the separation (almost *total*) from our servants (now we may spend three months in the year with them); and the trial of a cold climate on our constitutions; the uncertainty if I shall be able to fill the station, etc. These considerations must have their weight.

My friends are divided; yet the weight is for Philadelphia.

The fact is, I must go home and see my wife; and we must talk and pray over the matter and seek that conclusion which may be agreeable to God's will. You would not have me do otherwise. God willing, the students will complete their review for examination on the 10th or 11th of July *this week;* I shall leave for home on Tuesday the 25th, reach there the 27th, stay until July 6th, return to Columbia the 9th, and *will then endeavor to give the committee an answer.* Meantime pray for us. And *you must not give up*—if we conclude to accept—*until we can make arrangements to come on. This is a settled matter.*

Tell Brother Leyburn I thank him kindly for his letter. My best love to him.

Will it be too much trouble for you to write me again? Can board be had in a private boarding house? It might be in some respectable family (I do not care that it be some little distance from the office). And at how much *per week,* including everything but washing (or even that, if you please) *for three persons, requiring three rooms,* in a *pleasant* part of the city (I will not say *fashionable*) or *business* part? Again: are houses ever rented that are *already furnished?* Such things are done in cities. Or would it be best to rent and furnish and keep house? Boarding for the present would be best, I think. *Write as soon as you can.* I do not desire to raise expectations about coming to you; but these are items of no small value for us to know.

Oh, my valued friend and Christian brother, I desire first of all—and ever—to give myself away to God, and then let Him do with me according to His will. Oh, if I had that assurance of being His child which so many have— if all doubt and darkness were gone on that point, and I felt His love shed abroad in my soul, as I do desire it—then would I be happy in my God and Saviour! Then I could say: "Lord, *when* Thou wilt, *what* Thou wilt, *where* Thou wilt, and *as* Thou wilt." I find it hard for my depraved and wandering heart to crucify all its lusts, to throw down its idols, and to make God *truly my portion,* His service and glory *the end and happiness of my life,* and His heaven *my home.*

I have not replied to the committee formally, and beg you to let Dr. Janeway and Dr. John McDowell know that you have heard from me and how it is with me.

Most affectionately yours,
C. C. Jones.

Direct to *Columbia.*

Rev. C. C. Jones *to* Mr. Charles C. Jones, Jr.[t]

Columbia, *Monday,* June 17th, 1850

My dear Son,

I received your letter last week, and was much pleased to get it, and to know your mind in relation to the call which now occupies so much of our attention and serious thoughts.

It will be pleasant for you to graduate here under professors the most of whom have showed you special marks of favor; this is very natural. Entering senior in any other college, you could not expect a high appointment. But while appointments are very gratifying and are evidences in general of scholarship and character, yet they are not essential to an education, nor to one's success in after life. My great objection ever has been to this college— its want of discipline and of government upon correct principles, and its acknowledged immorality. A constant dripping will wear away a stone; and few young men—if the experience of those who have gone before is to be taken—can pass through the college without deterioration unless their principles are adamantine and their decision of that firmness which few can boast. I have felt very uneasy, my dear son, in respect to the general influence of the college over you.

Your late conduct on the rebellion of your class was very gratifying to your parents, who feel the deepest solicitude for you, and also to all your relatives and friends; but we can never feel at ease until you are soundly converted to God. Your immortal soul is yet uncared for, the awful retributions of eternity unprovided against; and I cannot bear the thought of your dying in your present state. The way of salvation you know, and the means of obtaining life you know; and let me urge upon you, my dear son, that you make your peace with God through Jesus Christ our Lord. I do not believe that you are at rest in your mind when you remember God and eternity;

43

and if the Holy Spirit still keeps your conscience tender and strives with you, do not resist those strivings but yield to them. And be careful especially to keep up the habit fixed in you from your infancy by your dear mother of daily reading the Word of God and of secret prayer night and morning. These are duties which, impressed upon your heart and conscience, you cannot lay aside without great injury to your soul.

Joseph and I have been together every Sabbath evening and united in prayer as usual, and it has been a great comfort to remember those we so dearly love and from whom we are now separated.

Tell Mother I received her first long letter, which has been answered, and her second one of the 12th and 13th this morning, for which I thank her; and hope she will continue to exercise, and be quite hearty when we get home *next week*. I wrote her in my last (which she gets *today*) that Joe and I would leave here the 25th and reach Liberty (Midway) the 27th in the stage; and the carriage must meet us at Midway; and we will bring Mary Sharpe out if she does not come out before. We can then talk over all our affairs in full.

The college is diligently reviewing for examination, and so is the seminary. Many candidates are spoken of in Colonel Preston's place, but it is not known who will be the successful one; but it is understood that the trustees *will not place a minister at the head*. How this comes out I cannot tell. Have seen but little of college since I came back. There are some fifteen or twenty almost every evening sitting under the porch of this hotel. They come in sometimes and take tea. Some of your classmates, Joe tells me, have come back. It will soon be known how many will be taken back. It is said a number will not come back at all.

We have nothing stirring in town but a plenty of dust—and warm weather. Have been taking tea out at various places, paying up Mother's calls for her and beguiling time. Expect to take tea this evening with Mrs. Macfie.

Saw Miss Sarah Jones on Saturday; all very busy at Barhamville. Examination takes place this week, and term closes. The poor crazy young lady— the teacher—is no better. Her mother has come to carry her home! An affecting thing!

It was expected that Colonel Elmore would lie in the town hall a day or more before his funeral; but his body could not be kept, and he had to be buried the evening he was brought up—by *torchlight!* Such poor creatures are we! I send you the paper containing Mr. Palmer's sermon on the occasion next day (Sabbath). Did not hear it; was attending the Odd Fellows' Sunday school with Joe.

Dr. Leland has come back in fine health and spirits.

Columbia with all the trees looks beautifully. I never saw the view from the steeple of the town house before Saturday. Joe and I went there; it is remarkably fine—better than that from the arsenal or from any other point I know.

The members of Mr. Palmer's congregation are proceeding with their subscription for the new church: something over $12,000 subscribed; subscription binding when it reaches $16,000. Hope they will succeed. They have not called on me yet. Suppose they may not, considering *the fire* and my present *unsettled state*. Can't give much anyhow. Dr. Howe gave $400.

Be careful how you break your pony. Do not run any risks. Hope the carriage horses are in good order.

Tell Mother she must read this letter, as it is for her too. Will write her again before I start for home, God willing. Kiss Mother for me. Love to Aunty and Uncle, to all at Woodville, and all friends. Howdy for the people by name. Joe is in my room, and unites in all this. Excuse this steel pen; it makes me write worse than usual. I remain, my dear son,

Your ever affectionate father,
C. C. Jones.

Rev. C. C. Jones *to* Miss Mary Sharpe Jones[t]

Columbia, *Wednesday,* June 19th, 1850

My dear Daughter,

I was very glad to receive your letter of the 10th. But you did not tell Father anything about your *throat*—whether it was better or not. Cousin Louisa said it was no better—that the caustic produced *no effect*. Then it might be well to stop it awhile and try something else. But I think it will be better as soon as your general health is improved.

These terrible steel pens! Can you read what I write?

And now let me tell you the latest news. Providence permitting, your brother Joe and myself will leave Columbia next Tuesday the 25th, be in Savannah Wednesday the 26th; and then we will all take the stage the next day, *Thursday the 27th;* and Mother will send the carriage to meet us at Midway; and so we will all go home together. Now, if you are still in Savannah, pack your trunk, get all ready for a start, *and be sure you pack Cousin Charlie off to the stage office and let him engage three seats for us—the stage to call for us at Aunt Susan's.* And tell Aunt Susan as my visit home is to consult friends about Philadelphia that she must think *fast,* and think *straight,* and have a right opinion to give me as soon as I get to her house Wednesday evening. I wish to see your dear mother and consult personally with her, as writing is very slow work, and return to Columbia the week after to the examination, and then back home again.

Your birthday was the 12th. I wish you, my dear child, every blessing, and hope God may spare you to usefulness, and fit you for the enjoyment of Him in another and a better world. My earnest prayers are ever directed heavenward for your conversion and sanctification. You have been a dutiful child to us, and we have had much comfort in you; and you know our love for you and our earnest desires for your every welfare. You owe everything to your dear mother, who has watched over you with the tenderest and most unceasing care from your very birth. May you ever be a good daughter and a constant comfort and support to her!

I long to see you once more. Hope you have given no trouble to your dear aunt and Cousin Laura, and that you have made some progress in your music.

Mr. and Mrs. Zimmerman send their special regards to you. They say you were their *favorite* scholar, and Mrs. Z. was much pleased when I told her that you had put her present in the form of a *brooch* to remember her kindness by. Joe and I went to see them, and they would hardly let us come away. The name of the nice vegetable they sent me is *kohlrabi;* it is sold under the name. Plant and set out like cabbage.

I will reserve all my talk and news until we meet, God willing. Mr. Donald Fraser will hand you this and tell you all he knows about Columbia. Mrs. Young and Miss Amanda send much love, and all friends also. Cousin Lou leaves next week: Wednesday. Pray excuse my bad pen, my trembling hand, my bad writing. It is *very hot* in my room. All Columbia smokes with heat. I long for a cool place and a cool breeze. Our love to Aunt Susan, Cousins Laura and Charlie, and respects to Messrs. M. and W. Cumming. All well at Mrs. Thompson's. And love to you. I remain, my dear daughter,

Your affectionate father,
C. C. Jones.

Mrs. Mary Jones *to* Rev. C. C. Jones[t]

Maybank, Wednesday, June 19th, 1850

My dear Husband,

Your last affectionate favor of the 13th is before me; at the same time I received those enclosed from Dr. Alexander, Mr. Gildersleeve, and Mr. Leyburn. Dr. A. writes cautiously; the other two decidedly in favor of *Philadelphia*.

Upon the point of duty my own mind is perfectly undecided. When the vast field of usefulness unfolds itself through the secretaryship, then comes the positive injury to the Southern church in your leaving the seminary. One view balances the other. The desolation which will probably come over our home and servants by entire absence presses heavily upon my heart and conscience. And yet if it be evident that you have been called of God to this work, He will take care of us and our interest if we give up houses and lands for His sake.

I have many fears for the effect which has been produced upon Charles by the breaking up of his class—arresting him in the most important period of college life. It has created a desultory state of mind. His plans and prospects, so flattering, have been suddenly arrested and crushed. He says if he goes to Princeton he knows that he will take no stand there, and speaks discouragingly of his future success in study. He has read frequently to me, but seems little disposed for systematic study. I have not urged this, as relaxation seemed necessary for a time; but it is over two months that he has been unemployed, and I shall feel thankful when he is again at regular work. I approve more and more of Joseph's wise decision to remain and prosecute his regular studies until the close of the term.

Mary is very anxious to return home, and her Uncle Henry and Aunt Abby will be in Savannah next week, and have offered her a seat out. I am delighted at the thought of seeing you so soon, and my dear Joseph too.

Mary Nisbet wrote Laura it was reported in Charleston that previously to the fire your mind had been very much exercised upon the point of having left the *black field,* and that you now viewed our calamities there as an intimation in providence that you ought to return to your duty amongst the blacks in Liberty. Laura replied that such views were entirely new to us; that your decision to go to Columbia arose from a conviction of duty, and your views were the same as ever. It must be to *such reports* as these that Mr. Gildersleeve alluded in his letter. I do long to see you and talk all my mind on the many subjects of interest now engrossing our attention.

Whilst I remember it, Miss Mary Mell begs you to obtain from Miss Jones as you pass through Charleston a likeness promised her of some friend there and bring it on with you.

I received a very interesting letter from Miss Clay a few mails since, and one from Cousin Mary.

Cousin Joseph Robarts speaks of leaving next Friday for Marietta. Poor fellow, all is not right with him. I fear it would break my dear aunt's heart to see him as I did on last Monday afternoon as we came through the Boro. Although he had left us in the morning, having spent Sabbath night with us, he promised to come and spend last night with us, but did not. I really thought if he came that I would try and speak to him on the subject; it might arrest his attention. At least it is duty to do all we can to rescue him from present and eternal ruin. Do not say anything of this to Louisa; it would only distress her uselessly.

This morning Sister Betsy and Miss Valeria Cassels rode to Maybank. Brother William was too unwell to come—with the same affection of his bowels. We ordered our carriage, and Charles drove us to Half Moon, Social Bluff, and Woodville; and they returned to Sunbury to dinner. Julia has heard from Mr. King and the boys: safely arrived after a long but pleasant passage.

Say to Joseph that I bought him two summer vests in Savannah, and a pair of plaid cassimere pants; and if he requires anything more, he must get Aunt Susan to choose them for him at Snider's as he comes through. Providence permitting, you may expect me to meet you certainly at Midway with the carriage and jersey. Mary must send her baggage along with yours in the stage. Sister Betsy will take no denial; she says *we must* come on and dine with her in Sunbury, as she intends to kill the fatted lamb for you. I have promised her to do so. Can you not bring Sister Susan and Laura and Charlie with you for the summer? It would be so pleasant to us all out here. I will give out extensively the notice of your preaching. . . . Do, my dear husband, if there is anything in your wardrobe that you need, bring the articles, that I may make them before you return.

I am expecting Sister Abby and Henry every moment to spend the night with me, and will leave my letter until morning.

They have not come, so I will close my letter tonight, as I wish to send it early in the morning.

Please when you come through Savannah bring a vial of *strong caustic* that may be diluted for Charles's throat; it is again in a bad condition, and he must persevere in the use of the caustic. He is scarcely able to sing or play his flute.

The servants all send many howdies for you, and are very much pleased to hear you are coming so soon. Mr. Shepard desires remembrance, and says I must tell you "he is very much cast down about the drought, but that it comes from above and we must not repine." The corn crops in the county are nearly destroyed. Our own prospects are sad in the provision line.

Present my best love to Dr. and Mrs. Howe, and the same to Mrs. Young, with grateful thanks for her kindness to Joseph. The same to all my other friends, not forgetting *Mrs. Thompson*. If you could procure a copy of "The Glory of Woman," I should like very much to have one presented to *Mrs. Zimmerman* in my name. I find the copy *you* gave me amongst my treasures at home.

And now, my dearest husband, good night. And good-bye until we meet. Charles unites with me in best love to you and Joseph, and to Louisa and Mr. Rogers. May the Lord bless and direct you, ever prays

Your affectionate wife,
Mary Jones.

What will it cost to put a head- and footstone to Jack's grave? We desire, you know, to have it done.

Rev. C. C. Jones *to* Mrs. Mary Jones[t]

Columbia, *Thursday,* June 20th, 1850

My dear Mary,

Another disappointment! No letter from you this evening. One came from Sister Betsy, for which I feel truly thankful to her; and one from Charles to Joseph, containing but little news. I have been away from home *five weeks* tomorrow, and in that time have received but *two letters* from you. I do not think you ever wrote as seldom; and I thought considering our recent trials and present unsettled circumstances you would have found much to say. Your letters, I am sure, would have been a great comfort to me. But Sister's letter enables me to account for it all. She says you have not been as much with her and Brother as they expected; that you have been fixing your household affairs and doing all sorts of things, and could not visit much until you got fixed. Well, it is all right. But I cannot repress my feeling of disappointment. Am glad to learn through Sister that you spend your time so socially and pleasantly with Mrs. King, your old friend and neighbor, and that both yourself and Charles look better.

My room in the afternoon is very warm, and I have adopted the plan of paying a visit or taking a cup of tea out, paying up your calls for you to the many kind friends we have met with here. I have taken tea at Dr. Howe's, Dr. Leland's, Mr. Snowden's, Mr. Thompson's, Mrs. Macfie's, Mrs. Young's; and called on Mrs. Taylor, Mrs. Beckett, and Mr. Zimmerman; and have received *one call*—and that from Mr. Snowden! Such is the society in which we have moved. As Dr. Trezevant (whom, by the way, I have called upon twice) says, all such sociability as these friendly social visits are nearly extinct in Columbia. Yet a friendly people otherwise. These visits have been pleasant, and in every instance the kindest inquiries made after you, and kindest remembrances sent you—Mrs. Beckett and Mrs. Taylor particularly.

Dr. Trezevant thinks the advantages accruing to the family by a removal to Philadelphia will be superior to those enjoyed here; nor would he be apprehensive of the *climate*. He seems to think a change desirable. Thus he expressed himself this afternoon.

The students seem to have come nearly to the conclusion that I will go. It is a kind of general impression in the town, though I have never said: "I will go." The dealings of Providence have been so remarkable they know not what to say.

Have been paying up the expenses incurred in consequence of our afflictions and the fire. Have not received Dr. Trezevant's bill. He told me I should have it before I left for home on next Tuesday *the 25th.* I do not know what it will be; but *I shall be glad if the salary up to July 1st pays up all.* I shall then leave Columbia without any pecuniary responsibilities behind. It is indeed a place for expenses. We have found it so.

The chimney and desolated lot remain as when you left. Have been there twice and tried to recall and realize God's judgments and mercies to us. May we learn wisdom!

I have come to no conclusion positively, but the preponderance in many points given is in favor of Philadelphia. There are some things I wish I could see clearer.

I asked Dr. Leland: "What if a person should conclude to go?"

He replied: "We should *lose* a great deal, and they would *gain* a great deal; that would be all."

I said: "Well, it is strange to me. I cannot see *that* either way."

"No," said he; "when John Newton's man came to him and told him that he (Newton's man himself) was like a shock of corn fully ripe and fit for the garner, Newton told him he was mistaken, for those who were so *never knew it.*"

I have recovered my course from the notes of the students in tolerable good form. They are now reviewing the questions and answers for examination. And am now trying to recover something of the lectures on unregeneracy in the ministry. Have been kept very busy. It seems hard for me ever to have a time of leisure.

Louisa goes next Wednesday in company with Mrs. Brown all the way to

Marietta. Mr. Brown sees them as far as Augusta. A good opportunity. She is looking very well, and seems to have enjoyed her visit.

I wrote to John some time since, but have received no answer. Have written to Dr. Talmage and Mr. Adger as you suggested.

I hope you have received my letter informing you that Joe and I would leave here next Tuesday the 25th and reach Liberty, God willing, on Thursday the 27th, and that you must send the carriage for us to Midway. Both his trunk and mine will be large and heavy, with some other baggage; and *the cart had better come with the carriage for the baggage.* It will be too much for the carriage alone. The weather is so warm and dry, *I think you had better stay at Maybank and not come to meet us;* and we will come directly down there. *I do not wish to go to Sunbury first.* The stage will not be at Midway much before 2 P.M., I suppose; but the carriage ought to be there by 12 M. Gilbert can bring a light feed for the horses, and they can be eating while he is waiting. Shall not write you again, as there will be no opportunity before we set out; and I trust a kind Providence may spare our lives to meet again in peace.

My love and thanks to Sister for her letter. And love to Brother; am sorry to hear he is unwell again. Our love to Charles; will tell him all the news of college when we come down. Joe's examination begins on Saturday. Howdy for the servants by name. Students all well. Mary Sharpe in her letter to Joe says she goes out this week with her Uncle Henry; had written her to get ready to go out with us. Received a long letter from General Cocke of sympathy and affection to us both and the children; he thinks Charles would do well at the university. My paper is out. I wonder if you will be glad to see me? Dr. Trezevant says if Mary Sharpe's throat continues affected that twenty grains of *iodine* rubbed up with cerate and rubbed on the *tonsils* externally will take the inflammation away.

Your ever affectionate husband,
C. C. Jones.

Rev. John McDowell *to* Rev. C. C. Jones[t]

Philadelphia, *Thursday,* June 27th, 1850

Reverend and dear Sir,

Your letter addressed to Rev. Dr. William A. McDowell, my brother, has been received, and was laid before the executive committee at their meeting last week. My brother has left the city, and the committee requested me to answer it. My brother saw your letter before he left, and will probably write you from his new residence. The board meet next Monday week, when your letter will be laid before them. I rejoice at the hope your letter inspires that you will come to us; and in the earnest desire that it may be so the members of the board individually, as far as I have heard, unite. And not only the members of the board, but the friends of the institution generally far and near. The domestic missionary cause is one of great and rapidly increasing

interest. I fully believe that there is no station in our church at this day of greater, if as great, importance as that of secretary of our domestic missionary board. The field of usefulness is immense.

We have created the office of assistant secretary, and have appointed Rev. R. Happersett to that office. He has been a very efficient agent for several years, during which time he has been so frequently in the office as to become acquainted with its routine of business. He will afford you valuable assistance.

I pray the Lord may direct you, as I believe He will, in deciding on the important question before you. And if it might be His will you should come, we will rejoice and thank Him; but if not, we ought to submit.

Philadelphia is a very healthy city; and as far as comfort is concerned, we have everything of a temporal nature to promote it. Board can be had at all prices according to location and accommodations—say, from $5 to $10. You can rent houses already furnished. Rents in Philadelphia compared with New York are moderate.

With fraternal respect yours,
John McDowell.

REV. J. J. JANEWAY *to* REV. C. C. JONES[t]

Philadelphia, *Thursday,* June 27th, 1850

Reverend and dear Sir,

At the request of Dr. McDowell I add that I cordially concur in what he has written, and hope and pray that God—if it be His holy will—may incline your heart to accept the important office which the Board of Missions has tendered to you.

Affectionately yours,
J. J. Janeway.

REV. C. C. JONES *to* MRS. MARY JONES[t]

Columbia, *Monday,* July 8th, 1850

My dear Mary,

I had a pleasant ride down to Savannah after spending near an hour in meditation in Midway graveyard, a place dear to me. Became acquainted with the son of Colonel Lewis Morris, of South Carolina, a young officer of the U.S. navy, and an interesting young man. Found Sister, Laura, and Charlie all well; and Cousin Charles West came and took tea with us; he is on his way with Cousin Evelyn and Maria to the North for Cousin Evelyn's health. He heard our statement about our call, etc., and said at once *we ought to go.* I was struck with his decision. John had told him of it before he came down the country.

Was a little seasick Saturday morning. Stayed with our kind friends the Misses Jones, who desire sincerest regards to you. They are all for Philadelphia. Miss Sarah says I will not live long if I remain in Columbia. Preached

51

twice for Mr. Adger's black people yesterday. Had some liberty; read several of Whitefield's sermons with profit—one on the benefit of afflictions in particular. He says "he never bore the Cross but he always found it *lined* with the love of God." How beautiful! And to God's own people how true! The sermons are very incomplete, being taken down in shorthand as he preached them.

Felt very badly this morning: too much effort yesterday. Do not think it will be unlawful for me to *rest awhile*. Warm ride up today; good company: Rev. Messrs. Adger and Palmer. Am at the hotel; did not go to Dr. Howe's, as I felt badly and wished for special reasons to be as much alone for a few days as I can. Besides, I thought the doctor would have some of his friends from the up country staying with him during the examination. He and Mr. Rogers called just as I finished dressing. All well.

Letters from several brethren. Dr. Talmage gives no advice; sees the importance of both fields, and thinks I must decide for myself. Dr. *John* McDowell and Dr. Janeway write expressing strong hope that I may accept. Board from $5 to $10 according to location and accommodations, and I suppose lower. Houses may be rented *furnished*. Never felt more the need of God's direction. Sometimes the way seems clear to go, then not. Have soon to decide; and pray the Lord to direct us. Know not exactly how to do, as my presbytery have not been consulted but in part. Must arrange all prudently and orderly.

I write by the mail, hoping you may get this Thursday; but it is very doubtful, as the letter if it arrives in Savannah late Wednesday evening is apt to lie over from want of activity in the office. If you get the letter, you can hold to our arrangement and send the carriage for me to Midway on Monday the 15th; and if anything should prevent my coming—more than I know—then send on Thursday. But my present hope is to be with you, my dear wife, God willing, on Monday the 15th. Love and kisses to my dear children. Have got a Princeton catalogue; the term of the college year begins *the 8th of August. Near at hand.* Love to my dear brother and sister, and kind regards to Mrs. King and family. Howdy for all the servants by name. The Lord bless and preserve you, my dear wife, and be your portion and everlasting reward!

Your true lover and devoted husband,
C. C. Jones.

Rev. C. C. Jones *to* The Presbyterian Board of Missions[t]
Columbia, Wednesday, July 10th, 1850

Reverend and dear Brethren,

Since the receipt of your letter informing me of the fact of my appointment by the Board of Missions to fill the vacancy occasioned by the resignation of Dr. W. A. McDowell as corresponding secretary of the board, I have been in communication with Dr. W. A. McDowell in relation to the appointment, and have had it under serious and I trust prayerful consideration. Last evening I sent in to the board of directors of our theological seminary, now in session here and in attendance upon the closing exercises of the term, my resignation of the professorship which I have held in the seminary; and I accept the office to which you have called me.

I accept it believing it to be a call from God, so far as I have been enabled to discern His will through His providences towards myself and family, and through the opinions of relatives and Christian brethren and the church generally. I enter this new field not knowing what may befall me, but let my trust and my rest be in the Lord, whose mercies are very great, whose grace He maketh sufficient for His people in their day, who even quickeneth the dead and calleth those things which be not as though they were. I feel also specially encouraged to undertake the work because of the hearty cooperation and direction which you have promised me for yourselves and the board, and because of your recent appointment of a brother as assistant secretary long tried and experienced. I cannot, however, disguise it: I have many fears and misgivings, and shall need your prayers, your counsel and kind indulgence. I can promise you nothing more than a willing mind and heart and a faithful endeavor to fulfill the duties of the office to the best of my ability. The Lord add the blessing!

It will be out of my power to remove to Philadelphia before the month of October—as early in the month as may be practicable—because we are obliged to make many arrangements in relation to our domestic affairs in prospect of long absence from home, which arrangements cannot be completed in a day. Added to this, the state of Mrs. Jones's health and my own demands some quiet, and that we make no changes during the heat of summer. Meanwhile I trust that my good friend and brother, the Rev. Mr. Happersett, with your assistance if necessary, may be able to carry on the business of the office, and the cause suffer no harm.

I shall embrace these weeks of retirement to make some preparations for my new field of labor, that at my coming I may enter upon my work without delay, and thus shall be profitably though not directly employed for the board.

Will you be kind enough to address me at *Riceboro, Liberty County, Georgia?*

With great respect and affection, I am, reverend and dear brethren,

Your brother in Christ our Lord,

C. C. Jones.

REV. JOHN McDOWELL *to* REV. C. C. JONES[t]

Philadelphia, *Friday,* July 19th, 1850

Reverend and dear Sir,

Your letter addressed to the committee of the Board of Missions, informing us of your acceptance of your appointment as secretary, has been received. As

I am the only member of the committee in the city, I have felt it my duty to drop you a line acknowledging the receipt of yours. The acceptance will be announced in *The Presbyterian* of tomorrow. I most cordially rejoice and thank the Lord for the result of this appointment; and as far as I have heard, all interested in our board are highly gratified with the intelligence. I believe, my dear brother, you have the confidence of the friends of domestic missions, and we view it as a smile of Providence that He has inclined you to accept.

I wrote to you about two weeks since and answered as far as I could your inquiries in a previous letter. Any information I can give you I shall be happy to communicate. Mr. Happersett, your assistant, is now the chief man in the office. I think you will find him a valuable assistant. Freely communicate with my brother the late secretary. He will be ready to give you any information you may need as to your duties. His whole soul is still devoted to this work, and he has had long experience, and is possessed of much practical wisdom. He was greatly interested in your acceptance, and will rejoice to hear of it. His post office address is Pluckemin, Somerset County, New Jersey.

The stated monthly meeting of the board will be the second Monday in August, when your letter will be laid before them.

With fraternal respect and affection yours,
John McDowell.

II

Rev. *and* Mrs. C. C. Jones *to* Messrs. Charles C. Jones, Jr., *and* Joseph Jones^g
Maybank, *Friday,* July 26th, 1850

Our very dear Sons,

It is for the first time in your lives that you are about to leave your home and the society of your parents to be absent for a length of time, and at great distance, among strangers. And we cannot forbear addressing to you a few parting counsels, which we hope you will regard as the expression of our deep interest in your welfare and our sincere affection for you. And it gives us pleasure to believe that they will receive not only consideration but be adopted by you as rules upon which you may frame your character and regulate your lives.

(1) In the first place, then, we trust that you will regularly *twice every day,* morning and evening, seriously, reverently, and teachably *read a portion of God's Holy Word and pray to Him in secret.* As you have been taught thus to do from your earliest years, so we hope you will never omit this sacred and necessary duty.

(2) That you will conscientiously *remember the Sabbath Day to keep it holy,* frequenting the House of God at least twice in the day, and spending the rest of its hours in reading the Scriptures and good books, and in meditation and prayer, and in consistent company and conversation.

(3) That you will shun with horror any suggestions or opinions, whether advocated by living men or advanced by authors in books, no matter how distinguished in the world for science or learning and wisdom, that would lead you to disbelieve or even to doubt in the least degree *the truth of God's Holy Word.* "Wherewithal shall a young man cleanse his way? By taking heed thereto according to Thy Word" (Psalm 119:9). That Word is a lamp unto our feet, and a light unto our path. *"Let God be true: though every man be a liar!"*

(4) That you will devote yourselves faithfully and conscientiously *to your studies,* and make every improvement in your power, and not misspend your time nor abuse your advantages. In order to this you must preserve your *health* by a rigid system of *diet, rest,* and *exercise.* Observe the appointed hours of study; be punctual to recitations and lectures and chapel prayers, and scrupulously observant of the laws and regulations of the college; and show all proper respect and obedience to your teachers and governors.

(5) As you have always been advocates of temperance and have discarded

as unnecessary, expensive, and positively injurious and therefore immoral *the use of ardent spirits and of tobacco* in all their forms, so we trust that you will never under any circumstances or influences depart from these good opinions and habits.

(6) We trust that you will avoid the company and association of *profane, Sabbath-breaking, idle, intemperate, immoral, and dissipated young men,* and on the contrary, cultivate and prize the society of young gentlemen of intelligence, integrity, and piety of character. For they that walk with the wise shall be wise; but the companion of fools shall be destroyed.

(7) That you will abstain from engaging *in all games of chance, as cards, dice, lotteries,* etc., and on no consideration hazard one cent in the way of *betting.*

(8) That you will go to *no theater nor circus nor horse race,* nor to any place of *dissipated* or of *low amusement,* however patronized and advocated by your fellow students, or by persons who may be considered the respectable, the wealthy, and the gay. *Frequent no eating or drinking houses.*

(9) That you will *not be out of your room at night,* except it be at some proper meeting connected with the college or the service of religion or at the house of respectable friends, spending a social evening with them. And *do not sleep out of your room* with other students or friends who may invite you.

(10) That you will avoid engaging in *any college riots or rebellions,* or in any *acts of the students* to disturb the town or to annoy the professors and tutors.

(11) That you will always endeavor *to respect the feelings and rights and circumstances of your fellow men,* and conduct yourselves as well-bred gentlemen, and men of character, dignity, principle, and honor, in all your associations and dealings with your officers and fellow students, and with the citizens of the town of Princeton, and all with whom you may have to do. And specially refrain from familiarity with persons of low character or inferior stations in society. Have self-respect.

(12) That you will be *economical in your expenditures and never run in debt,* but meet all your pecuniary engagements *upon your word and to your word.* If possible, borrow from none. Be careful to whom you lend. Generously give according to your means. Take care of your books, clothing, etc., that nothing may be lost or wasted through neglect or inattention. In order to this we recommend you to keep your room in a neat and orderly manner, to preserve an inventory of your clothing, a catalogue of your books, and a regular account of all your expenses, however minute.

(13) Embrace opportunities for a favorable introduction into respectable, religious, and honorable families, and improve yourselves by the best associations. Look upward, and while you enjoy the refining influences of elevated female society, lay aside all flippancy of behavior and excess of manner or dress, and form no connections beyond those of friendly intercourse. While we would deprecate promiscuous and excessive visiting as

decidedly injurious to your character and standing as scholars, we would recommend occasional visiting, in such families as those now indicated, as of essential benefit.

(14) You will always remember *that you are own and dear brothers.* Therefore be *respectful, kind, accommodating, patient, generous, and affectionate to each other;* and under all circumstances of trial or necessity or suffering *stand by each other as nearest friends;* and promote each other's peace, happiness, reputation, and success in life, without envy or jealousy, by every lawful and just means in your power.

(15) And we add in conclusion, our dear sons, what we have always endeavored to inculcate and impress upon you—*that you remember your God and your Redeemer, and the priceless value of your immortal souls, and the near approach of death, judgment, and eternity,* and never be at peace until you have obtained that good part which shall not be taken away from you. We can sincerely and freely say that nothing can come upon you in this life— no learning, no honor, no wealth, no reputation, no power—which will fill the hearts of your affectionate parents with greater or more lasting joy *than to know that you are the true children of God by faith in Jesus Christ our Lord.*

We shall hope and firmly anticipate your attention to these counsels. And we believe that you will take pleasure in endeavoring faithfully to observe them—for the happiness which it will afford your parents as well as for the good which will accrue to your own selves for this world and for that which is to come. *Ask God's aid.* As children of the covenant, early dedicated to your God and Redeemer, we commend you to His loving-kindness and tender mercy. And be assured that we shall ever do all in our power to promote your welfare, and that you will ever have the prayers and true affection of

> Your own dear father and mother,
> C. C. Jones
> Mary Jones.

Mr. Charles C. Jones, Jr., *to* Rev. *and* Mrs. C. C. Jones[t]
Savannah, Saturday, July 27th, 1850

My dear Parents,

Although this may be premature, still as I may not have a suitable opportunity of writing you from Charleston, this opportunity has been embraced of transmitting a few lines in order to state progress and assure you that we are both well. Brother, to use his own expression, feels *"first-rate,"* and we hope that he will have no return of his former indisposition.

Had a very pleasant ride from Riceboro to this place, enjoying the society of Mr. and Mrs. Spencer. Mrs. Spencer is really a very agreeable lady, and she and myself had a delightful ride, with the exception of the numerous jolts, which in consequence of the construction of our conveyance were very perceptible. One of the passengers, Mr. Spalding, appeared quite fond of the regular "brown stuff," and made no bones about indulging his propensities on every occasion, so that by the time we reached Savannah he was, to use a familiar expression, "pretty well corned." At Butler's two more persons (gentlemen) favored us with their company. We now numbered eight altogether, and owing to the heat of the day and the narrow compass of our accommodations did not enjoy the latter portion of our ride as much as the former. Arrived at Savannah at 5 P.M., and found all friends well and very glad to see us.

Cousin Laura has just heard from Cousin Louisa, who stated that all were well, and that Mr. Rogers was staying with them; preached twice on Sabbath, and expects to meet us in Charleston. Brother and myself obtained the checks by paying a small premium; they are upon the Philadelphia bank. I was invited to tea at Mr. Woodbridge's this evening, but in consequence of a rain did not comply with Miss Margaret's request. Will call, however, on Monday and see her. Aunt Susan wrote you upon a very important subject, and was much surprised that you had not received her letter. Cousin Laura has sent a small package, and says that there is no special news in this place. The gasworks are now in operation, and the lights in the streets and private houses, stores, etc., appear to great advantage, exhibiting a marked difference to the former dull oil lamps.

I have thus told you all that I have either seen or heard; not there there is anything herein contained which will prove very interesting, but as you, my kind mother, requested that we should communicate every circumstance, trivial though it be, which transpires, and this being a favorable opportunity of letting you know of our welfare, I embraced the chance.

In regard to our likenesses, we went this morning with Cousin Charles to the daguerreau rooms and sat twice. Both of the pictures were very much blurred, and we consequently did not take them. Upon our requesting the officiator to try again, he said that was as well as he could do, and accordingly refused to take another sitting, saying that the pictures were sufficiently correct. He is, I think, a man of limited abilities in his profession and withal very impertinent and coarse in his manners.

Brother, Aunt Susan, and family all unite with me in much love to yourselves and Sister. Remember me kindly to all at Woodville. Also give my best love to Aunty and Uncle; also to Uncle Henry and Aunt Abby. As ever, my dear parents,

Your affectionate son,

Charles C. Jones, Jr.

P.S. We expect to leave on Monday evening for Charleston, and you may expect to hear from us at every opportunity. This, as you will see, has been written in a great hurry, and consequently I hope that you will excuse errors if any there be.

C. C. J., Jr.

Mr. Charles C. Jones, Jr., *to* Rev. *and* Mrs. C. C. Jones[t]
Barroom of the American Hotel

Charleston, South Carolina, *Tuesday,* July 30th, 1850

My dear Parents,

Agreeable to promise, I embrace this opportunity of sending you a few lines, although present circumstances forbid that I should be at all lengthy. We left Savannah on Monday evening and arrived here this morning at nine o'clock. Had a delightful run, the weather being calm and the sea comparatively smooth. Our boat was the *General Clinch,* which is just from the stocks, where she has been entirely refitted, and is accordingly in fine order for travel.

Mr. Milton Bacon, the principal of the LaGrange Female Seminary, was one of the passengers. He appeared very glad to see us from Liberty, and he and myself had a very lengthy conversation, in which he gave me a complete description of the institute in which he is engaged; and from his account, and the interest manifested, I would infer that it must be in a most flourishing condition. We will have him as a fellow passenger as far as Philadelphia, his purpose and object being to visit those of the Northern female colleges which are of most note, see and examine their plans of operation, and thence deduce principles of improvement by which his own academy may be advanced and profited. His whole heart seems to be wrapped up in his present operations. He saw all our friends in Marietta; says that they are all with the exception of Aunt Eliza in the enjoyment of fine health.

Neither Brother nor myself were at all seasick.

We called upon Mr. Adger this morning; saw him and also Messrs. Law and Ellison from Columbia. They inquired particularly after you and Sister, and desired me to present their regards as soon as I wrote.

Mr. Rogers is not in this place, and I fear that we shall not have the pleasure of his company. We shall not wait, however, but intend sailing for Wilmington at 3 P.M. per ship *Gladiator*. Our through tickets are purchased, and our berths have been engaged.

We are here at this house for dinner only. The gong has sounded, and I must conclude. Brother unites in much love to yourselves, Sister, all friends in Liberty, and the servants. In great haste,
Your affectionate son,

Charles C. Jones, Jr.

Mr. Charles C. Jones, Jr., *to* Rev. *and* Mrs. C. C. Jones[t]
Jones's Hotel, Philadelphia, *Saturday,* August 3rd, 1850

My dear Parents,

Brother and Mr. Rogers have this evening gone to visit Barnum's Museum, and it is with much pleasure that I embrace a few moments to spend in converse with those of my own native land, and whom God has ordained as my best friends this side the grave. In consequence of the crowded rooms in Washington and the many circumstances conspiring to engage our attention, I did not write from Washington, and consequently will commence a brief narration of those events which transpired upon and after leaving Charleston, from which place you last heard from me.

Mr. Rogers arrived just in time to reach the boat (steamer *Gladiator*) before she left for Wilmington. We had a very pleasant and prosperous passage —the sea comparatively smooth and the heavens unclouded—so that although many of the passengers (who numbered 150) were sick, still neither Messrs. Rogers, Bacon, Brother, nor myself suffered in the least from seasickness. At night the weather was so warm in the cabin that we all (with the exception of Brother, who was too sleepy to realize the surrounding temperature) went up on the upper deck, crawled into a small boat which was laying there, and thus under the open canopy of the heavens laid ourselves down to rest—though, as Mr. Bacon remarked, there was too much romance about it to sleep. Arrived in Wilmington by breakfast hour.

There was one of my classmates along on board the *Gladiator:* Burgess Gordon. He appeared quite glad to see me, and expressed his regret at my intention to leave the class. Fifty-three have been admitted, the examination according to his account being a mere nominal thing.

At Washington we put up at the National Hotel, which is the finest by a great deal of any in the city; and there I met with another collegemate, John Moore, a very estimable young man, now studying law at Cambridge.

We went to the Capitol as soon as our baggage had all been safely taken care of, and there witnessed one of the most interesting sights I ever beheld. There were at least three thousand little children who were in attendance upon the schools, each schoolteacher attending his or her appropriate scholars dressed in different uniforms, and every company of them wearing various badges. After forming in the grounds of the Capitol around a stand erected for the occasion, they were addressed by the mayor of the town, who was succeeded by the Hon. Mr. Chandler, who delivered an appropriate and eloquent address. Those of the scholars who had distinguished themselves at a late examination of all the schools (by an appointed committee) were called by the mayor upon the stage, where they were presented with silver medals by the President, Mr. Fillmore, who did this in a manner as bland and mild as can be imagined, accompanying the presentation of the prizes with a separate encouraging word of commendation. The President is one of the finest men in his personal appearance that I ever have seen; in fact, he is what would commonly be called "a remarkably handsome man." On the whole it was a very pleasant sight indeed, and the performances were all conducted with great propriety and decorum.

On Friday morning we visited the Smithsonian Institute, a very unique and splendid edifice, constructed principally after the Lombard style of architecture. The material of which it is constructed is red freestone, obtained about twenty miles above Washington. As yet it is far from completion, although the work of construction is progressing rapidly. Saw there Professor Henry of Princeton, a robust and fine-looking man. They have there a splendid chemical apparatus, especially in regard to the branch of electricity.

From thence we proceeded to take a view of the Monument. It will indeed be a work worthy of our country. The Pantheon has as yet not been commenced, and will not be until the obelisk be completed. We saw several blocks from the states set in the shaft. The material employed in constructing the Monument is white marble.

We next took a view of the Observatory, and were very kindly attended throughout the building by one of the clerks, who explained the various instruments, many of which were exceedingly complicated, and showed to what a surprising degree the invention of man has arrived. We remarked that in going to such a place a man was forcibly impressed with the fact that he is a short-sighted and ignorant creature; for although those instruments appeared to be fully comprehended and understood by the operators, still many of them to us were as unintelligible as the Hottentot language. However, "what man has done man can do."

From this place we proceeded to the White House, where we took a view of several rooms, but saw no one except the porter, who by the way was an amusing Irishman. As we were entering, our hackman, a regular son of Erin, came and peeped in at the door, upon which the porter exclaimed: "Take your nose out of the passage and let the gentlemen pass!" Whereupon the other, drawing himself up in a very dignified posture, with the utmost gravity asked if the President was at home, and requested the porter to conduct him to the hall and let the President know that he had called upon him. It was quite a hard cut upon our driver, for he is a man not at all deficient in the development of his olfactories.

When we arrived at the Capitol after leaving the President's house, we found the houses in session. Brother preferred spending his time in the Patent Office, and accordingly did not accompany us to the Capitol. I saw Mr. Jackson, and had a pleasant conversation with him, in which he alluded to our meeting at the North in 1839. With apparently much satisfaction he said that he was very glad to see me, and desired his respects to be presented to yourself, Mother, Uncle William, Uncles Henry, Charles B., etc. Mr. Colcock and Mr. Gurley were not in the House, and consequently I did not see them, although I left the letters for them with the porter. Next, on my going to the Senate, I saw Mr. Barnwell, who immediately upon the reception of your note came out, and we entered upon an interesting conversation. He likewise inquired very particularly about yourself, Mother, and all the family, accompanying it with his kindest regards. His son John was to have been in Washington today.

It is the opinion of Messrs. Barnwell, Jackson, Haralson, etc., that the prospect for the Union was never so dull as it at present is. Mr. Clay, in consequence of his having lost the compromise bill, is very much chagrined and vexed, insomuch that he will hardly speak to anyone. Saw him in the Senate chamber. He appears to be in very bad health, and I would not be surprised if his days were not almost numbered.

There was today a little sharpshooting between Mr. Foote and Mr. Atchison, in which the former was entirely vanquished. Mr. Foote said that "in case the Union was dissolved they would place even the smallest of the Southern states in the mouth of the Mississippi (Carolina, for instance), and that with her alone they could stop every vessel and everything that floated on the Western waters." Mr. Atchison replied that "he was fully persuaded that the first freshet would sweep that little state, people and all, into the bosom of the Gulf." There was no business of importance transacted this day, for as one of the members remarked, "there had been a general wreck in both houses, and they were now just trying to find their whereabouts."

We were kindly shown the library by the Hon. Mr. Venable, whom we found to be a most interesting gentleman, and a strong Presbyterian. Those paintings in the rotunda appeared very beautiful, the day being clear and bright.

I recognized the features of the landscape along the Potomac, and knew Mount Vernon as soon as we came opposite. While we were passing, the bell of the steamboat was tolled—a circumstance which shows in strong light what lasting regard and veneration the people of this country pay to the greatest of men.

We also visited the Patent Office, and were highly entertained by the many and various curiosities with which this building was replete.

Our time in Washington passed most delightfully, and will long be remembered with pleasure and interest.

Mr. Bacon is one of the most agreeable men to travel with I ever saw, being full of life and making good use of everything he sees. We are always together, occupying seats adjoining, and stopping at the same hotels, etc.

Two of the passengers lost their hats in the cars, having fallen asleep. One of them, however, waking up about the time that his hat was going, made such a noise that he terrified everyone in the car. He persuaded the engineer to run back, and thus recovered it. When he returned from hunting his hat, and got upon the cars, we saluted him with a loud clapping which reminded me of college times.

It is now so dark that I cannot see to write, and the gong has sounded for supper. We are now at Jones's Hotel, Philadelphia, and will leave on Monday for Princeton. Brother and Mr. Rogers unite with me in best love to yourselves, Sister, Aunty and Uncle, Uncle Henry and Aunt Abby, Aunt Julia, and all at Woodville. Tell all the servants howdy for me, and accept the kindest wishes of

Your attached son,
Charles C. Jones, Jr.

Enclosed is a little sprig from a tree in the grounds of the Capitol at Washington for Sister.

Maybank, *Monday,* August 5th, 1850

My dear Sons,

If a kind Providence has favored your plans, you will this day reach Princeton. Our hearts have gone with you every step of the journey; and hour after hour as we spoke of and traced your progress from one place to another on to your final destination have our hearts risen in prayer for the divine blessing and protection of those dear to us as our own life.

Oh, my sons, could you but know the feelings of your mother as for the first time she saw you departing from the parental roof to go where none would look upon you with aught but a stranger's passing interest, where no warm homelike greetings would bid you welcome, no older and faithful voice of admonition and reproof would turn and win you from the paths of temptation and sin that snare so many promising youth, and from which to this period we have tried to shelter and protect you by our restraints, our counsels, and our poor prayers—I say to you, could you know my feelings at this trying period, it would convey to you some impression of the deep anxiety and intense desire I have for your eternal well-being in time and throughout eternity. You have been the objects of our tenderest solicitude and care; and from the hour of your birth to the present time, with the exception of a temporary absence on account of health, there has scarcely been any hour or day when we could not have said where our dear children were and how employed, either in the week or on the Sabbath, by day or by night. Perhaps you have thought us too watchful—too strict. You will not think so in years to come, if your lives are spared—or even *now* if you will look at those whom parental indulgence or neglect have abandoned to habits of indolence and worthlessness if not to decided profligacy.

But the days of your childhood are now passed. My heart felt as though it would burst as the carriage bore you away from the home of your infancy and youth, perhaps nevermore to return. When you were out of sight your sister and myself returned to the house. We went into the little corner room, fell upon our knees, and there committed you again to our faithful covenant-keeping God and Saviour. We arose; and my heart felt comforted with the hope that our Heavenly Father would never leave nor forsake you. *"In all your ways acknowledge Him, and He will direct your paths."* But if you *forget Him, He will forget you, and if you forsake Him, He will cast you off forever.* God grant that this last may never be the case with you, whom "goodness and mercy have followed all the days of your life," and who so recently with your sister and parents have been snatched from the devouring flame.

I need not tell you how desolate the house has been since your departure. Numberless times I would detect myself listening for your step below stairs, and sometimes almost sending Titus off to call you in from the heat of the sun or away from your fishing at the bluff. As evening comes on we miss the music of Charles's flute; and your sister's sweet voice sounds solitary and alone at family worship. The day after you left, the servants would walk about the rooms, and I would hear them saying to themselves: "Oh, how we miss Marse Charles and Marse Joe! It looks like somebody was dead in the house."

Yesterday, which was Sabbath, we assembled as usual in Patience's house. But you, my dear son, were not there to render me the accustomed assistance in reading to the people. In the afternoon the lesson in the catechism was on the sufferings and death of our Saviour. They were very attentive. Mary thought several of them appeared to feel, George amongst the number. How happy it would make us to see them inquiring: "What shall I do to be saved?" My greatest trouble in leaving the South is parting with your aunt and uncle and our poor servants. They all say when I write to tell you both for them *a thousand howdies*. Be sure and remember them when you write by some kind message.

How did you spend your Sabbath in Philadelphia, and where did you go to church? I always wish when you write especially to know something about the manner in which you pass the Lord's Day: who preaches, and the text and sermons. This will prove a bond of union between us on the holy day. When your parents know that you are faithful and attentive hearers of God's Word and ministers, they will have the sweet assurance that you "remember the Sabbath Day to keep it holy." My dear children, God's hand has been in your removal to Princeton, and we pray Him to bless it to your spiritual good as well as to your intellectual improvement.

When you write Mr. Rogers, give our love and thanks for all his kindness to you.

By the last mail I received an affectionate letter from your Aunt Mary Robarts. She sends warmest love and best wishes for you both. Says to you, my son Charles, that she wishes not only to hear *of* but always to hear *from* you, and hopes you will correspond with her. She has been one of *your own* and your mother's kindest relatives, and I hope you will write her at your earliest leisure, and that Joseph and yourself will write your *Uncle John,* your uncle and aunty, and Uncle Henry. I say nothing of the friends in Savannah, as they will be in Philadelphia the 1st of October, but hope you will find time to write them also. You must learn—*especially my son Joseph* —to write in *snatches of time,* and then you will have opportunities for doing so to all of your friends.

All of your little *valuables* left in your room have been carefully put away— Charles's letters and papers in his desk, and the guns, etc., in the wardrobe. Mary frequently examines the *bugs* and suns the flying squirrels. Your dog Rex comes regularly at meal times; we talk to him of his master, and he gets many pieces of bread and meat for your sake, although your sister has sometimes to scold him for interfering with the kittens I give daily charges about Lilly, Firefly, and Dove. The *last* is privileged to eat the fresh green grass in the yard, and sometimes to take her supper of corn on the front steps. Gilbert says Dr. King wishes to purchase Firefly, and told him so. If he was in *sober* earnest, I presume we shall hear from him. Mr. Rahn says he would have given $30 or $35 for the horse you sold. I think you ought to get $80 for Firefly. I shall direct the boys to proclaim his merits.

We cut the *mammoth* melon, and your sister and myself have preserved the rinds to send you. Aunt Julia spent the day with us and helped to cut them. I intend sending a part of them to Willie and Fred as a remembrancer from Maybank.

They write their parents every week, Fred in his last letter speaking of Willie *to Audley*. He says: "We are closely *linked together*. Willie's joys are my joys; his sorrows are my sorrows; and so mine are his." What a delightful picture of brotherly love! Would that the same could flow sincerely from the hearts and lips and pens of my two sons! I trust it will be so. *Love one another with true hearts fervently.* You were born of the same parents, nursed from the same fountain of love, lived in the same home, reared at the same board, kneeled at the same knee and around the same family altar, were educated in the same manner, and should know no division of feelings, interests, or affections. Oh, how it would grieve my heart to feel that you *did not love* and were not *kind* to *each other!*

Your aunt still continues very feeble. Last week she quilted her laid-work quilt at Mrs. Winn's at Dorchester. Your sister and myself went on Wednesday to assist. All the ladies of the village were present excepting Mrs. Dr. Delegal, and there was a tight squeeze for places.

Your Uncle James was kind enough to send out your letter with a bundle of music for your sister. We were very happy to receive it, and it greatly relieved our anxieties on Joseph's account. I hope, my dear son, you are quite well by this time.

Last Sabbath your dear father preached at Pleasant Grove and administered the Communion; he has not yet returned.

7th. Your dear father returned Monday night, having had an overflowing house and very pleasant day.

Yesterday your aunt and uncle rode out early and spent the day with us. In the afternoon your Aunt Julia and the little ones, Mr. King, Audley, and Messrs. John and *William Stevens* (the latter having just returned from Houston County) rode over and took tea with us. We sat in the end of the piazza, where we usually do at that hour, and took our tea—a fresh sea breeze fanning most luxuriously. It was delightful, but our hearts wandered away to our dear absent children.

How many thoughts do you cast homeward? And will you be faithful to write me every week? I read your letter to your aunts, and we all spoke of you both. It was your trial day—examination for entrance into college. I trust you have been enabled to maintain your stands; but should you not enter the classes you desired to do, it may prove all for the best. God hath moved to us in a "mysterious way" of late, and we must submissively walk where *He* directs. I do hope and pray that this removal to Princeton may be of infinite advantage to you. . . .

I must now leave room for Father. Your sister also wished to write, but has gone home with Aunty. The servants *all* send you a thousand howdies, and your friends all a great deal of love. God bless you, my dear sons, ever prays
Your own affectionate mother,
Mary Jones.

Rev. C. C. Jones *to* Messrs. Charles C. Jones, Jr., *and* Joseph Jones[g]
Maybank,*Wednesday,* August 7th, 1850

My dear Boys,

Your dear mother has left this half-sheet for me to fill up instead of letting me write a separate letter.

You will never know the depth of our feelings and our anxieties upon your departure until you are parents and in circumstances like our own—if Providence shall so will it with you. My constant prayer for you day by day is that you may be kept from the evil in the world, and that the evil of your own hearts may be restrained and removed by the gracious operations of the Spirit of God, and that you may faithfully improve all your privileges and advantages and be employed usefully on earth, to the glory of God and the good of your fellow men. Much, yea everything, under God, will depend upon yourselves. And much of your standing and success in college both in studies and in character will depend upon a good beginning. I am anxious to learn the result of your *examination*. If you fail of entering the classes you apply for, you must take the *next* classes. But I hope we shall hear that you have entered as you desired. Give us a particular account of your travel and first impressions. Your stay in Washington must have been a great treat to you in many respects.

Since you left we have had some very warm days. Both Sabbaths I preached (Midway and Pleasant Grove) I had nothing to speak of dry upon me but my outer clothing. The old ones said: "Long-look come at last!" I told them that I had not seen so many friends, I hardly thought, for two years. They were—old and young— very attentive to all the services.

We have had some refreshing rains, and our prospects are tolerably fair all to the provision crop of corn. That must necessarily be short. The prospect at Arcadia in cotton and rice somewhat better than at Montevideo. But we cannot calculate upon returns before harvest, there are so many contingencies.

Your little colt, my son, Mr. Rahn delivered to the purchaser.

I took up McGuire's *Religious Character of General Washington,* the small volume which was your grandfather's, and have been reading it with great interest since you left, and would recommend you both to read it; and you will come to the conclusion that the great man of his race was something more than a mere believer in Christianity. He seems to have felt the power of religion. Before finishing the book I loaned it to Mr. John Stevens, and shall then loan it to Mr. King.

Have received two more letters from distinguished ministers expressing their high gratification at my acceptance of the secretaryship, and saying that I would go into office with the confidence of the whole church. We can only look to God for His blessing, without which we can do nothing. Do not fail to write weekly, and we shall try to do the same. The Lord be with you and bless you, my dear sons!

Your ever affectionate father,
C. C. Jones.

Mr. Charles C. Jones, Jr., *to* Rev. *and* Mrs. C. C. Jones[t]

Nassau Hall, Princeton, New Jersey, *Friday,* August 9th, 1850

My dear Parents,

You will perceive from the date of this letter that we have at length reached Princeton.

The last time you heard from us was at Philadelphia. While we were there whom should we see but our respected professor Dr. Henry stopping at the same hotel. He appeared very glad to meet us, and had me to accompany him wherever he went. His baggage had been misplaced at the depot, and not being able to obtain it, he gave it over into my hands as the younger of the two, and better able to navigate among wrangling drivers, lumbering omnibuses, and other hangers-on (always the concomitants of such places). When we parted he said: "Good-bye, Jones. God bless you. May you have a pleasant term!" I feel much attached to him, and shall always remember his kindness to us when connected with the college at Columbia.

Mr. Rogers accompanied us to Princeton, where we arrived at nine in the morning, having left Philadelphia at half-past five. He remained, however, only until five in the evening, being in some haste to reach Western Pennsylvania.

I forgot to mention that during our stay in Philadelphia a gentleman at Jones's Hotel, the house where we were boarding, died of the cholera—or, as others said, of diarrhea. Which of these statements is true I am not capable of deciding, though the majority seemed inclined to believe that his death was in consequence of the former of these diseases.

Now to college matters. As Brother is writing I will not touch much upon his affairs, and will be more personal. I have been examined by Dr. Maclean in Greek, Dr. Carnahan in physiology and evidences of Christianity, Dr. Forsyth in Latin, and last but by no means least, Dr. Alexander on mathematics; also Professor Hope in belles-lettres. My examination on all of these professors was, I believe, satisfactory. At least, I was told there would be no difficulty in entering the senior class on their departments. But Dr. Alexander took us upon arithmetic first, next on algebra, geometry, plane and spherical trigonometry, and finally wound me up amid the intricate mazes of differential and integral calculus. In this department I must candidly say that my preparation was not competent for the requisitions of this institution. In the

South Carolina College very little attention is paid to plane and spherical trigonometry, and none in the junior year to the calculus, either integral or differential. So that in this respect "Tekel" was my portion. There is no institution (West Point scarcely excepted) where there is so complete and full a course of mathematics, and one upon which so great importance is imposed upon this branch, as is here the case. It appears to be their pride to maintain the highest stand in this particular, and consequently all who apply must meet their fullest requisitions to the letter.

It is my candid belief that I could not do justice to my senior year if entering under these disadvantages, for such a thing as taking lessons privately in mathematics would be next to an impossibility; for it would require all my time to learn the regular recitations, and the mathematics of the junior, senior, and I may say part of the sophomore years would be more than I could well get along with. Dr. Maclean has been very kind to us, and advises us as "brothers" (to use his own expression) to join the junior and sophomore classes in preference to the junior and senior. It is, I hope, my desire to do that which is for the best, to pursue that course which will meet your approbation, and secure that which will prove of lasting benefit in future life. We pushed the point quite sharply, and urged as far as we could your wish in the matter and our own preferences. But as I have said, in consequence of the importance attached to the mathematical course we are advised to enter the classes above-mentioned—viz., junior and sophomore. Accordingly we have determined to attend upon the regular duties of those classes until we shall hear from you, which we hope will be the case before long, as we will be anxiously expecting a reply. Dr. Maclean remarked that in the event of your taking us from this institution our dismissals shall be returned, and no charge shall be made for tuition during our stay here in connection with the college. This we believed would be the most advisable course, and one which under the existing circumstances would meet your approbation; for employment should always be preferable to idleness, and I do believe that if I remained here two weeks without employment there would be neither life nor spirit remaining.

We have a very good room: No. 17, North College. On the east wall of our room there are prints of balls fired by General Washington at a body of Hessians who had taken refuge in this building. In the picture gallery, which is in the opposite part of the building, there is a large frame which during the Revolution hung in here and encircled a portrait of George III. A ball from the American army at the battle of Princeton pierced the wall of this building and knocked the portrait out without injuring the frame; and subsequently a likeness of General Washington has been put in the place of King George into the identical frame. This causes quite a veneration to be attached to it, and it is preserved as quite a relic of ancient days.

I am very much pleased to see that there is a much higher moral tone of feeling and action prevailing here than at Columbia College; and although there has been some drunkenness and swearing, still it is nothing comparatively when we regard the fearful prevalence of these vices at the South Carolina College.

We have formed but few acquaintances as yet, and still feel ourselves "strangers in a strange land." Those, however, whom we do know were most of them converted during the recent revival, and are apparently very pious and moral men. One in particular—Mr. Lee, of Georgia—is a noble fellow, and is a man who will, I hope, be a true friend. He remarked to me that he thought that the revival had not altogether ceased in college yet, and I hope sincerely that its influence may be forcibly felt by your own sons.

The prayers in the chapel are conducted with due solemnity and respect, and present quite a contrast in appearance to those which we were formerly wont to hear.

Upon invitation I took dinner with Professor McCulloh (to whom I was introduced by Mr. Rogers) on Wednesday. Spent a very pleasant time, and found his lady and sister interesting and entertaining persons. She invited me to visit them as frequently as I could. Am struck with the freedom of intercourse here between students and professors; and I think in the case of Professor Maclean this is perhaps carried a little beyond the bounds of propriety, for the students joke him to his face about getting married, etc.

We shall not join either of the societies until we hear from you in regard to our future course. It is, however, our expectation to unite ourselves with the *Cliosophic* when we finally decide upon remaining.

Hope that this will find you all at home in full enjoyment of health. We often think of friends we have left behind, and anxiously apply at the office three times in the day to see if there are no letters from Liberty. I received a very kind letter from Mr. Snowden's sisters living near Princeton. Have seen no melons here at all, and the peaches and apples are hardly ripe. Do write us soon. Brother unites with me in best love to you, my best parents, and also Sister, Aunty and Uncle, Uncle Henry and Aunt Abby, Aunt Julia, Aud, and all at Woodville. Howdy for every one of the servants. It is time for the mail to close, and I must accordingly conclude. As ever,

Your affectionate son,
Charles C. Jones, Jr.

REV. C. C. JONES *to* MESSRS. CHARLES C. JONES, JR., *and* JOSEPH JONES[g]

Maybank, Monday, August 12th, 1850

My dear Sons,

We rose early and had breakfast shortly after five this morning. The carriage was at the door, and we were going up to Montevideo to meet Mr. Axson, who was to have some conversation with your dear sister previous to her application to the church for admission. The whole heavens lowered with clouds; rain appeared all around. The carriage was hastily put up, and we have had a torrent of rain with short intermissions until one o'clock.

When the clouds came over, you could not see the grove at Campbell's, nor the woods skirting the fields in any direction; and the whole morning has given us a succession of terrific discharges of electricity—the severest and the nearest we have had this season; and seldom have we any equal to it. The number I shall not attempt to estimate. The reports of thunder combined all of sublimity, grandeur, and awfulness that can be conceived. They rolled down on every side. The flash and the report most frequently came together. At one discharge of electricity, which left the clouds just over the house and fell towards Campbell's, I was sitting at my study table writing, and heard the clearing of the atmosphere as though some mighty sword in the swift hand of Omnipotence cut through it. It was nothing but the special providence of God, "who maketh a way for the lightnings," that preserved the dwelling and the houses from being struck, and so delivered us all from sudden death.

In such moments we realize our weakness, and the special care of God; and our hearts should be impressed with His mercy. But it is by His care that we are preserved in being every moment, for the powers of death are at His command at all times; and we should therefore endeavor to cultivate a sense of His presence and of our habitual dependence upon Him.

The low places in the lot were flowed with water; we enjoyed a concert of frogs—rather rare music this summer—from the ponds and ditches in the fields. And as we withdrew from the dinner table at two, the rain having nearly ceased, eight beautiful *ardea candidissimas* lit between the house and the hickory tree and busied themselves in the grass and weeds picking up something that the rain had brought for them.

"Oh, Father," said Mary Sharpe, "kill some for me!"

"Let these visitors live, my daughter. How tame they are! How beautiful they look! I will try and get you some another day."

But about the time I would have been ready, they took to their wings and bade us good-bye.

Mother thought the old oak was struck again, but we concluded it was only one of the decayed limbs broken down with its own weight. I think the rain was heavier on the Island than back in the country.

Had the rain of today occurred yesterday, we could have had no meeting. But a kind Providence blessed us with a fine day—no rain until night; and we had an excellent congregation of whites and blacks, and interesting services morning and afternoon. The services for the Negroes in the afternoon were specially encouraging, for although they have had no Sabbath school for months upon months, yet their recollection of the catechism was remarkable. Prime stayed home to mind the plantation. I told him he should be no loser by it, for I meant to preach the same sermon to him on my return, D.V., that I hoped to preach to the people in Sunbury. And I was as good as my word. I hope some good may come of it.

Sabbath evening, you know, is a special time to us in the family. Your mother and sister and myself were together and tried to remember you, my dear sons, at a throne of grace. Our greatest comfort is to commend you to God and our gracious Redeemer. We inquired how you spent your first Sabbath in Princeton, and whether you were careful to remember the Lord's Day to keep it holy. Let me beg you, my sons, to be extremely careful in respect to this duty. You are liable to visits, to interruptions in your room on this holy day from your collegemates if you lay yourself open and encourage visiting and worldly conversation. *Neither make nor receive visits on the Sabbath.* Take your stand at once; let it be known, and be *firm,* and you will not be troubled; and God will bless you in it. And never lounge and sit about the college doors nor in the campus on the Sabbath Day, nor take walks of recreation and pleasure. I most earnestly entreat you to observe the Sabbath. Now that you are in college, your principles and practice will be tested; but we hope and believe that you will be enabled to hold firm. Your conscientious regard for the Sabbath has always been a source of great comfort to your mother and myself.

You must write us particularly how you live and where you live, and how you spend your time, and how you are pleased with Princeton and your new acquaintances. Mr. Snowden wrote me that he had sent you a letter of introduction to a relative of his in Lawrenceville. Be sure and go and deliver it, and see Mrs. Snowden's sister, Miss Deer—an estimable lady. He also said he recommended you to a Mrs. Brewer in Princeton for board. He speaks highly of her. I wish you to make the arrangements about your board to suit yourselves. Consult your convenience and comfort, without being extravagant.

Tuesday, 13th. We came to Lodebar last evening after the rain. . . . Your sister and I are just going to Montevideo in faint hope of meeting Mr. Axson. The day looks promising. We have now *two mails a week* (*Monday* and *Thursday*), and hence we shall hear from you oftener. Write whenever you can, and tell us everything. Mother and Sister join in much love to you. They will write you soon. Breakfast is on table, and must drop the pen and take up the knife and fork. The Lord be with and bless you, my dear sons!

Your ever affectionate father,
C. C. Jones.

Mr. Charles C. Jones, Jr., *to* Rev. *and* Mrs. C. C. Jones[t]

Princeton, *Tuesday,* August 13th, 1850

My very dear Parents,

Another mail has arrived, and as yet there is no letter from home—no tidings of peace from the land of our childhood and the friends of our youth. We hope that the memory of us will not cease to remain, even though we be in a distant clime. To me the endearments of home are more realized now than ever. 'Tis often the case that when in the realization of many blessings and enjoyments, then we are apt to undervalue their importance, or from the fact that they exist, so to speak, without our personal effort, to conclude and regard such as trivial and commonplace. But when deprived of their kind and gentle influences, when borne from the bosom of family and home, 'tis then that in the land of the stranger we sigh for one sight of some well-known face, and eagerly listen for some message from kindred and friends.

Although pleasantly situated, still we have but few acquaintances. As a general thing the boys here are not so free in conduct as they are at Columbia, but are rather reserved and stiff, while at the same time you may say courteous, never speaking (although they may see you day after day) until introduced. This may all be very well, but there doubtless is, I think, such a thing as carrying it too far. For instance, to sit by a fellow student day after day in a recitation room, and yet have not the least intercourse with him, or even bow to him when meeting, is—no question about it—a kind of strait-jacket proceeding against which a good heart and an open hand would proclaim.

This college beyond a doubt affords the finest religious and moral training, if one will but improve it, of any I have ever known or heard. On last Sabbath (as an example of what was just stated) we had prayers at half-past six, prayer meeting at nine, church at eleven, Bible class at three, church in town at four, prayer meeting again at five, and church in the Presbyterian church at half-past seven P.M. Thus is the day almost totally occupied with the public and private exercises of devotion, prayer, and praise. Besides these ordinary hours of worship on Sabbath, we have during the week a prayer meeting every evening attended by some one of the professors—usually Dr. Maclean. Thus does this institution enjoy unusual spiritual advantages—such, too, as are perhaps equaled by few seminaries; so that everyone has the opportunity offered him of having a constant dispensation of the Word and prayer if such be his wish and desire. It is my purpose to be present at these meetings as often as practicable, and to endeavor to make a proper use of these means which the God of Heaven hath placed in our power.

Dr. Maclean sent me up into the choir last Sunday to help out in the singing, as there are but few who will go up. We soon hope, however, to have quite a respectable and efficient number. There is an organ which is played by one of the tutors, Mr. Hodge; and the singing, take it all in all, is pretty fair.

The boys have tonight been making quite a fuss: crying "Fire," blowing a horn, trying to make a large light in the third story with candles and paper, hallooing, howling, crowing, etc.—and all to get Dr. Maclean to come after them. In fact, when the noise was at its loudest state they were calling for him, and now are braying like so many jackasses with heads out of their windows.

Our board in the refectory is only tolerable: generally beef, Irish potatoes, and bread, accompanied now and then at dinner by a dish of stewed tomatoes. Usually, however, the fare is served up in a cleanly and orderly manner. Now and then, nevertheless, a stewed fly is found among the extra articles of diet.

The waiters are attentive and obliging—most of them sons of Erin fresh from the mother country apparently. It would amuse you to see a little French boy who waits upon our table. He has been but a few months in this country, and as yet is quite ignorant of our language. Chester, a classmate (son of Dr. Chester, who was with us last winter), understands a little of French, and we now most frequently call for what is wanted not in the language of our mother country but in French.

Although this is an extremely moral and quiet college, and notwithstanding the decorum and propriety with which the boys behave themselves in chapel, still there is much more noise in the recitation rooms—caused by the clapping of the students—than one would infer if left to his own decision. For instance, the junior class this morning stamped almost everyone who was called upon to recite; and upon the failure of one to solve the problem proposed, a member of the class exclaimed with great emphasis: "Crane *roweled!*"—which quite aroused the feelings of the professor, who threatened a repetition of the same offense with expulsion from the room. I would not be understood to say that such is the usual and habitual manner in which the students conduct themselves, for my short stay here has not as yet furnished experience on that point; but on the contrary it most probably may be the result of a present exuberant state of feeling arising from the relaxation of the past vacation.

There is a marked difference between the course of study pursued in this institution and that of South Carolina; and if the mathematical department was only a little more ably filled in the latter, I should decidedly prefer that of Columbia to this of Princeton; while at the same time there is no comparison between the two as regards the moral and religious advantages, for in the one case they are, you might almost say, wholly neglected, while in the latter due weight and importance is attached to them.

Nearly all of the servants here who attend about the college are Irish. They are respectful and attentive in the general, and are treated just as we do ours at home; and the only difference between them apparently is that in the one case they are white and in the other black. Some of the boys cuff them about a little, but this is entirely beneath gentlemen, and argues too little of self-respect and good breeding to be prevalent even to a limited extent.

I have enclosed sent Sister a little piece called a California coin, used as little rewards of merit, so she must take courage in her musical attempts upon the piano.

I find great profit arising to me both physically and mentally from my connection with the choir. At present I am the leader of "the baser sort."

Do write us soon and let us know how everything is progressing. How is that field of small cotton on the Island getting along? I think that it will do pretty well after all's said and done. We often think of the fine melons, peaches, and other fruit which you must now be enjoying. The only things of that kind which we get sight of are a few blackberries now and then.

I believe that my story is about done, and it is, according to an ancient philosopher, better to keep silence than to utter things unworthy of a hearing; so I will cease here until other circumstances and another occasion call for renewed transmissions. Brother unites with me in kindest love to you both, to Sister, Aunty and Uncle, Aunt Abby and Uncle Henry, Aunt Julia, and all at Woodville. As ever, my dear parents, I remain

Your affectionate son,
Charles C. Jones, Jr.

P.S. No attacks as yet from the *night marauders* concerning which we were so carefully warned, although I heard a student say that he found himself almost lugged off bed and bedding by them the other night. Rather prefer their room than their company.

C. C. J., Jr.

REV. C. C. JONES *to* MR. CHARLES C. JONES, JR.^g

Maybank, Monday, August 19th, 1850

My dear Son,

The mail today brought us three letters—one from Joe dated the 9th, one from you (same date), and another from you of the 13th. Why they should be so long on the way we cannot divine. We have written you *four* letters, including one from your sister. Two of them you should have received shortly after you reached Princeton. We shall write regularly, and hope that our new postmaster general will have our mails expedited.

You cannot think how much happiness your letters afford us. Your mother would have the first reading of them all. And our hearts were filled with gratitude to hear of the religious privileges which you now enjoy in the college, and our eyes with tears that the revival had not ceased, and that you would endeavor to use the means of grace thus mercifully placed within your reach. My dear sons, may you both be brought to the Saviour! I have seen and I trust felt more clearly and strongly within a few weeks than ever before that our sufficiency as lost sinners is in Christ Jesus alone. We never obtain the grace of repentance, the love of God, the ability even so much as to think a right thought until we come in faith to the Lord Jesus Christ. He is presented and freely offered to us as our only and all-sufficient Saviour, and we find everything in Him. We are indebted to Him for wisdom, righteousness, sanctification, redemption. Without a union by faith with Him we can receive none of these blessings and gifts. Keep Him before your souls as your all and in all.

The result of your examination has not surprised me—on two grounds: *First,* you had not *gotten through* with your junior year, and the course of study differs from that in the South Carolina College. Joseph had completed his sophomore year but *in part* also, and there was the difference in the course in his case also. *Second,* the faculty of Princeton have *a reputation* to maintain, and could not be expected to favor your application for a higher

position than that you had left. There was a *probability* that you might succeed, but not a *certainty*. Your mother and myself are therefore not disappointed, nor are we at all dissatisfied; but on the contrary we are *satisfied,*
and think on the whole it will result in your greater good. So you have done
exactly right to enter the classes to which you have been admitted by the
faculty. Now press on and make good use of your advantages, as I believe
you conscientiously will.

It will take you some little time to get accustomed to the college and its
mode of government and instruction, but hope you will continue to be
pleased and see no reason to regret the change you have made. You will undoubtedly be in a better moral and religious atmosphere, and that is what we
look to above all things else. Your feelings amidst new scenes, new manners,
new customs, new faces—all strangers—I well understand and sympathize
with you. We never know the sweets and comforts of home and the happiness we enjoy with dear relatives and friends until we are separated from
them. But you have gone to obtain an education of mind and heart and
manners to fit you for usefulness, and this you must keep before you. And
soon you will begin to form as many acquaintances as you desire. Young
gentlemen of real worth and character are seldom overlooked, and we hope
you will both commend yourselves as such to all around you. You will also
begin to have objects and pursuits of interest around you, become identified
with the society in which you live, pick up topics of conversation, and your
time will be beguiled of its heaviness. I think you will find Princeton a
pleasant place. We feel much indebted to Dr. Maclean for his kindness to you.

You must arrange your *boarding* so as to be agreeable to you, without
being extravagant. And I leave you to make any changes you may think
best. You will be able to judge of all things better after a little experience
and observation. Let me charge you about your *exercise. Take a plenty of it.*
Do not let your systems relax for want of it. Am glad you have joined the
choir; hope Joe may do so too after a while. He has a good voice, and only
needs cultivation. But do not let the music take up too much time from study,
as is sometimes the case. You must join whichever society you please, and
do not join the *Clio* because your father was an honorary member of it unless you have a preference. You must join where you think you will get most
benefit.

I write immediately on receipt of your letters, as you have not heard from
us, and to return you a speedy answer in relation to the classes you should
enter. Will send this letter in time for the mail tomorrow morning, D.V.
Will write more particularly of home and home friends and affairs in a few
days. Your sister thanks you for the California piece. Mother, Sister, and
Father send you, my dear sons, abundance of love. We miss you hourly, and
long for the time when we shall meet again. All friends and servants well,
and send love and howdy.

Your ever affectionate father,
C. C. Jones.

Mr. Charles C. Jones, Jr., *to* Rev. *and* Mrs. C. C. Jones[t]

Princeton, *Monday,* August 19th, 1850

My very dear Parents,

Your kind and highly prized letters have been duly received, and it is with pleasure that I now embrace this opportunity of replying to them. To hear from home and many kind friends is at all times pleasant and gratifying to one whom time and place may have separated; and to have such letters as those were—advising the right, counseling against the wrong, exhorting to the steady pursuit of known duties, brotherly affection, and above all to the fear of the Lord and the faith as it is in Jesus—is a privilege indeed which I hope is in part at least appreciated by your son, who hopes that the counsels therein contained may tend to lead him in the right and proper course.

You desired in your letter that we should give you an account of Sabbath occupations. On last Sunday we attended in the morning a prayer meeting had by one of the students; at eleven heard a very practical sermon to college students by Dr. Maclean; at three attended Bible recitation; 4 P.M. heard Dr. Forsyth, our Latin professor, preach in the Second Presbyterian Church; at five again attended a prayer meeting; and at 7 P.M. we heard Dr. Archibald Alexander in the First Presbyterian Church. Was struck with the force and pointedness of his discourse. He appears very aged, though apparently enjoying a green old age. His voice is very fine, and his neck is quite bent. He reminded me in his features of Uncle William, though in figure there was no similarity. I was so much pleased with his sermon that upon my return to my room I wrote a skeleton of it while fresh in the memory, his style striking me as a very lucid and clear one. This was the first of a course of lectures which he intends preaching to the young men of college, and others in general, delivering one every Sabbath night.

It may not be uninteresting to you to know his subject, and briefly the manner in which it was treated. First, then, his text was found in Proverbs 1:10—"My son, if sinners entice thee, consent thou not." First, the liability and exposure of young men to temptation, especially when absent from the watchful care and wholesome government of parents and guardians. The two great divisions were *to point out some of the temptations to which young men were liable* and then *offer some dissuasives to them from the yielding to such seductions.* Under the first head then he remarked that there were many companions of youth who by a show of kindness and good feeling won the confidence of unsuspecting youth, and thus led them from one step of sin to another, initiating them into the pathways of vice and folly until they were at length brought to a level with their seducers. (2) Temptation: enticements to the gratification of licentious passions. (3) To gaming and plays of chance and hazard. (4) To intemperance and all its concomitant vices. (5) That of novel-reading, and more especially the species of a light, immoral, and demoralizing nature. (6) To an avaricious and grasping desire of making fortunes, even if unfair means are resorted to for the accomplishment of the intended object or design. (7) Fear of the derisions of ungodly men deter

76

many from the performance of known and acknowledged duties. Secondly, the dissuasives offered to deter young men from giving in to these temptations: (1) Because God commands to yield not to the enticements of evildoers, and to disobey this mandate is to incur the wrath of that God who out of Christ is a consuming fire. (2) The ways of the sinner lead to hell, and to that lake of perdition from which no one ever returns. (3) To follow the wicked is to set at naught the precious Blood of the Redeemer, which was shed for guilty man. Third division embracing general corollaries: (1) No neutral ground can be taken. (2) All delay dangerous. (3) Life short and death certain. (4) Evil habits progressive. (5) No safety except in the true belief upon the merits and atonements of our Lord and Saviour Jesus Christ. (6) Assurances of success if the approach according to the rule laid down in the Holy Scriptures. (7) Promise in the Word of God. And (8) concluding with a general exhortation. I have thus briefly, though I am persuaded faithfully, given an outline of this excellent address; and my own interested state of mind may be a sufficient reason for having thus stated so much of it.

The class of which I am a member is a very large one, numbering over eighty, and also containing a number of talented young men. In proof of this assertion, the statistics of the last examination show that there were some twelve who stood above 98 (100 being the maximum), some few of them being perfect in every department, and a goodly number within only a fraction of it.

There was quite an excitement here in college a few nights ago. A parcel of town boys were in the habit of pillaging the garden and orchard of Professor McCulloh, often approaching very near his house, employing and using the most obscene and insulting language in the hearing of his wife and sister. He had several times driven them off, but on Thursday night they returned in increased numbers and were even more outrageous in their conduct. Seeing that they were too numerous for him to cope with single-handed and alone, he came over to our building (his house being in near proximity to the college) and requested one of the tutors, Mr. Giger, to select a few of the boys, and to accompany him in order to scare or drive them off. The news of their depredations, and especially their insolent language respecting the ladies of the house, acted as an electric shock to our feelings. A parcel of us accordingly were immediately in progress to the scene of the transaction; but "ere we reached the point proposed" they (as might have been expected), getting news of the approaching retribution, decided that prudence was, in their case at least, the better part of valor, and accordingly made good their retreat without even giving us a chance of forming a conjecture as to what course they had departed. On the whole I was rather glad that the affair terminated where it did, for I know that had we overtaken them in the then excited state in which we were, "Tarleton's quarters" would have been the only ones which would have been known or given.

Upon retiring, we heard some pistol shots in the streets, which proved to be a fight between a few of the college students and the town boys, or "snobs," as they are here universally denominated. One of them had his hat shot from his head, and several were struck with sticks. One of the students was hit by a rock, but not seriously injured. From the continued insults and depredations committed by these men upon the premises of Professor Mc-Culloh, it was necessary that some summary punishment should be inflicted upon the intruders; and on this account I almost regret that we did not over-take them in the very act, although it is to be presumed that this scare will deter them from future encroachments.

Mrs. McCulloh sent me over the other day some apples, for which I was much indebted to her, for every little helps in our present mode of living. Sunday is our best day for eating, strange to say, for we then have a little extra, which it is calculated will last us until another week rolls around.

There are some pretty walks around Princeton, though I have not had much opportunity to form a correct judgment of its beauties, my walks being for exercise and not so much by way of exploring the pleasures of landscape. By early rising we have an opportunity of taking a long and fast stroll before breakfast.

We are both pretty well, and fairly in the harness. I will write Sister pretty soon. Hope that you both and herself are well, and enjoying the pleasures of the season. With us the weather has been actually cold, insomuch that fire would be quite acceptable. Brother unites with me in kindest remembrances and love to you, my dear parents, Sister, Aunty and Uncle, Uncle Henry and Aunt Abby, Aunt Julia, Uncle Roswell, Audley, and all the little folks at Woodville. I wrote to Uncles William and Henry last week; hope they re-ceived my letters. As ever,

Your affectionate son,
Charles C. Jones, Jr.

Give our united howdies to each and every one of the servants.

Mr. Charles C. Jones, Jr., *to* Rev. *and* Mrs. C. C. Jones[t]
Princeton, *Monday,* August 26th, 1850

My very dear Parents,

Your two kind and instructive letters have both been received, for which we feel deeply obliged to you. Such advice and counsels as they contained are more precious than "fine gold," and I hope they will meet with due considera-tion and compliance from your attached sons. The welcome news in regard to our beloved sister was hailed as precious tidings of "great joy"—both because of the unspeakable satisfaction that it must bring to your own fond hearts to see the fruit of your longing prayers and ceaseless cares thus crowned with success, and moreover that she has now come out from the world and hence-forth will, I hope, be numbered among the true followers of the Lamb of God, who "died that we might live." Would that your boys could be brought so to see their own iniquities as to be led by divine guidance to turn from the evil of their ways and embrace "the truth as it is in Jesus."

Dr. Maclean left Princeton on Friday on his way to Scotland, his object being, I believe, to secure some possession in the line of property. His departure produced quite an impression among the students. Numbers of them went to his house to take a farewell of him; and over a hundred accompanied, or rather preceded, him to the depot, surrounding him on his arrival there. And as the cars moved off which bore him away, with hats off they gave nine long and loud cheers for the vice-president of Nassau Hall, which made the adjacent objects ring and reecho back again their joyous shouts. The bystanders were perfectly amazed, and were looking in every direction for that "great man" who was thus escorted. If we can only find out the day on which he will return, he will be welcomed back with demonstrations even more marked than those under which he left.

The other night (Saturday) it was rumored that the "snobs" were to make an attack upon North College, the building in which we reside, as a retaliation of that fight which I mentioned in a letter previous in which the town boys were routed. It appears, however, that upon second thought they abandoned the purposed design, and concluded that prudence in their case was the better part of valor. Happy it was for them that they came to this very just conclusion, for had they entered the campus they would have met with a reception so warm that more courageous hearts than dwelt in their bosoms would have recoiled and fled. In our part of North College there were three or four muskets loaded with fifteen slugs each, one rifle which discharges *thirty-one* balls a minute without any intermission, besides revolvers and clubs innumerable. So you see the affair would have doubtless proved fatal to some. Just as I was retiring there was a noise of numerous explosions heard in the entry. Immediately the thought occurred that the assault had been made, but upon examination the noise was found to originate from a pack of crackers which one of the boys had lighted in the entry. Thus terminated this noted invasion of the "snobs" of far-famed Princeton upon the courageous sons of Old Nassau.

We are hard at work, both as regards college and society duties. Have recited several times and succeeded pretty well. We have much to do in the way of writing lectures, compositions, and other exercises of a similar nature—that is, those of us who belong to the junior classes—Brother as yet not being required in his sophomore year to attend to anything of the kind.

I wrote Mr. Snowden a polite letter in reply to the one which I received.

There is at present little news afloat; a regular routine of duties is the usual order of the day. I am very glad that we entered the classes that we did, for I am confident that lasting benefit will accrue, and am also glad that our course met with your hearty approbation. We are confirmed Clios in every sense of the term, but neither bigoted nor exclusive in our faith.

Heard on last Sabbath two fine sermons, one of them a lecture to young men from Professor James Alexander.

Indulged ourselves today by way of variety in a basket of peaches. They were very juicy, but picked too soon and consequently not very sweet. There is a great tendency here to a looseness of the bowels; in fact, there have been scarcely two days in which I have not been more or less affected.

I thought of you last Sabbath and wished to have been an eyewitness to the interesting scenes which must have transpired at Midway. Hope that this will find you all well and enjoying yourselves both mentally and physically. We shall look for news from home every week. Wrote you both and also Sister a few days ago. Brother unites with me in best love to you, my dear parents, and to Sister, Aunty and Uncle, Uncle Henry and Aunt Abby, and all at Woodville. Will write Aud this week. As ever,

Your affectionate son,
Charles C. Jones, Jr.

Howdy for all of the servants.

REV. C. C. JONES *to* MR. CHARLES C. JONES, JR.[g]

Montevideo, *Thursday,* August 29th, 1850

My dear Son,

Your Uncle William and Uncle Henry received your letters last Monday, and they were with us yesterday and the day before and kindly brought the letters for us to read.

We were glad to hear of your health and welfare, and engagement in your studies. But we must beg you to keep in your room at night, and do not go out to mingle in the noise and contentions of the students and townspeople. If you go once, you will be tempted to go again, and the consequence will be that you will come—both of you—to be regarded as young men ripe for and ready for sprees of any kind. The professor was wrong to send for the students to expel thieves from his garden, knowing them to be of the town, as it would certainly lead to ill blood more or less. I hope, my dear sons, you will be considerate and firm in this matter. Your object at college is an education, and character of the right sort.

The last Sabbath was Communion at Midway. I preached from the words of our Lord: "I am the Good Shepherd; the Good Shepherd giveth His life for the sheep." The congregation above and below were attentive. I was enabled to speak freely, and hope good was done. And your mother and myself had the unspeakable satisfaction of seeing your dear sister make a public profession of religion and unite herself to the people of God. We longed to have you both there. Our prayers are offered for you daily, and we hope you will not put off the concerns of eternity, but speedily seek reconciliation with God through Jesus Christ and unite yourselves to the people of God. Think of your sister as a member of the church, and then inquire why you are not. The youngest has entered first. At the close of the Communion service I addressed the children and young people. They listened attentively and respectfully. Your young friends John Barnard (just graduated) and Audley King were there. In the afternoon I had an overflowing Sabbath school for the colored people. Great numbers out. It was one of the days of old. The weather excessively warm; my coat sleeves were wet, and the perspiration came through to my vest and wet that in part. We reached Maybank at dark: the days are growing shorter.

We shall begin next week, D.V., in earnest to make preparation for Philadelphia. The time is drawing near.

We saw most of the family from the Sand Hills. Your Uncle James Newton, who has been on a little travel up the country, arrived home Saturday night. Reports Aunt Eliza remarkably well, and all others well also. But everything *dear:* Marietta overrun with visitors. Your Uncle John quite popular, but his congregation does not increase much. Mr. O. W. Hart went up there to look at lands; comes back and says he would not give his place in Bryan for all Upper Georgia! No money to be made there.

I write for the mail, and am obliged now to start for Maybank and must close. Your mother and sister unite in much love to you both. We hope to get a letter from you today as I pass through the Boro. May the Lord watch over and bless you, my dear sons!

Your ever affectionate father,
C. C. Jones.

Poor steel pen!

MR. CHARLES C. JONES, JR., *to* REV. *and* MRS. C. C. JONES[t]
Princeton, Tuesday, September 3rd, 1850
My dear Parents,

Again I resume my pen, rather from a sense of duty and a feeling of pleasure than of anything new to be communicated. Brother received your letter, Father, dated from Montevideo. We were glad to hear that everything there was progressing so finely, and also that Mr. Shepard was recovering his wonted health. If the plan suggested and now in process of completion with regard to the erection of new buildings at Montevideo be accomplished, much will be added both to the value and appearance of that place.

We anticipate your arrival in Philadelphia with great joy, because we will then be in near proximity and will hope to see you frequently. It will doubtless be a source of great satisfaction for you to have the company of Aunt Susan and our cousins in the contemplated move, for then we will not be wholly without relations in a new place of residence. Would that our dear aunt and uncle could also find it convenient to do the same!

I am now hard at work in my college duties—or, as Horace would express it, *totus in illis.* We have entered upon a very difficult and abstract branch of mathematics: Young's *Analytics.* Oh, how it makes me feel when I think of the tremendous *"polling"* which I bestow upon this branch! . . . However, the discipline of mind and close application required in this study render its acquisition both useful and highly necessary.

We have much to do by way of taking notes and writing out lectures, as well as in attendance upon society duties. I made my first speech in Clio

Hall last Friday evening—with some effect, I am told by my friends. I have had reason to rejoice every time that I think of my entering the junior class, for lasting benefit will doubtless be the result of a two years' course at this institution if the advantages are rightly improved—as I confidently hope they will be.

It would amuse you to hear the tin horns blown in the entries every morning to arouse the sluggish sleepers. The sound is somewhat the following: *roont-a roont-a ra-a-ant-a rant-a roont,* etc., a most unwelcome noise to one who dislikes to leave a refreshing couch. This morning Dennis, one of the Irish waiters, was tooting loudly upon this instrument (which by the way is the only one on which he performs) near our door, when I suddenly sprang from bed and, rushing out, put an end to the pestiferous serenade. We have a very good little clock with an alarm, which arouses us every morning at any hour that we desire to be waked—a watcher at all times punctual and sleepless.

The boys are getting along very well with the exception of numerous shoutings and occasional hay-burnings in the entries, the floors of which fortunately are of brick, else they would certainly take fire.

Our regular routine in the refectory is bread (stale oftener than fresh), beef, potatoes, and again (by way of variety) potatoes, beef, bread. The regimen forces one to be abstemious, which perchance is well enough for the mental faculties; but physical appetites often exclaim: "Give! Give!" On the whole we prefer boarding there than in town, for it is both cheaper and more convenient. . . .

Jenny Lind is now in New York: tickets selling at $20. She was offered $200,000 to cross the Atlantic. Being a very benevolent lady she gives everything away, reserving only so much as will defray her expenses. Only wish her charity would find fit subjects for bestowal in No. 17, North College.

Although not very flush of money, still we are at present in no want, for our college bills are all settled, furniture for room purchased, society dues squared, books obtained, and a little surplus on hand. I hope you will not deem us expensive, for nothing has been purchased which was not needed. Our expenses this year will be heavier than any succeeding, for our room had to be fitted up and furnished, etc.

The exercises here on last Sabbath were very interesting, and our Bible class a source of great benefit, as well as a remembrancer of the many pleasant seasons of that nature which we have spent at home.

Brother wrote this week and I presume has told all the news. Although my frequent letters may appear unnecessary, still you will excuse them on the score of filial affection. Brother unites with me in much love to you both, my dear parents, to Sister, Uncle and Aunty, Uncle Henry and Aunt Abby, and to all at Woodville. Also our regards to Mr. John and William Stevens. Wrote Audley last week. As ever,

Your affectionate son,
Charles C. Jones, Jr.

MR. CHARLES C. JONES, JR., *to* REV. *and* MRS. C. C. JONES[t]

Beloved Parents,

We received a letter from you, dear Father, on Monday last, and are anticipating the arrival of another every mail.

You cannot think how it rejoiced my heart to learn that my sister had in very fact "come out from the world" and numbered herself among "the followers of the Lamb." I know how much joy and unspeakable satisfaction it afforded you thus to view a consummation of all your watchful care and anxiety in her behalf, as well as to feel that your fervent prayers had not been unheeded. And it gives me the strongest reason to hope that those same supplications which have and are still ascending to the throne of grace will be answered in behalf of your erring sons. I pray that my sister may have grace granted her from on high to act in a manner consistent with her high profession, and that she may be a chosen instrument in the hands of the Almighty for the advancement of His Kingdom on earth.

The holy ordinance of the Lord's Supper was administered in the First Presbyterian Church on last Sabbath. Such of the students as were members attended. We listened to our president, who officiated in the chapel, giving us a practical and pleasant sermon. His discourse, however, appeared to have failed of awakening the attention of one of our tutors sitting near me, for he slept it through, and appeared more refreshed by his slumber than by the preaching of the Word. In the afternoon the Rev. J. J. Prime (who by the way is a rank abolitionist) delivered a sermon in the Second Presbyterian Church. His discourse, however, partook of none of his persuasions in that respect, being a very solemn and impressive appeal. At night we heard Dr. Hale from the text, "Remember now thy Creator in the days of thy youth."

The seniors are now speaking in public from the chapel stage. None of their productions have as yet, however, struck me as peculiarly fine. On the whole the declamation of the boys in Columbia is superior to what it is here— that is, so far as there has been an opportunity of judging. It is, I believe, an established fact that Southerners are more remarkable for their oratorical powers than Northerners, though the latter may be more *"plodding"* than the former.

My college duties, I find, afford me as much employment as my time will allow. We have to attend the regular recitations, write up lectures, furnish compositions at stated periods, declaim, and prepare society exercises, which are far more numerous than those in which we were formerly engaged. It is all for the best, and I have made it a rule always to be doing something by way of improvement, and to read by *snatches,* if I may so express myself.

Brother is still zealous in the pursuit of the natural sciences, having demanded my attention this morning to some little water worms in a chrysalis state which he is preserving in order to notice their transformations. His alcohol vial stands on the shelf, containing some few insects—mournful examples of the pernicious effects of intoxicating drinks.

I had this evening a debate with one of my classmates on the subject of capital punishments. He is a veteran opposer, well versed in the arguments pro and con, and is as strong a debater as I have ever seen. He says that if I can show him a single direct command in the New Testament for such punishment, that he will yield the point. I wish that you would refer me to one, for I feel persuaded that some such there must be, and am not willing to give up the faith of my fathers thus easily.

Our class is one as remarkable for talent as the present senior is for the want of it, and I often hear numbers of the junior laughing in a pleasant manner at those of the senior.

One of the Georgia students, a classmate, lost his mother a few days ago. He was much affected by her death, remarking that "his only consolation was that she was a Christian"—though he himself is by no means such himself. His name is Lewis, from LaGrange.

Jenny Lind has excited and awakened quite an interest among the inhabitants of New York. One gentleman of that city is said to have paid $130 for a family ticket in order to be present at her first exhibition. Very foolish in him, however, thinks the subscriber.

A band of "Indians from the Northwest" passed through this place a short time previous and performed for one night. They have proved to be a company of students who, having become low in the purse, have left their accustomed exercises and resorted to this means to furnish themselves with the desired article.

There is, I believe, nothing new of interest here at present. Cattle pass in numbers every Friday morning on their way to Philadelphia and New York. Dr. Maclean has ere this reached Scotland if his passage was prosperous. My old complaint, the headache, has returned upon me with renewed strength. Hope, however, that it will speedily pass away, though I do not in the least cease on that account from any of my duties. As I have a composition to prepare tonight, I must bid you farewell, hoping to hear often from my dear parents and sister. Brother unites with me in best love to you both, to Sister, Aunty and Uncle, Uncle Henry, Aunt Abby, and all at Woodville. As ever,

Your attached son,
Charles C. Jones, Jr.

P.S. Excuse the ink in which this letter is written, for Brother had locked up the black and taken the key with him.

Howdy for each and every one of the servants.
C. C. J., Jr.

REV. C. C. JONES *to* MESSRS. CHARLES C. JONES, JR., *and* JOSEPH JONES[t]
Montevideo, *Thursday,* September 12th, 1850

My dear Sons,

Your welcome letters were received on Monday, and we feel grateful to God for His continued kindness and mercy to you; and it gives us sincere pleasure to know that you are both well satisfied with your change and are pursuing your studies with diligence and zeal. Make the best use of all your advantages; lay up your fortunes in learning and character; and devote yourselves to the love, honor, and glory of God.

Your dear mother and sister have been quite unwell, but hope they are both over it now. They are staying in Sunbury with your aunt and uncle till I return. Was to have gone from North Newport last Sabbath, where I preached to Jonesville, and thence next day to the Sand Hills to see some of our relatives and friends, but had to return the same evening to Maybank on account of your mother and sister's indisposition.

We have been making improvements at Maybank: clearing up the lot. Have left a row of cedars around the great hickory and formed a sort of cedar house by leaving and trimming the young cedars in a particular manner. Have had the road from the lot gate out to the gate at the causeway all finely cut, widened, trimmed, and worked upon, so that it looks handsomely and makes a clean and delightful walk. The road has long needed it; somebody will enjoy it if we do not; and I tell Andrew I am leaving some of my work for him to remember me by. He has been in a state of perfect excitement all the while, and taken as much interest in it as though it was to be the highway of the Czar of Russia.

Our crop of *little* cotton has shot up; is doing wonders, and putting on a marvelous top: a field of flowers. Andrew as usual most sanguine of results.

I came up here yesterday. We have had an ill child (Eve's little Elizabeth) from a fall out of the door. Better.

The books in the study have been so molded from damp since we have been away that your mother thinks they would be in a drier atmosphere at the Island, and Patience could keep a constant eye on them. So yesterday the removal began, and it brought along with it sad dismantlings and changes and great destruction. For shelves for the Island I had to invade your *museum!* The condition of the preparations in it was melancholy. The animals had scarcely a hair left on them, and the birds were fast losing their feathers and promised to be soon bereft of their plumage. The bugs were a mass of ruins. To keep them was impossible; they were past preservation. A council was held, and the decision was that all the perishable portion of the museum should perish.

Thereupon Gilbert and Andrew (who took the hen on the top to be a real live fowl) advanced with due solemnity bearing a great tub. Into that they deposited with great care the precious remains of your scientific handiwork. They were erected into a cone in the back yard. The great wood ibis was laid as a foundation; his worm-eaten legs stuck far out on one side; and his black, bald neck and head, with his wide, gaping beak with the wood rat in it, stuck out as far on the other side. Poor fellow, he seemed to lie resigned to his fate. Next around and over him were gathered all the *anser* tribe with their curved necks and wide bills, this in and that out, here cheek to cheek as if administering consolation and support to each other in such an hour.

Then the *ardeas,* some with their legs thrust in among the ducks standing, others upon their sides helping to raise the mound, tipping toe and stretching their long necks over, their sharp bills seen here and there. The *ardea caerulea* and *discors* were prominent. But the most doleful figure was the *platalea ajaja*—his pink robe in tatters, the wonderful spoon with which he fed himself all his life long gone. He seemed in a quiet agony. Here lay the *numenius longirostris;* he held his long nose clear of the whole group to preserve it if possible from insult. And now came the filling in. Here went the *muscicapas,* the *squatarolas,* the *orioles,* and all the smaller tribes. It was such a collection as is rarely seen, and had in it nearly all the colors of the rainbow. And the squirrels and rats were there: one fellow kept his head out grinning with his groundnut in his mouth, determined to save his dinner if possible. The tail of the great kite was then broken up and the papers placed within and around and all over; and finally the *great horned owl* was placed hovering with outstretched wings upon the apex, as if securing the richest variety of prey; and all being now ready, *Gilbert applied the torch!*

It was a burning! The papers roared; the feathers fried; the sealing-wax eyes of the birds wept out in melting tears. The cotton ignited; the smoke ascended; and the whole premises were fumigated with vapors of arsenic and burning legs and bills and skins and feathers and cotton and hair and snakeskins! Gilbert snorted and got himself out of the smoke, exclaiming: "Eh! De ting *smell!*"

This morning nothing remains but lumps of burnt cotton, a few calcined leg and wing bones, and the talons of the great owl.

I collected together and overhauled the mineralogical department and the department of Indian curiosities and saved a few that were worth anything; emptied the remainder in the vinehouse in Mother's flower garden.

Well, the museum has been good. It furnished you pleasant and innocent and profitable and instructive employment for many an hour that otherwise might have been dead on your hands—or worse than dead when spent in idleness and folly. It has been, too, a great source of amusement and of entertainment for your visitors and friends, and has given you a taste for natural objects and habits of observation that will never leave you. The value of our labors and engagements is not always to be estimated by their permanency. They bring their interest and improvement with them, and leave their benefits behind after they have passed away. This is the grand design of much of the education and training of youth—and indeed of the mind and heart through life. All life has for its end a brighter world to come. We are constantly—if we use life aright—*advancing;* and we should—to be perfect—be always *ascending.*

The day is beautifully clear and bright. The silent dog days in the feathered world are passing by, and the woods are again vocal with the few summer birds that still remain with us and our own native ones. Before breakfast a family of scarlet grosbeaks were hopping and chirping at the museum door. Now a cheerful yellow-breasted warbler is flitting from tree to tree uttering his notes, and his mate answers him in the grove. And the mockingbird is in the oak by the garden giving forth one of his sweetest lays of spring. All these sounds are music to me. I love the birds and the flowers and the green trees and the green earth, the flowing waters and the deep blue sky, the bright sun and the moving clouds. Our Father made them; His wisdom, goodness, power, and glory appear in all. They are sources of perpetual enjoyment to me. For that reason I love the country.

Little Andrew went down with the cart and most of the books this morning. He is to return for the balance this evening. Have some sermons left at Maybank that I did not carry to Columbia. Some valuable; the great part prepared in the first years of my ministry and not valuable. Have looked over them and burnt up a good parcel of them.

We are getting ready to leave here on the 1st of October (close at hand) if God permit: as fast as we can. Your mother says she will be in Princeton the day after she reaches Philadelphia. You may guess for what intent.

All our relatives and friends in Liberty are well at present. Mr. Axson has gone away on a short tour for recreation and health. Nothing new. Expect to spend next Sabbath, D.V., with the people at Arcadia.

Dove's colt is a little beauty. Lilly and Firefly in good order. Have not sold our carriage and horses yet; will not sacrifice them.

You will find an excellent review of Dr. Bachman's "unity" book in the last number but one of *The Princeton Review*. The reviewer puts the question on the right ground. It is not a question of pure science, but it is a *historical* question also. And we have an inspired history that settles it.

Have been all over your Aunt Susan's crop since I began to write, so time wears. Have several letters to write and must close. Cato and the people send howdy. Rosetta says you must finish your education soon and come home. The Lord be with you!

Your ever affectionate father,
C. C. Jones.

Mr. Charles C. Jones, Jr., *to* Rev. *and* Mrs. C. C. Jones[t]

Princeton, *Monday,* September 16th, 1850

My dear Parents,

The regular evening has again returned upon which my custom is to spend a few moments at least in holding converse with absent friends. To you in particular my heart turns with peculiar affection and gratitude. Never have I felt more fully what a debt of love I owe for all your sage counsels, watchful care, and unceasing petitions at a throne of grace. The remembrance of them will, I hope, act as a check when temptations assail.

Last evening, while walking in company with a classmate near the seminary, we passed a gentleman whom from his appearance we judged to be a professor. After proceeding a few paces he suddenly stopped, turned, and called aloud: "Charles Jones!" Immediately I advanced with "That is my name, sir"; and "Stebbins is mine," rejoined he. Instantly there was a full recognition and a hearty shake of the hands, accompanied by many general queries. Mr. Stebbins has become quite fat, and from his personal appearance one might easily conceive him a reverend D.D. Brother and myself called on him in the evening, and spent a pleasant hour with himself and wife. Mrs. Stebbins is an affable and agreeable lady—that is, judging from what we saw—and a member of one of the first families in Princeton. They have also a little responsibility—a daughter, of whom they appear very fond. On Monday evening he called at our room, and we had an extended conversation on everything relating to Liberty, beginning with each member of the family, the citizens in general, all the servants, and concluding with school days, Lightfoot, the jersey, and Gilbert. By way of recalling past recollections he played "The Stop Waltz" and "Lucy the Carrier Dove." It afforded us so much pleasure again to meet my former instructor, and he appeared also very glad to see us. He at present is on a visit to Princeton, but is engaged in building up a new church in Western New York.

A week ago a general celebration of Negro Sons of Temperance was held in this place, comprising four divisions, one from Trenton, two from Philadelphia, and one from Princeton. They marched through the streets, banners flying, drums beating, and with all the pomp and circumstance imaginable. Orations were delivered, I understand, by several of the order; and the whole procession, followed by women and children, proceeded a mile or two out of town to indulge themselves in a picnic. It was a strange sight to those of us who were from the slave states.

Last evening a lecture was delivered by a sailor on the question whether whipping and the allowance of liquor should be dispensed with in the navy. Brother went to hear him, and says he gave a horrible account of numerous chastisements inflicted, and of the injurious effects of intoxication. In the progress of his speech a cat-o'-nine-tails was exhibited, with which he demonstrated practically the manner of using it by repeatedly striking the table. Some say that this person was expelled the navy because of intemperance, others that being detected in a theft, and consequently chastised himself, he ran away, and is now going about the country denouncing this custom. To tell the truth, I verily am persuaded that his object is the procuring of money for himself, because this morning a subscription list is passing around. Whether he is justified in this course of proceeding I am rather inclined to doubt, for he is by this means circulating reports which must in the breasts of many prove subversive of the laws of the land.

So the museum has at last fallen—but in a good cause: formerly containing specimens of nature's handiwork, now sustaining the triumphs of genius. Your description of the hecatomb of birds was very perfect, and reminded me of some ancient sacrifice, accompanied as it was by so much care and reverence, as manifested in the conduct of Gilbert and Andrew. Apart from the fact that it was the museum, Gilbert's olfactories were doubtless considerably moved by the incense of burning cotton, feathers, bones, and arsenic.

Am glad to learn that the cotton on the Island is growing so finely, and hope that it may yield a plenteous harvest. A bad beginning, it is often re-marked, makes a good end. Although I am disposed to doubt the truth of this maxim in general, still in this particular case it would hold good—that is, in the event of a good crop.

Saw in a Southern paper the other day an account of a public meeting in Liberty, also the resolutions submitted by Uncle Berrien. Was pleased thus to see the county declaring her stand and belief in respect to the great ques-tion agitating the nation. The bill for prohibiting slavery in the District of Columbia has passed the Senate, but will, I hope, be killed in the House.

I am very sorry to hear of my dear mother's indisposition, as well as that of my sister.

We will soon be together again if nothing happens—that is, we will see you shortly subsequent to your arrival in Philadelphia.

Everything is getting along pretty well. A plenty to do. The lot must now appear to great advantage since your labors and pains with it. It is time for study, and I must close. Brother unites with me in much love to yourselves, Sister, Aunty and Uncle, Uncle Henry and Aunt Abby, and all at Woodville. I wrote Audley a short time since, and hope he received the letter. As ever,

Your affectionate son,
Charles C. Jones, Jr.

P.S. Tell all the servants individually howdy for me.

REV. C. C. JONES *to* MR. CHARLES C. JONES, JR.[g]

Montevideo, *Monday,* September 23rd, 1850

My dear Son,

Your letter came to hand last Thursday, and we were glad to hear of the mercies of life and health still granted to you, but were sorry to hear of the return of your old attacks of headache. You will probably discover the cause in sitting up too late at study: want of sufficient sleep and exercise. They most probably proceed from the state of the stomach, which makes its com-plaints by affecting the seat of reason. Therefore reform in these particulars if you have erred; and all, by God's blessing, may be well again.

The fallacy of your young friend on the capital punishment question, so far as the Scriptures are concerned, lies in setting the New Testament over and above the Old, whereas both are equally the Word of God, equally authoritative, and form *one* perfect revelation, one perfect rule of faith and practice. They are not in any respect antagonistic, but consonant, and mu-tually support the one the other. Nothing is set aside in the Old Testament in and by the New save the types and shadows and ceremonial laws, all which find their fulfillment in our Lord and Saviour Jesus Christ, and expire, as the

89

lawyers would say, by the statute of their own limitation. But all the laws of God that embody our duties to God and to men, whether socially or civilly, remain ever in force. These laws are recognized in the New Testament, but not repeated *in extenso,* there being no necessity for it. The morality of the New Testament is all founded on the laws of the Old; and the divine writers recognize their great principles, and that is all that is necessary. You do not find the law of the Sabbath repeated in so many words, but its existence is acknowledged both in the practice and teachings of the Lord and His apostles. The New Testament is built up out of and upon the Old, and is not contrary to it in anything whatever. It ever recognizes and supports the Old.

Another fallacy of your young friend is that we are not bound to do anything but what we are distinctly commanded in so many words by the New Testament to do. You perceive at once that this principle cannot be admitted without involving us in many difficulties. This fallacy grows out of the first and falls with it. All that is necessary is for the New Testament to acknowledge the Old, and the two be united in *one* perfect revelation. Neither is complete without the other. On the subject of capital punishment all that is necessary in the New Testament is that it recognize civil government as an institution of God. The great laws binding upon rulers and people as set down in various enactments in the Old Testament need not be repeated. This recognition you find in our Lord's command, "Render unto Caesar the things that are Caesar's," and in His *practice* and that of the Apostles. You find it recognized by Paul in Romans 13:1–7 *most fully,* and *"the bearing of the sword"* distinctly pointed at. The sword is an emblem in this connection of authority and power, even of life and death, where the power to take life is admitted. You can make nothing more nor less of it. This is a strong passage. The Apostle Peter (I Peter 2:17) recognizes civil government in "Honor the King."

I need not proceed any further. You can manage the controversy now, I think, with this little help. You are on the right side, and your friend is on the wrong side.

I write in much haste and offhand. We came up and spent yesterday here with the people. All well. Today we are arranging matters, and will take leave of the people in a few moments. Mother is with me. She is getting quite well again. Little Andrew has just come from the office with a letter from you. Glad to hear from you again. We hope, D.V., to leave the 1st of October for Philadelphia.

Mother sends much love to you. Mr. Shepard sends his kind regards to you. The Lord be with you and bless you, my dear sons!

Your ever affectionate father,

C. C. Jones.

III

Mrs. Mary Jones *to* Messrs. Charles C. Jones, Jr., *and* Joseph Jones[g]
American Hotel, Philadelphia, *Monday,* October 7th, 1850

My very dear Sons,

We left our quiet home at Maybank on the morning of the 1st, which was Tuesday of last week, arrived in Savannah about five o'clock, took tea, after which your aunt and cousins, father, sister, and myself started in the omnibus for the steamboat wharf, where we were kept waiting for the *Duncan Clinch* until after ten o'clock—the boat being occupied until that hour bringing in passengers from the *Isabel,* one of the West Indian steamers lying in the offing. We soon fired up, and with a sad heart I bade adieu to my own native state. I could not trust myself to express the feelings which had all day possessed my mind; but I hope it was in humble faith that we committed our bodies and our spirits and all our future prospects for time and for eternity to God, who hath a right to us and all we possess.

In consequence of our late start we did not reach Charleston before twelve o'clock, dined at the Planters' Hotel, and left at three o'clock in the *Gladiator.* We had a fine run all night, and reached Wilmington by half-past seven o'clock, where we took a walk and were in waiting until ten o'clock, when our train moved off at the rate of twenty miles an hour. We had a new and most beautiful car, and no interruption to our journey until we arrived within forty miles of Weldon. In consequence of a bridge being carried away by a whirlwind, we had to leave the cars and walk by torchlight a distance of a quarter of a mile. The baggage was transported in a *mule cart* denominated the "Halifax Omnibus." We supped at Weldon and traveled all night, reaching Richmond about seven o'clock, where we took an excellent breakfast furnished by a house just by the depot—a great convenience to travelers— soon after which we jumped into an omnibus and crossed the town for the northern train, which immediately moved off. Arrived on the shores of the beautiful Potomac, we went on board of the *Mount Vernon.* A number of persons coming South passed out as we went in, amongst them Major Hansell of Marietta. We had a delightful run, dined on board, passed Mount Vernon, which received the customary token of respect from the boat, tolling its bell. The approach to Washington you well remember. We passed through and arrived in Baltimore after night, took our supper at a house by the railroad depot, and left about ten o'clock. There were not a great many passengers in the ladies' car, so with extra cushions for our pillows we were enabled to sleep a little. Some of our party did a great deal. Within a short distance of Philadelphia I heard the jingling of bells, and found that our steam horse had been detached, and we were moving in the good old way. Throwing up the window, I could see here and there in the darkness and distance the gaslights at regular intervals, looking as if the stars of heaven had been reset on earth.

We arrived at the American Hotel about four o'clock, and are still boarding here, no other place being yet obtained—although your father and Cousin Charles are running all the time to get us fixed, and several gentlemen and ladies have called and kindly offered to assist us in any way. I hope we shall soon get suited, for my head is almost crazed from the noise in the street. Our room fronts the Old State House, and before its door all the political and every other kind of speech and noise seems to be made. We were all seasick, and even now whilst writing I am reeling from side to side in my chair. Your Aunt Susan is quite unwell, and so has Laura been since our arrival.

I have a box of articles coming on for you by the steamer, and as soon as it arrives want to come to Princeton to see you and bring the good things from home. Your Aunt Julia has sent you a jar of limes. I can scarcely realize, my beloved children, that I am so near you, and long to be with you. Your dear father has had a violent cold, affecting both lungs and head, and looks very badly. I hope the change will do him good. You must both be in want of warm clothing, and must be supplied shortly, as winter is coming on rapidly. Your purchases can be made to more advantage here than in Princeton. I want to come and see you the last of this week if possible. Your aunt and uncle and Uncle Henry and Aunt Abby and Aunt Julia and all at Woodville send much love to you. The servants all send howdies. Your father and sister and aunt and cousins unite with me in best love to you. As ever,

Your own affectionate mother,
Mary Jones.

Mr. Charles C. Jones, Jr., *to* Mrs. Mary Jones[t]
Princeton, *Tuesday,* October 8th, 1850
My dear Mother,

Your letter surprised me a little—that is, as regards its postmark—for although aware of your intention to leave home on the 1st, still I scarcely thought that you would reach Philadelphia so soon. Am glad to learn that you all enjoyed a speedy and pleasant trip. You happened to get on board the same steamers that we did when coming to this place, such as the *Gladiator* and *Vernon*. We regret to hear that Father is again laboring from an attack of cold. The change of climate and occupation may prove beneficial. Miss Alexander, a daughter of Dr. Archibald Alexander, sent for me a short time since, saying that she had received a communication from Cousin Laura stating that they expected to pass through Princeton on their way to Philadelphia. We anxiously awaited their arrival, but see now that they must have changed their route.

It is now a very busy time with us, having to stand the quarterly examination. Today we were wound up for three hours and a half in working original propositions in mathematics—the hardest examination I ever witnessed.

It gives us much pleasure to think that you are so near, and that we will see you so soon face to face. Hope that you will visit this place soon. We shall anxiously keep a bright lookout for the box of good things, as the fare in the refectory is by no means the best in the country.

You rightly judge, my dear parents, in regard to our clothing, for we have no warm clothing, and the weather has been quite cold.

Although I have much more to say, still I must close, for there is much to be done by way of preparing for the examination. Brother unites with me in best love to self, Father, Aunt Susan, Cousins Laura and Charlie, and my little sister. As ever,

Your affectionate son,
Charles C. Jones, Jr.

Mr. Charles C. Jones, Jr., *to* Rev. *and* Mrs. C. C. Jones[g]

Princeton, Monday, October 21st, 1850

My dear Parents,

Here we are again, refreshed by our pleasant trip to Philadelphia, hard at work, at one time searching diligently for hid treasure amid the abstruse problems of Young's *Analytics,* and at another delighting ourselves with the accurate reasonings of Blair and Alexander.

Everything is quiet at college, with the exception of those who prefer the service of Bacchus to that of Minerva. 'Tis strange how reckless many men are in this life, apparently regardless of the principles of honor, morality, and religion. Some with not even a pretension to anything that is just and proper pursue a course of iniquity which at best is short-lived, and certainly bearing the germs of that destruction so soon to overtake them. There are several in our entry who spend the most of their time in drunken revelings, their only aim being to entrap the inexperienced and incautious, and their motto, *Dum vivimus vivamus.* Even the ancients themselves, such as Juvenal and Socrates, with the early prejudices and untoward influences to which they were subject, could teach these lessons sufficient to put them to shame and confusion of face. What an amount of guilt will he have to answer for, who in opposition to the present enlightened age and the widely disseminated principles of religion and morality follows the teaching of a depraved and corrupted intellect!

Our return to Princeton from Philadelphia was speedy and pleasant. On Saturday I called at Dr. Alexander's and delivered the jar of limes with the regards of Cousin Laura. Miss Alexander was absent, and it was left in the hands of the old gentleman, who promised to deliver it on her return. He was very well, and desired me to remember him to you when I should write. I also called upon the Miss Brearleys and spent a very pleasant hour with them. We engaged to take a cup of tea with them on Wednesday evening.

Brother is busily engaged in his scientific reading, and his mind seems fully made up to be either a naturalist, chemist, or physiologist—or rather I should say all three.

I have derived much pleasure and profit lately from the perusal of Macaulay, Daubeny, Headley, and others, and am now deeply interested in *The Life of William Wirt,* by Kennedy. Macaulay is fine, but I cannot say that I think very much of Headley. True, his writings are of a popular character, but his narrations and sketches are in many instances overdrawn and too highly colored. If you will only notice, many scenes in *Bonaparte and His Marshals* are faulty in this respect.

Our grades are not out as yet, but you shall receive them as soon as practicable.

At present there is but little new and interesting in this place. Have you heard the renowned songstress? Professor Hope in one of his lectures advised us never to write when we had nothing to say, and always to stop when we had finished; so as I am bound to pay due deference to the instructions of those having the authority, and as I am somewhat in a similar condition to those whom he describes, I shall close. Give our united love to selves, Aunt Susan, Cousins Laura and Charlie, and to my little sister. My respects to the ladies of the house. As ever,

Your affectionate son,
Charles C. Jones, Jr.

P.S. The weather is quite cool, and our thick clothes are constant companions.

Mrs. Mary Jones *to* Mr. Charles C. Jones, Jr.[g]

Philadelphia, Monday, October 28th, 1850

This, my beloved son Charles, is your nineteenth birthday, and your mother's heart goes out to you with an interest and affection which has increased with every year of your existence. Nineteen years ago we received you as the gift of God, and early dedicated you to His holy service in the ordinance of baptism. I should say *publicly,* for I trust in faith we gave you away to Him from the first moment of your being. The indescribable feelings of tenderness, affection, and solemn responsibility which possessed my bosom as I looked upon you for the first time are as fresh as ever, and so is the memory of your infancy and boyhood. There are incidents which I had noted down of your own, your brother's, and sister's youth which I should like to recall with more distinctness. But the providence of God has obliterated their record from the earth, and it is only as memory rekindles the past that I live them over.

94

You have ever been to us a dutiful and affectionate child, and I desire to render increasing gratitude to our Heavenly Father that your brother and yourself have been kept from so many of the snares and follies of youth—the vices that debase and destroy both soul and body, and the wicked and disagreeable habits which are so prevalent. To know that you were Sabbath-breakers, to know that you were intemperate, to know that you used profane language, to know that you smoked or chewed tobacco, to know that you kept wicked company—either or all would wring my very soul. I *believe* you to be upright and honorable and free from these pollutions and sins. All this is most gratifying, but it cannot satisfy the fullest longings of your mother's heart. No, my dear son: *Christ* must be formed in your own soul the Hope of glory ere I can be at rest for you. *To be lost* it is not necessary that you become an infidel, an open blasphemer, a willful rejecter of the Divine Redeemer. No: you have only to live as you now live without a personal interest in His precious Blood and righteousness. And how can you escape if you *neglect* so great salvation? Think of this: it is only to *neglect salvation* and the soul is eternally lost. You esteem it no hardship to task your powers of mind and body to compass a liberal education. And will you not devote the energies of your soul in time to redeem it from eternal death throughout eternity? You must seek if you would find; you must knock or the door to the Kingdom of Heaven will never be opened to you. When I think of my sons as out of Christ, it daily bows my heart in anguish before God; and I should go sorrowing all the time if I could not lift up my eyes to the bleeding Lamb of God and remember the previous promises of His own covenant. May the blessed Holy Spirit, my dear child, touch your heart, give you genuine repentance for sin, and lead you by a living faith to Him who died that we might live!

We have received letters from your aunt, Uncle John, and Mr. Rahn since you were with us. All quite well. Your aunt writes in good spirits. We also received your affectionate letter, and were glad you returned safely. You must not be surprised to see us before long. The *preserves* were designed for the *Misses Brearley*. But never mind about the mistake—a part was kept back for Miss Alexander, which can now be sent to Misses B. I hope you will go and see them as often as you can.

We received Joseph's circular last week, but not yours. Tell him it gave us much pleasure to see his stand. In *behavior* and *industry* he stands 100, in studies 96.9. There were some three and four absences from prayers and room we did not exactly understand. He must take encouragement and go on. I know he will answer our fondest expectations if he will only apply himself diligently. I am looking every day for a letter from him.

Mr. Peace returned a week ago from Virginia. We saw him five or six times during his stay, and spent a very pleasant evening with his sister, Mrs. Ambrose White. He left on last Saturday for Columbia, looking very well. I hope his health may yet be restored and established. We feel a sincere interest in him.

Yesterday Dr. and Mrs. Chester called. It was delightful to meet and renew our acquaintance with Dr. C.

Last evening we took tea with Mr. and Mrs. Newkirk, where we met our old friend Rev. Daniel Baker, D.D., now of Texas. He is trying to interest the good folks here in behalf of our distant sister of the lone star—especially in the endowment of Austin College.

Your sister commenced school yesterday at the Misses Gill. They are pleasant ladies, and have a good reputation as teachers. We could not find a female school in which Greek was taught; consequently that language must be laid aside or pursued at home under Father's direction.

I hope your carpet has been made and put down. Be sure and let me know if at any time Joseph or yourself are in want of anything. This great city affords everything to gratify the tastes or satisfy the wants of any reasonable mortal.

Your dear father's cold is better, but he has suffered much from an overstrain of his eyes writing by a strong gaslight. Tell our dear son Joseph we are looking every mail for a letter from him. Your aunt and cousins and father and sister unite with me in warmest love to you both. Remember us to the Miss Brearleys affectionately.

Ever, my dear son, your affectionate mother,
Mary Jones.

REV. C. C. JONES *to* MESSRS. CHARLES C. JONES, JR., *and* JOSEPH JONES[g]

Philadelphia, *Thursday*, October 31st, 1850

My dearest Sons,

I suppose you think Father is so busy that he has forgotten you. Far from it. Not a day passes but you are in my thoughts and affections and prayers, and I have been much exercised in my prayers for you both. I feel that time is rapidly bearing you on in life, and you have not yet made your peace with God. My dear children, do not put off this most important of all your interests. Seek the forgiveness of your sins through the Divine Redeemer, and consecrate yourself in the morning of life to Him. I cannot express on paper my anxieties and the anxieties of your dear mother for you.

I have suffered from pain in the eyes from cold and an overstrain of them writing with a bad headache and before gaslights in the office. For a week they were very tender and painful, but are now nearly well. Two Sabbaths ago I preached for Dr. Boardman, and left the pulpit with fever and pain in the eyes and did not go out again the whole day. It is all gone now. Have been very much engaged in the office from $8\frac{1}{2}$ to 2 P.M. and from 3 to 6 doing up back work and attending to the treasurer's department, he having resigned and left his accounts in a sad condition! We hope to weather it all, by God's blessing. The post is not one of idleness—and no sinecure, I assure you. My great disappointment thus far has been no time for reading or study. Hope to gain time hereafter. Am really hungry for study.

We are getting along very pleasantly at Mrs. Price's. So far we find them very kind and accommodating and genteel ladies. We hope to have room for you in your vacation, and we anticipate great happiness in having you once more with us.

How do all your clothes please you? If you want anything, let me know it.

We have heard from your aunt and uncle in Sunbury. All well; and all well in Liberty. Also a letter of good news from your Aunt Mary Robarts last evening. All well in Marietta; and your Uncle John has something of a revival in his church. Mr. Russell's two oldest sons (William and ——) have professed conversion. The meetings are still in progress and very crowded; and your Uncle John preaching nobly and to crowded houses. Mr. Pratt has been to help him. This is good news indeed. Aunt Eliza goes to Liberty in December.

Your circulars have come. My younger son's came first. Behavior 100. Industry 100. Scholarship 96.9. This is very fine and satisfactory. But he has one prayers, three recitations, and four absences from room *not excused!* My older son's came today. Behavior 100. Industry 100. Can't be better. Scholarship 91.3! This is lower than we anticipated. Must be some mistake. No marks at all for prayers, recitations, or room: *good*. Try and be good students and good members of college. Give attention to *all* your studies, and do not let society duties interfere with your regular lessons. *And exercise and preserve your health.* Too much confinement at your books will not do. You will make less progress by it. Keep mind and body fresh and invigorated with exercise. Am glad you have been to see the Misses Brearley.

Mr. Rahn writes me all pretty well. Has succeeded in getting in all our rice; and cotton ahead of him in the field. A pretty good harvest. No news from Mr. Shepard as yet. You must write your friends at home as frequently as you can; and do not forget to do the same to all here. Mother and Sister and all send much love.

Your ever affectionate father,
C. C. Jones.

Mr. Charles C. Jones, Jr., *to* Rev. *and* Mrs. C. C. Jones[g]

Princeton, *Monday,* November 18th, 1850

My dear Parents,

I have just returned from the office, where I expected to have found a letter from someone of our relatives in Philadelphia, but it appears that that privilege is denied me this evening. You have doubtless much to engage your attention, and my desire to hear from you often leads me to expect a communication when such may not with propriety be looked for. Brother received your letter, my dear mother, and as it was addressed to him, I will leave a reply for him.

We are engaged in quietly—yet I am persuaded faithfully—meeting the regular routine of college duties, and are deriving much improvement from the same. Our professor of belles-lettres delivered an excellent lecture last Thursday to the junior class, the object of which was to suggest some practical hints in regard to a course of reading. He adopts the opinion of Lord Bacon, which is that "Some few books are to be chewed and digested, while the majority should only be tasted," recommending us to select some particular subject in which we feel deeply interested, to trace every other which flows from or bears any relation to it, and thence draw our own conclusions as well as preserve the thoughts suggested by its investigation.

He cited an example of the Reformation. Just fix the date 1520. Next, Luther appears as the great champion of this revolution in the religion and feelings of the Old World, together with his co-workers, such as Zwingli, Melancthon, etc. Then we are led to inquire into the principles of Leo X, the present Pope of Rome. We are now introduced to Tetzel and become acquainted with his several acts, such as the sale of indulgences: the effect produced by these upon the popular mind. Charles V next demands our attention, and through him we are introduced to Ferdinand and Isabella. Thence the fall of Granada, the expulsion of the Moors from Spain, the discovery of America, and other incidents of a similar character. Then in England we find Henry VIII figuring largely in this grand drama, and trace the connection which he bore. Queen Elizabeth next claims our attention, with that bright catalogue of great minds which graced her age, characterizing it as the Augustan Age of English literature. A little later and we become acquainted with that master spirit Lord Bacon and the unfortunate Queen Mary.

Thus we see how many events fraught with intense interest cling around that single date of 1520. It is by fixing our minds upon particular eras similar to this, by associating with them the most illustrious personages who then figured on the stage of action, and by tracing with a scrutinizing eye the several effects which each of them caused, that we fix any subject deeply and permanently, and derive that lasting, solid benefit which should be expected from a profitable course of reading. He advises to read with a pen in hand, not for the purpose of engaging in the pernicious habit of copying, but for the sake of marking whatever is valuable, and with a view to improvement. However vivid and bright may be the impression formed on the mind by any newly acquired knowledge, he suggests that it be written out, in black and white, as the surest method of impressing it upon the memory. He decries this false notion that many entertain in respect to their retentive faculties, and attributes forgetfulness more to a want of attention than to any fault of the memory. In this lecture I found much which was but a rehearsal of those valuable teachings which in early youth I received from your lips.

The *Oedipus Tyrannus* I find a very interesting and well-supported play, the which, I presume, is as chaste and elegant as any that can be gathered from the ancient Grecian poets, unless it be the *Hippolytus* of Euripides. Dr. Maclean is, I am persuaded, a good professor of the language he teaches, although (be it spoken with due reverence to his majesty) I believe that our old friend Dr. Henry is his superior.

A son of Dr. Wells is now in Princeton, as some say on a visit to his ladylove. I inquired after the welfare of his father and family, who, he stated, were in the enjoyment of health, and also that Willie was doing well. May every success attend him! He is a fine youth, and will, I hope, succeed in his collegiate studies.

Numbers of the students are leaving every day to hear the sweet music that falls from the lips of Jenny Lind. Madame Parodi also is, I have understood, attracting large audiences in New York, and is said to excel in her department. Although desirous to behold so distinguished a personage as the former, still so much is to be done that I scarce would feel satisfied to leave my present duties with such an object in view.

The little fresh escaped recitation the other evening by placing a large amount of asafetida upon the stool in their recitation room. The fumes pervaded the room to such a fearful extent that it was only at the imminent risk of one's olfactory nerves that the door even could be approached. Not content with contaminating the room, they spread throughout a great portion of the campus, imparting to the air a most disagreeable odor. This the fresh considered quite a feat, denominating it *the* spree of the session.

Tonight a lecture is delivered in this place by the Hon. Mr. Dayton for the benefit of the Second Presbyterian Church. His subject: "The Characteristics of the Age"; and admission 25¢.

It is said that Dr. Carnahan dismissed a young Dutchman in his employ for voting the Democratic ticket in the late election for governor, the old reverend himself being a strong Whig. Dutchie had a large handbill posted in the campus to this effect, also calling upon his Democratic friends to come to his rescue in this the time of his need. Whether this be true or only the saying of some of the boys, *Neque confirmare argumentis, neque repellere in animo est. Ex ingenio suo, quisque demat, vel addat fidem,* to use the words of Tacitus.

I was very sorry to hear of the loss the board had met with as well as the shameful conduct of one of its officers, and regard it as a providential thing that you, my dear father, were enabled thus early to detect the fraud.

Brother unites with me in love to yourselves, Aunt Susan, Cousin Laura, Sister, and Cousin Charlie. Hoping to hear from you soon, I remain, as ever,
Your affectionate son,
Charles C. Jones, Jr.

Mrs. Mary Jones *to* Messrs. Charles C. Jones, Jr., *and* Joseph Jones[g]
Philadelphia, *Thursday,* November 21st, 1850

With a most interesting book in hand I have sat for some moments debating whether I should continue to peruse its contents or lay it aside to converse awhile with my own dear children. Affection decides the question. Oh, my sons, you know not how much your father and mother love you, and how their hearts yearn to have you all once more gathered around us! In speaking of our past affliction (I allude to the destruction of everything by fire and the breaking up of our home in Columbia) your father often says to me: "Perhaps we loved our children too much, and were too anxious to keep them under our own watch and care. The Lord in wisdom saw it necessary to break up those earthly ties." Yes—and to invade the circle which our blind affection might have contracted into selfishness. The stroke was severe, and I realize more and more its sad consequences. But if for you, my dear children, it works out one good result, I shall rejoice. May your present privileges be sanctified to your spiritual and eternal good as well as to your mental improvement! "Let integrity and uprightness preserve you in all your ways." Set the Lord *before your face*. "In all your ways acknowledge Him, and He shall direct your paths."

On last Tuesday night we attended a most interesting meeting of the Pennsylvania Bible Society. There must have been three thousand persons present. Dr. Tyng of New York addressed the audience in a most eloquent strain; the spirit of his address was liberal and noble. Your sister thought she could not spare the time from her studies to accompany us, and remained at home. On our return I went immediately to her room, and was surprised to find her using a candle, and the lamp melted away on one side. She immediately informed me that during our absence she had gone down into our room for the purpose of filling her lamp. In doing so she placed it very near a lighted candle. In pouring out the fluid it leaped from the can. The flame communicated to that within the lamp. She attempted to remove it from the table to the hearth, but it burnt her hand so severely she was compelled to drop it on the floor. The blazing fluid communicated to the carpet, burning and scorching a large space, and melted away (such was the intensity of heat) the side of the britannia lamp. She ran to the pitcher and poured water upon the flames, thus extinguishing them. The ladies of the house were attracted by the smell of the burning carpet and ran in.

I cannot express to you what my feelings were upon the occasion. It has almost made me ill—and your sister too. Not one hour's sleep did I get that night. The past in all its terror was before my mind, and the dreadful vision of what my dear child has been brought nigh unto by her own carelessness. Had the lamp not burnt her hand and she had thrown it on the hearth, it would have come in contact with a highly heated stove, and she must instantly have been destroyed. Or if the contents had rolled down upon her dress, it would have caught and burnt her up. Or if it had not been put out upon the floor, the whole house must have been consumed. Oh, the goodness and mercy of God to us in thus preserving her life from destruction!

My children, let us fear before His great and terrible name, and tremble at His judgments. If His afflictions do not lead us to forsake our sins and draw us to Himself through Jesus Christ our Saviour, we may look out for sorer chastisements. "He that, being often reproved, hardeneth his neck shall suddenly be destroyed—and that without remedy." This is the *fourth warning* we have had touching the danger of using this *burning fluid*. You recollect in Columbia the can fired in your hands, my son Charles. My son Joseph spilled and burnt his table cover. Your father turned over his lamp and had his hand badly burnt. With these repeated warnings it would be worse than folly to persist in its use and call it harmless. And we must *positively prohibit your using one drop of it in college*. And when you come at vacation you must bring the lamps you have with you, and I will exchange them. You can have oil, or any kind of candles you desire, and just as many of them as you wish, for it is miserable economy to ruin your eyes by studying with a poor light. We have ceased using it ourselves, and I am convinced that it is a dangerous article.

Your affectionate and interesting letter, my dear son Charles, was received yesterday. It rejoices our hearts to receive such from you. I hope Joseph will write shortly. We received at the same time a letter from Mr. Shepard. He says our people are well, but mentions the death of Mrs. Moses Jones—a most afflictive event to her poor little children. Politics are running high in Liberty. What is to be the fate of our beloved country we cannot foretell. It seems to me the next Congress in its acts will decide the question.

[*Here Rev. C. C. Jones takes up the letter.*]

Your mother put down her pen here. I began where she left off. I sent you yesterday a paper containing an account of one of the most interesting and noble meetings I ever attended—*the great Union meeting* in the Chinese Museum Building. Had I foreseen the size, the character and patriotic nature of the meeting, I should have written for you both to have come down and attended it with me. It is estimated that between six and ten thousand persons were at the meeting, although but a portion could get in. The great hall and galleries were filled to their utmost capacity, and the roll of the multitude was like that of the waves of the sea upon a rocky shore. I wished for you a hundred times. It was an assemblage of rare excellence. The truth is, *the people of the United States*—North, East, South, and West—are true to the Union. It is the *ultras,* the factionists—few in comparison to the masses—that create excitements by their noise and impudence. I am still of the opinion all will come right.

When does your vacation occur? Let me know, and whether you are in any way short of funds. If we are spared, I think a vacation here may be spent profitably.

There is a letter this morning from your Aunt Betsy to your sister, and one from Mrs. King to your Cousin Laura. Not yet read, but hope all are well. We unite in love to you both, and pray every blessing may attend you.

Your affectionate father,
C. C. Jones.

MRS. MARY JONES *to* MR. CHARLES C. JONES, JR.ᵍ

Philadelphia, *Thursday,* December 5th, 1850

We were happy, my dear son, to receive your affectionate letter yesterday, but grieved to find your old and troublesome companion the headache had again visited you. I fear that you study too late at nights. You must not deprive yourself of necessary sleep—and that in its proper season. We are fully assured of your fidelity and application to your books, and whilst we rejoice in this, we do not want you to injure your health or impair your constitution.

Your intention to avoid all artifice or deception both in recitations and examinations is correct and honorable. It would surprise and distress us if either of our sons should ever condescend to mean and underhanded measures in anything.

I trust, my dear children, that your vacation will be beneficial to you both in point of health and many other ways. Our hearts long to have you once more with us, and Philadelphia will afford you all that is interesting and improving.

I wish you could have heard Jenny Lind. We did not feel that you had the time or we the means just now for that purpose. Your sister and cousins went one night to hear her, and your aunt, father, and myself attended her sacred concert. The clearness, power, and compass of her voice is beyond conception. A gentleman who has made her a life member of our Board of Domestic Missions, when handing her a certificate of membership, presented her also with a copy of your father's sermon, "The Glory of Woman." She was very much struck with the title; received it graciously and remarked that "her Bible and such reading was all she ever indulged in."

By the last mail we have very sad accounts from home. Mr. Rahn writes that our man Allen had had a stroke of palsy: his limbs were perfectly useless; neither could he speak a word. Poor fellow, he lies as helpless as an infant! I feel very much for his condition; his life has been a wicked one, and I know that he is not prepared for death. Mr. Shepard writes that the whole county was in a panic from smallpox in their midst. Some weeks since, Mr. Adam Dunham returned from New York with his winter goods; he put up at Mr. Stebbins' and was very soon dangerously ill. Dr. King pronounced it erysipelas. Continuing extremely sick, Dr. McConnell was called in, who pronounced it smallpox. Dr. K. disagreed with Dr. McC., Adam Dunham affirming that he had not been exposed to it. Old Dr. Harris was sent for, who confirmed the opinion expressed by Dr. McConnell. A.D. then confessed that before leaving New York he had seen a man with smallpox. During all this period his own family and many others had been with him. Mr. Allen had nursed him, and at the time Mr. Shepard writes had undoubtedly taken the disease. He was in an outhouse on his plantation, and they were going to remove him to Riceboro. Oscar, Mr. D.'s servant who waited on him, was taken with it also. He fears that Sandy and Porter may have received the infection, as they were working for Mr. Stebbins at the Boro at the time.

Every precaution is now used to stop all intercourse with the infected region; but we fear it is too late, as many must have come in contact with it already. Mr. Shepard has sent on for vaccine matter and will inoculate as soon as it arrives. Your father has written to him to communicate with us by every mail. As you may be assured, we are very anxious. May the Lord remember our dear friends and poor servants in mercy and stay the progress of this awful scourge! What lessons of our own *nothingness and vanity* is our Heavenly Father daily teaching us as a family! We are driven as chaff before the wind, or consumed as stubble before the devouring flame, when the hand of the Almighty is lifted up against us!

I have received a very interesting letter from your Aunt Howe. She sends love to you both; says she will ever feel a special interest in you, and hopes yet to hear you both preach "the unsearchable riches of Christ." The seminary is in a flourishing state: *thirty* students present, and Dr. McGill of this state elected by our Synod of Georgia to fill your father's place. Great political excitement prevails. I feel thankful that you are both away from the excitement, which necessarily must affect the college. *Mr. Peace* has again raised blood, and expects to go on to Florida for his health; he begins to fear himself that he will never be able to preach.

Your sister has received a letter from Mary Leland. She has united with the church, and her brother Samuel is married.

Is the sum sent by your father sufficient for all your expenses? Let us know, for you had best leave no debts unpaid. Bring all your clothes with you, as I want to overhaul and mend them up.

Next Sabbath is our Communion here; wish you could be with us. On the last Sabbath night your father preached the first of a series of sermons to young men in the city at the Central Church.

Your dear father and sister (who has been unwell all the week), aunt and cousins unite with me in best love to you both. Accept, my dear children, the best wishes and warmest love of her who never ceases to offer up her poor prayers for your present happiness and for your eternal welfare.

Your affectionate mother,
Mary Jones.

REV. C. C. JONES *to* MESSRS. CHARLES C. JONES, JR., *and* JOSEPH JONES[g]
Philadelphia, *Wednesday,* January 29th, 1851
My dear Sons,

Your letters have been received, and they were very welcome to us. Your interview with our kind friend Dr. Maclean was characteristic, and ended well. The same rule must apply to all.

You did not mention anything about your stove. Hope it came safely and answers your purpose. Be sure and keep the iron cup full of water on the top always. It makes the greatest difference in the atmosphere.

Read Dr. Hodge's article in *The Princeton Review* and since published in pamphlet form on civil government. It is *good*. Wish all Northern men would read it.

Heard Joe had himself vaccinated. Be careful, if it takes, until the inflammation subsides; and anyhow keep clear of Witherspoon Street and all black people coming about from that quarter of the town.

Your sister has been quite sick: taken with chill Monday morning before breakfast. Fever went off Tuesday morning. Dr. Hodge called in. Prescribed. She is sitting up today and much better. Hope she will have no more return. Mother very much pleased with Dr. Hodge. Rest all well.

Dr. Plumer gave a noble sermon to young men on Sunday evening.

Heard General Sam Houston of Texas deliver his noble lecture on Texas last night. Uncommonly fine. He is, I should think, six feet five inches high, well proportioned, and a man of mind, and speaks admirably. Fine impression. They talk of him for President.

Received a long letter from Mr. Shepard. Smallpox about over, but the citizens of Riceboro and the *outside* citizens in a quarrel, and the guard yet kept up. Says *Cato* has been very sick. Is better. Feel very uneasy about him. Wrote Cato a long letter yesterday. County well, and all friends well. Heard from your Aunt Betsy; you must write her and your Uncle William often. Everything at Montevideo and Maybank getting on pleasantly. Mr. Shepard says he will try and do the best with Pizarro or Firefly.

We all send much love. Write often. And give love to Cousin Laura. Let me know if you want anything.

Your affectionate father,

C. C. Jones.

Mr. Charles C. Jones, Jr., *to* Rev. *and* Mrs. C. C. Jones[t]

Princeton, *Thursday*, January 30th, 1851

My very dear Parents,

Your communication, Father, was this morning received, and for it I return my thanks. The items therein conveyed were all of them of a pleasing character except such as related to Sister's health. I sincerely regret that she has been (and perhaps still is) so much indisposed—both because of the interruption in her studies, which is unavoidable in such cases, and moreover in her time of life it must be very desirable that both mentally and physically the powers be preserved in an active and flourishing condition. Hope, however, that ere this she has recovered, and is again able to discharge her accustomed duties.

Last Saturday we enjoyed quite a treat in the line of temperance. Mr. John B. Gough delivered an address in Mercer Hall. Although he spoke more than two hours, yet the minds and attention of all were so much engaged, and the feelings so much enlisted in his favor, that we would with one accord have bade him continue longer—in fact, I might almost say indefinitely.

Never before have I listened to any speaker who so successfully commanded the attention of his auditors, or experienced the full import of that familiar sentence, *Populi mentem suasit ad voluntatem.* His peculiar power evidently consists in moving the passions. At one time the entire audience would be convulsed with laughter, and the very next moment the unbidden yet unrestrained tear must flow. His action and delivery evidently savored of the stage; and upon inquiry I subsequently learned that for a short period he occupied the station of an actor, although in a subordinate condition. His oratorical powers are truly extraordinary: imagination vivid, and powers of description as well as personification of different characters apt beyond measure. If our friend Judge O'Neall of Carolina could only have been present, doubtless his "ten-penny nail" and other hackneyed, time-worn jokes of that description would be exchanged for others a little more replete with life and point, and beyond a doubt exhibiting a greater degree of novelty. I felt it quite a treat, for although one's principles may be fixed upon any point, still the presentation of that truth in a forcible and attractive manner tends not a little to confirm his faith. When he concluded I felt like taking him by the hand and saying: "Mr. Gough, I heartily endorse every principle inculcated, every doctrine advanced." May success crown his laudable enterprise! Was glad that Cousin Laura enjoyed an opportunity of hearing this distinguished lecturer (I went for her to Dr. Alexander's and took her up), and that she appeared so much delighted.

Dr. Brown, the former president of Canonsburg—or rather the college at that town (for I forget at this moment its name), is now in Princeton. I saw him a short time since at Dr. Maclean's. As Mr. Gough was here, the conversation very naturally turned upon temperance in general and its various associations. To use his own words, "He despised everything that looked like temperance, especially as embodied in such organizations as the 'Sons,' etc. All this was a perfect humbug, the work of the— By what name shall I call the old boy? The greatest piece of tyranny and oppression the world ever had witnessed, and unworthy this enlightened republican age. Injurious to the state, religion, and the church. As for Mr. Gough, he was a scoundrel: had no faith at all in him; would not trust him out of his sight," etc. During these anathemas which fell from his lips (which by the way, judging from his age, I deemed should have been trained to utter wiser and more sensible sayings) nothing that either Dr. Maclean or the subscriber could say tended in the least to alter his opinion. In fact, every argument counter to those advanced by himself seemed but as so much fuel added to the flame. He accused me of ignorance—as being not aware of the nature of the association to which I had joined myself. Considering his age I thought it best to say little, regarding him as "joined to his idols," and therefore let him alone. Taking the old gentleman on another tack, I inquired whether he remembered Mr. Rogers. He did, and spoke very kindly of him, concluding by saying he was a student who could "decline *bonus* pretty well." Before leaving he said: "Do not appropriate what I have said to yourself—although I tell you, you are under a great mistake, etc. Come and see me if you are not afraid of entering a house where liquor is vended." To which I replied in a corresponding strain.

We see Cousin Laura every day. She appears to be having, as the doctor would say, "quite a nice time of it." This morning upon my persuasion she visited our room, and was much pleased with its appearance.

Our stove answers finely—better even than we anticipated. Now the temperature of the room is pretty nearly equalized, and not as it formerly was—a torrid heat in the chimney and freezing behind.

The college term has again fairly begun. Tomorrow we recite regularly. A few new students. Have been much interested in perusing the Oxford Prize Essays. Read Dean Swift's works; found much to amuse. His style rather quaint in the *Tale of a Tub* and some other pieces, but fine in *Gulliver's Travels*—that is, easy and natural. His sly hits at the particular factions and so forth of the day are capital. Here and there, however, he is exceptionable, being rather disposed to indecency.

Must now close. All well, and unite in best love to every member of the family in Philadelphia. I remain

Your attached son,
Charles C. Jones, Jr.

P.S. Do not send our session money until convenient, for there need be no hurry in that line.

Wish that I could have heard General Houston's address. Wish him success, for he is a good *Democrat*.

MR. CHARLES C. JONES, JR., *to* REV. *and* MRS. C. C. JONES[t]

Princeton, *Tuesday,* February 4th, 1851

My dear Parents,

Although I have no items claiming much interest to communicate, still a few lines from your Charles may not prove burdensome. In fact, more than once has this feeling forced itself upon my mind when taking my pen. Still, as I conceive it my duty, and certainly deem it a pleasing privilege, to hold frequent converse with you, on this ground you must excuse *aliam frequentiam scribendi.*

Fully equipped, or, as the South Carolinians would say, *animis opibusque parati,* we are zealously engaging in meeting the varied obligations devolving upon us; for the term has fully opened, and the "tug-of-war" is before us. The accession of new students is considerable; two Georgians among the number: Fraley and Cowles, the latter from Macon.

Yesterday evening I (upon invitation) in company with Cousin Laura and Miss Alexander spent with Mrs. Armstrong and daughter of this place. Everything passed quite pleasantly, and I retired impressed with the idea that they were *ladies.*

The death of Hon. David S. Kaufman was very sudden, and should prove a warning to those who are in authority. He delivered a speech before the literary societies of Nassau at the last commencement, and with much effect. One of the students—Mr. Hall, from Texas, an intimate friend of his—is now in Washington, and perhaps will accompany his remains home, if they are immediately removed. How many of our men high in public life have been smitten down in the very midst of their career during the last few years, or I might almost say months! Surely the honors and distinctions of men offer not a single safeguard against the shafts of death. Especially at Washington do our representatives and senators indulge in many excesses from which they ought as *men,* independently of their *stations,* to abstain. Yet such is man—at best the creature of a moment, a bubble tossed about by "every wind of doctrine," often the dupe of popular fancy, seeking the gratification of such pleasures as "perish with the using," or a blind devotee at the altar of self-aggrandizement.

Dr. Maclean has resumed his evening meetings, and I make it a point to attend regularly, for they are to me pleasant moments for reflection—a brief moment of leisure and respite from engagement.

The smallpox is rather on the increase. Eight cases reported this morning. A white man was buried yesterday who died from the effects of this disease. Do not imagine, however, that there is much danger to be apprehended, unless it get among the students. Brother has been vaccinated twice, and I intend following his example tomorrow.

We would be obliged if you would send our tuition bill for this session, as the time has arrived for paying up our dues. Say $120 apiece, as some must go to the society, for shoe leather, etc. We will endeavor to be as economical as possible this session.

Cousin Laura is very well. We see her almost every day—as often as our engagements will allow.

I make it a rule every night before retiring to read a chapter (or two, if they be short) in the Greek Testament. Also ten or twelve pages in Cicero's *De Oratore,* which I am perusing independently of the work we are collegiately studying—viz., Tacitus. When this is completed I shall take up Quintilian, which works will, I presume, occupy all the time to be spared this session. I am passionately fond of these old Latin authors. The style is so fine: great majesty of thought and expression. Gives one such a variety in the choice of words, etc. Have adopted the plan of taking permanent notes on what I read, which I find fixes everything deeply in the mind.

I must now close, hoping to hear from you soon. Brother unites with me in much love to selves, Aunt Susan, Sister, and the doctor. Hope my little sis has fully recovered.

Your affectionate son,
Charles C. Jones, Jr.
P.S. Remember me to Mr. Happersett and Mr. Powel.

REV. C. C. JONES *to* MR. CHARLES C. JONES, JR.[g]

Philadelphia, *Saturday,* February 8th, 1851

My dear Son,

Enclosed you have a check on the Southwark Bank of this city for $220, which you can get cashed at the bank in Princeton and then meet all your bills for the present term. You see the check is drawn to your order; and when they take it of you at the bank, they will require you to write your name on the back of it, which we call endorsing it.

Your dear mother wrote you both by your Cousin Charles Edward. He and your Cousin Laura reached here last evening in safety, the latter much improved. We are all well. Your sister has gone today to take her drawing lesson, and will commence school regularly on Monday.

A letter from Rev. Mr. Axson this morning conveys the melancholy intelligence of the death of our aged and venerable friend Dr. McWhir. He had been spending his winter in Liberty from one friend's house to another. Left Mr. Varnedoe's to go to Pleasant Grove Church; rode with Mrs. King; was taken unwell at her house; and after a few days calmly died at South Hampton Friday January 31st in the hope of a blessed immortality. Mr. Axson was with him; and Mr. and Mrs. King left no want unsupplied in his last hours. I am so glad he was with *them.* His funeral was attended at Midway last Sabbath, and at his own request his body was laid in Sunbury graveyard as near the body of Mrs. McWhir as it could be placed. Our friend Mr. Busby laid him in his grave. Thus, my dear sons, friend after friend departs! Gone, but not lost. The certainty of our own departure makes due preparation for it an imperative duty, and shows us that life is truly valuable only as it is spent for the good of our fellow men and the glory of God our Saviour. My name now stands first on the list of the members of the Presbytery of Georgia. Brother Quarterman and Dr. McWhir long stood before me. They are now gone. How long mine may stand is known to God only. I desire to be employed in the Master's work, and to be prepared by His grace for my latter end and for judgment.

Mother and Sister send much love.

Your ever affectionate father,
C. C. Jones.

MR. CHARLES C. JONES, JR., *to* MRS. MARY JONES *and* MISS M. S. JONES[t]

Princeton, *Monday,* February 10th, 1851

My dear Mother and Sister,

Your "sweet" favor was duly received at the hand of the doctor, and I now embrace this opportunity of returning you my warmest thanks for your kind remembrance. Although you may class me with those whose affections are quickest gained by a passage right down the throat (for they tell me that I, like Minerva of old, "sprang forth full armed for the contest" with a sugar bag in my mouth), still, apart from this, the recognition of well-known hands clearly pictured forth to my mind's eye a pleasant view of "the loved ones at home." It rejoiced me to know that you, my mother, were well, and more comfortably located, and that my little sis was again among the number of those who have no need for a physician.

You might have rejoined to Dr. Hodge after his fall: "Physician, heal thyself"; for while administering to the sick he himself experienced the mishap of a Daedalus.

By the way, this brings me to think experimentally of the slippery path we tread, especially in winter. Just imagine a sleepy junior, eyes half open, rushing out of Old North bound for the chapel. As he reaches the stone steps all covered with ice, see his feet how wild they fly! Oh, my countrymen, what a fall was that! A fip at least (or rather, not to appear extravagant, I will say three cents) would I have given to have had my coat wadded. But no such luck. Down I went, up again, every idea of sleep having disappeared, and rushed to the chapel with no equal mind.

Saturday I received a letter from Aunt Mary, and as it may prove interesting, and she appears to desire it, I will enclose it. You will there find much to interest. She mentions the death of Dr. McWhir, giving many of the particulars. It was truly providential that he died where he did, for he was certainly in the hands of the Good Samaritans. I can easily imagine to myself the care and kind attentions which Aunt Julia must have lavished upon him. Few men have reached the age that he has, or perchance accomplished so much real good. He doubtless rests with God, in that blest abode where "the wicked cease from troubling." May I die the death of the righteous, and may my last end be like his! How old was he, Sister? For you, I believe, always kept a record of his years.

I omitted to mention in my letters that the preserves were duly delivered to the Misses Brearley, who appeared much pleased with their presentation, inquired very particularly concerning the welfare of each of the family, and desired their kind acknowledgments for favors received to be presented. They appear very well, and were in fine spirits.

Cousin Laura has returned, and doubtless you have heard all of the news current in this little village. The smallpox is disappearing, and will probably soon entirely cease. We are progressing along quietly, and I hope with much profit.

Dr. Maclean still continues his evening meetings, which are rather thinly attended. He inquired of me this evening when Father expected to visit Princeton, and expressed a desire that he would do so soon. It would amuse you to see him walking about the campus in his buffalo robe, all muffled up. I verily believe that if it were required, he could hardly sit still two hours. Activity with him is certainly the vital principle.

Last Sabbath every twig and span of grass was covered with a perfect film of ice, insomuch that every tree and object appeared to the eye perfectly gray, bringing vividly before the mind the notion of "Him of the frosted locks." In the afternoon the weather moderated somewhat, and there came a hailstorm in miniature, for everything was shedding its robe of ice, and down came the frozen drops of water, rattling against the windows and roofs. Many of the boys have experienced much pleasure from skating, but as yet terra firma has been to me the safest foothold.

Have perused with much pleasure lately a work entitled *The Czar: His Court and People,* by Maxwell. It is well written, and is well deserving the attention of anyone. His descriptions of the palaces, festivals, civil government, military operations, inhabitants, serfs, tillage, improvements, etc., of Russia are very interesting, and are doubtless correct, for he went to that country as a minister plenipotentiary. What would you think! There are forty million serfs in this empire, one-half of which number belong to the king and the other to the nobles.

As news of any kind whatever is a very rare article, I will cease and wait for a more interesting occasion. Sister, did you open the portmanteau? Excuse the small token, remembering the old Latin maxim, *Non quid detur referet, sed qua mente.* Brother unites with me in best love to selves, Father, Aunt Susan, Cousin Laura, and Cousin Charlie. As ever,

Yours affectionately, at once brother and son,
Charles C. Jones, Jr.

P.S. The check came safely to hand, with which we will settle all college dues, and for which we feel much indebted.

C. C. J., Jr.

Mrs. Mary Jones *to* Mr. Charles C. Jones, Jr.[g]

Philadelphia, *Wednesday,* February 19th, 1851

My dear Son,

I was truly gratified at the pleasant tidings brought me of yourself and brother by your dear father, and sorry his stay was necessarily so short with you.

Directed to the care of Mr. Ross I have sent you, my dear children, a few little nice things for the 22nd. The cake is called a Washington cake, and will be appropriate to the day, whose returning anniversary I hope you will ever hail with grateful emotions. When we forget the birthday of our own national freedom and that of the Father of our Country, farewell to the spirit of true patriotism, to liberty and our Union! The character of Washington, his pure and incorruptible principles, his lofty integrity, and his exalted virtues should form the study of every American youth.

By the last mail your Cousin Laura received a long letter from your aunt. They are very happily fixed on the Island, and had just received a visit from Dr. Wells and Mary, Audley and Miss Rosa Jones. . . . By the same mail we received a joint letter from your Aunt Julia and Mr. King, and one from

Judge Harden with a copy of the will of our venerable friend Dr. McWhir. His estate is about equally divided between charitable bequests and legacies to friends. He names your father *first* in connection with three other gentlemen as executors, and has been pleased to remember *us* jointly in a legacy of $300, for which expression of friendship we feel very grateful; it was wholly unlooked for.

Lewis Pynchon called this morning and spent more than an hour with us. His term closes in a short time, and he is going next week to visit his grandmother in New England. He is very much improved in health and every respect.

And now, my dear son, I must bid you good night. Your sister and cousins say they feel quite jealous that I send all the good things to Princeton. All unite in best love to your brother and yourself. That the divine blessing may ever rest upon you, my dear son, and your dear brother, is the constant prayer of

Your affectionate mother,
Mary Jones.

REV. C. C. JONES *to* MESSRS. CHARLES C. JONES, JR., *and* JOSEPH JONES[g]
Philadelphia, *Thursday*, February 20th, 1851

My dear Sons,
Above you have receipt for a box of sundry little matters which Mother has put up for you, and to which I think you will do justice.

Your affectionate father,
C. C. Jones.

MR. CHARLES C. JONES, JR., *to* REV. *and* MRS. C. C. JONES[t]
Princeton, *Tuesday*, February 25th, 1851

My dear Mother and Father,
Your letter of last week was duly received, and would have been answered yesterday had not certain unavoidable engagements prevented. Today we were examined in the differential calculus, and during the latter portion of the past week I was much engaged in discharging hall duties. Considering these circumstances I hope that you will excuse my apparent neglect.

The box filled with every nicety which man can wish has been received, and we now return our sincerest thanks for your kind remembrances of us. It is a treat which the student seldom has the pleasure of enjoying during his collegiate course, and "the merits of the case" will be most entirely and scrupulously discussed—not with such a *secondary* zest as one is wont to manifest when investigating the *value* of some abstract question in mathematics, nor with the fancy of an epicurean, but with that gusto which sharpened appetites, the warm flow of kindred spirits, and a due appreciation of benefit received necessarily imparts. The oranges have been admired by all who have had the good fortune to partake of them, while the cake remains as yet untouched—but how long none can tell. Long may the memory of Washington remain—his fame be cherished; and would that he had been born twice a year, since his birthday brings with it such pleasing recollections!

However, to change the subject a little. Saw Mr. Green today. From him I learned that all our relatives in Philadelphia were well, and that you both expected to spend a Sabbath in Princeton before many days. Sincerely hope that you will, as soon as it may prove convenient, consummate your contemplated visit.

During the last few days two phrenologists have been engaged in delivering lectures in this town, as well as in examining the heads of any and everyone who might be desirous of having the secret workings and capacities of his mind unfolded. It is astonishing how many have been duped by them. In fact, few among the students can be found who have not submitted to the above-named operation. For my part I was prejudiced against these itinerant lecturers from the fact that whenever they spoke, all that candor and openness which should characterize the action of him who relied upon the truth of his cause was nowhere to be found. Causes were traced to effects which apparently had nothing to do with their production. Many assertions were boldly made which should have been proved—such, for example, as that the internal formation of the brain corresponded entirely with the external configuration of the cranium. In some instances they made egregious blunders with regard to the character of some of the students. It is, in fact, a very accommodating science (if it may be so termed); for if mistaken in one respect they can always find other bumps, the union of which will assist or counteract *ad libitum* the nature and operation of some other. The organ of faith will have to be more fully developed in some before they will be enabled to yield a ready belief to many of the principles therein inculcated.

Commodore Stockton was elected on Friday as the Democratic senator from this state. Doubtless he is much pleased, since he has, as is generally considered, an eye to the Presidency. In this respect, however, he will, I fear, have to remain with wishes ungratified until others more fitted for such a station shall have been served. Danbury's Hotel was open to everyone who chose to liquor—free of charge. This was the commodore's treat, and dearly, I am rather inclined to believe, did he "pay for his whistle." What a misfortune and disgrace is it to our country that such practices should be continued—equally unbecoming him by whom they are maintained, and deleterious to those who suffer themselves to be led away by such inducements. Such scenes as these argue badly for those whom we see in office, and the state of the community at large. Everyone has some influence either direct or indirect, and it is only by exerting this aright that the feelings and habits of mankind in general can be revolutionized.

I am much interested in perusing Hume's *History of England*. Find Chambers' *Encyclopædia* a most valuable book of reference, especially in the course of lectures now being delivered by Professor Hope. In fact, his lectures appear to many to consist of short epitomes of Chambers on like subjects.

As there is at present great scarcity of news (everything preserving the even tenor of its way), and I am just recovering from a most severe attack of headache, I must close. Brother unites with me in best love to selves, Aunt Susan, Cousin Laura, Sister, and the doctor.

Your affectionate son,
Charles C. Jones, Jr.

P.S. I met with quite a misfortune the other day. While writing up my lecture, suddenly one point of my gold pen flew off, and consequently it cannot write well. It is like parting with an old friend. You will find it herein enclosed, and I would be obliged to you if you could get it pointed anew. There is a shop for this purpose at the corner or rather between Chestnut and Market on 5th. I hope that it will not prove troublesome.

Yours,
C. C. J., Jr.

Rev. C. C. Jones *to* Messrs. Charles C. Jones, Jr., *and* Joseph Jones[g]

Philadelphia, *Wednesday*, February 26th, 1851

My dear Sons,

I write now to say that, Providence permitting, I hope to spend the coming Sabbath (March 2nd) *in Princeton*. Please tell Dr. Maclean of it at once, and that if he desires me to do so, will preach in the college chapel for him on *Sabbath morning,* having an engagement to preach for Mr. Schenck in the Presbyterian church *in the evening.*

Your dear mother will come with me, and I wish you would step over to Dr. Joline's and see if he can let us have a nice room in his hotel while we stay. We hope to return on Monday. There is no *family* in Princeton where I can take the liberty of going, stranger as I am.

Your mother has been quite sick with cold and fever, but is up again, in God's mercy to us. Did you get your box? Our love to you both. The Lord be with and bless you, my dear sons!

Your affectionate father,
C. C. Jones.

Mrs. Mary Jones *to* Mr. Charles C. Jones, Jr.[g]

Philadelphia, *Friday*, March 14th, 1851

My dear Son,

By your dear father I send your brother and yourself two cravats, and if you do not like them cut, write me and I will send the entire square. I wish you to buy a collar in Philadelphia of such size and shape as you like and are worn. And send me by your father as he returns also one of your shirts that fit you best—also one of your brother's—as I wish to cut out a number and send them home by your aunt to be made for you this summer. Do they wear tucked bosoms—I mean finely tucked—or not? Or how would you like the bosoms made? Do not fail to send these, as I have but a short time left to prepare them.

Kiss your dear brother for me. I have not time to write more, as it is past ten o'clock. With love from sister, aunt, and cousins,

Ever your affectionate mother,
Mary Jones.

Mr. Charles C. Jones, Jr., *to* Mrs. Mary Jones[t]
Princeton, *Monday,* March 17th, 1851

My dear Mother,

Your favor of the 14th was duly received. Permit me in reply first of all to return my warmest thanks for the present conveyed. The cravats prove very acceptable to us, and are very handsome indeed. In regard to the others, if it be convenient I should like to have mine entire. Brother desires that his may be divided. The collar I have sent, as you desired. It is the best that could be obtained. Perhaps it may be well to have those to be made a little longer. The shirt also, although not the *cleanest* that I have, is still the one that best fits; and therefore it has been chosen, hoping that you will excuse all other defects. In regard to the bosoms I do not imagine that there is any necessity to have them very finely tucked, although such are pretty generally worn. Hope, however, that you will act as is most convenient in that respect.

Have been looking for Father this morning, but he has not arrived as yet.

Today we received a joint epistle from Aunt Eliza. As it is quite interesting and you will doubtless desire to see the news, we send it by Father.

Miss Colwell is now in Princeton. Saw her on last Friday evening at Dr. Hope's, where upon invitation I spent quite a pleasant hour.

The catalogues are out, one of which Father will bring with him. You will there see the junior orators marked, and also what a numerous class we have.

They have a report that Dr. Maclean is thinking of taking to himself a rib. For the truth of this report, however, I cannot answer.

We have snow today and quite unpleasant weather. The bell for recitation is about to ring, and I must close. With much love to all, I remain

Your affectionate son,
Charles C. Jones, Jr.

Rev. C. C. Jones *to* Messrs. Charles C. Jones, Jr., *and* Joseph Jones[g]
Philadelphia, *Wednesday,* March 19th, 1851

My dear Sons,

Enclosed you have the amount of your subscriptions to the hall; and if you need anything at any time, give me due notice of it.

We got aground in the river and lost an hour. Got home at eleven, and

Mother was so startled at my unexpected appearance that she nearly fainted. Your sister and I stood in amazement.

We had many things all together. A heavy snowstorm all night. A fire at 3 A.M. a square above us which burnt the assembly buildings through and through, and burnt all day *in* the walls: did not spread. Mr. Watson opened his house and furnished the firemen with hot coffee. Poor fellows, in snow and fire, in cold and water, they worked on. Then to mend the matter, the companies got into a fight; some marched off to the "lock-up." Then came out a bridal party all before the Markoe House. And the same night down fell Dr. McDowell's church roof and side walls—smash down: total ruin. Defect in building materials and construction of roof. The same, my son, we went to up 11th Street one evening in the winter.

Your Aunt Susan has been quite unwell with cold and fever: up and out again. Cousin Laura suffering with cold in eyes, but up and about. All the rest up, through God's goodness.

Am as busy as usual. Write soon. All join in love. The Lord be with and bless you, my dear sons! Do not forget your obligations to live to His honor and glory.

Your ever affectionate father,
C. C. Jones.

MRS. MARY JONES *to* MESSRS. CHARLES C. JONES, JR., *and* JOSEPH JONES[g]
Philadelphia, *Sunday,* March 30th, 1851
I have but one moment to say, my dear children, that we are all well, through God's mercy, and your aunt and cousin expect to leave next week. Your box was packed on Friday, and would have been sent Saturday, but we feared it might be delayed over Sabbath and thus cause a breach of the holy day. And now I am all in a hurry to get it off for the morning train.

You, my son Charles, must give the cut cravats sent you last to your brother, with one of the whole ones now sent. The satin and other two are for yourself; also the collars. I send a knife found in my workbag, and presume it must belong to one of you.

May God bless and prosper you, my dear sons, and keep you from all evil—especially the *greatest,* which is *sin*—ever prays

Your own affectionate mother,
Mary Jones.

Write soon.

REV. C. C. JONES *to* MESSRS. CHARLES C. JONES, JR., *and* JOSEPH JONES[g]
Philadelphia, *Wednesday,* April 2nd, 1851
My dear Sons,

Your two letters have been received, and we are glad to hear of your continued good health. The Lord be praised for His unnumbered mercies!

Your Aunt Susan leaves us next Tuesday with your Cousins Laura and Charles, and we wish you both to come down and see them before they leave. You can take the early train on Saturday morning and spend the time with us until Monday or Tuesday. Let Dr. Maclean know, and obtain leave of absence. Enclosed is a bill for your expenses down.

I expect, D.V., to go to New York on Saturday, but not until the afternoon train. Call at the office as you come up. We will have quarters provided for you at the Markoe House. We are all well, and unite in love to you.

Your ever affectionate father,
C. C. Jones.

Your mother sent you a box of sundries on Monday, care of Mr. Ross. Hope you received it.

Mr. Charles C. Jones, Jr., *to* Rev. C. C. Jones[t]

Princeton, *Thursday*, April 3rd, 1851

My dear Father,

Your letter of the 2nd inst. was duly received this morning. We are very busy indeed this week, the quarterly examination coming on Monday. I presume that you had not received my last communication when you wrote. In consequence of our engagements next week we will be in Philadelphia by tomorrow morning's train if nothing unforeseen prevent. Hope, however, that you will not object to our returning on Saturday. It will be a source of gratification to us, as well as a mark of respect due to our kind relatives, to bid them farewell in person; and therefore college engagements, however pressing, must be dispensed with for a short time. If, therefore, we do not hear anything further from you this evening, you may expect us at eleven on Friday.

With much love to all our kind relatives, I remain, in haste,

Your affectionate son,
Charles C. Jones, Jr.

Rev. C. C. Jones *to* Mr. Charles C. Jones, Jr.[g]

Philadelphia, *Thursday*, April 3rd, 1851
7 A.M.

Your letter, my dear son, was received last evening just as mine to you was put into the post office. I write now to say that *you must use your discretion about coming down.* Your aunt and cousins would be very glad to see you, but do not wish you to be interrupted in your examination, which is very *important to you.* Should you get through your examination by Monday, you might come down and spend Monday night with us and see them off on Tuesday.

If you cannot come down on account of your examination, then take an hour and write your aunt.

We rely upon your prudence and decision and good principles that you both will have nothing to do with the foolish and hurtful proceedings which you witness around you from time to time. Keep your minds fixed upon the great end for which you are in college, and the great end of life. Besides, it is sinful in God's eyes to act as many do in college, though they consider it all fun and frolic.

We are all well, D.G., this pleasant morning: up bright and early, and send much love.

Your ever affectionate father, my dear boys,
C. C. Jones.

MR. CHARLES C. JONES, JR., *to* REV. *and* MRS. C. C. JONES[t]

Princeton, *Friday*, April 11th, 1851

My very dear Parents,

As the examination, which has continued all this week, is now completed, I will do myself the pleasure of conversing with you for an hour or two. One of the peculiar privileges which man enjoys is that, although far removed from those we love, still every facility is afforded of a speedy and untrammeled intercourse. Ours is no Russian despotism, where even private letters must pass before the eye of a scrutinizing and suspecting spy of the tyrant; nor yet the unenlightened abode of the Baghirmi, where ignorance coupled with superstition rules supreme; but a free independent nation, acknowledging not those restrictions imposed upon oppressed and benighted regions, calling no man master save Him who formed "the earth and all that therein is." With what a filial attachment should each American citizen cleave to this "sweet land of liberty," and use every endeavor to promote her welfare and prosperity!

Since our return to Princeton we have been busily engaged in reviewing for the quarterly examination, and have in this way found much to enlist the attention. Brother is not, I believe, entirely through with his, but as for myself I am glad to say that "the gentleman has done." It was on the whole satisfactory. In consequence of our visit to Philadelphia I was not able to review the differential calculus as carefully as I might have. Still, here I succeeded pretty well, and in the remaining studies as much so as could be desired.

The faculty have held more meetings this week than in any four or five previous. This was not without a cause, nor wanting in effect; for several of the students have received walking tickets, or rather *traveling passports,* duly signed *secundum artem legemque.* Several others are in much trepidation of soul in regard to their fate, halting between two opinions—viz., their own and that of the reverend judiciary: strongly inclined to remain in college, and yet almost persuaded that full permission will be granted to rusticate for a while amid the interesting sand hills of the Jersey pines. So much for college sprees, drinking, etc. Let those who enter into them bear in mind the rewards

117

which such interesting scenes afford. Those who sow tares cannot expect to reap wheat. Yet boys are so foolish that they rush on regardless of order, rule, their individual reputation, and the wishes of parents and relatives.

I deposited the jar of limes very carefully in the hands of Dr. Maclean, who seemed much pleased upon the presentation, and desired me to present his warmest thanks and kind remembrances.

Dr. Lord still continues his lectures, which are attended with great interest.

A student from Athens, Georgia, has just arrived in Princeton and joined our class—the *immortal junior* of 1852, containing ninety-one members. He reports all friends there well, and that the "major" maintains an excellent stand.

I suppose that our kind relatives left at the appointed season. Hope that they may be prospered in their homeward-bound passage. You doubtless feel their loss; yet I always find that employment and plenty of labor makes one forget present troubles.

No news at all in Princeton except that a little house is in process of erection; and one of the college servants has again resumed his accustomed appearance, his visage having been somewhat marred by the concurrence of his nose and a billet of wood—the former the property of Dennis, the latter guided by the arm of one of the barring company.

Spring is again robing the earth in a garb of green, and all nature seems buoyant with life. However, there is not very much of nature here. More of art—yet but a little of that; for you are aware that Jersey is rather a lukewarm state, remarkable for nothing.

As I have a miserable headache, I must now close, hoping to hear from you as often as convenient. With much love to selves and Sister, in which Brother unites, I remain, my dear father and mother,

Your affectionate son,
Charles C. Jones, Jr.

Mr. Charles C. Jones, Jr., *to* Mrs. Mary Jones[t]

Princeton, Wednesday, April 23rd, 1851

My dear Mother,

Your precious letter of last Saturday was duly received on Monday, and I improve the present moment to reply. This season does indeed remind us of one replete with calamity and sorrow, yet at the same time full of merciful kindness. May the remembrance of that occurrence never fail from our breasts, but serve continually to awaken within us stronger emotions of gratitude and praise to that God who literally "plucked us as brands from the burning."

Am glad to learn that our relatives have reached their much loved home in safety. Doubtless they are in the enjoyment of the many pleasures which cluster around that Island home; and I hope that ere many months shall have elapsed, you also will be there to share in them.

Wrote Mr. Rogers last week, wishing him every success in his laudable undertaking, and declining his offer. Though it would be pleasant indeed to see him taking upon himself the responsible vows of Hymen, to stand by him in that *trying* or (to utter my own sentiments) most auspicious hour, yet engagements are such that I cannot for a moment think of such a thing.

When does Father leave for the General Assembly? It is rumored that Dr. Maclean intends going, but for the truth of this I will not vouch. Tacitus, however, has justly remarked: *Haud semper errat fama et aliquando elegit.* If Uncle John be there, and they return in company to Georgia, it will be indeed a delightful trip—one which Father needs much, for he is already wearied by continued application and confinement to his official duties. I think that it would be rather imprudent for you to accompany him, because upon those Western waters many diseases malignant in their character are often prevalent, and you would be much incommoded by lengthy travel. Hope that during his absence if you at any time stand in the least need of anything that you will just let me know, and you will find me by your side— always, I hope, a faithful boy.

In regard to the watches, if it *were perfectly convenient* I would be pleased to have mine, for as it will be necessary to act somewhat of a prominent part at the ensuing commencement, "it behooveth to appear suitably," as the ancient author says. However, as regards this I hope that you and Father will suit your convenience, for that will suit me.

Am now engaged in writing my speech for the junior stage. Find it rather hard to select a subject, and, when chosen, to treat it in a manner which will appear pleasing to the audience. Will write most probably upon the sublime— as exhibited in nature, displaying the majesty of a God; as linked with mystery, connected with association; and appearing in the highest and noblest efforts of man, forming the moral sublime. It is one which can hardly be stated in the short space of ten minutes, and I will have therefore to touch barely upon the most prominent points.

Have been reading with interest the *Astoria* of Irving, whose works I am now perusing in course. His *Conquest of Granada* is also fine.

Our grades will most probably be out the first of next week, when you will receive them. If mathematics were only dispensed with, I would stand as high as any in the class.

Did Sister receive my letter? If so, say to her that I shall expect a reply so soon as it may prove convenient.

Am so much engaged that I have seen no ladies since our visit to Philadelphia, and can therefore give no account in regard to the welfare of friends in this town.

In relation to Brother's watch he will write on Saturday and speak for himself, although I think he prefers waiting a season. Mine has been given to stopping whenever the idea strikes it, and therefore cannot be relied on as a faithful watchman of the flight of time.

Hoping that this may find you in the enjoyment of every temporal and spiritual blessing, I remain, with much love to self, Father, and Sister, in which Brother unites with me,

Your affectionate son,
Charles C. Jones, Jr.

MR. CHARLES C. JONES, JR., *to* REV. C. C. JONES[t]
Princeton, Wednesday, April 23rd, 1851

My dear Father,

Enclosed is a letter which, although directed to Mother, is written to both of my respected parents. Having therein communicated whatever of interest could be gathered, it only remains for me to request that you would give me *ten dollars* ($10). The reason why this is asked is this: the junior orators have to get out *bills of the proceedings* of the night when they speak, and also assist in defraying the *expenses for music* then incurred. Besides, we are on the eve of commencing several new studies, and of course textbooks must be obtained. This amount will, I believe, cover these contingencies. With much love, I remain

Your attached son,
Charles C. Jones, Jr.

REV. C. C. JONES *to* MR. CHARLES C. JONES, JR.[g]
Philadelphia, Thursday, April 24th, 1851

My dear Son,

Enclosed is $15 for your incidentals, and $5 for Joe. And when he gets to be junior orator, he must draw on me for what he wants, if I am alive and able to help him.

I have never been more busy than lately, getting ready for the assembly; and still am busy. This office is all work. Have invited your mother to go with me, but she has been hesitating very much, not wishing to leave your sister and yourselves. And especially does she wish to be at the commencement and hear your oration, which she cannot do if she goes with me. She will decide shortly what she will do. I think your letter will have some weight with her.

We have received letters lately from home. All well. Some *frost.* Mr. Shepard says it makes the cotton look sickly. Nothing new in the county.

Must try and see you before I leave. May not set off before the 5th of May.

I have been feeling and praying for you very much lately. *When,* my dear sons, will you seek the Lord and openly and forever through His grace make your peace with Him? You are exposed to many adverse influences, and need watchfulness and decision. And now only is the accepted time. I pray God in mercy to keep you from the evil and to call you effectually by His grace into His Kingdom. Your mother and sister unite in love to you both.

Your ever affectionate father,
C. C. Jones.

IV

Philadelphia, *Tuesday,* May 6th, 1851

My dear Son,

We had a comfortable journey home after the pleasant day spent in Princeton, and yesterday your dear father left us. My heart was sad indeed in saying farewell. Never before in my life have I felt myself so entirely amongst strangers; but I strive to look up to my Heavenly Father, my Almighty Friend: "God over all, blessed forever!"

These feelings have been increased by the indisposition of your dear sister. For several weeks there has been a kind of eruptive disease prevailing in Miss Gill's School resembling measles. Mary must have contracted them there, for on Saturday they made their appearance; and she has been confined to her room ever since, but not in bed. She is up and dressed, without fever, suffering only from pain in her limbs and the disagreeable irritation of the surface. Dr. Hodge has paid her two visits, and treats it as a thing of little consequence. She *diets* by eating no meat, but a plenty of brown bread and butter for breakfast and vegetables for dinner. So you will not imagine that she suffers from abstinence.

Today's mail brought a long and interesting letter from your Cousin Laura written from South Hampton. Your aunt and uncle and Charlie had gone to the Sand Hills, *she* to have a tumor or something of the kind removed from her arm by Drs. Troup and C. E. Maxwell. I hope the operation will be successful and reflect credit upon their surgical skill. She says your Uncle James Newton will not be married before fall. Mr. Peace very much improved and enjoying himself hunting and horseback-riding. Montevideo, our dear old home, looking beautifully—only trees and flowers growing after their own inclination. None to bend the twig or train the vine. We were permitted as a family to enjoy many, many happy and peaceful and I trust useful years there; and if they come not to us again in this life, they will ever dwell in our grateful recollections of the past. They were to me the sunniest hours of existence—blessed with the affections and kind attentions of your dear father, cheered with the presence of my good, obedient, healthy, and active children, surrounded by the comforts of a bountiful and delightful home, with the numerous social enjoyments that spring from a circle of intelligent and affectionate friends, with faithful servants and many precious religious privileges. Was there not everything to be grateful for? We too often do not appreciate our blessings until after they have passed away. I do not feel that I was as thankful to God for those mercies or improved them as I should have done. But in the retrospect there is a consciousness of great happiness and enjoyment during the period of their possession.

Today the Board of Domestic Missions has been informed of a most afflictive and awful event. About two months since, Mr. Geary from Ohio, a most active, intelligent, and superior man, with his wife and three children sailed for Oregon. When they reached the Isthmus he took a boat *as usual* and proceeded up the Chagres River; but before reaching the point where the water conveyance ceases and they take the mules and wagons, the boatman ran up into some obscure creek and there murdered Mr. Geary, wife, and three little helpless children! Did you ever hear of anything more truly awful occurring in a Christian (or *nominally* so) land? It is thought that they mistook a chest of carpenter's tools for treasure. *Four* of the men have been arrested; *six* were concerned. How dark and mysterious seems such a providence as this! But "what we know not *now* we shall know *hereafter*." Would that from this murdered Christian brother's grave a voice may arise to engage many soldiers of the Cross to enter the field which now stretches from the Atlantic to the Pacific!

Oh, my dear son, you were consecrated to the service of a Blessed Saviour. When will you enlist under His banner and become a messenger of salvation to dying man? Not for ten thousand worlds would I urge you to take the sacred office uncalled upon yourself; but I must urge you to the *first great duty* of giving your heart to Christ and securing your eternal happiness. I rejoice to see that there is a revival in Yale College, and hope that Willie may be made a partaker of its blessed influences.

I wish you had found time to read your speech to your father. I can but feel solicitous that it be something that will reflect credit upon your head and heart—I mean in intellect and sentiment. You will rightly judge when you think that your mother is but poorly qualified to criticize a literary production. You had much that was classical and beautiful, but some things which struck me as out of taste, such as "pearly gem." Pearls are from the ocean, gems from the mine. And your quotation from the prophet, in which the Lord is said not to be in the whirlwind or the tempest, is *irrelevant*. As the speech now stands it wants distinctness of conception and expression, and will consequently not impress unless you improve it. *I feel assured that you are capable of writing a good speech, and I do not want you to have any other, for it would be doing yourself injustice.* Your subject is a noble and elevated one, and calls for corresponding feelings and expressions. The natural world teems with objects of sublimity which cannot fail to excite and elevate the soul. The lofty mountain, the butting crag, the fearful precipice, the foaming cataract; ocean, restless and ever varying, beating with tremendous pulse from continent to continent; earth's caverns, dark and deep, with mysteries untold; the heavens above of unmeasured space, where thought is lost in unknown worlds. In the moral world every great and noble action conveys an impression akin to sublimity, or perhaps it is so of the highest order. Nothing to my feelings has ever been more awfully sublime than the passage of an immortal soul from a world of sight and sense, from the companionship and associations of time, alone and unfettered into the presence of the Infinite Majesty of heaven—a spirit disenthralled and clothed with immortality.

It is quite late, and I must cease, for my arm is so painful from rheumatism I can scarcely write. Sister if awake would join in warmest love to Brother and self. My next shall be especially to him. May Heaven's best blessing rest upon you both, ever prays

Your affectionate mother,
Mary Jones.

P.S. Do not play shinny or bull with your watch in your pocket.

MRS. MARY JONES *to* REV. C. C. JONES[t]

Philadelphia, *Wednesday,* May 7th, 1851

My dear Husband,

After you left us on Monday my heart was so sad it could do nothing but vent itself in floods of tears, and I fear it rose up in murmurings at my desolate state. To be alone amidst thousands is the worst kind of solitude; but "God is over all, blessed forever," and I strive to look up and cast you and myself and our dear children upon His almighty care. If it was His good pleasure to bring us here, I hope He will not leave nor forsake us.

On Tuesday morning Mr. Happersett called and offered in the kindest manner to do anything that he possibly could for us in your absence, and brought me a long and interesting letter from Laura. She wrote from South Hampton. Brother William, Sister Betsy, and Charlie had gone to the Sand Hills, *she* to have a tumor or mole removed from her arm by Drs. Troup and C. E. Maxwell. She complained of feeling uneasy about it last summer, and I presume must have thought it proper to have a surgical operation, which I trust will be successful.

Mr. H. informed me of the awful murder of our missionary Mr. Geary and his entire family in his passage of the Chagres River in crossing the Isthmus. The boatman ran into an obscure creek and there perpetrated one of the blackest crimes that was ever committed in a heathen land. Mr. H. said he would write you *immediately* all the particulars. It is supposed that a box of carpenter's tools which he was carrying out was mistaken for something more valuable, and caused them to commit the murder. If they had only taken everything and thrown them upon the shore alive! The impression of the awful scene is ever before my eyes. Oh, how mysterious are the ways of Providence! In such events as this, when all is shrouded in darkness, faith alone can patiently endure, believing that "what we know not now we shall know hereafter." I know your heart will be filled with grief at this awful affliction. I heard you so often speak of the eminent qualifications of Mr. Geary as a domestic missionary. Four of the murderers are said to have been arrested, and were to be executed. Six were concerned.

My kind friend Mrs. Newkirk called yesterday, making every demonstration of kindness. Mr. N. was ill for several days last week; two physicians employed; they pronounced it a neuralgic affection. He is better, and able to ride out, but Mrs. N. says is very weak.

In the course of the morning after you left we had a heavy shower of sleet. The earth and atmosphere were so warm that it soon melted away; but it has been cool and damp ever since. Just now the sun is peeping into our western window with somewhat of a smiling face; and when this is finished I must try and take a walk, for I have not had my feet out of the house since you left.

Yesterday the good Dr. Hodge "looked in upon Mary," as he said, and bade her not expose, and be careful of her diet; says there is much of this kind of disease prevailing, and some cases (severe) very like scarlet and others like *broken-bone* fever. Mary is quite bright today, and tired of her quarantine; but I am afraid not only on her own but that of the boarders' account to let her go down. You know how much they all dread in this country coming in contact with diseases. When I go to table, I feel like "a sparrow alone upon the housetop," and would not go at all but Mary says: "Do, Mother, go; they will think and say so much about my sickness if you do not."

Mrs. Marvin and her son and daughter have arrived; and our neighbors who occupied the corner room in our entry left rather precipitately. The *gentleman,* it seems, was very suddenly called home on Friday; and on Sabbath a hack drove up to the door, and the lady and her *trunks* were about to be handed into it by her brother-in-law when Mr. Watson stepped up and ordered the trunks detained, which she refused to have done; but he insisted that they should be, as her board had not been paid, and he had previously learned that that was the style in which the *gentleman* usually left his boardinghouse. So off she went, and the trunks came back, and I know not if they have been yet ransomed. Mr. and Mrs. Wood left this morning.

I wrote Charles a long letter last night making such suggestions as seemed to me to be necessary about his speech.

We take the map and trace your journey out as well as we can, and pray that it may prove a safe and prosperous one. I have always had a dread of those Western waters. I trust the Great Head of the Church will preside at the meeting of the assembly and guide all of the deliberations for His own glory and the advancement of the Redeemer's Kingdom! Do, if there are any papers with the proceedings from day to day, send them to me. My heart is with you every hour, and the two long months of your absence is an age in prospect. Mary says tell you we miss you too much; indeed I cannot describe my loneliness when evening closes in and no dear husband comes to bless me with his presence and affection.

I have not yet completed my commissions for home; Mary's sickness and the weather have prevented. I must now close for the mail. Mary sends love and kisses for her dear father. And accept the sincere and devoted affection of

Your

Mary J.

My dear Mr. J., I had just signed my name in a hurry to send off my letter when John came up and said two gentlemen had called. And who should it be but your venerable friend Dr. Woods and Mr. Daniel Woods, his son. He expressed the *sincerest disappointment* at not meeting you, and said I must give his unfeigned love to you. He looks well—astonishingly so for his age. His eye is undimmed, but his step is rather feeble. They stayed some time, and his visit was most delightful and refreshing. He told me many precious instances of answers to faithful prayers in the conversion of children, and said we must never despair on that subject, and that he hoped the Lord would bless and convert our sons and make all our children useful in His Kingdom. Says all his children are married but Dr. Leonard; that he is an admirer and fond of ladies' society, but cannot concentrate his affections on any particular one. The dear old gentleman—I could sit at his feet for hours and drink in lessons of usefulness from the fountain of his rich experience. Mrs. Woods is with him in Philadelphia, and I hope to see her if Mary is well enough for me to leave. Adieu again—with love from your daughter, who is now awake.

Your
Mary.

Do not be uneasy on Mary's account. I hope she will now soon be well. Sometimes I think she has the *mumps*.

Rev. C. C. Jones *to* Mrs. Mary Jones[t]
Steamboat *Cincinnati*, Ohio River, *Wednesday*, May 7th, 1851

My ever dearest Wife,

We left Pittsburgh at 12 M. today. I telegraphed you from there; hope you received it.

It rained when we started from Philadelphia on Monday, and it rained the whole day. My seatmate was a Hicksite Quaker. He says the Hicksites are the true followers of *Penn* and *Fox,* and are two to one more in numbers than the *orthodox*. They have large funds in dispute, but have not as yet gone to law. No love between them to spare. My next seatmate, a German from Lancaster County, Pennsylvania, says *Lititz,* a Moravian town eight miles from Lancaster, is one of the pleasantest villages in Pennsylvania—a good place to spend a summer, and cheap; beautiful country. The railroad takes up the Juniata. You remember the scenery on the Susquehanna in 1839; it is almost identical. Too rainy to be enjoyed. All night in the cars. Not much sleep. Crossed the Allegheny at daylight on ten inclined planes—five up and five down; and the highest peak is *tunneled*.

Took the canal on the west side of the mountains at Johnstown, a poor-looking place. Canal skirts the River Conemaugh; this enters the Kiskiminetas, and this again into the Allegheny; and this brings us to Pittsburgh, where, meeting the Monongahela, they form the Ohio. Dr. Krebs of New York joined us at Harrisburg. The canal skirts the rivers named, and it is not until it reaches the Allegheny that the country improves from the wildness of mountains (cold and barren for the most part) into farms and cultivation and some beauty. Monday night was *cold;* Tuesday morning *heavy frost and ice,* and my feet colder than any day last winter that I remember of; Wednesday morning *frost* again, and must have been ice, but saw none: deck of canalboat *"slippy"* with frost. Passengers all pleasant—as great a crowd *almost* as we had in 1839.

On Tuesday afternoon we were detained an hour by the breaking of a lock. In the evening we had *preaching.* The preacher was your weary husband, and he was much assisted in proclaiming the goodness of salvation to a most respectful and attentive assembly, male and female. Felt thankful for the privilege. As I proposed it, the brethren put the work on me. The good Lord bless the seed sown! I have seldom preached with more comfort and peace than all this winter past, whereof I desire to be grateful.

Dr. Krebs says the young man impressed under my sermon in his church is giving happy evidence of a true change. Let God be praised for His mercy!

The canal passes through a *tunnel* to cut off a bend in the river, and the passage through—with a deck crowded, all stooping, some alarmed, and all excited—was an incident. Looking back as you passed along, the effect was fine: the long dark deck way above; the even canal below reflecting the light streaming in from the arched entrance in the distance, and the bright day outside of all; our boat, like a great, quiet living thing, gliding along; and the silver light from our disturbance of the water dancing on the wet vault overhead. Part of the way there is no masonry—only the *solid rock* cut through. It is three hundred yards long, about.

The cabin at night *strewed* with men, and berths three tier high! One man with nightmare tumbled out of the berth in and upon the sleepers on the floor below, crying "No! No!" to the no small consternation of some and the infinite amusement of others. Brother Latta, who slept by my berth, scuffled up, crying "Hello! Hello! What's the matter, sir?"—pushing the man aside and trying to get out of his way. His bedfellow resigned himself to his fate. The man deliberately laid down on him, holding him, and inquired "if there was any fox hunt there." Some thought the boat was on fire, and ran in alarm; and the confusion for a few seconds was great—all waking up and crying: "What's the matter? What's the matter?" I was perfectly cool, and did not stir, but have not had so hearty a laugh for many a day. Now while I write, the scene convulses me.

Had my hat knocked off into the canal as we were coming into Pittsburgh, but recovered it with no damage. As soon as Mr. Martien and I had deposited our baggage on board the packet steamer *Cincinnati* we went up to the telegraph office. We left at twelve, and are now plowing down the far-famed and beautiful Ohio.

Must close, and give you an account in another letter. Do not know if you will be able to read this; the boat jars, and it is written with the *gold pen,* I make it pay you the first tribute of its excellencies. I have greatly desired your society, and think you would have enjoyed the scenes of this day a great deal. I have been not well: worn-down feeling. The brethren say: "You look badly; you work too much." My thoughts and heart have been with you. I feel most anxious to hear of my dear child. Hope she continues to amend. If she is not decidedly better, telegraph me to Louisville on Saturday, care of Rev. W. W. Hill. I will immediately return if necessary. Kiss my dear daughter for me. She must take my place and be your comfort while I am gone. Love to the boys. Must close to get my letter in at *Wheeling*. Kind regards to Mrs. Roser and Mrs. Watson and to our kind friends Mr. and Mrs. Newkirk. Will write you every chance I can get. The Lord be ever with and bless you, my dearest one! As ever,

Your affectionate husband,
C. C. Jones.

Rev. C. C. Jones *to* Miss Mary Sharpe Jones[t]
Steam Packet Cincinnati, Ohio River 300 Miles below Pittsburgh
Thursday, May 8th, 1851

My dear Daughter,

I wrote your dear mother yesterday, and have sat down this morning to write you. You have been much upon my mind, and trust ere this reaches you that a kind Providence will have restored you to usual health. All God's dealings are intended for our good, and our lightest sicknesses should be improved. You will find in your experience as a Christian that afflictions are ofttimes sanctified to our great and rapid advance in holiness, and in weariedness from this world. Certain it is if we are God's children He intends to fit us for His presence in glory; and we must quietly yield in all things to His will, and have but one desire—that He may glorify Himself in, through, and by us.

Last evening Dr. Krebs of New York preached for us. Almost all the passengers most respectfully came aft and attended our service. The doctor stood in the ladies' cabin near the door so that all might hear. But the jar of the engine and the escape of the steam at every revolution created considerable noise, and sometimes we heard indistinctly. But he preached well on "All the promises of God are in Him; yea and amen"—that passage; do not think I have quoted it exactly right. Our captain kept the boat as still as possible, though not a professor of religion.

The Ohio is a beautiful river. It flows in a tortuous course through a hilly country: the hills of various height and outline, now precipitous to the river's bank, and now sloping back, or yielding a margin or a level promontory for farms and villages, which run all along in almost unbroken succession. The land is fertile; green fields stretch away, swelling up the sides and over the tops of the hills, and farmhouses sit on the sunny sides embosomed in trees; and the forests are clothed in the earliest tints of spring, dotted with the white dogwood and the blush of the redbud. We pass low islands in the river (some inhabited), formed by the deposits of years. They are skirted

with the common forest willow and the sycamore. The waters are now tur-
bid from a fresh, and we meet with no obstructions. I think Mother would
have enjoyed the trip down the river if no more, and nearly all my pleasure
is taken away because she is not here to see what I see and partake in all
things with me. I have seen too the birds once more, and occasionally catch
a sweet note of the oriole, or the icterus of our own loved home. As I was
gazing on the bank, who should suddenly fly up but a real *ardea virescens!*
There he was, snapping his short tail, and raising the feathers of his neck,
and singing out his salutation: "Squow! Squow!" There is a gull with a
dark blue scalp, white and lead-colored tips to his wings, that inhabits these
Western waters; and a passenger said they were found all down to New
Orleans—a new fact to me.

Our steamer, however, is a small wonder. She sits low on the water, her
fire deck not above three or four feet above it. You enter at *her bows,* ascend
a flight of stairs, and enter the reception room, to the right of which is the
clerk's office. Here extras of baggage, etc., are stored, and men smoke—a sort
of "omnium-gatherum." It has front and side windows, and you can look out
and see the progress of the boat and the scenery on either hand. Passing
through this, you enter a saloon (guessing) from 150 to 200 feet long by 15
or 18 broad, with staterooms on each side for the accommodation of two persons, running the whole length; the upper end (about 30 feet) cut off by
folding doors, and constitutes the ladies' apartment. These doors are thrown
open during the day, and the room is all in one. The windows in the ladies'
apartment look out over the stern. Height of ceiling: 9 or 10 feet. Here meals
are served up in excellent style and of good quality; and some 150 or 200
passengers three times a day satisfy their appetites. The ladies are all brought
in and seated first; then our good captain waves his hand, the bell rings, and
the coarser lords of creation are then allowed to take their seats. The saloon
is all carpeted, plainly but well furnished; after meals it is the sitting room,
and the passengers read, write, converse, or walk as they please.

It is very like a hotel, and saving the jar and noise of the machinery you
would scarcely know you were in a boat. And I never was in a steamboat so
free from all disagreeable smells of the oil, etc., that makes one sick. You are
away and above it all. If you go on the hurricane deck, you are 20 or 25 feet
above the water, and have a fine view all around. There go up the huge and
towering smoke pipes rolling out their black volumes of smoke; and between
them is the steersman's house still above you; and then on each side the
steam pipes, puffing and roaring like two lions down in their throats, responsive to each other. There she goes—the black column of smoke trailing and
ascending from the smoke pipes, and the milk-white and smaller columns
of steam ascending by their sides and mingling with them, and a torrent of
foam and spray bursting from her stern and wheelhouses, and all the river
lashing its sides as she displaces the water and it rushes back to its former
level. Off goes her shrill and powerful whistle to be heard for miles, telling

her approach to some landing place; and then her great bell tolls like a church bell. Things are on a larger scale out here than east of the mountains.

But I must stop. Kiss dear Mother for me over and over, and take good care of her for me till the Lord brings me back to you. The boat shaking and the hand shaking makes very shaky writing. You must, however, try to spell it out. Would write better if I could. The Lord bless and keep you, my dear child!

From your ever affectionate father,
C. C. Jones.

Rev. C. C. Jones *to* Messrs. Charles C. Jones, Jr., *and* Joseph Jones[g]
Steam Packet Cincinnati, Ohio River 300 Miles below Pittsburgh
Thursday, May 8th, 1851

My dear Sons,

I left Philadelphia on Monday morning at eight, sorry at parting with your dear mother and sister, and especially as your sister was still sick with the peculiar epidemic resembling measles that is going through Miss Gill's School. Dr. Hodge, however, assured me that it would be over in a few days, and hope ere this she is restored by divine goodness.

We went in the railroad, crossing the Allegheny on inclined planes, to Johnstown, where Tuesday morning at sunrise, amid *frost and ice,* we took the canalboat, and finally reached Pittsburgh Wednesday morning at eleven o'clock. A full load of passengers: pleasant company; and I preached on the boat in the evening to a most interesting and attentive audience. Thus "As ye go, preach," said our Lord. May He bless the seed sown by the wayside! The country through which you pass is interesting, varying in fertility and improvement, all rolling, hilly, some mountainous, but the ranges not very lofty. On the Allegheny as you near Pittsburgh it melts into the beautiful, giving you some charming views in the sweep of the river.

Pittsburgh, you know, is built upon the site of old Fort Duquesne of Washington and ante-Revolutionary memory. The land comes down in a promontory and flats off at the base and end of the hills into a plain where the Allegheny and Monongahela Rivers come together and form the Ohio. And there you have Pittsburgh—a city well called the City of Smoke, full of iron furnaces and factories, and every fire made with bituminous coal. There hangs over the city a dense cloud of smoke, and the tops of the houses are colored black, and all the buildings are dingy and black, and even the fences and bodies of the trees are blackened. The houses lately built look sixty years old. Wash your face and walk out and come home, and your handkerchief is soiled as you use it. But a great business is done here. The riverside is a sight. The bank is paved down from the upper level of the town to the water's edge, and this long, wide slope is covered with people, drays, carriages, and goods moving up and down. And the shore is one line of great steamboats, and a forest of smoke pipes and steam pipes. Bells are ringing and steam escaping, and the river is foaming with paddle wheels. It is altogether unlike the East, and you feel that you have come into a new part of your great country. Things are done with a rush, and the people are pushing, and every man seems very independent of his neighbor.

We are in a fine, large packet: large number of passengers and good accommodations, all things well regulated and orderly, much like a hotel. We had preaching last night by Dr. Krebs of New York. Almost all the passengers attended. My business was to go among and notify and invite all to join us, and so they did with few exceptions.

The peculiar wildness of which you have heard so much on these Western waters is wearing away. The Ohio is a beautiful river. Runs through a hilly country, and you have all the varieties that such a country affords of scenery. Occasionally a low island. We passed Blennerhassett Island in the night; will tell you about it when we are spared to meet again. This, you know, is the great coal country. Along the sides of the hills you will see holes, and railways running up into them, or deposits of coal about them. These are entrances into coal pits: numerous indeed. The people dig in almost anywhere and there is coal, and a great business is done in the article, and numerous iron foundries are scattered about. A country of great agricultural and mineral resources. The spring was very backward in Western Pennsylvania and the upper part of the Ohio River, but as we make more *southing* the forests are more advanced.

I am much interested in the trip, but would be more so if Mother was with me. Write her frequently while I am away. And Joe, you must write me and direct to Riceboro, and put in your letter what books you wish me to bring on for you; and Charles may want some also. The memorandum you gave me was on a letter left in the office in Philadelphia. Do not forget it.

We hope to be in Louisville on Saturday morning, spend Sabbath, and reach St. Louis about Wednesday night or Thursday morning, God willing.

Have met on board a brother of Rev. Mr. Ross of Savannah, who has given me most interesting accounts of Missouri, New Mexico, etc. He was in Colonel Doniphan's expedition.

You can write me on receipt of this after a few days to *Marietta, Georgia,* care of your Aunt Eliza. Will write you every chance I can get, but expect to be very busy while the assembly is in session.

Be good boys. Improve your opportunities. Am sorry, my son, you did not read me your piece. Did not know you had read it to your mother till we got to Philadelphia. *Study clearness.* Do not aim too high.

The Lord be with and bless you, my dear children! Remember your Creator in the days of your youth. I never cease praying for you. Excuse the handwriting; the boat shaking a great deal. You can make it out, I hope.

Your ever affectionate father,

C. C. Jones.

REV. C. C. JONES *to* MRS. MARY JONES[t]
Louisville Hotel, Louisville, Kentucky, *Saturday,* May 10th, 1851[*]
My dearest One,

Oh, how I miss you! Have just taken out your miniature and looked at it and kissed it. You are my own dear sweet wife, and I am as ever your true lover and devoted husband. Everything pleasant that I have seen and met with I have said in my heart: "I wish Mary was with me"; and everything that has been hurried and unpleasant I have said: "I am glad she has not this to bear." You are my own dear sweet wife, and I wish I was good enough and kind enough and able to make you perfectly happy in all things. The Lord bless and reward you, my dear wife, for all your kindness and goodness to me and mine, and pardon me in all my waywardness and shortcomings as a husband to you!

I sent you a telegraphic dispatch from Pittsburgh, and one again from Cincinnati, and mailed a letter to you at Wheeling, and one to my dear daughter and one to my dear sons at Cincinnati. Hope you will all be able to spell them out, as the boat would not keep still for me to write.

Pittsburgh is finely situated, and is, you know, a most important and flourishing city. But oh, how dingy and black! Looks aged. Roofs, walls, doors, windows, fences, even *trees* and shrubbery all black and rusty—the effect of the smoke and cinder of the bituminous coal, which is universally burnt, and in numerous furnaces and factories; and there is a widespread smoke continually ascending from the plain of the city. A passenger in the canalboat said it looked like the smoke from the plain of Sodom and Gomorrah, he supposed!

Allegheny City is on the opposite side of the River Allegheny, and the position of the seminary is the most ridiculous imaginable. Conceive of a huge hog, and the sharp ridge of his back cut through so as to give sufficient foundation for a building, and you have the sharp, odd, and perched appearance of the seminary building. The approach is from the less precipitous side of the two. The hill is sold, the building to be taken down and put up in a better position.

The bank of the river, where the business of the city is done, is cut and sloped down from the front street to the water's edge, making what I believe they call a landing or levee. This construction of the landings is peculiar to all the towns on the Western waters, because from the overflowings of the rivers they can have no wharves. This open-wide slope, stretching perhaps the whole length of the town on the river, affords ample space for the landing and shipment of goods, and is walled in on the river side by huge steamboats, lying side by side with their heads against the shore, and a forest of smoke and steam pipes—decks crowded with goods and people, goods landing and taking in, drays and carriages ascending and descending to and from the ranges of stairs; and town on the high bank, where the street runs and a multitude of people thronging all the space, the whole stretch of the levee

131

alive with them; and the rattling and calling and conversation, and paddling and puffing of boats—the whole presents to your eye a most novel yet animating and interesting scene. When you have seen one, you have seen all. They have at the towns and landing places on the river *floating wharves*—that is, reception boats having a regular *house* on the flat deck. The steamboat comes alongside and takes in or puts out goods. This is to prevent the steamboats from grounding when they come to the shore.

There is nothing grand in the scenery of the Ohio, but it is always pleasing, and frequently changes into the beautiful. You have every variety of hill and margin scenery. The hills when they slope immediately down to the water's edge on one side, on the opposite side they have receded; and there lies a wide margin or plain, sometimes almost level; and so plain and high hills alternate from side to side all the way down to Louisville. It is upon these margins or plains that the towns and villages and farms are located; and as you pass from one to another you see that you are passing through a settled country. Now and then a stream or river empties into the noble river itself. It is indeed a noble river, varying in width from a third to a half mile, and still wider in places: the great highway opened by a kind Providence into this great country. Iron and coal abound in all the upper regions through which it runs, and you see the coal pits on the sides of the hills, with their black mouths and railways running down the slope, and furnaces sending up their smoke, and here and there piles of iron on the shore. On the right bank is the free and on the left the slave state. The improvement is about the same on either shore, with perhaps a predominance of villages and towns on the free side.

We reached Cincinnati before daylight. We went and breakfasted on shore, and then I pushed for *Dr. Law's,* our old friend. Found him sitting in his apothecary's store reading a morning paper.

"Howdy do, Doctor!"

"Oh! Oh, Charles, how do you do! How do you do!"

Perfect surprise; not more surprising than agreeable.

Away we went to see his family. Lives in his own nice brick house in a pleasant part of the city with fine furniture and every comfort. Mrs. Law quite well; children well; all perfectly satisfied; prospering greatly in pecuniary matters. His money lent out—and realizing ten, twelve, and fifteen percent interest, etc., etc. He is delighted with his change. Does not practice; his apothecary's shop supports his family. Belongs to Dr. Rice's church. They wished to make him an elder; he declined. Looks like his father. Not as fresh and full as when at White Bluff, but hearty.

Not a moment to spare. We hastened to Mr. William Neff's house. Fine mansion: $27,000! New purchase. Saw Mrs. Neff. Retains her identity, but years and cares have made their impression. Pleasant interview; sent her respects to you.

Hurried off to Mr. Neff's *pork house.* He was reading.

"Howdy do, Mr. Neff!"

"Why, *Charles!* How *do you do!*"

And he was as glad to see me as I was to see him. Looking remarkably well. His son *Clifford* in business with him; tall like his mother.

We revived old recollections.

"Well, Mr. Neff, don't you want another *clerk*? My constitution is wearing under my present work; suppose I come and begin the world with you again?"

"Ah," said he, "if I had *such* a clerk again, I should not now need *two*."

He was the same mild, gentlemanly man, but now all softened, with the grace of God. Time *flew* away, and I reluctantly took my leave of him after receiving a hearty invitation to visit him with you and our children at Yellow Springs, his summer retreat in the country.

Dr. Law then showed me several buildings, among others the celebrated hotel, the Burnet House, and as much of the town as our few moments would allow. It is a great city—120,000 inhabitants counting in the suburbs; full of life, enterprise, and business; and a faithful worshiper of Mammon, as report goes.

At 12 M. about, after sending a telegraphic dispatch to you, and taking leave of my kind friend, the steamer *Telegraph No. 2* backed out, and we were off, and soon out of sight of this queen city of the West. Dr. Krebs preached for us in the evening; or rather he preached for us between Pittsburgh and Cincinnati, and a Mr. Dabney from Virginia and Dr. McKinney between Cincinnati and Louisville. We had a noble run of 120 or 130 miles, going at the rate of about fifteen miles per hour, and arrived at Louisville at ten in the evening. Put up at the Louisville Hotel.

All this morning and most of this afternoon have been engaged with Brothers Hill and Humphrey in settling up the business between the Western Executive Committee and the board of paying up the missionaries. Think we have it all right now, and will endeavor to keep it so. Have engaged to preach tomorrow afternoon for Dr. Humphrey's people, and in the evening for the Negroes in the Baptist church. Could not well get off, though would have liked to be a hearer. Work, work while the day lasts. The brethren are about, walking, riding, seeing, and being seen. Have been busy all day, and am now trying to refresh myself with an hour or more with my dearest of all friends.

Louisville is situated just above the falls in the Ohio on a fine plain. Very well built; some fine houses private and public of course. Country around superior. City growing rapidly; much business. Destined to grow, for railroads are centering here from all quarters. In all this West the people have an air of freedom and individuality; are offhand in address and argument; more of the active than the contemplative; and rather more open and free than polished; and pervaded with a spirit of progress and adventure. Dr. Law says he never knew a place in which human life appeared less precious than in Cincinnati.

I just now telegraphed you a note by Morse's line to sweeten your cup of tea; and as no telegraph has come from you to me here, I fondly hope my dear child is better.

We purpose leaving in a boat for St. Louis on Monday morning—a very large company of ministers and elders; and if prospered, hope to arrive there on Thursday morning. The meeting promises to be one of importance. Two professors to elect. Dr. McGill, it is said, will go to Cincinnati; there seems to be a doubt about it. Then there may be some movement about a different mode of conducting our domestic missionary operations. Then there is a desire to establish committees of the other boards West, etc., etc. The Lord will order everything aright. My earnest prayer is that He would enable me so to speak and act that in all things His holy name may be glorified. The more I mingle with men and with God's own people and have to do with the affairs of His Kingdom, the more do I feel the hourly need of the teachings of the Holy Ghost—of that wisdom which cometh from above. Pray for me, my dear wife, as I do most constantly for you.

Kiss my dear child for me, and send much love to the boys. Am very glad I wore my old suit for traveling. The weather has become quite warm; vegetation two weeks in advance of Pennsylvania. Felt a soft *south* wind yesterday afternoon. Farewell for the present, my dear wife.

Your ever affectionate husband,
C. C. Jones.

Rev. C. C. Jones *to* Mrs. Mary Jones[t]
Steam Packet *Fashion,* Below Louisville, *Monday,* May 12th, 1851
A week today, my dear Mary, I took leave of you and my dear child, and by the good hand of God we are thus far on our way.

I preached yesterday afternoon in Dr. Humphrey's church, and in the evening to the Negroes. Was much assisted in both services, and trust a blessing may ensue. The meeting in the evening was the greatest treat I have had since leaving home. Between five and seven hundred Negroes present. House *"crammed."* The pastor a genteel educated mulatto of excellent character and standing, and much esteemed, and *a native of Georgia!* Born and reared in Middle Georgia; has been here eleven years. He added a word after the sermon: "My Christian friends, we have long heard of Dr. Jones, and of his great success in *reformation.* But we could never understand the mystery before. Now the mystery is solved. He preaches the *pure gospel.*" And then sat down. All Baptists: a noble congregation and pleasant season. After service at Dr. Humphrey's a Baptist brother introduced himself saying: "I am grateful for your discourse. A lady came with me who has been endeavoring to believe in the annihilation of the wicked; but the discourse I hope will settle her mind."

Feel better today than I expected. The boat is new; the company of brethren large. We trust in a kind Providence to carry us safely on our way. He has been very merciful to us thus far. We would trust Him in all time to come. Wrote you and telegraphed you also on Saturday, and have come into the stateroom and embraced a moment before the boat leaves to send my dear wife a line.

Louisville is *a city!* Situated upon a beautiful plain; many fine residences; excellent churches: a great Popish church building; a great deal of business. You know it is just above the falls in the Ohio River; a canal runs around them. Tolls high. A Southern city: you see the difference as soon as you enter it, and it is agreeable. New Albany, where we have a theological seminary, is opposite on the Indiana side, but lower down—at the lower end of the canal.

The engineer says if we are prospered we shall reach St. Louis on Wednesday evening about teatime. Kiss Mary for me. Hope she has quite recovered. Farewell for the present, my dearest wife. The Lord watch over and bless you and my dear children!

Your ever affectionate husband,
C. C. Jones.

Mr. Charles C. Jones, Jr., *to* Mrs. Mary Jones and Miss M. S. Jones[t]
Princeton, *Monday,* May 12th, 1851

My dear Mother and Sister,

Your letter, my beloved parent, was duly received, for which I return you my warmest thanks. Father's departure has doubtless caused a feeling of sadness to steal over the soul whenever you think of him far away. Yet we hope his presence at the General Assembly will prove highly beneficial to the "great cause." If he there meets with Uncle John, what a delightful trip they will have in company to Liberty! And then the seeing of friends and relations, servants and all—how many pleasant associations will in a moment be revived! The scenes of other years—how fast they come crowding upon the soul! Truly has it been remarked by an able author: "The memory of joys that are past is sweet and mournfully soothing to the soul." Sweet, because of a satisfaction springing therefrom; mournfully pleasant, for at the same instant we look back upon such times as golden moments hallowed by many endearing recollections, but they are flown never to return. You and Sister must look forward with much interest to the time when you shall revisit those fine seats where so many cheerful days have been spent.

To change the theme somewhat, the account of that missionary's death was one of the most awful that I ever heard of. What inhuman wretches those boatmen must have been—at the same time cowards of the meanest sort! Such brutality scarce meets with a parallel amid the benighted tribes of Africa, the deluded Hindus, or savage Malays. Men talk of the enlightened and civilized condition of this country. Well, comparatively speaking it is enjoying many privileges. Yet how much remains yet to be accomplished ere

135

the veil of darkness shall be wholly lifted from the face of this land! The board suffers much also in a pecuniary light, for if I remember rightly, Father stated that it required $1,500 to defray the expenses of the missionary and family to their place of destination. Perhaps this outrage may nerve the arm of justice to increased vigilance and direct the attention of the church to that quarter.

We have had a death recently among our number. Mr. William H. Timlow, a member of our class, died at the residence of his parents in Amity, Orange County, New York. He was a devotedly pious young man, beloved by all, diligent in his studies, unpretending in all his duties. The disease which terminated his mortal career was dropsy. Before leaving college he looked very badly; and as I bade him farewell the thought was impressed upon my mind that I should nevermore behold him. You are aware how fatal such attacks are with us. We are about to make an effort to erect a monument over him similar to that you remember in the graveyard. Speaking to his brother, who is also a member of our class, he remarked that such a token of our respect for the dead would be very gratifying to his parents and relatives. You have perhaps noticed the resolutions adopted by the hall —published in *The Presbyterian, New York Observer,* etc.

On last Sabbath Dr. Carnahan delivered his farewell sermon to the graduating class. His remarks were very touching, and the old gentleman appeared to feel every word that he uttered. We have already taken their places, and if nothing prevents will in one year take our leave of Old Nassau. Although a student desires to leave college, and is delighted when the season of graduation comes, still there are many ties binding his soul which are very hard to separate. Friendships are made with fellow mates, with the faculty; and around every feature gathers an association which time itself can scarce dissolve.

Listened with much pleasure and interest to an address delivered by a minister lately returned from a visit to the Waldenses. Judging from the statements made, they must indeed be a noble people—pious and fond of liberty. They manifest the highest regard for Americans, esteeming them the most favored people of earth.

Am sorry to say that my old friend the sore throat has again paid me a visit, and seems demanding penance for the long vacation that has been allowed. Have this morning taken a dose of blue pill and salts, with a gargle of alum. Think that it was brought on by cold, my eyes being red and very painful. Hope, however, that by taking care of myself for a day or two that I shall recover.

My dear mother and sister, if you have the least need of my services at any time, be it night or day, just let me know, and you will immediately find me by your sides. Have received no letters from home for some time, and therefore no news from that quarter. I suppose that you have noticed the action of the legislature of South Carolina; she seems determined to leave the

Union. Hoping that this will find you both in good health and fine spirits, I remain, with best love, in which Brother unites,

Your affectionate son and brother,

Charles C. Jones, Jr.

Many thanks, my dear mother, for your just criticisms and good advice. Shall try to profit by them.

Mrs. Mary Jones *to* Rev. C. C. Jones[t]

Philadelphia, *Monday,* May 12th, 1851

My dear Husband,

Your letter of the 9th to Mary has just been handed to us by John, and we feel grateful for your kind remembrance of us. The telegraphic dispatches were both received about five o'clock of the day on which they were sent. I never realized before what streams of happiness are thus conveyed rapidly almost as thought itself throughout our land. It cheered and rejoiced my sad and desolate heart to know almost from day to day your progress and situation. Then came your welcome letter from Wheeling. And you cannot rest even on a journey! I hope those religious services may bring forth fruit for a happy eternity though sown by the wayside.

By Saturday's mail we received a long letter from Laura to you with a note from Mr. Peace, and one from Cousin Mary. Brother John will tell you all the Marietta news. Also one from Mr. Douglas with an order for the Bible and the remainder in a piece of silver for Mrs. Davis.

Our dear child was so much recovered from the eruption as to walk out and go to church once on Sabbath; but she has taken a cold which affects her teeth, ears, face, neck, and whole head, which is swollen. Tonight I sent for the doctor; not that I was alarmed, but I thought she needed medicine, and did not like to prescribe myself. He has just gone, having ordered some cathartic pills, which I trust through God's blessing will relieve her. He says "she is suffering rather from an *excess of health* than a want of it, and he likes to see a constitution of vigor such as she appears to have; that although disease seizes upon it with violence, there is something to work upon; but it is the poor, feeble, nervous creatures that it is difficult to do anything for." You must not be distressed on her account; he will visit her until she is relieved.

He told me there must be some mistake touching the reported murder of Mr. Geary. I trust it may be false.

Oh, my dearest, how shall I get through the two long months that lie in prospect ere you return? My poor child being sick, I wander down alone to my meals and eat them as quick as possible and hurry back to my room. All is so cold and desolate and cheerless in this land of strangers; not a generous or even a polite emotion seems to move the hearts of those around me. I must, however, except our good friends Mr. and Mrs. Newkirk; and I spoke par-

137

ticularly of the dwellers under this roof. I pray daily to be delivered from the sin of murmuring, which excited the just anger of the Lord so often against the children of Israel.

The weather has been very hot, though pleasant to myself. Today President Fillmore arrived, but I am told his reception was a cold, tame thing. My paper is dancing, and I must close until morning.

13th. According to Dr. Hodge's directions I gave the pills every three hours. Mary had an uneasy night, and of course I did not *sleep* much from anxiety and the giving of medicine. She suffers very much. Her whole mouth within and without is so swollen it is with difficulty she takes nourishment. From a letter received from Charles today I fear he may be taking the same disease, as he complains of his eyes and throat, and it has been prevailing in Princeton. One of his classmates has recently died of dropsy: from Orange County, New York.

I called to see Mrs. Chester the other day, and she told me what pleasant arrangements she had whilst boarding—just a square above this in Chestnut at precisely what we now pay: twice the room and more than twice the conveniences. Our quarters certainly could not be more contracted, and I shall be on the lookout whilst you are away for some improvement. It may be all owing to a want of enterprise and attention to these things that we are not better situated. Mrs. Harrison would have given us three rooms for a trifle more. I hear constantly high recommendations of her house. If Mrs. Watson asks $6 apiece for the three rooms in a row on this entry, we had better take them than to take but *two* at the same price, thus paying $12 for one which is only a few feet larger. I will only be on the *lookout,* and *not engage* until you return.

I trust, my dear husband, that a pleasant journey, pleasant company, and a trip home will do much to refresh and revive your health and feelings; for you needed a change, and were very much worn down by your constant and arduous duties before you left Philadelphia. I shall be often in spirit with Brother John and yourself on your homeward journey. I have been so constantly occupied with Mary that I have not procured the remainder of the articles for the servants; will do so and have them shipped as early as possible. I am sure your visit home will be greatly promotive of our interest there; indeed, humanly speaking, your presence there occasionally is absolutely necessary, for you cannot expect others to attend to our affairs if we neglect them ourselves. We had a lesson upon that point when they were wholly entrusted to managers before.

Strange to say, I have not received one of your newspapers since you left, and feel quite lost about the affairs of church and state.

I will write you next to Marietta. Cousin Mary's letter was put in on the 6th, and I received it on the 10th. *Mr. Powel* is very kind to bring them every one himself, and makes the kindest inquiries after you, and offers to attend to any business for me; and I feel that we have a *friend* in him.

Tonight is the twenty-seventh anniversary of the Sunday School Union, to be held at the Musical Fund Hall. Mrs. White kindly sent me three tickets of admission yesterday; but I shall not leave my dear child.

Give a great deal of love to my dear brother. I often wish he was settled near us, but really believe himself and family better off in Marietta than they would be here. I rejoice in the increase and prosperity of his church. Tell him one of his best friends said once to me: "If he could only conquer that dreadful habit of procrastination, he would make an able minister of the gospel." It is sad when the influences of a noble character are marred by the prevalence of one bad habit.

Excuse my letter; it has been written almost in the dark, for Mary cannot bear the light. Best regards to Dr. Leland. The ladies of the house send respects to you. The Lord watch over and preserve you, my dear husband, ever prays

Your affectionate wife,
Mary Jones.

Rev. C. C. Jones *to* Mrs. Mary Jones[t]

Steam Packet *Fashion*, Mississippi River 80 Miles below St. Louis
Wednesday, May 14th, 1851

Here am I, far off in this Western world, shut up in my stateroom to write to you, my own dear sweet wife. My heart turns to you with fondest love; I am your true and devoted lover, and here you are sitting before me and looking me full in the face while my soul is knit to yours and converses with you above a thousand miles distant. I feast my eyes upon your miniature, and recognize every line and feature; and could it start into life, I should overwhelm you with caresses. This clear forehead which I have so often smoothed, these eyes of love, these lips and cheeks so warm and sweet to me, these hands of ready affection, the true and noble heart that beats for me within this sacred bosom, this precious person—it is my own dearest, sweetest one, my own beloved Mary. What can I do to make you love me? I wish you the fullness of the blessings of heaven from above, and the fatness of the earth beneath.

Our married life has flowed a river of love to me most free and full—uneven at times from the imperfect heart within me, yet nevertheless a river free and full. Clouds have cast their shadows upon it, but those shadows have never tinged its purity. Would that I had the power to set up in your memory all along the many years of our union the happiest hours, the brightest scenes, the sweetest joys, so that every shadow should be gone, and on looking back you would see and remember me in the light of my love and in nothing else. It is so that I look back and remember you. Increase of years has brought its cares, and time is making his lasting furrows upon me; but thanks be to God, my heart does not grow old. My wife is still my *bride,* and I can walk with her under these blue skies and upon this green earth, and

139

our young love shall give brightness and beauty to everything, and she shall be more than all the world to me. Into her lap would I pour the fullness of my best labors for her good; and into her bosom all my heart, that she might have everything, and find her happiness in me, as I do mine in her, and as perfect and complete as our Heavenly Father permitteth us to enjoy in each other here below. I bless Him for my wife; I praise Him for His wonderful mercies and loving-kindness to us all our life long, and to our dear, dear children. Oh, may He continue to be our God and their God, and unite us together eternally in His Kingdom of Glory!

I have over and over wished for you in my present wonderful voyage, although I know you decided to remain for the best of reasons. But I have wanted your eyes to see what mine see, and your ears to hear what mine hear, and your heart to enjoy what mine enjoys. You can form but a poor conception of this world out here from books and descriptions. Think of navigating a noble river a thousand miles before you reach its mouth, with but one solitary obstruction; and when you reach its mouth you see it mingle its waters with the parent stem which flows a thousand miles more before the waters mingle with the sea! Then turning up that same main river, you may travel up into the heart of our continent in more directions than one above a thousand miles further! The width of the Mississippi where the Ohio enters it is little if any greater than the Ohio itself. But it is much deeper, and immediately above and below the junction spreads wider. Well has it been called the Father of Waters. For fifty miles up from the mouth of the Ohio the banks are low, and then on the Missouri side they rise into undulating hills that come to the water's edge sometimes, but the great bottom of the river spreads far on either side. There is a silent majesty in the flow of the river, and an apparent consciousness of worth and power! Intent upon its great way, it notices nothing. The long reaches, the luxuriant banks, the wide curves and sweeps embosoming great islands—all give an impression of majesty and magnificence to the stream. As we ascend, now some sixty miles below St. Louis, the right bank (Missouri side) is hilly and beautiful. The banks remind you, in the *lower* parts, of our Southern rivers: soil alluvial, foliage dense and green and luxuriant, and climate unhealthy. A scattered population stretches along and furnishes wood for steamboats. Here and there a little settlement or village. But I will not tire you with descriptions; will lay them up to talk of with you when God shall please to bring us together again.

Interrupted by a call to attend a meeting of the passengers to pass resolutions expressive of their feelings in respect to our boat and voyage and mercies. Dr. Krebs in the chair; Dr. Leyburn secretary; Dr. C. C. Jones of Georgia chairman of committee on resolutions, etc. All over pleasantly; and Dr. Hall of Connecticut made an interesting and impressive prayer in conclusion. We have been wonderfully blessed. The Lord be praised! Our steamer has done nobly. We hope, the Lord permitting, to reach St. Louis this afternoon.

Hope all my letters have reached you. Kiss my dear daughter for me, and send love to the boys. Do walk out with Mary Sharpe and take good care of your health every way. My remembrance to Mr. and Mrs. Newkirk, and respects to Mrs. Roser, etc. God be with and bless you, my dear wife!

Your ever affectionate and devoted husband,
C. C. Jones.

Rev. C. C. Jones *to* Mrs. Mary Jones[t]

St. Louis, Missouri, *Saturday*, May 17th, 1851

And now, *my darling wife,* I must write you, having just got my report all ready for the assembly. It is made the order of the day for Tuesday ten o'clock. Have been very little in the assembly owing to the preparation of the report.

Our boat reached the levee on Wednesday at 4 P.M. On going ashore, who should be there but *John himself!* We simultaneously cried out as far as we could see each other in the crowd, and then rushed into each other's arms, the gladdest fellows you ever saw. He had made a most pleasant arrangement for me at Mrs. Annan's, one of Brother Nat Pratt's most intimate friends. And here I am, with a pleasant room all to myself, and most kindly entertained by Mr. and Mrs. Annan. If you were only here to share it with me! On the same afternoon we reached here I telegraphed you by Morse's line. The clerk said you would get it at *teatime.* Hope you did, for I know it would sweeten your cup of tea. I also sent you a special *love letter* written to you on the bosom of the broad-flowing Mississippi by myself, your *old true lover.* I look at you and kiss you every day.

John is very hearty; left all well; and is delighted with your *likeness,* and thanks you for it heartily, and prefers it to mine. He and *Dr. Leland* came by way of Nashville together; arrived three days before us, and are quartered in a fine establishment—at *Mr. and Mrs. Charless'.* The doctor same as ever: rejoiced to see me, and made the kindest inquiries after you and our dear children; reports all as usual in Columbia, and brought me a most affectionate letter from Brother Howe. He would have me to go into the pulpit and assist him in his opening sermon; Dr. Magee also. Have ordered the sermon sent you in the paper which is printed daily containing the proceedings of the assembly. It will reach you every day until the assembly closes. The first evening I came *John* preached an excellent sermon in Dr. Potts's church, and I went into the pulpit with him.

You will see my name was put up with several others for moderator. I let it quietly go, knowing that Dr. Humphrey would be elected, as the West has the moderator this year.

The assembly moves on very quietly and successfully, and our promise is of a pleasant session. St. Louis pours out its hospitality, and attends the meetings well. Have seen a number of missionaries of the board; and my visit, by God's blessing, will not be in vain. Several of my old *Princeton* classmates here: Bristol, Huntington, Gillespie, Johnson. Everybody has heard of me if not seen me, so notable have my *black* labors made me. Last night Dr. Van Rensselaer had a meeting in favor of the Board of Education. Only tolerable; speaking moderate. Would have been glad to have spoken for him on *ministerial responsibility for ministerial supplies*—a subject that needs much pressing home on our church at this time; but was not asked, you know.

Your precious letter of May 7th came yesterday. John and I were at the office together. Thank you for it and all the news in it from my dear child and from home, and for all your expressions of love to me. The Lord be with and bless you, my dearest one! *Look up* always; that is the best way to do. Hope my dear child is well now. Wrote Charles also about his speech. We have hopes it is *a mistake about Brother Geary!* The *last* steamers, Mr. Lowrie tells me, bring *not one word of it.* Awful, mysterious, heartrending if true! The Lord sanctify it to us and all the church!

Mr. Shotwell and Mr. Singletary are here, and Mr. Bishop and Mr. Telford, from South Carolina. Mr. Telford tells me his *wife died one month ago*— twenty days after the birth of an infant! And he is here! Well, we don't understand these things. Married about a year!

Last night we had a Southern thunderstorm, and now (3 P.M.) another. How the wind blows! Trees streaming. There fly the coats and hats. Pantaloons shivering; the people running in every direction; a cloud of dust; carts and drays dashing by all wildness. And the dark cloud obscures my lines as I write; and the lightning and thunder are succeeding each other; and here comes the welcome rain and the cool air after a most sultry day.

Will give you some idea of St. Louis in a subsequent letter. No room in this. Kiss Mary Sharpe for me. Hope she and you have been receiving my letters all along as I came. Have been appointed to preach Sabbath evening; *declined;* believe John was put in my place. And now, my dear wife, I must close. Have begun to count the days for my return to your bosom, my own sweet Mary. Oh, how I do love you! Be sure and write me to Marietta and to Riceboro. We have some hope the assembly may close *next week*. Then, if God please, we shall leave for home. Blessed be His name for His great mercy to me unworthy! I pray for you and our dear children morning, noon, and night. You are my own dear, sweet wife. Mrs. Annan's little canary bird is singing so joyfully; I think my heart would sing for joy if I could see *my love.*

From your own dear husband,
C. C. Jones.

MR. CHARLES C. JONES, JR., *to* MRS. MARY JONES *and* MISS M. S. JONES[t]
Princeton, *Saturday,* May 17th, 1851

My dearly beloved Mother and Sis,

You know not the pleasure that I experience when, laying aside the accustomed routine of college engagements, I bid my pen trace the feelings of my soul, and politely bargain with Uncle Sam for the safe transmission of a few words of love to those whom my bosom ever holds most dear. A continued repetition of "the same old news" at once tires the receiver and is at best but a nominal way of interchanging views with correspondents. I will therefore endeavor to interest you, for a few moments at least, with such reflections as forced themselves upon my mind this evening while taking a short stroll. First, however, let me thank my kind parent for her remembrance of "the boys," and congratulate my sister upon the prospect of a speedy recovery.

I love to walk alone. Not that company is disagreeable; far from it: an interchange of sentiment is pleasant. But there are seasons when one should leave the busy throng, view nature in her silent operations, mark an attraction in the thousand objects that present themselves, and above all commune with nature's God. Such a time as this is sweet to me, for then, forsaking the giddy circle, the pressure of business and close application, the mind finds an opportunity calmly to listen to its own suggestions. Then, catching the spirit of evening vespers, it speaks only of freedom and love, of joy from a better land.

The sunset this eve was beautiful. Just before the King of Day hasted to plunge beneath those western waters, he seemed loath to leave so lovely a world to the sway of darkness, and turning his full-orbed face full against the horizon, shed his farewell rays, mantling this azure vault with gorgeous drapery, as if he would say: "Good night, loved spot of God's creation. Ere I leave thee, take this beauteous covering and wear it in remembrance of me till Phaëthon shall again harness his horses to my chariot, and Aurora once more unlock the golden portals of the east." Just then a lovely cloud arose, resembling some vast mountain in the distance, whose summit looms aloft high above the plain. To my mind the form of giant Gonah was forcibly recalled as alone in silent grandeur he towers monarch of Nacoochee.

That is a beautiful prospect, but hark! Is that the neighing of some war-horse snuffing the battle from afar? 'Tis something yet more terrible, for yonder appears some huge iron monster, whose tread is like the sound of a mighty earthquake. In his nostrils dwell fire and smoke. His mission is onward, his trust three hundred souls. Yet this mighty engine is subservient to the will and guidance of a single man; in fine, it is but the resultant of those powerful intellectual forces of which he is the sole possessor. What a triumph of mind over matter! Truly man, though his visage be badly marred by sin, still bears about him the impress of omnipotence. In the subjection of the natural elements he displays in a faint degree the power of Him at whose simple fiat worlds spring into being, perform their rotations, and disappear.

Then, just by his side, a fit companion came—the steamboat puffing along the canal. And on its very brink stand the posts of the telegraphic wires. Yes, the telegraph, that great annihilator of time, is also an offspring of the same great inventive genius. Send a dispatch from New York at ten o'clock, and they will receive it in St. Louis a quarter before that hour. Is it not then truly an annihilator of time? Could we make the communication around the globe perfect and unbroken, in a single moment would this winged messenger perform his circuit.

Truly we live in an age of wonders. Could the ancient Roman have arisen from his sleep of ages and stood where I then did, how completely would he have been lost in amazement! Surely he would have imagined that Jupiter and Neptune were running a race, and I fear that his most vivid conceptions regarding the swiftness of a Mercury would have fallen far short of the rapidity of the telegraph. We may well conceive what ideas the ancient Puritans would have entertained, and what their conduct would have been, should anyone have dared to foretell such a period. "A witch! A witch!" would they all exclaim. "His brain is turned: he bolted through Mrs. Quankum's keyhole last night and bewitched her darling babes. No such person should live. Let us burn him! No such broomstick-flying is in accordance with the good old go-to-mill jog."

Thanks, however, these days have passed, and we reap the rewards of an enlightened, encouraged, enterprising spirit. What need for action, then, that one keep pace with the age? Keep pace, did I say? Nay, this is not sufficient— but of laborious exertion that we be not found among the common herd, but of those who live in advance of their period and yield encouragement to its progress.

Yet there is a dark side to this picture. For although we are making such rapid strides in arts, sciences, and manufactures, I verily fear that there is a marked declension in morality and religion. "Moral suasion," so much lauded by many nowadays, is in the main, I believe, not worth much. In fact, if I ever have any little "responsibilities" to bring up, they shall know that such a moralist as Solomon lived, and be *sensibly* aware of his precepts. I have, I hope, my dear mother, imbibed some at least of your noble principles, and will endeavor to transmit them unsullied. We were just speaking of the astonishment with which the Puritan would have viewed our achievements in the arts; and we may also add that in view of our multifarious iniquities his righteous soul would have experienced much holy indignation. So what we have gained in one way we have in some degree at least lost in another.

Have you seen a notice of a recent invention in Washington, by means of which it is proposed to propel the locomotives by means of galvanic batteries, thus dispensing with coal, wood, fire, and water? It is truly a grand one if it be carried out.

Received a very interesting letter from Cousin Laura on Saturday. She, together with all our dear friends in Georgia, is quite well. They are anticipating much pleasure there this summer, and desire their best love to be presented. Heard also from Father. He was upon the Ohio between Pittsburgh and Cincinnati, much pleased with the scenery.

Have handed in my speech to the president for perusal. It is not entirely completed; and my throat is yet so soar that I fear I will be unable for some time to practice it. Never in my life have I had such a sore throat. The larynx has so much closed that I could scarcely swallow water. By taking blue pill, salts, Dover's powders, etc., and by using an alum gargle with caustic it has in a great degree recovered.

Have much to say, but must now close. Am so short run for pantaloons that I will have to have one made today. A dark or light gray coat, one pair of pants, and a white vest for Junior Orator Night will be all the thin clothes that I shall require this session—or rather this summer. The orators all speak in vests of that color, and mine that I now have I find upon examination to be rather small. We can have our clothes made here very well, and perhaps as cheaply as in Philadelphia. I have now two light pair of pants, and will need another of a dark drab just between a winter and summer cloth (one which can be worn every day and will not require washing), and a coat of the same material. However, I will leave it all to you, although I would like to have them made here to my liking. Brother unites with me in much love to self and Sister. With every feeling of love, regard, and affection, I remain

Your obedient son,
Charles C. Jones, Jr.

If you ever need my services in the least, I hope that you will let me know, and you will find your boy present so soon as the cars can carry him.

Your son,
Charles C. Jones, Jr.

Rev. C. C. Jones *to* Mrs. Mary Jones[t]

St. Louis, *Wednesday Evening,* May 21st, 1851

My dearest Wife,

Your welcome letter of the 12th and 13th came today (yours of 7th also received); and I was thankful for God's mercies to you and to our dear daughter, yet much distressed at her relapse, and all your anxieties and cares and loneliness and want of larger accommodations.

I do not know what the Lord has in store for us. We thought we were doing His will in our removal, and it may be—as I have no doubt it is—for the best of purposes for our good that we are where we are and undergo what we do. I often think of Job's reply to his wife: "What! Shall we receive good at the hand of God, and shall we not receive evil?" We have certainly lived long enough to know, and have had the Lord's dealings with us enough to know, that we have here no abiding city, and this is not our rest. Go where we may, we are still in the flesh, still in the world where sin and all its bitter consequences abound; and we must make up our minds to care and trials and troubles, and pray for patience and a quiet trust and rejoicing in God as our portion and heaven as our final home. We have had unnumbered mercies. We are advancing through life, and must lay our account to come to its end. The Lord prepare us for it!

I immediately telegraphed you on reception of your letter today, begging you to let me hear from you immediately in the same way. You do not men-

145

tion hearing by telegraph from me from Louisville. The *lines* so far west are uncertain. I comfort myself, however, with the reflection that if my dear child were worse you would, as I requested, telegraph me without delay.

Let me beg you to remove from the Markoe to where Mrs. Chester is, whom you mention, or anywhere else you may prefer without awaiting my return if it be at all necessary to your convenience and comfort; and request Mr. Powel to pay Mr. Watson his bill in case you do so.

We must lay our account for a *cold* climate in Philadelphia. People are proverbial there for what we have observed in them. We are happy to know that there are exceptions. But we must be grateful and draw comfort beyond the reach of men. The longer I live and see the real character of men, and the more I understand the real draft of life and the emptiness of creature things, the more am I inclined to retirement and to a search after that hidden life with God which is the true peace and happiness of the soul.

Yesterday I delivered my report to the assembly, making use of the ecclesiastical map of the Presbyterian Church by way of illustration. I did not read, but *delivered* it; was above one hour and a half, and met with every attention and success that I had any reason to expect, and beyond my most sanguine expectations. I was much assisted. The assembly in very many members confesses that the subject of domestic missions was never so presented nor understood before. Many very high and extravagant compliments were paid me, and our Southern brethren were specially delighted. Dr. Leland —none more gratified: "Brother Jones, you went beyond yourself altogether; you did the thing, you may depend!" I leave it with God. I asked His blessing before I spoke; I asked His blessing after it was over. The moderator, Dr. Humphrey, delivered an effective sermon in the evening on domestic missions which the assembly has ordered printed.

The Princeton matter came up today. There were some turnings over, and by a large majority the assembly fell on the plan which has long occupied the professors and board of trustees of transferring Dr. Addison Alexander to the chair of ecclesiastical history and putting Mr. Green, our pastor, in his place. The first was done today; the second will no doubt be done tomorrow. I opposed the arrangement, with Dr. Krebs and others; but the Princeton influence prevailed—in my judgment to its own injury: wheels within wheels. Am sorry to say it. So our good friend Mr. Newkirk will be afloat in his church again.

Tonight Dr. Plumer delivers his sermon on popery; I have preferred the quiet converse with my dear wife, and am here in my room; I have lost nothing by it.

The meeting of the assembly thus far has been very harmonious and pleasant, and I hope it may result in great good to the church. The people of the town take considerable interest in the meeting. Have had three invitations to preach, and I am weary; if I preach at all, it will be, God willing, to the Negroes.

146

Somehow I feel lonely. John says we are loving each other too much. He sends this message about *procrastination:* "that he has had the credit of it so long he could not recover from it however he might reform; but on *Sundays* there is no mistake; he is to the minute." Do kiss my dear child for me; tell her Father is more than troubled on her account, but hope she may be recovered before this reaches you. And now, my dear wife, I must close. I dream of you, and long, long to embrace you again.

Your ever devoted husband,
C. C. Jones.

Miss Mary Sharpe Jones *to* Rev. C. C. Jones[t]

Philadelphia, *Wednesday,* May 21st, 1851

My very dear Father,

We were very happy to be informed a few evenings ago by the telegraph of your safe arrival in St. Louis. Last evening Mother received your letter written from Louisville, and we felt thankful to know that you have had so pleasant and prosperous a journey, although you seem to have preached whenever an opportunity offered. It must have been very gratifying to you to have a congregation of colored persons to listen to your preaching. They are all looking anxiously for you in Liberty.

You cannot think how very much we have missed you—especially, too, as I have been sick. I walked out yesterday for the first time. For a week after you left I think the boarders were—some of them—very much afraid of me. My face has been very much swollen, owing to a cold which I took before the rash had quite disappeared. Dr. Hodge said perhaps it would be necessary to extract my front tooth, but Mother objected to having anything of the kind done. As the tooth is now becoming firm, I hope I will suffer no more. Dr. Hodge has been very kind indeed. I have not been to school yet.

We heard from Brothers Charlie and Joe last evening. Brother Charlie has been quite unwell with a severe sore throat, which has confined him to his room for a day or two. He has submitted his speech to the president for criticism. He is afraid his throat will not allow him to practice it as much as he desires.

We have just had a visit from Miss Ann Sanford. She has been sick here for a week, and we did not know she was in town until she knocked at our door this morning. She begs to be remembered particularly to you.

How is your own health, my dear father? Do you think it is improving? I often wish Mother and I could accompany you home. Cousin Laura says everything *there* is looking so beautifully. I am glad you have Uncle John with you.

Mother received a letter from Aunt Mary Robarts a short time since; she mentions that they have reason to hope that Lilla has experienced a change of heart. How pleasant this is!

In a letter which I received from Mary Leland she says that there has been

147

a great deal of sickness in Columbia, especially among the theological students.

We have heard nothing more about the reported murder of Mr. Geary and family. Mother seems half inclined to hope that it may be false. I hope it may be so.

Mr. Powel has been very kind in bringing our papers and letters and in doing everything he can for Mother. Mr. Happersett has been to see her several times. Day before yesterday Mother packed and sent to your office the box of dresses and caps; Mr. Powel marked and shipped it. All of the dresses are marked. Mother has purchased the Bible for Mr. Davis and a silver goblet for Mrs. Davis; the latter was presented by the ladies also.

About a week ago Mother and I visited the Academy of Fine Arts. There are some very beautiful paintings there. I recognized the painting of Queen Victoria instantly; I saw it, you remember, in 1839. I was very much pleased with West's painting of "Death on the Pale Horse." This is truly a picture for study. They have two executed in watercolors which are equally rich, and I think much finer than those done in oil. Mother and Mrs. Roser have gone there this afternoon.

No notice has as yet appeared in the papers of the meeting of the General Assembly.

Spring is making very rapid advances here; the market is full of flowers, and this morning Mother and I noticed a great many strawberries. They reminded us very much of our own home and garden.

Please give a great deal of love to our friends in Marietta when you reach there. The telegraphic dispatch which you sent from Louisville never arrived. We now feel that we can appreciate the value and usefulness of the telegraphic wires more than ever. The last Savannah paper gives quite a spirited account of a tournament which was held at Pineville, South Carolina. Will you be so kind, my dear father, as to bring Bancroft's *History of the United States?* I think it is at Maybank if it was not burned up. Please give our love to Uncle John. Mother unites with me in best love to you, and hope you will soon come back again, for we are so lonely without you. I remain, dear Father,

Your affectionate child,
Mary S. Jones.

Please give a kiss to the dear little baby and Dunwody; also to Mary Sophia, Lilla, Ellen, and Joe.

Mrs. Mary Jones *to* Mr. Charles C. Jones, Jr.[g]
Philadelphia, *Thursday,* May 22nd, 1851

My very dear Son,

Your interesting and affectionate letter has been received, and at the same time one from your dear father dated May 12th, written from Louisville just on the eve of departure for St. Louis, from which place I hope to hear from him this evening or tomorrow. In due course of mail it takes nine days between this and St. Louis.

I feel very much concerned, my dear child, to hear of the state of your health and a return of the sore (not *soar*) throat, and am thankful that my dear Joseph has thus far been preserved from the same affection. I think since you have taken active medicine that it would do you good now to brace up your system by tonics, and wish that you would take five grains of quinine every day immediately after your breakfast, or two grains three times a day. Your sister's throat was very much benefited in the winter by quinine, and I have no doubt but it often proceeds from debility and the state of the stomach, and in your case often from want of rest. If you would persevere like your brother in the use of the cold bath, you would find it of essential service—adding to it a free use of the flesh brush. I find it very beneficial to myself; and from a constant use of the bath and brush during your sister's sickness, although shut out from all exercise, I felt no special want of it. I wish, my son, that you would have some very strong *green* (not *black*) tea drawn, add to it a piece of alum, and sweeten with honey if you can get it (if not, with sugar). Use it constantly as a gargle. Dr. Hodge prescribed this for your sister, and she thought it did her more good than any other remedy. I hope and pray through God's goodness and mercy that you may be relieved from this painful affection. I know how depressing it is to the feelings, and wearing to the constitution, from what I have seen of its effects upon others; for I have always been blessed with great freedom from everything of the kind myself.

In practicing your speech do not overstrain your voice. I do not think the most effective and agreeable oratory consists in violent and unnatural declamation; but to feel the subject and be fired with suitable animation is absolutely necessary. Eloquence is a great gift, and one which had I been of your sex I should have greatly coveted and sought after. As it is, there is nothing which has so much the power to charm my soul. I would willingly barter the finest scenes that my eye ever rested upon, or the loftiest strains of music, for the intellectual excitement and enjoyment of a *good speech* upon a *good subject*. In "thoughts that breathe and words that burn" man seems to give out more of his immortality than in any other way.

If you think, my dear son, that your brother and yourself can have your summer clothes made in Princeton as *well* and nearly as reasonably as in Philadelphia, you can have them done at once. You might at least have *two pair of pants made apiece,* and the white vest you spoke of, and *if there is anything else you wish* for your dress on the important night. Be sure and have all made of *good* and *serviceable* materials—*genteel* and *neat* in appearance. The summer coats also, if you require them before vacation. Write me *immediately* what the cost will be, and anything else that you wish.

You did not say if the hats and caps fit you. And how does your watch keep time? I would like to know particularly. Have you no badges connected with your society?

149

Thank Joseph for his affectionate letter. Will write him soon. Received a long one from your Aunt Susan. All quite well and happy at Social Bluff. If you have an opportunity do send your Aunt Julia's and Aunt Howe's letters; you can do so by mail; I wish to answer them.

I received a paper from Savannah with an account of a tournament at Pineville, South Carolina, where your old flame Miss Inglesby flourishes, and there are names of college memory. I will send it to you when it comes home; I loaned it to Miss Cunningham for her amusement.

Yesterday we were most agreeably surprised by a visit from *Miss Sanford*. She made particular inquiries after you both. Will leave tomorrow.

I must now close to be in time for the mail. Would have done so earlier, but have been sitting with a very sick lady recently come to the Markoe. I fear she is very near eternity. I look at her with indescribable feelings; she is too weak to converse, and I know not what are her hopes beyond the grave. *Sister* is much better, and unites with me in tenderest love to you both.

Ever, my beloved child, your affectionate mother,
Mary Jones.

Do not stint yourselves in anything necessary. I have confidence that you will not be extravagant.

Mrs. Mary Jones *to* Rev. C. C. Jones[t]

Philadelphia, *Friday,* May 23rd, 1851

Your precious letter, my beloved husband, mailed from St. Louis was handed me by Mr. Powel yesterday afternoon just as our tea bell was ringing. You may be assured I stopped first to sip the delicious draught of love, and felt as if I wanted nothing more. After reading your dear letters I always feel as if I had been under the influence of exhilarating gas, and can hardly restrain my feelings. You cannot make an expression of affection that does not meet a response in my own bosom; and there is nothing on earth which I would not do to promote your happiness, health, influence, and usefulness as a minister of the everlasting gospel. I am grateful to God for your safe and pleasant trip; only fear that you have been too much occupied. You will never spare or take care of yourself.

My last letter, I fear, will not reach you before you leave St. Louis; and I almost hope it may not, for it was a sad and gloomy one. I feel better now, for my dear child is at my side again and able to be out walking. The doctor continues to pay her occasional visits, and has *just left*. He examined her mouth and probed it deeply, scraping the bone of the roof, which he still fears is affected. I asked him the consequence of such an affection; he said particles of the bone would be thrown off. The lump continues, although it has diminished in size. At his recommendation she is taking Blair's Compound Syrup of Sarsaparilla as an alterative. Her whole system was thrown into a dreadful state of excitement by those *French measles*. I always do associate *French* with everything that is effervescent in character and influence.

I still feel very anxious about my dear child's mouth; but it is, I presume, one of those cases where we must wait *patiently*.

Our dear Charles, too, has been very sick with sore throat. He writes me that the passage of his throat was so closed up that with difficulty he could swallow even water. If it does not improve very much, he fears it will unfit him for speaking at the junior exhibition. He has taken a plenty of medicine, and I wrote him yesterday that he must take quinine or some tonic and use a gargle of green tea, alum, and honey. Much of that eruptive affection and sore throat has been prevailing here and in Princeton. Joseph has been quite well, and thinks his prudent and persevering habit of bathing in cold water twice a day—in the morning and at night—exempts or protects him from prevailing epidemics.

They have been good boys to write me frequently in your absence. Charles's last was a deeply interesting letter. Oh, that they were truly converted and entirely consecrated to the service of our Blessed Redeemer! They are all dear and precious children to us, and we have reason to be grateful to God for His mercy and goodness in sparing their lives and preserving them from many of the sins and follies of youth. They wrote me that they wanted some summer clothing, and could have them made as well in Princeton as here; and as it is more convenient I wrote them to do so—whatever was necessary—and I will draw upon Mr. Powel for the cash. The payment of Mary's tuition in music, with the purchase of the caps for the servants, Hannah's washing account, medicines, etc., etc., has made a pretty good hole in what you handed me before leaving. I strive to be prudent and economical in all things.

Evening before the last (Tuesday) Mr. Green and one of the elders of the Central Church (Mr. Barnes, I believe) called and passed an hour or more with me after tea. I thought it very kind and polite. They desired their regards to you. So do Mr. Happersett and Mr. Powel from the office, Mr. and Mrs. Watson, Mrs. Roser and Mrs. Clayter, and Mr. and Mrs. Newkirk. *She* says *you* are her dependence in the assembly for keeping their pastor. Dr. Boardman's people likewise seem to be thrown into a state of excitement about the professorship.

Day before yesterday Miss *Sanford* paid us a delightful visit. She has been a week in Philadelphia, but quite sick from a cold. It grieved me that I did not know it earlier. She and her uncle leave tomorrow for Petersburg, Virginia, where they are now located.

A few days since, a lady and her husband—*Mrs. Lewis*—arrived from St. Louis at the Markoe. She is now very ill. I have been in several times to see her. Yesterday she had a hemorrhage which Dr. Hodge, who attends her, says was from the stomach. Her intention was to make a voyage to Europe, but from present appearances I think it doubtful if she lives to leave this house again. I know not if she is a Christian, or what her spiritual state is. She is too weak to converse much. Was married but a few months since, and this is her—*third husband!*

After reading your dear letter last night I went to bed and dreamed delightfully of you all night. Oh, how happy I shall be when you return—but do not want you to hasten back on our account. I wrote your sisters that they must keep you as long as they could and recruit you for the summer's campaign.

It is very warm today. Mr. Banks asked if I would venture out in such hot weather. I told him yes, I delighted in it, for I came from where the sun shone hot. Everybody is complaining, but I am luxuriating in the warm breath of spring. It seems to come from my own native land. Near my window hangs a cage with a nonpareil and canary bird that are now singing their morning hymn of praises most delightfully. Oh, that I could but look out upon the sweet flowers and green fields of the country!

I will write you to Savannah touching the things in the *box*.

You know I never liked the *steamboating* to Princeton. A few days since, the *Ohio* from Baltimore was run into by the *Stockton* from this place and sunk at Kaighn Point, just below the city. Several persons drowned, and all their baggage submerged; but they are now recovering it.

Give to my dear brother and Sister Jane sincerest love, and kisses for the sweet baby and Dunwody. And the same sincerest love to my dear and respected aunt and own dear cousins. I will write Cousin Mary very shortly. And love to each of the children. . . . And now, my own beloved husband, farewell for the present. The Lord bless and keep you in all your ways!

Your devotedly attached

Mary.

Howdy for Nanny, Clarissa, Sam, Peggy.

REV. C. C. JONES *to* MRS. MARY JONES[t]

St. Louis, Saturday, May 24th, 1851

I sent a telegraphic dispatch to you, my dear wife, on the 21st, and begged you to answer it, that I might know how my dear child was, and how Charles was; but after anxiously waiting two days I conclude that my dispatch never reached you, as they report some interruption on the lines. I was almost ready to pack up and start back when your letter came. I answered it by mail immediately, concluding that I might rely upon your good judgment to let me hear from you every mail if Mary Sharpe was ill or worse. Am sorry you have not written more frequently. I have faithfully embraced every moment that could be commanded to write you. It is my greatest comfort and pleasure to remember your sweet person, and all your faithfulness and love. Every day I open your miniature and gaze upon it, and kiss it, and long once more to see you and embrace you and tell you all my love. May a kind Providence grant me this happiness!

The business of the assembly has moved on with dispatch and good feeling; and we are hoping to get through on Monday the 26th if not before. The

Board of Missions seems much in the thoughts and affections of the assembly; and the impression made by the report seems to have been most deep and satisfactory, which of course is matter of great thankfulness to me. John thinks it has been remarkable, and considers our situation one of the most important and influential in the church. There has been some discussion about the Princeton professorships, and some of us in the assembly have dissented from the *cut-and-dry* system. Your husband was put in nomination and declined it; and when referred to the assembly, forty-six voted against granting me leave to decline. Will tell you all about these things when we meet, please Providence.

Miss Legare is here; calls me most kindly Cousin *Colcock*. Has done—is doing—wonderfully well at Cedar Rapids, Iowa. Has five families in her colony—her nieces and nephews. Donald McIntosh, *Major McIntosh's son,* married a niece of hers the other day *(fifteen years of age!)* at Cedar Rapids; and Don is there, and expects to cast in his lot with the colony. But *the fever* they have all had! These new countries are as sickly, taking *epidemics* and cholera, etc., etc., into consideration, as ever Liberty County was. They are becoming more healthy as they become more settled and cultivated. This city of St. Louis is a *graveyard for children.* They died mainly in the second year, the period of dentition; families have been desolated.

The persons *now in nomination* for the professorship at Princeton are our Mr. Green; a reverend gentleman of Washington College, Pennsylvania (I now forget his name); and Messrs. Smyth and Thornwell of South Carolina. The election will go in favor of Mr. Green. Have had five invitations to preach tomorrow, but have declined them all on account of constant occupation and desire of rest. So many here to preach. May perhaps preach for the Negroes somewhere. Have to distribute the wine at our Communion tomorrow. The Lord bless that Communion to His servants! We had considerable and interesting speaking yesterday afternoon on domestic missions —on the final passage of the assembly's resolutions on the report. Dr. Baker of Texas spoke, and as usual with favor and effect; and several others. I prefer these spontaneous expressions of feeling to set addresses.

The weather has suddenly changed from *hot* to *cool,* and fires are made up this morning. Was wise enough to keep on my flannel. We have not as yet fixed upon our route. One of two anyhow: either by the Cumberland River to Nashville, and thence by stage to Chattanooga; or by the Tennessee River to Tuscumbia, and thence by railroad and steamboat to Chattanooga. Many brethren will go together. Dr. Leland wishes to take the Tennessee River route to avoid the staging.

My kind host and hostess, Mr. and Mrs. Annan, make me perfectly at home. I could not have been better situated. They have no children. Originally from Virginia. A great many Virginians, Kentuckians, and Tennesseans here; and a mixture of all nations almost.

My darling wife, you must be cheerful. Take exercise; employ some time every day in reading; fill the mind with food. Visit your more special acquaintances; and if my dear child can go out, take her out to walk and visit with you. We will try and make everything as comfortable and pleasant as possible when we return. Then you and the children must take a trip off and enjoy the country air; and if possible, will go with you. I will try and be the best husband to you in the world, and will love you with all my heart, and do all I can to make you love me. I often wish I had nothing to do but to wait on you, and be with you, and gratify all your wishes, and take away all your cares, and bear all your troubles, and let you be in perfect peace, and so make you as happy as it is possible for you to be this side of the true rest which Christ has purchased for us. You must forgive all my shortcomings, and remember not my evil against me. Kiss my dear daughter for me. And believe me, my darling Mary, to be, as ever,

Your own most faithful lover and devoted husband,
C. C. Jones.

Mr. Charles C. Jones, Jr., *to* Mrs. Mary Jones[t]
Princeton, *Monday,* May 26th, 1851

My dear Mother,

Your welcome letter was duly received, and permit me in return to render you my warmest thanks. The hats and caps were brought on Wednesday of last week—all safe except my straw hat, which by some means or other was a good deal mashed and broken in one place on the top. However, this is of little consequence, for it is in such a position as almost entirely to escape observation.

Barnum's Museum was in Princeton on Saturday exhibiting their "wonderful curiosities"—viz., Tom Thumb, elephants with their Asiatic drivers, camels, animals, the man without arms, etc. Above all these, however, he seemed to have imagined that his "car of Juggernaut" would have excited most admiration, for it was introduced with great pomp, drawn by eight horses, carrying on its top the band. From the very name you doubtless feel an interest in the appearance of this prodigy. I expected to find a moving temple, with hideous images of heathen deities, horrid countenances, unearthly forms. At least I thought that it would bear some shadow of resemblance to its great prototype, the object of supreme veneration of the Hindu. But how far from reality was such a supposition! Instead of this it consists merely in a large square box on wheels, with a few elephants painted upon its sides, and several attempts to represent a double-headed god—and that in lead-colored paint. *A perfect Barnum humbug.*

Well, this immense affair, in view of their not being able to deposit it in any enclosure, was left in the street just in front of Dr. Maclean's house. About twelve midnight seventy or eighty of the boys went to it and examined whether any person was sleeping within or not. Seeing that all was quiet, and the townfolks slumbering in their beds, a large party laid hold of it, rolled it out of Princeton, down to the canal (a distance of about a mile), and there tumbled it in. An iron steamer ran against it in the night, injuring it seriously. So much for this spree. Everyone in town thought it the best frolic that the students had ever had, and appeared truly rejoiced to see such a great humbug thus treated.

The drivers (about sixty in number) first discovered that it was missing about four in the morning, when they were preparing to take up the line of march for Brunswick. Provoked beyond measure at seeing their boasted "Juggernaut" missing, they tracked it to the canal; and you may well imagine their chagrin when they found it there, filled with water, covered with slimy mud, and tilted by the steamer into the shape of a rhombus. They made many threats—yet not in hearing of the students. "If we only could catch those chaps," said they, "we would tie them and cast them one by one into the canal." One declared that he single-handed could whip any twenty students. Having with much difficulty drawn the famous car from its watery grave, they proceeded to mend it up, and by the application of oil or turpentine to remove the dirty deposit upon its sides and top.

Having completed this renovating process, harnessing horses, they proceeded to Princeton. Many of the boys were down while they performed this job, and excited them by many jocose remarks with regard to the dignity of this sacred curricle. Several, in spite of the prohibition of the driver, mounted upon the top and joined in the ride. As they entered the town you could hear them crying: "Here comes the holy car of Juggernaut!" "This is Barnum's grand humbug!" "Been taking a bath," etc. As they left town you could see the breasts of at least two hundred joining in one long shout. Strange is it that the waters of the Ganges were not pure enough to cleanse the seat of the great god.

Barnum is certainly one of the humbugs of the age, and this one of his poorest efforts. Hope that he may learn a lesson for the future. He will doubtless avoid Princeton most carefully in after tours. The townsfolk are delighted, and especially an old man who keeps the drawbridge. His chief source of rejoicing is that he made $2 by hiring his boat to assist in raising the car.

On Saturday evening the boys entered into a horn spree, but failed in a great measure.

In neither of these were your boys engaged.

Received a paper today directed to Father from South Carolina, containing some interesting intelligence. You will find it enclosed.

We are both well and quite busy. Have been troubled a little with sore eyes, a complaint to which until this time I have been totally free. They are now, however, stronger and let me study by candlelight.

My watch is almost regulated, and runs finely.

Have ordered a white vest and one pair of pants to be made. They will be completed on Wednesday. The pants cost three and a half, the vests the same. I will be very much obliged to you, my dear mother, if you will send me ten dollars ($10) if it is convenient, as I will have to pay for those clothes, and need a little more to assist in defraying the publishing of bills for commencement. It required much of what Father last sent to buy textbooks, which were rather high.

Hoping that this will find you in the enjoyment of every blessing, both temporal and spiritual, and that my little sister has entirely recovered, I remain, with all manner of love to self and Sis, in which Brother unites,

Your most affectionate son,

Charles C. Jones, Jr.

Hope, my dear parent, that you will let me know if at any time you will need my services.

C. C. J., Jr.

Mrs. Mary Jones *to* Mr. Charles C. Jones, Jr.[g]

Philadelphia, *Tuesday,* May 27th, 1851

My dear Son,

It is late, but I must stop to send you a line ere I retire. Your affectionate favor was this afternoon received, and I herein enclose you $30—$20 for yourself and $10 for your brother. And he must have a pair or a couple of pair of pants made for himself unless he prefers to wait, and a vest if his are too small or he needs more. I have two summer cravats for each of you. You must be careful of your money, as it is a scarce article with me. Tell my son Joseph he must not suppose I have made a distinction between you in the sums sent. You both must feel assured of my feelings in this matter. I have always tried to be equally just and affectionate to each of my children, but in consequence of your increased expenses as junior orator and subscription to the monument of your deceased classmate, I have sent you $20. His turn will come next year when he is junior orator. Be sure and keep an account of your expenses.

The Barnum humbug amused me greatly, in spite of my abhorrence of all college sprees. I am thankful that my dear children avoid all such doings. My daily and constant prayer for you is that you may be kept from all evil and led in the narrow path that leads to everlasting life.

I must now close, for I am disturbing your sister with the light, and feel weary from a long walk. The paper from South Carolina is very interesting. The injury to your hat must have been from pure carelessness. Sister if awake would send warmest love. Accept the same for yourself and brother, with constant prayers for your best welfare, from

Your devotedly attached mother,

Mary Jones.

Your hat ought to have reached you on Monday evening.

REV. C. C. JONES *to* MRS. MARY JONES[t]

St. Louis, *Tuesday,* May 27th, 1851
12 M.

My ever dearest Wife,

After two days of anxiety and suspense, having telegraphed you on the reception of your letter, John and I on Saturday afternoon walked down to the telegraph office.

"Have you any dispatch for me?"

"Yes, sir. It has just gone up to Dr. Potts."

"Come, John, let us go."

Said he: "The original is here, and you had better see it."

The man of the office turned to it, and with great relief and thankfulness I read: "Love. Mary, Charles well. Satisfied. Mary Jones." Dated May 23rd, Philadelphia; received St. Louis, May 24th. Oh, these telegraphic wires! The wonder and comfort of the age!

Sabbath we heard Dr. Humphrey preach in the morning: an excellent sermon. In the afternoon we had our usual Communion. Dr. Swift and I were at the table, and we distributed the elements and addressed the brethren. A calm, impressive hour. At night preached in the Methodist colored church upon the invitation of *the bishop,* a real African: fine, large, good-looking, and intelligent man: *Bird Parker.* Had much conversation with him. The abolitionists tell all sorts of stories of the South, and in the absence of better information people believe them. There was a good attendance and good attention, and a number of whites drawn to hear and to see from curiosity perhaps.

The assembly closed its sittings last night a little before eleven in a calm, impressive manner, our moderator making a modest and effective parting address. It has been a meeting of considerable business, some discussion, and general harmony and good feeling, and must be of benefit. The people of St. Louis much gratified. All the benevolent schemes of the church are represented as being in a flourishing state. The Rev. Dr. Wheeler of *Vermont,* delegate from the Congregational association of that state, made a capital address to the assembly, full of good spirit and full of correct sentiments. I gave him my hand afterwards in expression of a cordial reciprocation. The Rev. Mr. Comingo received a letter from his wife in which there was information flatly contradicting the murder of Mr. Geary. He had been heard from *by letter* from Panama. The assembly received the intelligence with lively demonstrations of gratitude; and thereupon I obtained an order from the assembly *for the constitution of a presbytery in Oregon.* I have all along been somewhat incredulous. The assembly indefinitely postponed the big-church-in-Washington-City scheme; so that folly dies.

This morning the members are leaving in every direction, and will all soon be gone—all pleased with St. Louis and happy in our meeting. Dr. Leland, John, and I and many others have taken passage in the steamer *Schuylkill* for

Paducah at the mouth of the Tennessee River; and there we take another boat either for Nashville on the Cumberland River or for Tuscumbia on the Tennessee River as Providence may open the way. We prefer to go by Nashville and thence by stage to Chattanooga and so by railroad to Marietta, as it is the shorter route of the two. We expect, God willing, to leave at 5 P.M.

We called this morning to see Mrs. Isaiah Davenport (Martha Fairfax that was). Very glad to see us. Sent her kind regards to you and to all her Southern friends. She has been here some two years. Time and changes and illnesses have left their traces. Has three children living. Mr. D. very well. Then I called on Mr. William Neff's sister and daughter, who I knew above twenty years ago in *Frankford:* Mrs. Patterson and Mrs. Budd. Astonishing! The old lady without form or ceremony saluted me spang on the mouth! Very glad to see me. Both retaining their identity in a remarkable manner; been here some twelve or fifteen years. All my engagements and calls are now completed, and I have come home to write my dear wife and pack up and dine and take leave of my very kind and hospitable friends Mr. and Mrs. Annan. They have done everything to render my stay under their roof agreeable. Mrs. Patterson, although unknown to you, begged me to present her love to you.

St. Louis has between eighty and ninety thousand inhabitants! Would you think it? Great numbers of foreigners. Between forty and sixty steamers along the levee; about the busiest place I have ever seen: some half a mile or more long. Crowded; piled up with produce and goods of all sorts; a mass of businessmen, horses, drays—all mixed, moving, driving, calling. John said to be in it he should lose his wits. The city founded upon a rock: strata of soft cream-colored limestone. The dirtiest place in parts I ever saw; no wonder they have cholera. Streets partly paved: generally macadamized. Rain, *mud;* sun, *clouds of dust!* In every direction improvements. Growth wonderful! To be a great city! Churches many, very good. Every effort made to drain and cleanse and improve it. Supported by the immense trade of the West.

Must stop. Here you are by me. Have just looked at you and kissed you. Oh, you sweet wife, my own darling Mary, why don't you speak to me? You just look at me so? Never mind, please a kind Providence, if I don't make you talk to me and love me when I get back to you with all your heart. I do love you so much! Kiss my dear daughter for me; I rejoice she is well again. And our dear son. Received a letter dated the 17th from Mr. Happersett this morning. And now, my dear, sweet wife, my good wife, farewell for the present. God be with you and bless you and my dear children evermore!

Your own affectionate and devoted husband,
C. C. Jones.

V

Rev. C. C. Jones *to* Messrs. Charles C. Jones, Jr., *and* Joseph Jones^g
Steamboat *W. H. Day,* Cumberland River, *Thursday,* May 29th, 1851
My dear Sons,

Many engagements prevented me from writing you from St. Louis, where I received my dear son's letter. I arrived there on the 14th and left on the 27th—just two weeks' stay. Was about half the time in attendance upon the assembly, and the other half occupied in duties connected with the secretary-ship. My report was listened to with profound attention, and produced a most decided impression upon the assembly. Many were free to say that "it is the first time for a number of years that the subject of domestic missions has been fully set before the church in its true light and importance." I was much assisted in the delivery of it, and made use of my ecclesiastical map of the Presbyterian Church in the United States in illustration of it. The meeting of the assembly was characterized by harmony and efficiency, and must be productive of good. You will see that we meet next year in Charleston, South Carolina. So we have no idea that South Carolina will go out of the Union. The citizens of St. Louis were very hospitable, and did all in their power to render our stay pleasant.

As usual in going into a strange place, I made myself as well acquainted with St. Louis as time and opportunity allowed. For many miles below, the Mississippi cuts and washes the base of rolling high land—a deposit of soft cream-colored limestone. The strata without dip, and the face and cliffs of the hills bare or broken, are sometimes like walls of fortifications, and are worn in places into shapes of arches, and become pleasing. The trees skirt their base, and cling and hang upon their sides. But the soil on the top is thin and the growth stunted. This extensive deposit extends beyond St. Louis, and the city is built upon it—in its location literally founded upon a rock. They obtain stone enough nearly in excavating their cellars to build their houses, so they say. The land on which the city is built is uneven, with a general slope to the river.

As you approach, you are impressed with the size of the place, extended on the hills and slopes and along the river, and a number of spires and the dome of the courthouse conspicuous over all. The levee (the wharf or landing) is crowded with steamboats—three-deckers, as I call them: a forest of smoke pipes, and lie with their bows ashore and their sterns a little down the stream. They take in and discharge their cargoes over the bows, and when ready to sail, they back out, draw out their noses, and paddle off. The river bank slopes to the water's edge and is paved, and this is a peculiarity of all the landing places on these Western waters, for the rise and the fall of the rivers will admit of no other plan. Between the slope and the range of stores is a wide street. Over a mile long is this levee, and it presents one of the busiest scenes imaginable. The goods and produce landing and shipping cover the levee from end to end, with little room to move about; and the drays and carts and wagons are mixed up in endless streams and crossings, and sometimes are jammed up in apparently inextricable confusion, while a countless throng is pouring along the sidewalks and mingling everywhere.

St. Louis stands upon the first available ground for a city below the Missouri, and must ever be a great place. Its growth is wonderful. It contains nearly if not quite ninety thousand inhabitants, and bears the most unmistakable evidences of rapid growth of any city I was ever in. The old part of the town—and it is but a small part—has the appearance of being some time built, but hardly that, as improvements are going on. But take your walk in any direction—north, west, or south, and it is a city *building up:* streets laying and grading, excavations, foundations laid, walls going up, roofing. Private, public houses, churches building here, there, everywhere. They cannot keep pace with the growth. The streets are universally macadamized with the said soft limestone. The paved streets are the exception. In a dry time you are choked with dust; in a wet time you slip in mud; and it is, taken as a whole, a dirty place. The city corporation cannot keep it generally clean, and I do not wonder that cholera does its fearful work there, or that the city is not healthy. And what makes the difficulty greater is the immense number of foreigners who locate in the place—and they are not cleanly. Property is very high, and changes hands frequently. You know it has been one of the chief seats of the papists in the West; but the Protestants are outnumbering them fast.

Missouri is a great state, and is rapidly improving every way. Hemp and tobacco are becoming great staples.

You would be impressed with the vastness of our country traveling on these Western streams. Think of floating down a broad and beautiful stream a thousand miles with but one obstruction, and then be launched upon the bosom of another, and you may then follow it down a thousand miles ere you reach the sea, or stem its current and go up into the heart of the continent between two thousand and twenty-five hundred miles in different directions! And there is a calm, quiet magnificence in these streams, especially the Mississippi—the views far-reaching before you, the long line of the forest banks diminishing in perspective, the vast bends and curves, with islands reposing on their glassy bosoms. Well, you exclaim, is this the Father of Waters—an inland sea?

But after all I seem rather to prefer the older portions of our country. The great West is more pleasant to visit than to dwell in. So much mixture of people from all places; so much driving, speculating, selfishness; a world of strangers, a world of changes; moving, pushing, sickening, dying. Many like its ideas of greatness, its excitements, its adventures, its creations and annihilations. At some convenient time, if Providence permit, I wish you both to visit all this Western country, and at such a stage of your education as may be most profitable to you. The whole visit has been of undiminished interest to me, and one full of the loving-kindness of the Lord. Have seen many places and many things, and made many pleasant and profitable acquaintances.

We left St. Louis on Tuesday at 5 P.M. in a fine steamer, and her captain indulged his pride in showing her off when we left the levee. At Paducah, at the mouth of the Tennessee River, we left our old friend Dr. Leland, who preferred to ascend that river and escape staging. Your Uncle John and I came to Smithland at the mouth of the Cumberland—to reach Georgia by way of Nashville. We lay over last night there, and I preached in the Methodist church to a good and an attentive audience.

As the sun was declining I enjoyed a great treat. I walked out alone to the back part of the village, and ascended the hill upon which is situated the cemetery. On the apex of the hill is the monument of an Episcopal clergyman, and from this point, turning to the village, the view may be called beautiful. In the dish or valley below lies the village; and before it the Ohio, and its green banks beyond, stretching away down to the left; and on the right the great river running up for miles until shut in by its banks; and the soft skies of light were mirrored on its surface. The Cumberland flows in at the upper end of the village, and the swelling hills are here and there crowned with settlements. It was what I have longed for many days: *solitude*. I leaned on the fence and gazed on the tranquil scene before me. The heavens were blue; the summer clouds were catching the reddening rays of the setting sun. The earth was all green, and no sounds fell on the ear but the music so familiar and sweet of the birds—the bluebird and the wood robin and the catbird. And what made the solitude more impressive, I heard far down in the forests between the hills the faint cawing of the crow, and the long hoot of our common swamp owl; and he was answered by his mate still far beyond him still. The tinkling of the cowbell came too to fill up the measure of the impression of repose. I love this quiet in nature; and I embraced it to remember your dear mother and sister and both of you before the ever-present God, and to beseech for you all His richest blessings.

We took passage this morning in a light small steamer with the wheel in the stern—the *W. H. Day*—and are puffing along, and hope, Providence permitting, to reach Nashville tomorrow evening in time to take the stage for Chattanooga. Our passengers are all pleasant, and we have two men on their return from California. Not much success: they both represent gold-digging as excessively laborious, full of exposures morally and physically, and few succeeding in it.

I trust, my dear son, you have quite recovered from your sore throat, and have a pretty good speech for your society. And I hope, Joe, you have written me to Riceboro to let me know what books you wish me to bring for you from home. You must be watchful and not suffer the constant wear and tear of college association to weaken down your good resolutions and habits. Continue through as you have begun—only improve upon it. And my constant prayer and hope is to hear that you are both converted to God. I cannot be at peace until your everlasting peace is made with God.

My letter is very long, and you may be puzzled to read it, written as it is on the boat. Your uncle sends much love to you. Write your mother often. The Lord be with and bless you, my dear sons!

Your ever affectionate father,
C. C. Jones.

Mrs. Mary Jones *to* Rev. C. C. Jones[t]

Philadelphia, Friday, May 30th, 1851

My dearest Husband,

Your most welcome letter of the 21st, mailed the 23rd, was this afternoon brought me by Mr. Happersett, who has been as kind and attentive as possible to us in every way that was in his power; also Mr. Powel. Did you get the telegraphic dispatch on the 23rd? Yours of the 21st did not reach me until the afternoon of that day, when Mr. *H.* took my reply and went immediately to the office and had it sent to St. Louis. I hope it reached you, for I felt very unhappy at the thought of your anxiety and suspense.

Our dear Mary has been at school the past week and much improved. The swelling in her mouth is not entirely relieved, and I think will not be until her front tooth is operated on. I hope this may be deferred until you return. Charles is much better, but writes me that his eyes are weak. This, I have no doubt, is consequent upon his recent attack. Mary's were in the same situation. I have written him what to do for them, and hope they will soon be strong again.

Mary and myself both wrote you to Marietta, and this will come to greet you in our own dear home.

The St. Louis *Presbyterian* has interested me much, and I am grateful that my dear husband was enabled to present a report that was acceptable to the assembly and that shall be for the good of the church and our whole country. If called by the Great Head of the Church to occupy this responsible station, I trust that you will be made useful in it.

The thought of your being in the path of duty reconciles me to being here; and as I trust that conviction alone brought us, so can it, by God's grace supporting, enable us to continue. I told Mr. Happersett the other day that *socially* considered I thought the situation of a secretary, particularly that of his *family,* one of the most undesirable in the community. There were no special ties to any church or any people, and no one thought of them with any feelings of interest. The situation of a pastor or professor was one of spiritual and social relations. He said he was almost afraid they would call you again to Columbia. *I told him I did not care if they did;* that my situation was more pleasant there than here. In all this, however, I trust that I am willing to submit entirely to the will of my Heavenly Father, who for so many years granted us all the comforts of home and the happy intercourse of friends. These are now removed—many of them forever. The soul as long as it is an inhabitant of the body and a resident of earth must have desires connected with life. I strive to put away every worldly hope and expectation, and my constant prayer is that I may be prepared for death and judgment.

There is at this time a sick lady here from St. Louis in whom I feel a deep interest, and she seems to appreciate it. Every day I visit her sick chamber, and today had a pleasant conversation with her on religion. She is a member of Dr. Potts's church; her husband is a Methodist. They are named Lewis. She seems very surely and rapidly passing to her grave. I often look upon her and fancy myself in the same situation, with eternity just in view. Oh, how precious is an Almighty Saviour to a poor, suffering, dying sinner! There is no comfort or peace but in the atoning Blood and justifying righteousness of Christ.

Thus far had I written, my dear husband, last night when I began to feel so lonely and sad that I closed with a hearty cry and went to bed. Mrs. Smith has just left me. She has been sitting with me in my room for two hours—a delightful visit. General S. has also called *twice* to see me in your absence. Their daughter has just returned from Florida. Mrs. S. desires love to Sister Susan, Laura, and yourself; hopes you saw her brother and sister in St. Louis.

This morning's mail brought me a letter from our dear Sister Betsy to you and one from Laura to myself detailing the particulars of little Mary Delegal's death—one of the most remarkable and heartrending providences I ever heard of. She seemed to glorify God even in the flames. She always interested me particularly, and her countenance is so perfectly impressed on my memory that if I had the power I could sketch her likeness. Dear, precious child! I pray that it may be sanctified to her father and family and that whole community. If an angel from heaven were to descend, he could scarcely bear stronger testimony to the power and truth of religion. It is pleasant to remember your instructions to the little children of Dorchester. The rich experience of her deathbed may have sprung from seed then sown. I remember how attentive she used to be to you, and how her little hand was always thrust over the pew in Sunbury to bid me welcome on Sabbath. It brought to mind our own deliverance in Columbia: not a hair of our heads was touched. Awful beyond description it was, but how much more so it might have been! The situation of that sweet child can tell us.

I received also a letter from Charles, and hope he is quite recovered, as he does not complain. I sent himself and Joseph $30 from what you left with me, which brings it down to a small sum in the locker. They needed it for some articles of clothing before commencement and other little items of expense. They are good children, and few parents have less cause to complain of a want of prudence in the use of money. They spend but little on selfish gratifications. I shall call upon Mr. Powel to advance me whatever is required. In view of the boys' and Mary's expenses in the opening term of college and her school, had you not best bring on $400 or $500 with you? It will certainly be required.

I have received no answer from Mr. Rahn in reply to my letter about the butter. I wish he would keep an account of it and engage it this year as the last; and Mr. Shepard also to engage that at Montevideo. If Mr. Stebbins would take it, it would be convenient in our plantation accounts. Do make arrangements *for this*. We have so many expenses it is our duty to turn these things to some account, and they will *not* be attended to without *positive arrangements*. If you think best, some of the best hams can be reserved, and with the lard sent down to Patience for proper attention until I come in the fall—if my life is spared to spend the most of the winter at home. The rest of the bacon can be used on the plantation; and if any syrup was reserved, that can go to the people too. The barrel of sugar will be improved by keeping. Do ask how many pounds of wool there is *in all* of the last; we never received an account. No doubt you think these very small matters to trouble *you* with.

Mr. Shepard writes that the rice planted in the marsh had failed again. It is a pity they had not tried cotton at first, or corn. I trust with the blessing of Providence we may do more there this year than the last, for it is a *growing* and expensive place.

I wish *Tony* to devote himself to keeping up my flower garden and destroying the nut grass in both; I was surprised at the increase when I returned last spring. And he must have a good heap of rotted leaves for me when I come in the fall, as I shall bring—if spared to do so—some new flowers for the garden.

I feel quite incensed at the depredations upon my cedar trees and garden, and wish that Mr. Shepard would inform me who did the mischief. I must positively object to people from the Boro visiting it, as Tony and Rose told me they were in the habit of doing last year. It is a liberty which Mr. Shepard must *positively forbid*. Most persons think when the owners of a place are away that things are for the *public,* and often those least acquainted will take the greatest liberties. I am inclined to believe that the wood gate makes our place somewhat of a thoroughfare; if so, I would take it away altogether and put a lock and key on the Boro gate if there is no other way of defending the place from intruders. It costs me no trouble to be kind, polite, and obliging to everyone; *but—but—I—will—not—submit—to—impositions. Mr. Shepard can hear this—and tell all the county too!*

No doubt the box of articles reached home before you did. I had to pack it in such a hurry that I did not mark three or four small caps designed for *Titus and Niger* and any other of the small ones—Little Prime, perhaps, as he waits on Mrs. Rahn. All the grown ones had best be served first, and if there are over, give to them, I put in thirty-six dresses and thirty-six caps. Also a piece of shirting on the top for Mary, about which I have written asking the favor of Sister Susan to cut them out for me and make Phoebe make them. If she does her work properly, she may remain at Montevideo and send it down to the Island every week by Porter; but if there is any difficulty about it, *she* and *Victoria* (to mind her youngest) with Lafayette must be moved down; Cash and Jane to continue in the field at Montevideo. Cato must be careful of Jane, as it is her first summer in the field.

I will bring a present for all the infants born since we left home when I come; and each mother should have an additional blanket in the fall who has a newborn infant.

Charlie writes me he has had Kate removed to the Island to be under Brother William's care, and that without doubt she is a clay-eater. *That* was certainly the case with cross-eyed Titus last year. I told Mr. Rahn about it, and that from his symptoms and appearance if not stopped he would become seriously diseased and die. You had best examine him yourself. The only remedy, as Charles remarked, is that which effected a cure with Sarey and Moll—a *mouthpiece* to prevent access to the poison. I have no doubt his frequent indisposition is owing to that practice.

Do tell all the people howdy for us, from the oldest to the youngest. I want to see them every one. I hope they attend Mr. Winn's preaching.

Mr. Green, I presume, will certainly go to Princeton. He has been very kind and polite to me, and has called *three times* in your absence; his sister also. He is certainly a most excellent young man.

Mary unites with me in best love to Sister Betsy and Brother William, Sister Susan and Laura, Julia and her family, Henry and Sister Abby, and all friends. I wrote H. this week, and to James: I must congratulate him on his future prospects. Remember us to Mr. Peace. Affectionate regards to Mr. and Mrs. Axson and Mrs. Harden and family if you see them. Tell Mama and Daddy Pulaski howdy; I have sent a dress for her in the box. And now, my own dearest one, I must close in time for the mail. Your daughter sends love and a kiss for dear Father. May the best of Heaven's blessings abide with you!

Your ever affectionate
Mary J.

My kind regards to Mr. and Mrs. Shepard and to Mr. and Mrs. Rahn.

Rev. C. C. Jones *to* Mrs. Mary Jones[t]

Steamboat *W. H. Day,* Cumberland River, *Friday,* May 30th, 1851

Yesterday I wrote my dear children two long letters, and I must now write one to my *true love,* who is more to me than all the world beside—the wife of my youth, the faithful and tender mother of our dear children. I have been alone on the upper deck reading my Testament and meditating and praying and remembering you all; and then I walked for exercise, and set up your loved image in my heart, and conversed in spirit with you, and recalled all your tenderness and sweetness, and thought over all our love. Oh, may God ever bless you, my ever dear Mary, with the fullness of His mercies from heaven above and from the earth beneath, and reward you for all your kindness to me and mine, and give you in that day a crown of life! So prays your husband continually.

Our little boat makes but slow progress, and the fog on the river obliged us to tie up the better part of the night. To use General Cocke's expression, I should say the concern is "not very enterprising." We are a hundred miles below Nashville, and will not in all probability reach the city until after the Chattanooga stages are gone, which may throw us back two or three days. Well, Providence orders all things right.

John preached very well last evening in the cabin; some twenty men present of all sorts.

At breakfast (as you must have a sketch of manners as they rise) there was much pleasantry. One passenger, who had slept in the ladies' cabin with our party, was told by another, who had not done so, that "the captain would charge him a dollar more for it."

"Well," said the Tennessee farmer, "it's worth a dollar more to be in the *right kind of a crowd*."

Here the joke passed over to the other side and created a great roar against the gentlemen's cabin.

"*Where* did you sleep?" said one to the tallest man on board, a seven-footer.

"Ah, he could find no berth long enough for him."

"Fact," replied the tall man, "I tried this berth, and there was no window to stick my feet out of, and I was sorely put to it."

Mr. Putnam came in: "Oh, you could *shut yourself up like a jackknife,* and then you could lie."

The idea was irresistible. We were convulsed. Our tall friend enjoyed it as much as any.

I put out some *tracts,* and the passengers—some of them—read them. I find the portable desk and Mary Sharpe's portable little inkstand a great comfort, affording me pleasant occupation with the pen and filling up many an hour usefully. Time may be improved or wasted in traveling as men are disposed; some doze and sleep it away.

The Cumberland River is for its length a narrow stream, not above three or four hundred yards broad with tolerably high banks, and is a pretty river, but has nothing striking about it. Not much improvement to be seen as you pass up, though the country is rich. Tennessee is a fine state. In one of the finest counties of the state, *Murray,* in which Columbia is situated (Mr. Polk's former residence), lands average from $20 to $30 per acre improved. Can be bought at any time, as the people are disposed to move off to Texas and Arkansas, etc. This disposition to emigrate has brought down the price of lands in all the older Western and Southwestern states. Society is very changeable in all this Western world, and the more I see the more I am convinced that good and evil, in the kind providence of God, are more evenly distributed to men in this life than most are inclined to admit; and they

166

who are comfortably and successfully settled should be slow to break up and to move off.

Brother Huntington tells me *Nashville* is a most fashionable place, and wicked. His impressions of the state of society are not the most favorable. His vision may be discolored. He lost his wife, her two sisters, and their brother with cholera—four out of five—all out of one house and within a short time of each other! It is amazing how we bear up under the deepest afflictions and live beyond them, so as to come out again into the sunshine of pleasure and of renewed hope.

I look out of the cabin door down the river; it flows and bends far away. How rich and green are the banks—the shore lined with rocks, and the trees bending over and dipping their boughs in. The summer clouds are above, and the sun sheds on all his brilliant rays. I learn a lesson. Yesterday the clouds were black; the thunder was heavy; the rain fell. Today all is changed. Let us see God in everything, and ask a heart of Him to respond to all His dispensations, that the day of affliction and the day of prosperity may alike be sanctified to us. I should have rejoiced in you as my companion in travel many, many times; and yet you would have been subjected to some inconveniences. But it would have been so pleasant to have had you to share in all my sights and thoughts, and for me to have waited on you and made you happy in all things. Never mind: we will have much to talk about when we meet, and our separation will make us happier then.

Afternoon. Slowly moving over the shoals forty-five miles below Nashville, and no prospect of being in time for the stage. Passengers lounging about, and some sleeping, and some reading. But the day has been on the whole pleasant. Have been reading Hugh Miller's *Footprints of the Creator.* Do not know enough to appreciate him as he should be, but much interested as it is. We are coming now to the region of the *beech tree;* the forests of them along the river banks are beautiful: the green is deep and brilliant. The cottonwood is almost identical with our aspen at home; it bears flower and seed here, and is borne on winds and waters—thick covering over sandbars, banks, and islands, growing in the water as well as out of it.

John sends love. Kiss Daughter for me. I remain, my darling wife,
Your attached and devoted husband,
C. C. Jones.

REV. C. C. JONES *to* MRS. MARY JONES[t]
Nashville, Tennessee, *Saturday,* May 31st, 1851
My darling Wife,

We reached this city this morning at four o'clock. How accustomed and indifferent we become to dangers of which we have heard a great deal! The front deck of our little steamer, the pleasantest part of the boat, where we usually sat and walked to enjoy the cool breeze, was right over the boilers.

167

There we sat and there we walked as unconcerned as if we were upon the bosom of Mother Earth. The Rev. Mr. Clark from Astoria, near New York, gave us an excellent little sermon in the evening.

After coming up to the Veranda House, it being early, I undressed (the first time for two nights), and putting on my nightgown went into bed and dozed above an hour, then rose up, shaved and washed and bathed, and changed all my clothing, and felt most delightfully. Breakfast being over, John, Brother Moore, and I sallied out to see the town. First we went to the post office, where I put in letters for my dear wife and for my dear children. Then we bent our steps to the stage office. No possibility of leaving before Monday night—unless we should break the Sabbath. This we could by no means consent to do. Down went our names on the book for *Monday* night.

Our steps were turned next to Morse's telegraph office.

"Are you in connection with Philadelphia?"

"Yes, sir."

"Then forward this dispatch for me; and put your private mark—44—on it, that it may be answered immediately."

He did so; and now while I write I trust my dear Mary is reading that dispatch, and is preparing to send me another to make my heart glad. Miss Legare, my cousin in Iowa, says she ranks great men thus: Washington, Fulton, Morse. Surely these wires are wonders. What messages of love, of joy, of sorrow, of hope and fear, of life and death, tremble with viewless speed along them!

I must now take you to Capitol Hill and give you a view of Nashville. Conceive of an immense swell of land, rising by rather a gradual ascent on all sides, and the side on the river cut square down by the stream and revealing the strata of limestone rock of which the entire swell or hill is composed; and then a plain all around the base spreading out for miles, gradually undulating as it recedes until it terminates in hills; and then ranges of hills still above and beyond these as far as the eye can reach; and now upon the very summit of this great swell there rises a hill gradually that overtops all. Having fixed this conception, then let us ascend this topmost hill, and there behold the splendid state capitol in process of erection. It crowns all. Come to the story above—as far as it is completed—and look down! What a view! Here is the city built up around this capitol hill, and reaching down the great swell on every hand, and then the houses receding on the plain, becoming more and more scattered as they go into the distance until they disperse and settle themselves upon the hills, with green fields and lawns around them and they half-embosomed in trees. See the hills rising and encircling the entire horizon, some altogether crowned with forests and others bearing the green fields upon their rounding forms. And see! You catch a glimpse of the river winding its way in its deep bed and the fields and country houses and hills beyond. It is springtime. The freshness of spring is on everything. And now throw over the city with its spires and roofs and streets and buildings and busy multitudes, and over the plain and on the river and on the fields and country seats and upon the hills that would emulate mountains all around, the glorious light of the sun; and you have Nashville as it sits in unrivaled beauty before you. One of the most beautiful views I have ever beheld. I do not know how I have succeeded in the description, but I know how much I wished my loved one with me this morning, that she might enjoy the prospect with me. John urged me to walk out on the wall and stand on the outer wall and take in the whole at one view. I did so, but my head inclined to topple, and I made him come and steady me with his umbrella and help me back again.

We then walked to Mrs. Polk's residence. It is situated in the heart of the city, but is not as splendid a mansion as I was led to believe it to be; nor are the grounds about it as spacious as I had supposed. Yet it is imposing, and merges into elegance. The structure is of brick, with columns, and wears the appearance of the residence of a wealthy man. The grounds had not been fully improved at Mr. Polk's death, and have but been kept up since, Mrs. Polk having until recently been secluded from society. She had her noble husband, to whom she was ardently attached, interred in the lawn on the back of the mansion (back or front as you please); and she has erected a monument over him with suitable inscriptions to his public and private virtues; and the covering is supported by four pillars, the whole standing upon a green mound with a gravel walk around it. All simple, chaste, appropriate. He lies below in a vault, where I presume she desires in due time to lie. You open the iron gate of the iron fence that encloses the lawn next the street and enter and visit the tomb without ceremony, seeing no one, hearing no one. A lady passed us going to the house (not Mrs. Polk), to whom I lifted my hat; and she politely returned my courtesy.

We called on Dr. Edgar: not at home. When we reached our hotel, there he had just entered to call on us. He has insisted so strenuously on our all going to his house that we are obliged in all kindness and brotherly love to do so. He walked with us to the courthouse, and we had the pleasure of hearing two aspirants for a seat in Congress take the stand against each other. A large table was set under the shady trees, and a small table to hold papers and water was put upon it, leaving space enough for the speaker to move about and turn around. One took the table and spoke an hour; and his competitor followed, and in the midst of his speech we came off for dinner. This is the way they do things out here, and they go through their district addressing the people in this wise. Folks think a great deal out here of *personal bravery*. A man must have nerve to go through the campaigns.

The present prospect is that I shall have, if God spares my life, to preach tomorrow morning, and visit Dr. Edgar's flourishing Sabbath school for the Negroes, and hold a domestic missionary meeting in the evening.

Monday, June 2nd. Did not preach yesterday, but delivered an address in the evening in Dr. Edgar's lecture room; and although a damp evening, we had a fine audience.

Today we rode out to *the Hermitage,* and thus made a pilgrimage to General Jackson's tomb. Time fails now; but will give you the first opportunity an account of our ride and all we saw.

We have taken our seats and paid for them, and leave this evening at eight o'clock on our route to Chattanooga, where, if God permit, we shall arrive sometime on Wednesday. We shall be obliged to ride two nights. Our stay has been very pleasant, and Dr. Edgar and his family have done everything to make us at home. We have been "courteously entreated."

And now, my dear, dear wife, farewell from this place. Be assured of the ardent love of your own dear husband, and his constant prayers for your happiness. Love to Daughter and sons.

C. C. Jones.

Mrs. Mary Jones *to* Rev. C. C. Jones[t]
Philadelphia, Monday, June 2nd, 1851

Your sweet, loving letter, my dear husband, from St. Louis dated the 24th reached me this morning, and the telegraphic dispatch from Nashville of the 31st of May on the afternoon of the same day. I am so sorry you did not get the one I sent you in reply to your anxious inquiries after Charles and Mary. Mr. Happersett went himself and attended to it. Yours had been three days in coming. My reply must have gone into the clouds, and perhaps will yet come down upon some electric flash. I would certainly have written you oftener, but it seemed such a time to go ere they reached St. Louis that I was constantly under the impression they would never arrive in time before you left. Mary and myself both wrote you to Marietta, and on Saturday sent a long epistle to welcome you on your arrival home, and now hasten with this to Savannah, that you may feel assured that I am not unmindful of you.

Our dear child is looking again quite like herself, and in another respect is relieved. Her teeth still are troublesome, but I want to delay any operation upon them until you return. Dr. Hodge advised me to give her Blair's Compound Syrup of Sarsaparilla. She is now taking the second bottle, and I think has been benefited, for her system was thrown into a terrible state of excitement by the eruptive fever. Everything *French* seems turbulent and excitable. Her vacation will soon occur, and then I want her to avail herself of all the air and exercise she can get. Dr. *H.* says he *hates* schools. He has quite won Mary's heart by his kindness, and she threatens Miss Cunningham with her rivalry.

Give our best love to Charlie, and thanks for his kind favor, which Mary and I will answer very soon. I am sure he will make a first-rate physician, and cannot be excelled in his description of *baby-tending.* Tell him his letter was next to a visit; gave us a hearty laugh (the first in a month), and cheered our spirits. His table, tub, bucket, and comforter are quite well.

Two charming old ladies from Charleston have arrived at the Markoe and occupy Mary's room, which *Sallie* the chambermaid tells me they are going to keep. If that be the case, *ex necessitate* we will have to look elsewhere.

Mrs. Harrison is still unrivaled, and is enlarging her bounds by having the adjoining building fitted up and attached as a boardinghouse. The Girard House next to the Mission rooms has a flag with an eagle and stars and stripes floating from its battlement, which I presume is the signal of its near completion; from the signs of the times we may reasonably conclude that there will soon be *room for all*. I am not particularly fond of changes, but old enough and resolute enough to make them whenever they appear for the better. If God spares our lives and designs to keep us here, I do not conceive it wrong to make ourselves comfortable. I no more believe in unnecessary privations than I do in any other self-inflicted torments or austerities.

The Central Church are very much troubled at the prospect of losing Mr. Green. They seem to feel that he has no voice in the matter, but is arbitrarily compelled by the assembly to accept. This afternoon they are to have a meeting expressive of their feelings. Mr. Newkirk asked me on Sabbath if I did not intend to present our certificates and unite with them at this Communion, which will be next Sabbath. I told him *no;* that I believed your connection, which you retained with Presbytery, was sufficient for you, and we did not feel settled in Philadelphia. He said in his peculiar and earnest manner he hoped you did not think to *dodge* the secretaryship. We certainly are under more obligations to that church than to any other and would most naturally cast in our lot with theirs; but if Mr. Green leaves, they will be thrown into a distracted state, and there may be no regular ordinances or services.

The sick lady of whom I wrote you is extremely ill. Drs. Hodge and Jackson pronounce her case hopeless. So her husband has just informed me, and says she may depart at any moment. Poor man, he asked my opinion in that event about the removal of her body; said he would like to have her by him at home, but knew that could not now be done, and did not like the thought of disturbing her afterwards. I told him if it were myself I should like to be buried where I died, particularly if it was in a Christian place; that the changes of life were so frequent we could never calculate on our own resting place; and at the resurrection we should all be raised to life again. Distance will not separate friends at that moment, when the work will be done in the twinkling of an eye. He said she had once expressed her own objection to the removal of dead bodies; so I presume that she will be laid in Laurel Hill whenever her spirit departs to a better world, as I hope it will. Mr. Barnes called to see her yesterday, and she derived much comfort from his visit; said she wished I had been with her. She appears to have a firm hold upon the Saviour, and her peace with God made years ago; but I do not think she has any idea that her end is so near. We have conversed frequently together, and she always appears so glad to see me when I enter her room; asked me some days since if you thought of removing to St. Louis; said she would be so glad to see me there.

Will you, my dear, be so good as to get two spools of No. 40, two of No. 46, and two of No. 50 (*six* in all) and three dozen pearl buttons, and take them to Sister Susan for me? They are for Mary's garments. Please give best love to Charlie, and remember us to Major and Mrs. Porter, Mrs. Vanyeverine, and Mrs. Gilmer, and to Messrs. M. and W. Cumming; and when you reach home unnumbered loves and kisses to all at Social Bluff and Woodville. Mary is at school or would join with me in all that is loving *to you*. Do not hurry back, but enjoy and recruit yourself. The Lord bless and preserve you, and favor you spiritually and temporally, ever prays

Your ever affectionate wife,

Mary Jones.

Mrs. Mary Jones *to* Rev. C. C. Jones[t]

Philadelphia, *Thursday,* June 5th, 1851

I looked this morning, my own dear husband, for a letter from you, and felt disappointed when it did not arrive. Perhaps it was unreasonable that I should feel so, but in your absence all my comfort and happiness is to receive the expressions of your love and remembrance. If God spares our lives to meet again, will we not strive to be and to make each other happy? I know that I have often failed in the performance, and always come far short in my duty to you in many things; but my heart has ever had with it a fountain of sincere affection ever flowing out to you, and an undivided feeling of interest in your every welfare. There is nothing in this world which I would not do to advance your happiness, your honor, and your usefulness. I know that you are noble and generous and affectionate in your nature, and I ask but the love and tender sympathy which my heart so much craves and without which I would gladly rest in my grave. . . .

Day before yesterday Mrs. Chester called to see me; and yesterday she wrote me one of the kindest notes I ever received, saying that the rooms she once occupied at Mrs. McMurtrie's were vacant, and Mrs. *M.* would be glad to have me see them. So after breakfast I walked over to her house, which is two doors below the assembly building that was burnt. I found her a perfect lady, as she truly is in manner, and has that character with all who know her. She showed me the rooms; they are in the second story, back building. You enter the front, which is a small, neat parlor with two windows furnished with sofa, chairs, and table; the next, communicating with a door, is a chamber, larger than the one we now occupy, with two windows and closets; and communicating with that by a door another, larger than Mary's here, with two windows and closets; and last of all, beyond *that* is a large closet or baggage room with shelves on each side from the floor to the ceiling, and a bathroom with a marble bathing tub and other conveniences—all perfectly private and attached to those rooms alone. Fixtures for gas in every room. She asks for this suite of rooms $20 a week with three persons, which makes in the year but $100 more than we pay here for two small rooms and no conveniences. I forget to mention at the end of the large closet is a door opening into the yard below; so that by throwing open all the doors you have a current of air directly through and a long walk from one end to the other. It would of course be preferable if you had not to go through one room to get into the others, but just with Mary we would not mind it. Fuel, of course, and lights would be extra.

I told her I could not give a decided answer until I heard from you, and at least we should not want them before July. Some provision must then be made for the summer; I shall not feel like leaving you when you return to go anywhere. Everything about the house bears the impression of order and neatness and quiet. Dr. and Mrs. Chester always boarded there, and I think we could be pleased with accommodations that suited them.

One thing is certain: if we expect Mary to improve in music we must hire a piano for her to practice on; for she has a poor opportunity now, and here we would have no place to put it. I do desire for her every opportunity of obtaining an accomplished education, and I cannot bear to withhold from our children any means of improvement that our circumstances will admit of. We cannot board in Philadelphia and educate our children under $2,500 or $3,000 a year; but we must remember the expenses of a college course would have to be met anywhere, and so of Mary if we design giving her liberal advantages. I have just called again upon Mrs. McMurtrie and asked in the event of our taking her rooms if she could make some provision for our sons during their vacation, which she said that she could do.

I wish that you were only here to look and decide. I am so much accustomed to your counsel and decisions that I am really fearful to act lest I should go wrong. Do write me by the very first mail; and if you think best, we could postpone the decision until you come, which I would much prefer. Only write me immediately, for I have promised to let her know something in nine or ten days. In winter they will be warm, sunny rooms. Everything in the future looks at times to me so chaotic that I feel like a feeble boat drifting upon the waves of time.

I sat up alone night before last with the poor sick lady. She is still very ill, but astonishes everyone by holding out so long. No one can say how long she may not be preserved in a life of suffering. Sometimes when I go in, she throws her emaciated arms around me and draws me to her and kisses me. She says: "I love Mrs. Jones, and I hope she will come and live in St. Louis." It is a satisfaction to me to render any attention to this poor sick and dying stranger.

And now, my ever dear friend, I must close to be in time for the mail. Mary unites with me in love and kisses to dear Father, and love to Sister Betsy and Brother William, Sister Susan and Laura, Julia and family, Henry and Sister Abby, James, Mr. and Mrs. Axson, and all friends. Do tell all the servants howdy for us. Write as soon as you can and as often as possible to

Your sincerely attached wife,

Mary Jones.

Mary's room is now occupied and probably will be for the summer, so some change must probably take place.

M. J.

173

Princeton, *Thursday*, June 5th, 1851

My dear Father,

As you are now free from those numerous and pressing engagements which devolved upon you while in St. Louis, perhaps a line or two from Princeton may not prove unacceptable. Doubtless ere this you have reached that spot so dear to us all, and are enjoying those many pleasures which flow so sweetly from social intercourse. The excitement of debate, cool deliberation, and metaphysical reasonings have all been left behind with office duties; and like an uncaged bird you again visit in freedom those scenes around which unnumbered associations of bygone joys are wont to cluster. Once more is the noisy city exchanged for the quiet retreat, the narrow street for the wide-spreading field and verdant forest, while the rattling of carts is heard no more: naught save the warbling notes of the feathered songsters singing of love and content, the gentle lowings of pasturing herds. But above all these, dearer to the heart and more charming to the ear, fall the soft accents of friendly words—relations whose voices have long been silent save when faintly echoed from a distance by the pen. Yet I know your soul often turns to one who is left behind, and as often finds a response: "I'll think of thee." As you doubtless would wish to hear of her welfare I will say that we heard from Philadelphia last week: Mother and Sister both quite well.

I perused with great interest the letters from the General Assembly, and was much pleased to see with what marked approbation your report was accepted. The manner of its presentation apparently was quite novel, but very impressive and uncommonly commanding. *The Presbyterian* was lavish with its commendations, praises, etc.

Commencement is now near at hand, and we are as busy as "bees in a tar barrel." It seems that an ill fate must be my guardian deity. Again my throat has been so sore that I could scarcely swallow water. Each attack is more severe than the former, and it almost takes away all my spirits; for I begin to believe that I can never apply myself closely to any profession, and especially to the law, which requires above any other a sound larynx and good lungs. If this be my lot, then good-bye to many aerial castles. As yet I have been totally unable even to read aloud my speech; consequently have not practiced it, and necessarily will labor under a disadvantage in its delivery. The junior orators speak in a little more than two weeks. My dear mother and sister will probably be with us on the 23rd. Am sorry that you cannot also be present at that season. Dr. Schanck has me under his charge. The fever and headache have been relieved, and I hope in a week my throat also will have pretty nearly recovered. The caustic will, we think, do its work.

Suppose that you have heard of our spree here a short time since. I refer to the overthrow of Barnum's great "Juggernaut" into the canal by the college boys. For particulars see a letter written to Aunt and Uncle a week or two since.

I wish that we had some items worthy of communication, but it does really seem that nothing of interest can be found. Hoping, therefore, that you will excuse this mere apology for a letter, for the reason just alleged and also in view of the many pressing engagements now demanding attention, I will close. Brother unites with me in kindest love to self, Aunts Betsy and Susan, Cousin Laura, and Uncle; also to all relatives and friends in the county; and to the servants howdy.

Ever your affectionate son,
Charles C. Jones, Jr.

REV. C. C. JONES *to* MRS. MARY JONES[t]

Marietta, Georgia, *Thursday,* June 5th, 1851

It is one month this day since I embraced my own dearest Mary and took leave of her for my Western travel; and it seems an age. My heart is full of the tenderest affection for you, and if it pleases God to restore me to you, I shall be the happiest husband in the world.

I promised to give you an account of our visit to *the Hermitage.* Dr. Edgar ordered a hack, and we drove out of Nashville Monday morning; and after a ride of twelve miles through a beautiful country we turned in the road to the Hermitage. The broad fields and woods embraced in the estate stretched away over hill and meadow towards the river, impressing you with the idea of wealth and comfort and thrift. An iron gate let us into the lawn immediately before the mansion; nor had we in our approach seen anything more than the top of a chimney or the glimpse of a wall or pillar; nor did we see anything now, so embosomed is it in trees, and so full of small cedars and shrubbery is the lawn. The road winds around an enclosed plat in shape resembling a guitar, shut in by low white posts connected by a small rope with one another. The grass in this lot was much grown, and we observed that the mower had commenced to smooth it off with his scythe. The carriage drew up at the piazza, resembling the Mount Vernon piazza, paved with limestone flags, and with the fluted columns running to the cornice above the second story. It is built of brick, a center with wings, plain, substantial, and evidently for the convenience and comfort of a noble and retired gentleman.

You enter a wide passage, furnished with sofas and chairs; and the walls are hung with fine paintings; and some busts of the general's friends are there in different positions. This was a favorite lounge for the general in warm weather, as the passage with its doors open at either end, and shaded, always gives a pleasant draft of air. Turning to the left, you enter a spacious drawing room; and folding doors connect it with the common parlor in the rear, of equal dimensions; the two rooms most handsomely furnished, and lighted with chandeliers; and the entry is lighted in the same manner. A door leads from the side of one of these rooms into the dining room. The walls are hung with portraits—two of General Jackson himself, the last completed

175

not above six days before his death by the French artist Healy, who was sent over for the purpose by Louis Philippe: a remarkably fine painting. You see Mrs. Jackson when some fifty years old, the picture of health, benevolence, and peace: rotund, decidedly engaging, and must have been attractive in all her life—a lady whose character for piety, virtue, amiability, and charity and unbounded kindness has seldom had its equal. The love of the general for her was chivalrous, ardent, undying; and her influence over him was unbounded. In his wildest days and wildest scenes of excitement, if he caught her eye, he left everything and went to her; and when her voice fell upon his ear and her hand touched his person, he was her captive knight. He loved her with his heart, and this was the bright spot in his character all his life. He was one of the finest men in principle and in life in his intercourse with the sex, and to his wife the tenderest husband. Dr. Edgar says he has visited her tomb with him, and he has wept bitterly. There is a picture of him in general's uniform on his charger on a field of review. Other portraits of his personal, civil, and military friends adorn the walls. You know the Hermitage was burnt while he was at Washington, and this mansion he had built while he was President. His own chamber, with all its furniture, I did not see. John and Brother Moore saw it. I happened to be out when Mr. Jackson opened it to them.

We walked through a neat and extensive vegetable and flower garden on the right of the mansion; and in one corner of it is *the tomb*. Eight pillars uphold a circular cornice, which gives support to a dome that is covered with copper, with an urn on the point above. Beneath this dome lie General and Mrs. Jackson, and a shaft upon a pedestal rises from the center of the floor between the two plain slabs that cover the bodies of the dead. Mrs. Jackson is on the right, and the general on the left. Her epitaph is simple, affectionate, touching. His slab bears the inscription: "General Andrew Jackson," with the dates of his birth and death. The whole tomb is made of the native cream-colored limestone. The floor of the tomb is perhaps two feet from the ground. It is all unostentatious, plain, impressive; and General Jackson built it for his wife before he went to Washington, and left a place for himself by her side, which he now fills.

Our little party retired to the house, and I lingered at the tomb. Four willows, set one at each corner, threw their pendant boughs over the dome and around the tomb, and were almost motionless in the morning air. The sun shone without a cloud, and his light fell upon the floor of the tomb. Thick shrubbery shut in this consecrated spot. Roses and tuberoses, pinks and shrubs and hollyhocks and other flowers bloomed around; and the birds were flitting from tree to tree, chasing each other, with merry notes, or alone in some upper branch were sending forth their enlivening song. The fields outside the garden lay in richest green. A peaceful repose pervaded all nature, and before me lay the man whose life and actions are identified forever with the history of his country and with a worldwide fame. All that remains of him is in this dark vault! He is gone. I reviewed his animated, troubled, eventful life in the field and in the cabinet, and recalled his distinguished services and acts, and honored him in his independence, decision, magnanimity, and patriotism. But I turned with the highest pleasure and satisfaction to the closing years of his life, when he was called by the grace of God and made a subject of that Kingdom which can never be moved. He was a soundly converted man some years before he died, and his Bible and hymnbook and Confession of Faith were always upon his stand. He led a life of devotion, and you remember his calm triumph in death in the merits and intercession of the Divine Redeemer. The Hermitage church, a neat brick edifice, which he assisted to build, stands immediately opposite the road leading to his house, where it comes into the public turnpike leading to Nashville. It stands upon his own grounds, and it was in this building that Dr. Edgar received him into the communion of the Presbyterian Church. Yes, it was the fact that this extraordinary man died a Christian that interested me most of all when I stood at his tomb.

I followed the gentlemen into the house after conversing a few moments with the gardener and picking some sweet shrubs. Mr. Andrew Jackson, the general's adopted son, now heirs the estate: a calm, pleasant, gentlemanly man and a consistent and hearty member of the Presbyterian Church. He received and entertained us during our call with a graceful and generous hospitality, and I felt my heart drawn towards him for the virtues which seemed to exhibit themselves in his whole conversation and manner. His intelligent and accomplished lady was confined to her chamber by very severe illness, and we learned with pain that her health was seriously impaired.

The hour for our return came, and taking leave of Mr. Jackson we drove to the Rev. Mr. Kerr's, a Presbyterian minister. Here we dined, and then went on to Nashville.

This visit to the Hermitage was grateful to me, and I wished for you and my children many, many times. Dr. Edgar, who was an intimate friend of General Jackson, interested us with a fund of anecdotes of his life, and reminiscences of his Christian life, which I must try to remember and tell you when we meet.

We took leave of Dr. Edgar and his family, where we received unbounded hospitality, at eight Monday evening, and rode all night, all next day, and all the next night, and reached Chattanooga at six in the morning Wednesday. Our company consisted of John, Brothers Moore and Bishop, and Elders Hemphill and Morrison, and two ladies (relatives of Mr. Morrison). We could not have been more favored. The road lies through a fine country.

On Tuesday afternoon we commenced crossing the Cumberland Mountains. The driver begged all that could to walk, and so relieve his horses. Four of us got out. Onward and upward we trudged. The clouds thickened; the lightnings flashed; the thunder rolled over the mountains; and down came the storm. Soon the streams were rushing down the road. We plodded on in mud and rain, protected by our umbrellas. On the summit we resumed our seats. The sun came out, and we enjoyed a ride of three miles across the top of the mountain. The honeysuckles and kalmias were in bloom. When we had reached the descent, we got out again and traveled down the mountain till we reached the valley, in which flows *Battle Creek*.

I now took my seat with the driver, and enjoyed as pleasant and enchanting a ride as I ever did down this narrow but beautiful valley till night shut in upon us. The Cumberland Mountains are on either side of you in all the richness of their forests and hues and varied outline; and a succession of well-cultivated farms, patched with different shades of green, of wheat and rye and oats and corn and clover fields, keep you company all the way. The sun went down gloriously over the mountains. Now I sighed for my love. One remarkable feature in this valley is several large springs which issue out of the sides of the mountains from yawning caverns, and the water is so abundant that it is sufficient for milling purposes. We had "songs in the night." Brother Bishop and John and the ladies sang many spiritual songs.

When we reached the Tennessee River, we drove along its banks, the road being cut out of the side of the hill or mountain; and the stage lamps threw their light down the steep bank to the water below, and above into the dense forest of trees. We looked across. The dark mountains on the other side were shadowed in blackness upon the waters; and on all the smooth and brighter part of the river the stars were reflected in immeasurable depths. Strange, impressive scene. We crossed the river in a dense fog in a large flat, and were soon over the Lookout Mountain and in Chattanooga. The mountain and river were so enveloped in mist we could see nothing.

Leaving Chattanooga at seven, we reached Marietta at 2½ P.M., finding all our dear relatives well and overjoyed to see us. All *looking* well except Sister Jane and little Mary; both are thin. The baby has been sick; a fine child, and begins to talk. *All* the children much grown.

Will go to Roswell today after breakfast (June 6th) and return this afternoon or tomorrow morning. Will try and write you again before starting for Columbia on Monday. Kiss my dear child for me. I hope she may speedily recover, and that the affliction of her face may pass away without serious injury. I feel much concerned about her. Love to the boys. Tell them all my travels. Sister Jane and John, and Aunt and Cousin Mary and Lou, and all the little folks send a world of love. Would fill out my sheet, but must dress for breakfast and Roswell. God bless and keep you, my dear, dear wife! Your husband longs to see and to embrace you and tell you all his love, and is ever
Yours most faithfully and affectionately,
C. C. Jones.

REV. C. C. JONES *to* MRS. MARY JONES[t]

Marietta, Monday, June 9th, 1851

My darling Mary,

Before leaving Marietta I must write you a line. . . . Have just come from Aunt's, where I spent the night. . . . Will now pack up my concerns and get ready to leave in the cars at 2½ P.M. *for Columbia;* reach there tomorrow evening, spend Wednesday, leave Thursday, and return by Augusta to Berzelia, seven miles from Bath; take carriage and spend Friday with Messrs. Rogers and Dowse at Bath; go to the Central Railroad Saturday, and be in Savannah Saturday evening; spend Sabbath, and go out home in stage Monday the 16th. All is *if God will.*

I need not tell you, my dear wife, how I long to see you. Oh, these absences! Yet it is not my business I am on, but the Lord's; and He will see that all will be well with me and mine. But you are so bound up in my heart, and my happiness is so bound up in you, I never want to be a day nor an hour away from you.

I hope you will go to Princeton with Mary Sharpe and see the commencement exercises; and go some week or two beforehand if you can get good accommodations, and enjoy the fresh air of the country. I wish you all to take a summer visit somewhere, and you must lay out some plan that you would like.

Will write you particularly about what time you may expect me in Philadelphia. Hope you will write me to Riceboro and let me know what you wish me to do for you at home. Will attend to the box and distribute the presents as you have marked them.

Your letter was precious to me, and one also from Mary S., and one from Joe. . . . Have just time to pack my trunk and eat dinner and be off. Everybody, black and white, sends love to you and the children. Kiss my daughter for me. Hope she is well.

From your ever affectionate husband,
C. C. Jones.

Mrs. Mary Jones *to* Rev. C. C. Jones[t]

Philadelphia, *Tuesday,* June 10th, 1851

Your affectionate letter, my ever dear husband, from Marietta has just reached me, and as I closed it I could but fall upon my knees and bless God for His goodness and mercy and preserving care over yourself and my brother amidst all the exposure of travel and cholera. I felt very uneasy after your letter from Nashville, fearing that you might come in contact with that awful scourge upon the riverboats. I am thankful you found all friends so well; and as you speak of first visiting Columbia, all my letters awaiting your arrival in Liberty will be so old that I must hasten this dispatch to meet you in Savannah.

Charles has just left me this morning. He came to Philadelphia on Saturday at the solicitation of his friends in Princeton, who saw that if he did not obtain some relief he could not possibly speak at commencement; for he has been suffering for weeks with his throat: fever frequently and violent headaches. I consulted Dr. Hodge; he prescribed salts and astringent gargles, and says just what Dr. Trezevant used to do—that it arises from the state of his stomach altogether, and he will not be free from those affections unless he regulates his diet and takes exercise. He took hold of his limbs and said there was quite too much muscle and flesh to talk of serious indisposition, and *I* must not persuade him to it. I told him *by no means;* I only felt uneasy, fearing it would affect his general health. He says if he is particular with his habits and diet he will be relieved.

Jenny Lind sang last night, and Charles had the great pleasure of hearing her, and came home in ecstasies. He improved wonderfully the two days he was with me, and returned in good spirits this morning. Whilst sitting with us on Saturday evening he said: "I have not been so happy for a long time as I am this night, Mother, with you and Sister. For weeks in college I have felt so sick and depressed that I have scarcely smiled." I feel thankful that their vacation is so near at hand.

Joseph wants to pay General Cocke a visit; and if convenient you had best write to him and ask if it would be agreeable.

Last week I wrote you a full account of an offer made me by Mrs. Mc-Murtrie; and as I am desirous to hear from you on the subject, will mention here again and direct to Savannah. The only reason I have for knowing your wishes is to secure the rooms she offers: a *small* parlor furnished with sofa, chairs, and table (two windows and closets), back of which (separated by a narrow space from which passes a flight of private steps) is a bedroom larger than the one we now occupy, with two windows and two closets. This room opens by a door into another nearly as large; and at the end is a bathroom, etc., and a very large closet with shelves on each side from the floor to the ceiling for books, baggage, or anything else. By opening these connecting doors you have a current of air through the whole; and in the bathroom and large closet are windows, one of which opens to the floor and looks down upon a great plat of grass. They are all on the southwestern side, and would be delightful in winter: warm and sunny. They are in the second story, and have been all newly painted and whitewashed, and the little parlor repapered; so they present a neat and comfortable appearance, and are as quiet and retired as could be found. She offers us this suite of rooms for $20 a week. We are now paying $18 for two most contracted rooms. In the year it would only be $104 difference.

Mrs. McMurtrie has the reputation of being a perfect lady, and her house is occupied only with the most respectable. It was through the kindness of Mrs. Chester that the offer has been made. Mrs. Roser says no one stands higher than Mrs. M., and she receives none but the genuinely respectable as boarders. I feel that such an association—as we are compelled to board— would be far preferable for Mary and our boys when they are with us than our present society. Everyone treats us with great respect and politeness too, but there is wanting a refined and elevating influence. Dr. and Mrs. Chester and their daughter boarded there for years. We certainly cannot remain here without some change.

I informed Mrs. McMurtrie that I could not give her an answer under ten days, and requested that she would not consider us in the way if she had an advantageous offer, as you might like to postpone your decision until you could see the rooms; but in the meantime do write and let me know as early as possible what you think of the change.

I met Dr. Talmage a few days since. He says he expects they will have to bring you back to Columbia. I trust the Lord will guide and direct you into the path of truth and duty!

Charles begs that you will bring on his pistol. I believe it is in the wardrobe in their room. He says he wants it to amuse himself with in vacation.

We might take these rooms for the summer; the only objection is that it binds us down when the children might like a few weeks elsewhere during their vacation. And then I want to go home in the winter. The Markoe House is thinning every day, and there is much dissatisfaction amongst the boarders. They say it does not compare with what it formerly was.

Sabbath was Communion in the Central Church. Eight members added. One quite a youth; a most touching sight: his back was broken, and he looked as if he was on the borders of the grave. The ill lady, to the astonishment of physicians and everybody, is better. I have made the acquaintance of *Mrs. Wheaton,* whose husband you saw in St. Louis. Mary is quite well again, and sends love and kisses for her dear father. I look upon your likeness and kiss it and long to have my original back. Our very best love to *Charlie* and all friends in Savannah. And now, my darling husband, I hope you have improved from your travel and will enjoy your visit home. Stay as long as you can, for I know it will do you good. May the divine blessing ever abide with you!

Your own affectionate wife,
Mary Jones.

Mr. Charles C. Jones, Jr., *to* Mrs. Mary Jones *and* Miss M. S. Jones[t]

Princeton, *Wednesday,* June 11th, 1851

My dear Mother and Sister,

Here I am again, sitting in our room in Old Nassau, looking out upon the beautiful campus which has just been mown—all ready for commencement. My visit to Philadelphia was exceedingly pleasant to me, and I also hope has proved profitable: pleasant, because the opportunity was thereby afforded of enjoying a few days of personal intercourse with those whom relationship and love have placed dear and near to my soul; profitable, in that I hope my throat has been much benefited. The wharves were crowded with boats and steamers all busily plying in the Delaware; and the river, whitened by numerous sails, appeared beautifully as we plowed through its waters. Reached Princeton in safety, and once more am at the student's desk, preparing for the final examination of the junior year.

My indisposition and absence just at the time when close application was most needed will, I am afraid, have their effect upon my grade. Barring the satisfaction which I know a good grade affords you and Father, I care not myself what kind I have, if it be only a respectable average standing. A good mark does not afford true gratification to the student if he feels that it was obtained by chance—by being called up on an easy passage, etc.—for he is conscious that it came not from desert but fortune; while on the other hand, one who has regularly and attentively performed his duties, even though he be not placed among the first, still the fact that his mind has been improved, that knowledge has been obtained, outweighs every petty ambition in the way of show and mere éclat. Stood this morning upon Professor Alexander's differential, etc. Succeeded pretty well after a hard night's study.

Received a letter from Father and Cousin Laura yesterday. Both quite well. Father's was written from Nashville. Cousin Laura mentions the death of Mr. Moses Jones. What a melancholy occurrence, and sad bereavement to his orphan children! A father and mother both taken away in a short time! Surely the old proverb is often verified—viz., that afflictions do not come singly.

They are making many preparations for the approaching commencement, etc. We will all look as fine as a fiddle by that time. What a pleasure it will be for us to have you up here at that time! From all accounts such anniversaries must be well attended. Ladies flock to Princeton from New York, Philadelphia, Trenton, and all the country around. Enclosed you will find a bill of our junior speaking.

Am sorry that I have nothing new to communicate. However, one of these days something will turn up worthy of note, and you shall know it all. Whenever you feel disposed to visit Princeton, just let us know and we will have everything prepared. Hope to see you on Monday week. Do persuade Mr. and Mrs. Smith to accompany you; the trip will be pleasant and their company very agreeable. Has Mrs. Roser and family left as yet for New York? Please excuse this short epistle, for a pressure of study and scarcity of news warn me that the hour of closing has arrived. With all love to you, my dear mother, and also to Sis, in which Brother unites, I remain

Your sincerely attached son and brother,
Charles C. Jones, Jr.

P.S. The sweet notes of Jenny's voice are still sounding in my ear. Charming lady, may you never catch *the sore throat!*

Rev. C. C. Jones *to* Mrs. Mary Jones[t]

Richmond Baths, Georgia, *Friday,* June 13th, 1851

My ever dearest Mary,

Let me continue my journey with you. Left Marietta after dining with our dear aunt and family—each and every one, white and black, sending you a world of love; and parting with John at the depot, reached Augusta Tuesday morning about four or five o'clock. Took the cars at Hamburg, and at 3½ P.M. was in Columbia. There I found Walthour and Willie with Joe and the carriage waiting for me. Our kind friends Dr. and Mrs. Howe gave me the most cordial welcome imaginable, and presently Dr. Leland called over, and his heart was full at meeting me. Then Mr. and Mrs. Palmer; and then Mrs. Young and Miss Grazier. Mrs. Howe gave me dinner and *curds;* was hungry, and enjoyed my meal heartily and thankfully. Made arrangements to address the students in domestic missions this evening in the chapel.

Interrupted: called to prayers and breakfast.

Ninety-Mile Station, Burke County, Georgia, Saturday, June 14th. Resume my journal. Addressed the students in the chapel in Columbia, and a good many old friends came out to hear me, male and female. Students of senior class about all engaged.

Wednesday, June 11th, went out after breakfast to call on our old friends. During the day called on *Mr. and Mrs. Law.* The old gentleman up again, but still feeble; Mrs. Ellison well, but absent. *Mr. and Mrs. Palmer:* all well. He has bought the lot next Dr. Howe's and is putting up a nice story-and-a-half house of wood. A gate will let them into Dr. H.'s garden, so the families are as near as they can be. Happy arrangements for all concerned. New church not yet commenced, but plan settled; to be commenced soon. *Mrs. Peck:* hearty as usual. *Mrs. Macfie:* all well except her son: threatened *with consumption! Mr. and Mrs. John Crawford:* all well. *Mr. and Mrs. Snowden:* all well, and *Miss King;* Mr. Snowden much better. *Mr. and Mrs. Beck:* saw Mrs. Beck; all well. *Dr. and Mrs. Wells:* board at Clarke's old hotel; Mary thin; happy; the doctor doing better than he anticipated in Columbia. *Dr. and Mrs. Trezevant:* exceedingly pleased to see me. She has been very unwell: now as well as usual. He hearty. Says I have added five years to my life; carry the appearance of a man not reduced by disease but wearied down with too much labor. Described my state accurately, and gave me valuable advice; says if I find I have to force myself to carry on the duties of my office and am weary, I must instantly resign; *after forty-five,* slips in constitution may be *checked* but *never recovered.* He was very kind and friendly. *Dr. Fair:* well. *Mrs. Young and Miss Grazier:* well; as ever the same. *Dr. and Mrs. Leland:* all well; took tea with them. *Mr. and Mrs. Thompson and Mrs. Shelton:* all well and happy; going to the North this summer.

You cannot imagine the hearty expressions of friendship I received in all these calls from our old friends and acquaintances, and the feeling and special inquiries made after my dear wife and children. Have had so few exhibitions of the warmth of love for so many months past that it was strange to me. Dr. Howe says we have a great many friends in Columbia; and Mr. Palmer says: "You are great favorites here." Surely we should be thankful to have it so. I know our feelings are strongly interested in Columbia. I told Mrs. Wells "she would find the people in Columbia the most kind and friendly in the world; and if she was only *burnt out,* she would *know* it perfectly." Mr. Stockton called; they have a remarkably fine infant boy. Attended chapel prayers. Seminary needing a third professor; hope still for Dr. McGill. Could call on no more. Several friends invited to dine with me at Dr. Howe's. Professor Brumby's family all well. Dr. Thornwell and family in Charleston. Colonel Preston much better. Major Williams acts as chaplain but does not preach.

Town looking beautifully. Visited the old spot! Sorrowful recollections! Mrs. Ewart has four cottages from the corner to the end of the lot, all fronting toward Lyons', as the old house did. She had *three* built *for the insurance money on the old house and a quarter of the lot,* on which Mr. Killian has put up a cottage for himself. I saw her at Mrs. Young's, and said to her that "I was glad our misfortunes had resulted in her benefit." She seemed pleased. Occupies one cottage, and rents the other two for $450. DeLeon's house unoccupied; going to ruin. Dr. Gibbs's fine house shut up and for sale; he occupies Dr. Toland's house. *Living dearer* than ever, Dr. Trezevant says. *Mrs. Waddle, Mrs. Gladden,* and *Mr. James* all dead! Old Mrs. Beckett still lives! Mrs. Taylor declining very much. Mrs. Bell as well as usual.

Left Thursday morning. Short visit, but most delightful one. You are remembered with sincere affection, and everyone without exception *sent abundant and warmest love to you over and over.*

The first thing my eyes rested upon on coming up to the depot in Columbia was *Jack and Marcia's grave;* and I rode there and looked at it the last thing before I came away on Thursday morning. Nothing has disturbed them. I shed tears over them. Jack is identified with all our married life and with our children from their infancy!

Took leave of Drs. Leland and Howe and Donald and James Stacy, and arrived at Augusta in the evening. Met Dr. Talmage in the cars on my way out to Berzelia; rejoiced to hear him say he saw you last Friday. *All well!* The Lord be praised! Berzelia is twenty miles from Augusta on the road to Marietta. Stopped here, took tea at Kirkpatrick's, and went over seven miles to Bath in Judge Davis' buggy, which happened to be there. Mr. Rogers surprised and delighted to see me. Went to Mr. Dowse's, and of course was most hospitably entertained. Mrs. Dowse, Miss Susan, and his son, Mr. John Dowse, make up the family. Miss Philo is in New York at Madame *Chegaray's* (I don't know how to spell French names). Friday Judge Whitehead, Mr. Gideon Dowse, and Dr. C. W. West called. Preached at 10½ on missions. Dined with our cousin Dr. West; has *five* fine children, and his lady the picture of health and happiness. Called on Mr. and Mrs. Rogers. Board with Mr. Gideon Dowse; occupy a small cottage alone, and they are love in a cottage. Both well and happy, and delighted at their recent change: married just one week. Prospects good. Sent much love to you and the children.

Mr. Dowse kindly sent me down to Waynesboro twenty-one miles, where I could take the stage for the ninety-mile station on the Central Road. Waynesboro at dark. Bad night: slept or lay on slats with crowds of mosquitoes and hot room! Off in stage at six, and reached ninety-mile station eleven o'clock. Took out my little desk and commenced writing to you. Saw Judge Law here on his way to superior court in Hawkinsville. Railroad in fine order. *Savannah* at 6¼ P.M. Put up at Mr. W. P. Clark's, west end of the academy. Saw Brother Ross, Charles Edward, and Cousin Joseph Robarts; he has been and still is quite indisposed and confined to the house.

Sabbath, June 15th, preached in morning at First Presbyterian Church; afternoon heard Brother Ross; evening nowhere. Remembered my dear wife and children as usual. Called a moment at Major Porter's; Mrs. Vanyeverine died on Monday last the 9th, falling asleep like an infant. Louisa much afflicted, but Christian in all her feelings and deportment.

On Saturday I received your letter of the 2nd, and on Sabbath Mr. M. Cumming sent me your last of the 10th, a sweeter and more loving letter than that of the 2nd. I thank you kindly for them, and the Lord for His great mercies to us. I have got up at four this morning to finish this letter in answer to yours before the stage calls.

Then to business. I leave the change to Mrs. McMurtrie's to your own judgment. My earnest desire is that we may secure such accommodations as may be every way agreeable and comfortable, for there is nothing in this world which I do not wish my dearest wife to have that will make her comfortable and happy. As to the matter of taking the rooms and having to pay for them while we are away—or the children—that we cannot help. We must either do that or be ever changing. This expense of living has to be put *by itself;* other things *extra*. You might take the rooms, which by your description are good, for the summer at any rate; and we may regulate the winter afterwards, if we are spared so long. If you think it best, and are willing to take the trouble, *take the rooms and move at once, and enjoy the comfort of them,* and request Mr. Powel to pay up our board to Mr. Watson. You will find my last bill paid up to the 1st of May or thereabouts in the book in the little box marked "Bills Paid." Mr. P. can draw out a bill exactly like it for the time being (throwing *me* out) and pay Mr. Watson. This may be the best arrangement; and anything you do which meets your views will please me. Then you will have a new home ready for me when I come, God willing. Will Mrs. McMurtrie charge anything extra for our boys when they are with us?

Hope our dear boy is better, and will be able to speak. Will write General Cocke about Joe's visit. I wish you all to take a vacation as soon as I get back. You must do it.

Must close, as the hour for the stage is near at hand. Love and kisses for my dear daughter and sons. You give me leave to stay as long as I can. I want to see my dear Mary too much to stay longer than is absolutely necessary; and then the office needs me. My kind regards to Mr. Happersett and Mr. Powel. They must keep in good heart, and I will be with them shortly.

Mr. Moses L. Jones is dead! Mr. Joe Bacon has lost a child. Mr. Edward Delegal had his poor little daughter by his first wife burnt to death! All lately. And my old and Christian friend *Driver Paris* (Mr. King's) has recently gone to his heavenly rest. Changes! Changes! God be merciful to us and prepare us for them and for Himself! Will write you from home if spared. The box has come; not yet sent out.

And now, my dear wife, my darling Mary, my sweetest one, tell me when you write that you love me. Let me *read* your love. I long, long to embrace you and tell you all my love. May we be spared to meet in health and peace! Will write you when to expect me: somewhere between 4th and 6th of July. Shall count the days! God be with you, my dearest wife!

Your ever affectionate and devoted husband,
C. C. Jones.

Savannah, *Monday Morning,* June 16th, 1851.

Mr. Charles C. Jones, Jr., *to* Mrs. Mary Jones[t]

Princeton, *Monday,* June 16th, 1851

My dear Mother,

Although we are in the midst of a severe examination, still I must lay aside my books for a moment and discharge a filial as well as a delightful duty. Often does my mind turn to you, and in imagination I view you seated in the rocking chair, now perchance thinking of one on whom above all others your soul loves to dwell, now far away in that balmy clime revisiting those lovely spots hallowed by many a pleasing recollection, around which memory fondly clings, calling up associations at once endearing and soothing, where reside those around whose hearts the golden chain of friendship is closely entwined, to whose joys and sorrows your own leaps with responsive feelings. Again, when the shades of eve draw near, and all nature prepares to rest, methinks I hear that sainted voice as it raises in anthems of praise to the great "I Am," and then breathes a prayer for an absent husband, a dutiful daughter, and two erring sons. Though the heart be corrupt, and the affections stray from the paths of rectitude, though the young man forget for a while the instructions of his earlier days, yet there is one thought which above all others will bring him back to duty, and that is: "A Christian mother prays for me." Though he be a wanderer upon some dreary waste, though he tread those lonely regions where the foot of man has never trod, the remembrance that the guardian spirit of her who begat him still lingers around his footsteps, and accompanies in its votive offerings his every action, is enough of itself to throw about him a mantle of protection and inspire him with noble aspirations to prove himself worthy of her love.

In relation to commencement, I wish that you would let me know whether Mr. Happersett will accompany self and Sister. If he does not, then one of us must come down and bring you up, for we are very anxious that you should be present. Mrs. Hope expressed to me the other night her deep regret that she had no room to offer you. "Tell your mother," said she, "I wish that she would do everything else—eat and sit with me all day—except sleep." Wishes that hers was "an india-rubber establishment" which might be drawn out on one side. Will try to make every preparation for you in the hotel.

The locusts are here now in great abundance. They are of that kind which comes from the ground every seventeenth year, and their sting is said to be poisonous. A few days since, a boy in Newark was bitten by one and came very near dying, and several persons have been killed by them. Fortunately, however, they generally keep upon the trees in the woods, where their singing may be likened to the noise of a pond filled with frogs. What must the locusts be in Egypt!

As I am very busily engaged in preparation for tomorrow, I hope that you will excuse any further particulars. When have you heard from Father last? Do mention my *pistol* when you write. Hoping that this will find you and my little sis in good spirits, and that you will acquaint us if our services be needed, I remain, with best love to self and Sister, in which Brother unites,

Your ever affectionate son,

Charles C. Jones, Jr.

"U. S. S." *in futuro*

P.S. Noticed today that Senator Dawson had his leg broken by being thrown by a young and fractious horse against a rail. Mr. Stephens also (our representative) lies dangerously ill.

C. C. J., Jr.

REV. C. C. JONES *to* MRS. MARY JONES[t]

Montevideo, *Tuesday*, June 17th, 1851

See, my dearest Mary, *where,* by God's good hand upon me, I now am! In our old and quiet and happy home! And oh, how my heart and soul yearns for my love, my sweet wife! If she were here what love, what peace, what happiness!

I gave Charles Edward my letter to you to be put into the post office in answer to yours of the 10th about the rooms, and also containing an account of my travels up to the time, *yesterday morning.* Came out in stage; fellow passengers: Mr. J. B. Barnard, Dr. B. B. King, Mrs. Bailey, and the servant women. Dined in Riceboro; there met Charles Berrien and Henry and Mr. Shepard. Rode with Mr. S. to Montevideo. Saw Phillis, Maria, and Daphne in McAllister field, and Tony at the foot of Carlawter hill; Niger and Sue in their corn field; Rose at the house. And the whole plantation in the course of the evening came over, little and big, expressing great pleasure and satisfaction at seeing me once more. They made many inquiries after you and the children, and begged to be remembered to you, with a hundred howdies. They are all well, and are looking remarkably well. The old man Tony looks uncommonly well. Flora is declining, as much from her inveterate *quietude,* sitting almost universally, as from any other cause. There have been five mothers since we left: Dinah, Clarissa, Bella, Eve, and Fanny. Children fine and healthy.

There has been an extraordinary drought over all the state, and indeed over several states, with occasional veins of good seasons; and the conse-

187

quence is that all the provision crops are seriously and fearfully injured—in many places beyond recovery—which must make provisions scarce and high next year. We have suffered seriously in common with others in the provision line. Cotton very good on the whole here; of course I have seen nor heard anything from Arcadia and Maybank. Yesterday afternoon, an hour or two after I came, we were mercifully visited with a copious and refreshing shower, which was renewed again at night; and today the wind has been northeast: *very cool indeed* and *considerable more rain*. The immediate hand of a kind Providence. This rain will, we hope, save the provision crop, which of course must be shorter than common. It is a general rain, and we rejoice in the blessings of others. The people said: "You have brought the rain, sir." I told them they might be twice glad—first to see me, and then the rain—either way they pleased. It was God's goodness. Mr. Shepard and Cato much delighted. We attempted to walk into the fields this morning, but were driven back by the storm.

Have just distributed your presents to the men and women, with which they are greatly pleased, and send you many thanks. The variety in the color of the dresses is specially acceptable, and the caps are more valued than anything you could have sent. I told the little children who came also that you would bring their present when you came in the fall, God willing. Little Andrew brought up the shirts for Phoebe to make this morning with a note from Sister to Mr. Shepard. Will give her the work with directions. The piece of cotton for Mary Sharpe I will carry down to the Island, and when cut out Phoebe will make it up. She is looking pretty well, and has been doing well. The change of employment will be very good. She will leave the shirts in the house and take out two at a time as she makes them. Have taken a memorandum of your inquiries and commands about matters and things from your letters, and will attend to them and report to you on all when we meet. Had no opportunity of getting the spools of cotton you wrote for in Savannah for Mary's clothes, as your two letters to Savannah were received one on Saturday night and the other Sabbath morning. I did not go to the post office; Montgomery sent it to me by a servant. Will get them at the Boro.

Your dispatch to me in St. Louis was received the day after you sent it, *much to my relief;* and I thought I had acknowledged it. Your two letters directed to Riceboro, and one from Charles Colcock and one from Mr. Happersett, Mr. Stebbins handed me yesterday. They were all pleasant to me. But whose letters are like my Mary's? She is my friend, my best friend, my dear wife, my sweet wife, the precious one of my heart. I have not a thought or remembrance of you in all our lives together, my darling one, but it is of *pleasantness and love.* You have been God's richest blessing to me on earth, and to my children. And it seems to me, if we are spared to meet again, I will strive to be everything to you as your own affectionate and devoted husband which you could desire. I reciprocate from the bottom of my heart every expression of confidence and affection in your letters. I only wish I could embrace my dear wife and tell her all my love.

You must take the rooms at Mrs. McMurtrie's if you like them, and move and make yourself comfortable at once. If you are pleased and satisfied with them, you may be sure I will be. And you must *write and let me know immediately;* and don't forget to mention *the street and number,* for what a fix would I be in to arrive in Philadelphia and not be able *to find my wife!*

We will endeavor to arrange about a piano when we reach Philadelphia if you do not anticipate me in it. I have every confidence in your prudence and good judgment. I agree with you that we must do everything we can to secure our dear children the best advantages for an education; and our constant fervent prayer must be that God would crown our efforts with His blessing, and regenerate and sanctify them, and fit them for His service here and for His glory hereafter.

Am sorry our good friends of the Central Church are to be deprived of their minister. It is presumed he will go, although his election was far from being unanimous, there being over forty votes cast against him. There were strong objections in the minds of many in the assembly against the Princeton arrangements. You see by the papers that your husband was, in company with Dr. Krebs and others, opposed to them. The whole matter as passed by the assembly lost ground daily, the more the members came to understand and to reflect upon it. But it is all over; and if my friend Mr. Green goes to Princeton, I shall wish him every blessing and success for the sake of Christ's Church and for his own sake. And I shall wish the Central Church a pastor whom God shall send for His own glory and their best good.

We are *where* we trust God in His providence has placed us. As yet He gives us no intimations of a decided character that He would have us remove elsewhere. *Let us be without care, casting our care upon Him, for He careth for us.* And so marvelous have been His dealings towards us, it would be the height of presumption and wickedness in us to take one step without His special direction. Sometimes our kind friends *fear* something may happen which perhaps they *wish* may happen. It may be so in respect to our removal. Am sure I do not know. My business is not with men but with my Master in Heaven. Let us ask God's direction and blessing, and by His holy and almighty assistance discharge the duties of our office to the best of our ability. He will order all aright.

Evening. The northeast wind and rain has continued all day off and on. This evening the rain increases. No harm done. It is astonishingly *cool.* Rosetta has had a fire made in my chamber, and added a blanket to my covering.

The rose leaves you sent in your letter were very fragrant. One lies before me which has fallen out.

Jackson—the last—has just come in for his cap. Were you in possession of the fact that *the heads* of the *Negro* race are much smaller than those of the *Caucasian?* It is so. And there are no heads found here large enough, except where the hair is abundant, for the larger-sized caps. Boys' caps suit the men. As the sailors say, they will have to take *a reef* in some of them.

Let me send you some notices of a religious nature which Mr. Shepard took out to publish from this house today: "Rev. C. C. Jones will preach in Sunbury Sabbath, June 22nd. In Jonesville Monday evening, June 23rd. In Walthourville Tuesday evening, June 24th. In Dorchester Thursday evening, June 26th. And at Midway Sabbath, June 29th, Providence permitting." This is an old and excellent way to see one's friends. It leaves good impressions behind. The Lord be with and bless the preacher and the hearers!

Should the weather permit, and I am spared, hope to go to Arcadia in the morning, stay with Henry at night, and go to the Island on Thursday morning. Mr. Shepard has kindly given me the use of his horse and buggy while in the county; for our gig, you know, is done; the sulky not well to use, the harness being much gone; and no horse that can well be driven with Jackson in the carriage. Lilly has a young colt.

You would be surprised to see how the trees around the house and in the lot and the shrubbery have grown. Some of the trees are beautiful. The cedar rows are fine, and the double row down to the river will be an ornament, though the view may be too much obstructed. Kept at a certain height, would do well. The house is almost hidden in trees. The drought has affected the flowers; few are blooming, but the bushes much grown. Thought of setting Gilbert to trimming, but as the time was short, thought you could amuse yourself with this work when you come home next winter. A better time— and better hands.

When I came home yesterday the first living object that met my eyes was a large rabbit hopping about on the main walk in the flower garden, much at his ease. He pricked up his ears and turned his head, as much as to say: "Pray, sir, who are you?" and then slowly hopped off. After the rain the sun came out, and the air was cool and sweet; the rays glittered in the trees and on the lawn; and the birds were pouring forth their melody on every hand. The red-winged blackbird was upon the river's side; the mockingbird sported himself on the housetop; and the sweet thrush turned his bosom to the setting sun from the highest branch in the grove. The quail whistled and courted his mate on the green; the lark twittered and hid himself in the grass; the woodpecker piped and hammered the old oak; the soft and measured cooing of the turtle dove came I could not tell from where; and the redbird and the oriole came in; and even the impudent crows joined the choir; while the nighthawk mounted and sailed and turned and stooped and screamed at his bugs and mosquitoes high up in the heavens, intent upon winning and enjoying his supper, for he had no idea of going to roost with an empty crop. I enjoyed it all. My Father made them all. Think you I did not lift my heart to Him? I remembered *the past, the present, my loved ones, the bright world to come,* and *Him who bought it for us.*

You must be tired of my long letter. Kiss my dear daughter for Father. Love to the boys. God bless you all! My darling wife, *love your husband,*

Your own ever affectionate husband,

C. C. Jones.

Mr. Charles C. Jones, Jr., *to* Mrs. Mary Jones[t]

Princeton, *Tuesday,* June 17th, 1851

My dear Mother,

I write to convey to yourself and Sister a very pressing invitation from Mrs. and Mr. McCulloh that you will both remain with them during commencement. She sent for me this morning to request that I should write and urge it upon you, and would have written herself, but I told her that I would comply with her wishes. They say that the hotel at that season is so much crowded with country people, and frequented by drinking characters, that it would not only be very unpleasant but almost impossible to put up there. Besides, they conceive it a duty and pleasure to entertain guests at that time. You will, if you accept, spend a delightful period with them, for they are truly Southern in their hospitality and feeling. No refusal will be taken, for she requested me to bring you there immediately upon your arrival, and says that she will expect you on Monday. I scarcely see how you can refuse so kind an invitation. However, of this you must be the judge.

Hope that you will excuse this short note, for we are in the midst of an examination, and I must close for the mail. With feelings of love, I remain

Your ever affectionate son,

Charles C. Jones, Jr.

P.S. Do not let any consideration of my having engaged rooms at the hotel weigh with you, for I can attend to that satisfactorily.

Mrs. Mary Jones *to* Messrs. Charles C. Jones, Jr., *and* Joseph Jones[g]

Philadelphia, *Wednesday,* June 18th, 1851

My dear Sons,

I have delayed to the last moment writing you, hoping for a letter from your dear father. I am indebted to you both, and now send a few hurried lines to request you to meet us at the depot on Friday evening at the usual hour— I think about seven o'clock. Mr. Happersett will certainly, if Providence favors our plans, accompany us as far as Tacony and probably all the way. Please say to Dr. Joline we shall be there to tea. I feel very grateful to Mrs. Hope for her kind invitation, and beg that you will say so to her for me.

It is eleven, and I must close. Your sister unites in best love to you both.

Ever, my beloved children, your affectionate mother,

Mary Jones.

P.S. Excuse the sheet: I did not observe that it was torn until I had finished. It would be well to inquire the price of board per week.

Mrs. Mary Jones *to* Rev. C. C. Jones[t]

Philadelphia, *Friday,* June 20th, 1851

It is a whole week, my dearest husband, since I have received a line from you, and it seems a month. Morning and evening I have looked in vain for a letter. Your last, put in on your way to Columbia, has been received; and from the arrangements in prospect I know you would scarcely find time for writing before reaching Liberty; and yet I am so anxious and unhappy if your dear letters do not come at the expected moment. Not that I am displaying these feelings to all around. I know how useless it is to make demands upon human sympathy, and conceal them in my own bosom.

Our trunks are all packed, and at five o'clock this afternoon (Friday) Mr. Happersett is to accompany us as far as Tacony at least on our way to Princeton, where I propose spending a week or ten days, feeling that Mary needs the change, for she has never recovered entirely. Yesterday I received a very kind invitation from Mrs. McCulloh to pass our time with her; but as she is an entire stranger, and I wish to tarry beyond an ordinary visit, and would like to be so situated that the boys could be with me at all times, I shall go to the hotel, where they have already engaged me a comfortable room. Mr. Happersett and Mr. Powel have rendered me every kindness and attention in your absence, and I feel very grateful to them for it. Since you left we have been invited to spend the evening out with the Misses Gill, Mrs. Janeway, Mrs. Dr. Mitchell, and with Mrs. Newkirk, but have declined them all, as I really did not feel like enjoying society *alone;* and now it would be very irksome to me to go to a private house in Princeton.

The good folks in the Central Church are very much troubled in prospect of losing Mr. Green, and place *all* the blame on the assembly. I tell them no; Mr. Green is a free agent, and the assembly has no compulsory power. Some of them say they will never regard the seminary with interest again. I have no doubt but there was a perfect understanding amongst the parties concerned before the election.

Not knowing what to do with my things, I have packed up all the books and clothes in the trunks, and the other articles put away in the closet, and put all the papers from your desk into the portmanteau, which I have left with Mrs. Watson, begging in case of fire that she would try to save it, as it is your little all. The key of the room I will leave with her. I have had a conversation with her about our plans, and told her we might make a change when you returned, as it was absolutely necessary that we should have more room, and that we could obtain a suite of rooms at Mrs. McMurtrie's. I also took the occasion of saying that if we should make such a change it would be from no feelings of discontent, as I had always been treated with politeness and attention by the servants. She said very politely that the waiters had often remarked: "If all ladies were like Mrs. Jones, there would be no trouble in getting along"; that she would regret exceedingly to have us leave the house, and if we could be accommodated by the use of a third room, we should have them at a lower rate than anybody else; and when I proposed paying our bill, requested that it might lie over until I returned. Lately there has been quite a spirit of dissatisfaction with the house; a great many have spoken of leaving, and Dr. Wheaton and daughter and daughter-in-law have actually done so. Mrs. McMurtrie is the sister of Bishop McIlvaine of

Ohio, and is spoken of in the highest terms by her boarders. The accommodations she offers us are superior to anything in point of comfort that this house affords.

Captain Smith of the army and his wife sit above us at the table, and I find them very agreeable. They have been very polite and attentive to Mary and myself. She is a sweet little lady from St. Louis—very much like Sister Betsy in character and manners, and looks like the picture of her grandmother that hangs over the mantelpiece.

I hope, my dearest, that you will not expose too much to the sun whilst you are at home. I believe my former letters contain all I have to say of business matters. Do charge Mr. Shepard about my flower garden. I hope he and Mr. Rahn will take care of things in our absence. There is much in impressing persons with the idea that we expect fidelity and have the wit to observe omissions. I see from the papers that a distressing drought has prevailed through Georgia and Carolina.

Captain *Cunningham* is now here, and has called twice to see me. Miss C. has been quite sick recently.

What think you of Mr. Webster's speech at Buffalo? He does not mean to open our veins and bleed us to death by abolishing the Fugitive Slave Bill; but by confining us and our property to the original limits he will put his hand around our necks and strangle us to death. This seems to my mind to be his present position with regard to the rights of the South.

You will find many afflicted hearts in Liberty. I felt shocked to hear of the death of Mr. M. L. Jones. How truly desolate has his family been made!

I must now close, as it is dinner time, and we leave soon after. Give from Mary and myself the best love to Brother William and Sister Betsy, Sister Susan and dear Laura, Julia and her family, and to all friends. Respects to Mr. Shepard. Tell all the servants howdy for us at home and the Island. I want to see them all. May the blessing of the Lord ever abide with you, prays
Your affectionate and devoted wife,
Mary Jones.
Charles begs you to bring on his pistol.

REV. C. C. JONES *to* MRS. MARY JONES[t]

Maybank, Saturday, June 21st, 1851

My dearest Mary,

I am upstairs in my old quiet pleasant study. Not a sound about the house. Perfect quiet within. But the whole world without is filled with the melody and notes of a hundred birds. Their voices are not silent a second of time. They seem to have entered in and taken possession more perfectly than when we were here. The calmness, the quiet is delightful. The lot looks so grown, so fresh and green. The house all open, so clean and pleasant from top to bottom. Everything just as you left it, and all reminding me of my love, my sweet Mary. If I look out on the flowers and smell their fragrance, she planted and trained them with her own hands; if I look at the trees and the garden with its fruits, its oranges and figs and pomegranates, its pears and peaches and plums and apples, they were all set out under her eye and pruned and fostered by her care; if I walk in the piazza, in imagination she is at my side, and we are leaning in the cool breeze upon the shaded banister, sharing our thoughts and our love together. In the parlor, in the passage, in our chamber, her image is before me. There is not a part of the dwelling—no, not a single part of it—which does not furnish some scene of affection, some moments of love between us. Oh, if you were here, you would know how my heart beats towards you, my own, my dearest Mary! Then my children are associated with all around me too. If you were all here, would I not be a happy husband and a happy father?

I left Montevideo Wednesday; put a letter into the office for you as I passed through the Boro; and went on to Arcadia, finding all our people well and glad to see me and to hear from Mistress and the children. They thank you kindly for your presents, with which they seem much pleased. You will be happy to know that a considerable change has passed over some of them of late for the better: Charles and Lucy, Pharaoh, Clarissa, Kate Jones and Agrippa, and Bella and some others. They are more sober, and regular at church and in the house of prayer; and it is hoped they may be under the influence of the Spirit of God. And all the plantation affairs are moving on successfully. Kate Cumming has been very unwell, and is now here at Maybank, and for some days past is improving. I took a short walk into the fields with Stepney (Mr. Rahn, not knowing that I was coming, had gone home), and we returned on account of the present rain.

Sue gave me quite a nice dinner, and I drove on to Henry's. Sister Abby and their two children (Joe and little Miss *Nameless*) *well*. The baby is small, but sprightly and healthy. They received me with the greatest affection, and made every inquiry after you and the children.

Next morning Henry drove me to the Island. We first came up *here*. The people ran out the field to see me, and all made their *toilet* before they came except Andrew; he made no tarrying. All well and hearty; thank you over and over for your presents, and are too glad to hear that you are coming home this winter. "Hope *all* will come, and don't go back." Patience is thin, but otherwise well. Will give you special accounts of everyone individually, little and big, when we meet, if God will.

At Social Bluff we found Brother and Sisters Betsy and Susan and Laura, each in *excellent health and spirits;* Laura uncommonly fat and hearty, with Mr. Peace for her beau. He has been staying down between Brother's and Mr. King's several days; went to Walthourville this morning. Is thin, but has no cough, and looks much better than I had expected to find him; and he says he is stronger and much better. Let Mrs. White know when you see her. After dinner Julia and Belle and Mr. Joseph E. Maxwell and Audley rode over and sat an hour or two. Mr. King weather-bound at North Hampton. Northeaster still continues.

Yesterday dined at Brother's, and we went and took tea at Woodville. Carried your likeness over to show it. Mr. Maxwell and Julia thought it better than the one Sister has with the bonnet on. Mr. King had arrived, and it was a real old-fashioned evening party *all to my wife and children.* They were not there, although they were not forgotten, for everyone wished for you many times over. We closed with family worship as you have often seen it: the stand and books in the corner, Mr. King on my left in the rocking chair with one of the little fellows in his lap, the family and friends disposed around, the folding door thrown open, and the dining room filled with the servants. It was a pleasant season, and we remembered the *present* and the *absent!* The presence and grace of God and of our Lord sweetens everything. As I *walked over,* so I walked *back* in the dark from choice, although I had the offer of a saddle horse both ways. Mr. Peace rode his white horse ahead of the carriage so that Brother might have something to guide by.

Sister Susan is re-silling and repairing the house, and expects to put it in complete order.

The rains from the northeast have been general, copious, and abundant for the present. A great mercy from the Lord. Walked over to Maybank this morning to spend the day alone preparing for tomorrow and for my appointments next week, and to write my love, my sweet wife.

What would you have thought of me—how would you have felt towards me—had you been able to see me yesterday holding your miniature for an hour in my hands, looking at it through Brother's spectacles, which magnified it and made it almost instinct with life and preparing to speak to me? Then if you could have read my *thoughts* and my *affections,* I think you would have been convinced that you had a *true lover* if there was any such a being in this world, and a *devoted husband* that loves you as his life.

Sister Susan has the piece of cotton shirting you sent in the box to be made up for Mary Sharpe; also the spools and buttons you requested me to get for her; and she says she will see it all attended to. I set Laura to darning my socks yesterday, and Mr. Peace, wishing her to play for him on the piano, said: "Miss Laura, that sock requires more darning than any sock I ever saw. I do wish it was in a more perfect state. Let me try it." She gave him the sock and needle, and he very methodically set to work. They were at the piano shortly after, and I suppose the darning amusement was laid aside for the time being.

Afternoon. Have looked over my library. The volumes are like old and familiar and—some of them—most valued friends. Everything invites to study and recalls other days before me. Took the letters detailing our afflictions in Columbia from your little desk, and will get Laura to copy them for me, and will then put the originals back.

Have walked with Andrew over all the crop. Corn and cotton most *seriously injured* with the long drought, but better on the whole than last year. There are a considerable number of peaches and pears and some pomegranates; and the orange trees, both sweet and sour, give promise of a much larger crop than ever before. The ground immediately under them is strewed with dead and dying leaves and withered oranges fallen off, so great has been the effect of the dry weather. The sea breeze is in, and the piazza is delightful. The drought nearly destroyed your geese. None of the old ones have died, and there are fine goslings. They had to be turned out in the pasture, and the water dried up and the grass burnt hard, and they were watered in the trough. They laid but few eggs. They could not be suffered to go about the spring on account of the crop. They are now doing better. Patience keeps everything about the house in good order. Am just going to look at the stock on my way back to Social Bluff. So farewell, my love, for the present.

Montevideo, Monday, June 23rd. The stock at Maybank looks remarkably well considering the dry weather. Picked out a small beef for the people, and had one killed at the place, and one at Arcadia also.

Yesterday we had an excellent turnout of white and black. I preached with freedom and interest in the morning, and Mr. Winn catechized the children and preached in the afternoon. All seemed glad to have me once more in the pulpit. I was thankful to be there. It was old times and employment over again. Sunbury is done up. Mr. William Screven has moved to the Sand Hills, and the place is abandoned to the poor white people, who, now left wholly to themselves, it is to be feared will wax worse and worse. Mr. Roe and two of his children, Mrs. Somersall and old Mrs. Ennis, and one of Captain Speers's children were all of them in church. Mr. Winn left his *fourth son,* a *few hours old* only, to come down and preach, and on account of the rain *stayed all night* at Mr. O. W. Stevens'! Henry says "he thinks he would have let the people be disappointed for one day on such an occasion for once." Mr. Winn thinks of calling it *Thomas Clay.* Hope he may. Rode home in the rain with Henry and Sister Abby. The first time she had left her baby. Left a little sugar on a piece of cloth for its comfort; the little thing happy all day. They think of calling it *Ella Sturges.* Found Cousin Joseph Robarts at Henry's: better. Some six inquirers came after tea whom Henry is instructing, and I took his place. All so natural: could begin and go on with my old labors as if my absence from them had never been. Henry drove me to the Boro this morning, and I walked home. Saw Dr. Harry Alexander on the road. The old man hearty, happy to see me, and sends his best respects to yourself and the children. The rains continue: a great blessing.

Have been thinking about Mrs. McMurtrie's rooms. I suppose you have taken them. If so, how would it do for us to occupy *the small parlor* as our sleeping apartment? You know how we like our chamber to be perfectly private. Would the parlor not be more private than the chamber opening into another? Or suppose Daughter takes the parlor and *we occupy the other two?* Would not this latter be the better arrangement? But I leave it all with you, and will be satisfied whichever way you arrange it. We could use one of the rooms as a sort of parlor or sitting room, and it would be very convenient as such opening into the other. Our calls we could receive in the common company room of the house, and if you have special friends, you could receive them into your own little sitting room.

I feel grateful to all who have been attentive to you, and long to be able to pay you my personal attentions myself. We must show ourselves friendly, and make all the friends we can. Tell Mr. Happersett I have received his last letter and thank him for it, and as my time is so near run out, will defer answering it till I can do so in person. My kindest remembrance to him and my good friend Mr. Powel. Hope his wife is well. Ere this reaches you, you will have visited Princeton. Hope our dear boy will be able to speak, and will acquit himself creditably. They have given him the place of honor in the speaking. The people all send howdy. Go to Jonesville this afternoon, God willing. Will try and write you by Friday's mail: my last letter from home, if spared. Kiss my dear children for me. God's presence and blessing be with you! I remain, my precious wife,

Your ever affectionate and devoted husband,
C. C. Jones.

Rev. C. C. Jones *to* Mrs. Mary Jones[t]

Montevideo, Thursday, June 26th, 1851

My ever dearest Mary,

How are you and my dear children today? I suppose you are all at Princeton. Yesterday was the junior exhibition day, and sincerely hope my son was well enough to deliver his piece, and that Mother was more than gratified with his performance. It is matter of sincere regret that I could not be present. You must give me a full account of all the college exercises when I come, if God spares us all to meet again.

Mr. Shepard and I on Monday afternoon rode over to the Retreat. Old Mom Clarissa appears nearly as well as usual with the exception of her eyesight, which has failed considerably; and she says she is obliged to trust to her ear more than to her eye in recognizing persons. She is in good spirits, contented with her daughter Rachel, and sends howdy and best remembrance to you and the children, and hopes she may live to see you come back. While sitting in her house Silvia came, expressing much joy and making every inquiry after you, thanking you for the present and sending love to all. She is looking remarkably well. Went to see Pulaski. He is suffering with an inflamed eye; otherwise well. Very glad to see me and to hear from Mistress and "the small family," and begs to be particularly remembered to you. All the people at the Retreat well and doing well, and their numbers are increasing.

I visited *Father's grave!* The musk-cluster planted by the side of the monument is a large bush, and sheds its fragrance over his grave. May his memory be ever fragrant in our hearts! The cape jessamine covers the head of your mother's tomb. The yard is kept clean, and wore the appearance of attention. Here I stood and recalled the past and present, and silently lifted up my full heart to God.

Jimma was at home, and Miss Newell and Helen and little Evelyn had come down to spend the day. All hearty. Jimma rode all the way to Maybank last week to see me while I was up here. His inquiries were most affectionate and particular after you and the children, and sends much love. He has made an addition to the house (in the rear joining the back piazza) of a couple of pantries and a passageway open on the west side, so that the room corresponding to our old *bridal chamber* will hereafter be used as a bedroom. A very good idea. Miss Newell and his mother are to purchase carpets and furniture for him, that in the fall he may take his bride to a comfortable home. I imagine he has made a judicious choice.

After spending an agreeable half hour Mr. Shepard and I left for Jonesville, and Miss Newell and the children followed on for the Sand Hills. Stopped at Mr. Axson's; all well, and happy to see me and hear from you. Mrs. Harden and her four children (all much grown) staying with Mrs. Axson until Mr. Barnard sets out on his summer travel, and then she moves into Mr. B.'s house. Mrs. Varnedoe there when I arrived; most pleasant interview. Brother Axson's children much grown also, and everything happy and pleasant about them. All sent as much love as I could bear you, and will, if spared, give you a hearty welcome home in the winter.

Called over to see the afflicted family of Mr. M. L. Jones. Laura begged us to excuse her, as she was at the moment putting mustards upon Miss Kate McConnell, who was suffering from headache, etc. They sent for Mrs. Axson. Saw only one of the children. The community sympathizes deeply with the family. Surely God's hand has been *heavy* upon them! Eight children—both parents gone!

Preached with interest by Brother A.'s request on domestic missions to an attentive audience in the evening. Spoke to everybody almost. Felt grateful for this privilege. Rode home and spent the night with Mrs. Shepard. Mrs. S. and he and his daughter send kindest regards to you. They are excellent people, and fear God.

Took up my line of march after breakfast Tuesday morning for the Sand Hills, and arrived at Charles Berrien's about eleven. He and Sister Marion received me with great affection. They have four fine children, and well behaved, and his house and lot one of the best and pleasantest on the Sand Hills. They built on the spot they said "*I* had selected for them." I remember Charles asking me to give him my judgment when he was about to build. I dined with them and passed a most agreeable day. They send warmest love to you and the children. Aunt Hetty has gone to travel North with Sally and her husband. Sally very happy.

Rode over and took tea with the family on the other hill. Received very kindly. It was a great pleasure to see the little girls. They were dressed neatly, and kissed me affectionately. They are much grown and improved. Miss Newell does a good part by them. Helen and Laura Matilda played a duet on the piano quite prettily. Mr. Peace and Mr. William J. King's daughter and nephew and Mrs. Dr. Anderson and Charles Berrien and Sister Marion took tea with us. I felt grateful for the visit. *Alfred* in all his identity inquired particularly after *"Missy,"* and sent "a heap of howdy, and long to see her."

Preached on missions again in the evening to a tolerable good audience. You would be surprised to see the young people. They are now entering fast into manhood and womanhood. Spent the night with my old and valued friend Mr. W. Quarterman Baker. He has sixteen or seventeen living children, four or five *(all boys)* by his last wife, who is in her usual health, and bears her responsibilities with ease, efficiency, and *kindness*. Had a most pleasant visit here.

Reached Montevideo Wednesday at 11 A.M.

But we are not our own keepers! How little know we of the day or hour of our death! The sun being hot, I attempted to draw the umbrella from the boot of the buggy; it ran into the spokes of the front wheel, making a prodigious rattling, when in a second Mr. Shepard's horse took to his heels. He ran some thirty or forty yards. I drew the umbrella partly out of the wheel, and being a very tender-mouthed horse, through a kind Providence I succeeded in stopping him. Precisely the manner in which Father lost his life. This happened just after passing Hargrave's old place. The Lord keep us in a state of preparation for His coming!

Walked over the whole crop with Mr. Shepard (who came from Jonesville to meet me) and Cato. Was gratified. The crop as promising as the season and lands would permit. The taking in of the swamp and marsh some fifty or sixty acres on the Springfield tract has been a great work, and has added very much to the value of the plantation. It is all under bank, and needs now only to be raised in place; and the way is now open to bring the whole swamp above into successful cultivation and give us as fine provision land as need be desired.

I wish to have the yard and gardens and the whole lot put into thorough repair for you this fall, and will give no final direction about it until we meet, and then will have it all done just as you may wish it. And we must send Mr. Shepard word also how we wish the lawn cleaned up.

It is very pleasant here, I assure you. The people did but half work today, and I met them in the chapel in the afternoon and held meeting with them, and afterwards catechized the children and youth, and gave all the exhortations and good advice I could. My visit home here has been every way agreeable. The people all well and apparently doing well, and things bearing the marks of attention, and in as good repair as you could expect with the master away, whose eye and hand, you know, are so necessary on a plantation. Mr. Shepard is improving the plantation, and is anxious to do all he can to promote our interests and to please us, and says he only desires to know what our wishes are, and he will do his best to fulfill them. The people have nearly all taken leave of me, little and big, and send howdy for Mistress and Miss Mary Sharpe and Masters Charles and Joseph, and hope you will soon come home.

Will leave my letter open and finish it at Arcadia this afternoon, D.V.

Arcadia, 3½ P.M. Have walked over everything, and consider the cotton (seventy-five acres) excellent; corn with seasons will come out; rice much injured, but there may be a tolerable yield from above half of what is planted. Everything wears the appearance of attention except the yard, which Mr. Rahn is to repair this fall. People all well, and send howdy for Mistress and Masters Charles and Joseph and Miss Mary Sharpe. Have just concluded service with the people. A pleasant season, and hope a profitable one. They seem more sober and considerate. They were delighted to see your miniature. Our old friend Rhina came over to see me, and sends a thousand remembrances to you and to the children. Am gratified with my visit here also. A kind Providence has smiled in mercy upon us, and we have a thousand blessings showered upon us unworthy sinners.

Have now to go to Dorchester and preach this evening and return to the Island tomorrow, spend Saturday with the people at Maybank, preach at Midway Sabbath, and set out on Tuesday on my return to my dear wife and family. So this will be my last letter to you before I see you, God willing.

I saw a letter from you to Mrs. King postmarked June 18th in the post office, and none to your own dear husband! And was greatly disappointed in receiving none from you today. Will live in hope of one next Monday. At any rate, I have tried to keep you in remembrance of me. My love to my dear children. I hope God will make my way prosperous and permit me once more the inexpressible happiness of embracing my ever dearest wife. As ever,

Your affectionate and devoted husband,

C. C. Jones.

Mr. Rahn sends his best respects for himself and for Mrs. Rahn.

Mrs. Mary Jones *to* Miss Laura E. Maxwell[t]

Joline's Hotel, Princeton, *Friday*, June 27th, 1851

My very dear Laura,

The 105th commencement of the College of New Jersey—Old Nassau Hall —was held day before yesterday. As you may well imagine, the whole town of Princeton was thrown into a state of perfect excitement, which is just now subsiding into somewhat of a calm—at least sufficiently so to allow an attempt at letter-writing, although my descriptive powers feel rather enfeebled after a sleepless night, interrupted by various sounds and serenades of doubtful harmony. I really think the quiet good folks will be thankful when all the noisy boys are away. It has really done me good to sit at the window and see with what light and happy hearts they would give the parting shake to each other and with merry steps bound into Mr. Ross's old carryalls and hurry away to the railroad and off to their respective homes, free as imprisoned birds restored to liberty.

We came here this day week in the afternoon train, escorted by Mr. Happersett as far as Tacony, our boys meeting us at the depot. We drove up to Dr. Joline's, where our coming had been anticipated; and the important little gentleman ushered us into our bedroom with the annunciation that everything in it was new and clean; and we found it even so. It had been newly painted, whitewashed, and furnished, and was indeed the coolest and most retired room in his house. We felt very much pleased with the selection, and proceeded immediately to making ourselves at home by shaking out our dresses and hanging them up in the closets, of which our room has two.

On Saturday we called to see the Misses Brearley, and received a visit from Miss Miller and Miss Breckinridge and Dr. Maclean.

On Sabbath we attended the First Church and heard an excellent sermon from Mr. Schenck on the general judgment, and in the afternoon had the great privilege of hearing the venerable Dr. Alexander in the Second Presbyterian Church. His discourse can never be erased from my memory—at least, I hope not. I listened to it as if one of the old prophets was again addressing us. It was a written sermon, and said by those who heard him to be one of his best efforts in manner and matter. I shall never forget his appearance and the tones of his voice as he rose and gave out the 39th Psalm: "Teach me the measure of my days," etc. The Scriptures were read and prayer offered by Mr. Duffield, the pastor; then again broke forth that voice so peculiar in its tones and emphasis that you never expect to hear its like again in the 90th Psalm, beginning with (I think) "Alas, our mortal frame!" I cannot now remember the precise words, but you can hunt them out. Then followed the text: Numbers 23:10—"Let me die the death of the righteous, and let my last end be like his!" . . . He alluded most touchingly to the changes that had come over Princeton since he first settled here; said scarcely one remained of those he first knew—that an entire generation had taken their places; and closed with a most solemn and earnest exhortation to all present to prepare for death. Just before me sat the venerable Mrs. Miller, and I thought with what feelings she must listen to him; she afterwards remarked to me that Dr. A.'s discourse had put her mind into the happiest frame ever since she heard it.

I think I saw Miss Alexander in church on Sabbath, but have not heard a word from her, and am under the impression that she has been absent since. Will try and call before I leave.

On Tuesday afternoon Mr. Venable of North Carolina addressed the literary societies on "The Duties of the Citizen-Scholar." It was characterized by good sound sense and an interesting address. He was escorted in by the eight junior orators, and the stage was filled by the learned and venerable of the land.

That evening we took tea by invitation with Professor and Mrs. Hope in company with some dozen persons, amongst which were Ex-Governor Hayne of New Jersey and your friends Miss Henry and Miss Rowley. We left soon after tea, and arriving at the church found it already crammed. But the polite governor carried Mary and myself forward to most delightful seats, from which I believe he had routed somebody; and when I expressed regret at being served at the expense of others, he said: "No, Madam, it is your right this evening." The splendid New York Band struck up most inspiring strains; and soon appeared two by two up the aisles the junior orators for the evening, robed in flowing black silk gowns, like judges or divines. There they sat, eight of them: fine-looking youths. Here and there you might discover the blanched cheek; and the free circulation of cold water, and a fan most diligently plied by one and another, told of expectations yet unfulfilled. My boy sat up as if he were already a statesman.

And now you must forgive anything that savors of *pride, partiality, prejudice.* (I do always try to mind my *p*'s.) I will send you the order of exercises. The speakers take their places by *lot,* and Charles came last. You may be assured as it drew on to the close I listened with palpitating interest. When James Taylor Jones closed, and the sweet music that followed died away in gentle strains, and the voice of the venerable president was heard introducing **Mr. C. Jones** of Georgia to the audience, I felt a deadening chill run over; but no sooner had our boy made his bow than I felt assured from his calm collected manner that he would do himself and his society justice.

His speech seems to have met with general approbation. Governor Hayne came up immediately and congratulated me in a very flattering manner, and so did everyone in the house that I knew, and some that I did not know taking that occasion for an introduction. Mr. Stebbins, their old teacher, rushed through the crowd with a beaming face and said "he felt proud and happy to congratulate me; that whilst Charles was speaking it seemed as if all those that had gone before were pygmies, and he was like a giant amongst them." Now, you must *not repeat* any of these vain things, they are so foolish. I only write them knowing they will interest you all, and then do not speak of them. The success of his speech was certainly greater than I anticipated, as it was a laudable undertaking. When I took my seat I could but lift up my heart to God and ask Him to strengthen my child for the task, and I returned thanks for His goodness and mercy. But oh, how I dread the influence of worldly ambition upon his soul! My great desire for them both is that every power of mind and body may be consecrated to the service of God in the way that He shall by His providence point out.

On Wednesday (Commencement Day) the church was jammed—the galleries back to the walls and benches down the aisles, with persons standing wherever they could find room. It was interesting, but I thought the speaking inferior to the juniors. Some came near a failure, and of others it might be said as the old woman did of the minister: "If his text had the smallpox, his sermon would not catch it." Mr. and Mrs. Newkirk, Miss Green, and Mrs. Barnes were there; and the lady who flung the most bouquets was a young widow engaged to one of the graduating class. We dined on Wednesday with Mrs. and Professor McCulloh, and by the time we returned to the church every seat was occupied, so that we did not see the closing exercises of conferring degrees and hearing the valedictory. At six o'clock we went over and took tea with the venerable Mrs. Miller. Her daughters and daughter-in-law and son-in-law Mr. Hageman and granddaughters with Mr. Nixon the valedictorian were all the company present besides ourselves; and we passed a most agreeable time, regaling our tastes with the choicest of cherries from her orchard.

Friday evening we spent with the Misses Brearley; and Saturday Dr. Maclean invited us to pass the evening with him in company with Mrs. Chester and son, and he entertained us in lordly style with all the delicacies of the season. He inquired particularly after Charles Edward, and said I must *not* put Mary to boarding school away from me; that he regarded colleges and boarding schools only as *necessary evils*. During the commencement his house was filled with ladies, and he is certainly a noble old gentleman.

Would you believe it? I did not see Miss Alexander to speak with her during my stay in Princeton. I was told by someone that the family were absent, and under that impression did not call at the house. On last Sabbath, observing the old gentleman and lady in their pew as I went into church, I walked up to them and spoke, inquiring after Miss Janetta. She came in afterwards, and was there also at the night service; and although she walked out of church just before me, she did not recognize us.

I believe it is fully determined that Mr. Green enter upon his professional duties by the opening of the next term in August. His church feel the matter keenly. No doubt there was a perfect understanding of the matter and arrangement beforehand. Mrs. Hope told me it was reported and believed that he would be married very shortly to Miss Colwell, who has returned from the West Indies in perfect health so far as appearances go. I am inclined to believe this true from my own observation. Soon after Miss C. returned home I called to see her in the afternoon quite early—too much so perhaps for etiquette, as Mrs. C. inquired if I did not find it warm so early in the afternoon when she came down. The servant ushered me unceremoniously into the drawing room, the doors and every window of which was drawn to so as to give a dim light. And who should I pounce upon and startle like birds from a covert but Mr. G. and Miss C. seated on the sofa *close together!* They flew apart hastily. Miss C. maintained her composure, but Mr. G. was evidently much confused and did not recover during the visit.

Your friends often inquire after you and desire to be remembered. Your Sunday school scholars are always delighted to hear from you, and your *note* affected many of them to tears. Caroline Gauss brought me a bookmark and a little glass box to send you, and Amelia Wohlgemuth wrote on a slip of paper that she wanted to see you. She is one of the most promising girls in the class. M. J. Williams is very smart, but needs control. I feel a great interest in them all. The church, it is feared, will be thrown into a very distracted state by the loss of their pastor, and some prognosticate a dissolution; but I trust there is no ground for this fear. Mrs. Newkirk and Mrs. Riesch desire especial love to Sister S. and yourself.

Philadelphia, July 1st. We returned yesterday from Princeton, my dear Laura, and I have been trying to finish my letter for the office, but have been prevented. We are overjoyed at the prospect of having our best earthly friend with us by the close of the week. It is more than probable we shall change our lodgings to Mrs. McMurtrie's when he returns, as we can have more room there, and are heartily tired of our cramped quarters at the Markoe. Our room is warm beyond description; for two days past the thermometer has been 99° in the shade and over 105° exposed to the sun.

Mrs. Roser and family have left for Newport. Mr. Wood arrived a few days before. He and Clara are devoted to each other; I think there can be no doubt of the termination.

Mrs. Smith is quite well, and will be very busy for the remainder of the summer providing for Mrs. Baird's *anticipations.* The air of Florida has improved the lady in every respect, and Mrs. S. now finds her a happy and satisfied daughter. "Experience is a great teacher." I selected and had inscribed an elegant Bible and silver goblet (in this last Mrs. Smith aided with her taste) for Dr. and Mrs. Davis, presented by the ladies of Camden.

I am happy to hear that everything is so revived and improved at Social Bluff. It is a delightful and comfortable home. I long to be again at our own dear home. If there are any pinks at Maybank living, do take them; and I promised Aunt Law a cutting: do see that she gets it if to be had.

Mary and the boys will embrace their vacation to write you all. She and Charles are suffering from sore throat. I believe it is constitutional with them. Joe as usual is rapt in his scientific pursuits. Mrs. White has removed from the city for the summer. Am happy to hear that Mr. Peace is so much improved. His niece never returned Mary's visit after she came to the Markoe. The children unite in best love to Sister Betsy and Sister Susan, Brother William, and yourself, and to your Aunt Julia and the family. You see how long a letter I have written to the *household* in general and *you* in particular. It has been done in snatches of time, and I fear you may not be able to read it. Do tell all the servants howdy for me. Miss and Mrs. Clayter send love to you. I feel very grateful to Sister Susan for her kindness in cutting out the work and taking so much trouble for us. My poor boys have brought a beggarly account of shirts from college. I begin mending operations tomorrow. Where, alas, will the ending be! Do write soon and long and everything you think or hear of. May the best of Heaven's blessings abide with you all!

Ever your attached aunt,
Mary Jones.

VI

Mrs. Mary Jones *to* Rev. C. C. Jones[t]

Saratoga Springs, New York, *Thursday*, July 17th, 1851

My own dear Husband,

After bidding you good-bye yesterday we had a pleasant run without recognizing anyone that we knew, and arrived in New York about two o'clock. As we crossed over it was most delightful to breathe the soft sea air and look out upon the expanse of ocean whitened with the commerce of many nations. We landed amidst the importunities of hackmen and crowds of people, amongst them scores of emigrants just arrived—from their rosy and robust appearance and peculiar dress fresh from the *vaterland*. The women wore no covering to the head but a thick woolen shawl put on without any reference to taste. Some of them were arrayed in a kind of red jacket trimmed with tinsel and a petticoat usually of blue, which gave them a grotesque and fanciful look. Amongst them were many children, and their baggage such as would be found in our Negro houses of the most ordinary kind: old boxes, barrels, etc., etc. Our captain said trip before the last he had five hundred passengers, and three hundred of them were emigrants.

Charles attended to the baggage, and we walked immediately to the *Troy,* a splendid steamboat, where we registered our names and selected a stateroom delightfully situated and contiguous to the promenade deck. This boat must be over three hundred feet long, and there is an open way or saloon from one end to the other, beautifully furnished with center tables, sofas, rocking chairs, conversation chairs, carpeted with rich tapestry and hung with cut-glass lamps and mirrors, which when lighted has a gorgeous effect, and on each side of which are the staterooms, nicely and conveniently furnished for two persons. Charles insisted that we should take one of these, and it only cost a dollar more apiece than the cabin berths below, and bore no comparison in point of comfort.

We washed and refreshed ourselves, and depositing all the baggage sallied forth in search of a restaurant. Turning into Broadway, we walked quite beyond the Park and Astor and American houses before we reached a desirable one. But we were compensated for our trouble. Entering a large saloon furnished around with marble tables and chairs, we seated ourselves; and the waiter brought us three plates of sliced tongue, three rolls as large as small loaves, three pieces of butter, three tumblers of iced water and the casters. I called for a cup of green tea, which was immediately handed hot and strong. The lunch ended, Charles and Mary ordered creams, and I another

205

cup of tea. The creams were superior; I told the waiter I had always heard Philadelphia creams praised, but these surpassed them. He said: "All ladies and gentlemen praised them." For this refreshment they charged us $1.12½, which we thought high; but it was more agreeable than going to a hotel. We then walked down Broadway and visited the American Museum, where the children saw much to interest them. The Chinese department is very good.

We returned to the boat at half-past five o'clock and by six o'clock were under way. A mist from the ocean obscured the view of the harbor, but cleared off as we proceeded up the Hudson. We passed three boats returning as full as it was possible for them to do with picnic parties. They cheered us loudly as we passed. Just in our wake the *Isaac Newton* came plunging on, and I feared we might have a race; but our captain wisely kept on "the even tenor of his way," and the other boat shot ahead. But that was all, for they did not arrive twenty minutes before us. We sat upon the deck admiring the beautiful country seats as we passed up the noble Hudson. Some of these were magnificent—of all descriptions of architecture. We had a very fine view of the Palisades, looking like huge battlements along the shore.

The summons to tea was quickly obeyed. The captain gave Charles the head of the table, and we at his side. There was such a bountiful display of luxuries that it was perplexing to choose; after tender young duck and fresh fried oysters we wound up with creams, berries, and watermelon.

Returning to the deck, we found night gathering around us unusually soon owing to an extensive black cloud that now curtained a large part of the heavens, through which the lightnings darted with fierce and rapid glare, whilst the thunders rolled in low mutterings amongst the distant hills. Our boat plunged bravely on to the west and outran the storm, which broke away to the east. The night was intensely dark, and the lights from the little craft that lined the river looked like brilliant stars reflected in the mirror below. When we neared Stony Point, a Drummond light shed down a brilliant pillar of light that looked on the water like the rising beams of a full moon. It was too dark to discover West Point.

We read our Bible, of which the boat has several in each cabin, and retired early to rest after asking the blessing and protection of our Heavenly Father. I did not sleep well—scarcely at all, rising frequently and looking out upon the dim outline of the distant hills. I thought of you, my own beloved husband, and missed you every step I took. You are always so good and kind in traveling to interest and instruct us about everything. If you were here and I was "by your side, my love," I should enjoy myself greatly. But away from you I am always lonely and sad.

At Troy we took the cars, started at six, and arrived between seven and eight o'clock at Saratoga. Charles was attending to the baggage and Mary and myself on the platform, when who should step up but Brother Joe Anderson! He and the whole party had been here for ten days and were just leaving: Mr. and Mrs. Walthour and daughter and Mrs. James Winn and

child. There was so much confusion I did not see them: they were just starting, and we just arrived. Charles went into the car and saw them. Helen and
Laura were both sick whilst here.

We drove directly to the house they left, and now find ourselves delightfully situated with *Mrs. Andrews,* a widow lady. Everything is neat, genteel,
and good fare for $7 per week—a price as low as it can be obtained in Sara-
toga. It is the very spot Dr. North would have engaged for us. We have a
much larger and nicer room than the one just above us. *I wish you and Joe
were here too. Mr. and Mrs. Mallard (Sarah Way that was)* and *Ann Baker*
that was at Dorchester are here, and everything is so neat and quiet it
charms my spirit. The large hotels are overflowing, and charge $2 a day. A
kind Providence has arranged for us; had we come earlier, we could not
have got in. Mrs. J. has just vacated in time, and I have her room.

I hope you will be able to make some arrangements for us ere we return.
Suppose you look over at the building going up near us by Mrs. Brown's;
and inquire of Mrs. McMurtrie. Only remember I am not discontented at the
Markoe if we can get more room. Mary is asleep, and Charles in his room. I
have seized the first moment to write you. Love to my dear boy. Do write
soon to

Your affectionate and devoted
Mary.

Mr. Charles C. Jones, Jr., *to* Rev. C. C. Jones[g]

Saratoga Springs, *Saturday,* July 19th, 1851

My dear Father,

It was my intention to have written sooner, but Mother, having the preference, communicated with you yesterday; and this being my turn, I will
proceed to state our incidents of travel, impressions of Saratoga, etc.

After parting with you at the boat we moved down the river under a fine
pressure of steam, remarking the many fine vessels passing to and fro upon
the broad bosom of the Delaware, ships on the stocks in the lower part of the
city, and whatever else of interest we could discover along the shore. After
a pleasant though rather dusty ride, we reached New York with its forests
of masts and towering steeples.

It is really astonishing to behold the subjugation which the little creature
man has effected over the elements. Could the Indian once conversant with
every feature of Manhattan now stand upon that island, would he recognize
his once loved domain? Would he in the form of those vast edifices trace a
relationship with his rude wigwam, or claim the stately steamer as his once
loved canoe? Surely civilization with its mighty, transforming power has
been abroad in the land, and where the council fires of the aborigines formerly glowed, we behold the busy mart; instead of the rude altar erected to
Manitou, the portals of the temples of salvation.

Having secured our berths, we went on shore, walked into Broadway, and enjoyed a very fine lunch, after which we visited Barnum's Museum, which contains perhaps the finest Chinese collection in this country. It is really interesting, and well worth a quarter, to view the many curiosities there exhibited. In one of the hotels we saw Mr. Gracey from Columbia, sitting quite at his ease, although he beheld us not. On the wharf any quantity of emigrants, seemingly Dutch and German, were assembled. Some were robed in old English regimentals, others in knee breeches, while all the females had black gowns, trimmed with red, heads covered with a dark shawl, and a little tunic reaching scarce below the shoulder blades. Taking them all in all, they presented as singular and curious an appearance as one could well imagine. Some three hundred of them took passage on the same boat with us for Troy. Their baggage was beyond compute. In fact, the bow and undercabin was so filled that no one could get aft.

Leaving New York at six, we obtained pleasant seats on the upper deck, where we easily saw all the fine residences upon the left bank of the river, the Palisades, etc. Several thunderstorms passed over, so obscuring the heavens that it was with difficulty that we could trace even the outlines of the hills on either hand. Passed Stony Point at nine. Upon the top of the hill was a beautiful light, reminding one of that upon the museum in Philadelphia: very nearly as brilliant as the Drummond. We reached West Point at ten, and could distinguish nothing save the lights of the hotel. Sat down to a very bountiful supper; nothing was wanting that could please even the most fastidious taste.

Woke up in the morning and found ourselves alongside of the Troy wharf. At half-past six we took the train of cars for Saratoga, where we arrived at a quarter before eight. Found Grandmother, Uncle Joe Anderson, the little ladies, Miss Newell, Mr. Walthour and lady, etc. They all inquired after you and desired their remembrances. All were leaving Saratoga, where they had been spending two weeks, for Niagara. Much to our pleasure and relief, Uncle Joe directed us to the private house where they had been staying near the depot, and a very eligible place of residence. There we met Miss Ann Baker and little Mr. Mallard with his young bride. All this tends much to our enjoyment.

Immediately upon our arrival, after seeing Mother, Sister, and baggage safely lodged, I called upon Dr. North. He was not at home. His lady, however, a very mild and pleasant person, received me hospitably, and upon my mentioning our whereabouts stated that it was just the place where Dr. North had intended to direct us.

Our hostess is a regular Old School Presbyterian, with two daughters, and one of the best old ladies possible. Mother and Sister have a large, delightful room, and are entirely satisfied with the location. Board: $7 a week. The charge at the United States Hotel is $14. Some seven or eight hundred are now boarding there: dancing every night, and as much noise as you can expect from so large an assemblage.

We go to the spring (Congress) twice every day: once in the morning before breakfast and then after tea in the evening. Have not been able to take more than five glasses at a time. The water is remarkably fine, and has as great an *effect* as if one should take so much Seidlitz powder. We are all improving rapidly. I have never felt better in my life. No headache, and all sore throat frightened far away, I hope.

Called upon Mr. Woodbridge, the pastor of the Presbyterian church in this village. I found himself and family very pleasant. He promised to call with his wife and sister upon Mother.

Saratoga is truly a beautiful spot. My recollections of the place since our visit in '39 were very few. The principal street (Broadway) was on one side entirely burned down, and in the place of wooden buildings fine brick ones have been substituted. The United States Hotel now embraces almost an entire square, with very pretty grounds and with accommodations for eight hundred persons.

An evening or two since, we visited the cemetery, which although it cannot compare in magnificence with Laurel Hill, still contains many elegant monuments, chaste and suitable.

On our return we passed through an encampment of Indians from Canada. They come to Saratoga every summer, and are engaged in making baskets, bows and arrows, embroidered moccasins, bags, and other fancy articles. It is surprising what ingenuity, skill, and precision they manifest in the manufacture of their trinkets and toys. The Indian mothers are very particular to cover their babes if visitors approach, and seem indisposed to permit them to be seen. These infants are lashed to a board and then suspended from two trees in a little hammock. The Indian boys are running around, shooting their bows and arrows, and it is surprising with what accuracy they can strike a cent, although placed at some distance. Every one strives to hit it, and he succeeding immediately pockets it as his earned treasure. They will not, however, shoot at any mark unless some piece of money be upon it. *Indian beauties* have been long and far famed, but if we may judge of them by the representation now here, we should pronounce all stories of similar import apocryphal. They are of a light complexion, and are, I presume, rather mixed with the white race, although they all speak in the Indian tongue, and with but a few exceptions cannot understand English. The matrons and young maidens are highly ornamented with rings of silver, trinkets, etc. All smoke cigars—indiscriminately, both male and female.

The grounds around the spring are highly improved, and present quite an inviting aspect to strangers. They have the valley so fully under control that all fresh water is carried off by machinery arranged for that purpose, and the mineral properties are thus preserved separate and unimpaired.

We are much interested in Hugh Miller, and I have already read more than one third of it aloud to Mother. If not interrupted, shall finish it on Wednesday—or Tuesday.

Often do we wish that Brother and yourself could be with us and enjoy the water and pleasing retirement. By walking about four or five hundred yards you arrive at a beautiful grove. The weather is a little warm, although we have most of the day a cool, fresh breeze.

Will now close and write again soon, hoping also that we may hear from you. Mother and Sister unite with me in warmest love to yourself and Brother. I remain, as ever,

Your affectionate son,
Charles C. Jones, Jr.

Respects to Mr. Powel, Mr. Happersett, Captain Smith and lady.

Rev. C. C. Jones *to* Mrs. Mary Jones[t]

Philadelphia, *Tuesday,* July 22nd, 1851

My dearest Wife,

Your welcome and affectionate letter of the 17th I found upon my desk this morning on my return from up the Hudson River, and am truly glad that you had so remarkably a pleasant trip and enjoyed everything so much. It would have been delightful for me to have accompanied you and participated with you in all you saw and felt. Life loses with me more—far more—than half its happiness when separated from you. The passage up the Hudson is peculiarly fine. Few rivers in the world, I apprehend, can surpass it. You will return by the day boat and see it all. How well all your Saratoga settlement worked! It would have gratified you to have seen the party of relatives and friends from Liberty; am sorry it so happened that you did not. And now that you are so pleasantly and economically situated, I wish you to remain just as long as you and Charles and Mary are improving. You need not return when Charles returns to college, which will be about the 7th of August. He can return alone and reach Princeton or Philadelphia in one day from Troy or Albany. And when you are ready to come home (*that word* in these regions?) I can take a run up for you. Think of it.

Since you have left I have been looking at *houses.* There is a good house, large enough for us, in 9th just below Walnut, belonging to Glenn, the fancy-store man, who lives next door, for $475, most conveniently situated for my business. Two parlors (not large) and small dining room in back part of the house, *two* good chambers in *second* story (door between), two in *third* story, and one over entry (*a third*), and two *garret* rooms. Kitchen and cellar for wood, etc., *in basement or cellar.* Quite a little green yard back. Water in kitchen (hot and cold) and bathroom and fixtures in second story. Good neighborhood. Gas in parlors; not above. There is another just below where Dr. Chester lived, which I am going to see. All tell me it will cost no more to keep house than to board, and you have privacy, liberty, room, and comfort and self-control into the bargain—and, as I believe, *more religion.* The difficulty about servants we may meet with, but it is not insurmountable, for see how many keep house. There are others I will look at, and then will make an estimate about furniture and see how it will be; but will make no change of the kind *unless it is approved by your judgment and inclination*.

Joe and I had a most delightful visit to Rondout. He enjoyed himself greatly, and will give you the particulars of his journey. I preached twice on Sabbath and attended a funeral. Left on Monday at 10½ A.M. and reached Philadelphia at 9½ P.M., and am today at my usual work.

Joe's coat was torn in the shoulder, and the button broke off his shirt collar; and I darned the one and sewed on the other for him. Could not find our washerwoman, so we had to go on a short allowance of clean clothes, but made out. Elizabeth, the chambermaid, washed a garment for me. All I needed was a *ribbon*. She has kept the room very nicely.

Captain Smith and lady are at Carlisle, and will not return to the Markoe. Few boarders: many left on excursions. Did not see Mrs. Clayter nor the South Carolinians this morning. Mrs. Banks yet indisposed. Mrs. Watson has lost her mother. Paid your visit to Mrs. General Smith; his daughter got back from Florida. Will go and see Mr. and Mrs. Riesch soon.

Received a letter from General Cocke. Has been very sick; goes to Virginia springs first week in August. Wishes Joe to visit him. So late and time of stay so short Joe declines going now. A wise conclusion. Will write the general in a day or two. Sends much love to you and the children.

Heard from Major Porter: all well, and desire remembrance. The legacy of $262.50 paid and to my credit in bank.

Enclose you Mr. Shepard's interesting letter from home, thinking you would like to see it. The Lord's mercies to us and ours are very great!

Letter also from Brother Axson: all well, and send love. Liberty County generally very healthy. He encloses $20 for a Sunday school library for *Dorchester:* good; and $5 from our old friend Mrs. Mallard to buy some books for her: *big print.*

And now, my own sweet wife, enjoy the mercies of God around you, and improve your spirits and health, and do not stint yourself in anything. If your funds give out, write and I will send you all you want. Love to my dear boy, and tell him he must fill my place, and take the best care of you and my dear daughter; and he and Mary Sharpe must exercise and drink the waters and get rid of the throat troubles if possible. Kiss my dear daughter for me. Joe sends his love. I can but be glad and grateful to think how a kind Providence ordered everything so happily for you. Remember me most particularly to Mr. and Mrs. J. B. Mallard and Miss Baker. Excuse this perverse pen and trembling hand. But *the heart* is all right, for it is all your own.

Your devoted lover and tender husband,

C. C. Jones.

Sent Charles's letter with his check from his Cousin C. E. M. by mail today. Check needs his endorsement to be available.

Rev. C. C. Jones *to* Mrs. Mary Jones[t]

Philadelphia, *Wednesday,* July 23rd, 1851

Enclosed, my darling wife, you find two letters from home. I will not forestall either your pleasure or merriment by touching on their contents.

A letter also from Mr. Rahn. Sue relieved. Crop affected both by rain and drought. People generally well. Measles rife on Gravel Hill. Shall write him to keep it off the place if possible.

Miss Houstoun and Mrs. McDonald sent me their cards yesterday. They are at No. 5, Portico Row. Mrs. McD. has come on for the benefit of her eyes; left husband and children. Joe and I called on them last evening. The Cunninghams at Cape May. Miss H. and Mrs. McD. regret your absence, and desire love to you.

Weather warm. Very busy. Will try and write you as frequently as possible. A pleasant day to you all!

Your affectionate husband,
C. C. Jones.

Rev. C. C. Jones *to* Mrs. Mary Jones[t]

Philadelphia, *Saturday,* July 26th, 1851

My dearest Wife,

The weather has been very warm for the past two days, and it still continues so, and am glad to know that you are away in a cool and pleasant location, where I hope God may bestow upon you health of mind and body and abundance of grace and peace. Joe and I keep up our "small family," and have worship morning and afternoon, and never fail to remember the loved ones who are absent. He is poring over his Cuvier and kindred books, but is careful to exercise, and we are out walking every day. Mr. Happersett has gone down to Cape May for a week or ten days. I asked Joe if he would like to go. He declined—"preferred staying at home and reading."

Yesterday we took Mrs. McDonald and Miss Houstoun to the Academy of Natural Sciences, and they were gratified beyond measure. They take a seat with us in our pew on Sabbath. Do not know who preaches.

Mr. Newkirk was in the office a moment this week; looked worried; said all were well.

Rather discouraged over going to housekeeping. Have seen two more houses. One $500: *complete* in every part. The other $360: small; sufficient room; gas; bathroom; kitchen below; grates; small yard; good street: 13th below Chestnut, corner of George; newly fitted up. But have been thinking more maturely since I last wrote. We are now, through divine favor, *free of debt:* a great mercy. To go to housekeeping *will exhaust our little surplus and put us in debt—or come in very little of it.* We cannot furnish a house of any decent size under $700 or $1,000. That settles the question. It will not do to run into debt unless upon a *necessity.* Then on every hand the cry is. "Servants! Servants! Servants!" So much plague and bother. My great desire is *your comfort;* if you are accommodated as you wish to be, and have just what you wish, then I shall be satisfied. Have heard nothing more from Mrs. McMurtrie. Paid Mr. Watson his bill last night, and *squared off everything up to July 16th, the day you left:* $148.40. And then requested him to let me know what was his lowest price for the chamber we *now* occupy and two adjoining. He is to let me know today. I prefer the chamber we now occupy to any in the house on account of its quiet and privacy. We might convert it into a sitting room and study, and Mary could have her piano in it, and her present room be our chamber; and by putting the outer door in the passage farther down the entry we could shut out the three rooms together. This would be good. When Mr. Watson reports, will consider further and "look around some," as customers say. We might go farther and fare worse.

We have no news in town saving warm weather and closed churches. Generally healthy.

We have some twenty boarders; keep about at that.

Had a real touch of depression yesterday: lonely; no friends to go to see; none to come to see me; bound up in the office; load to carry every day; no respite; warm; tired; feet ached.

"Bang-bang-bang," went old Independence bell.

"Where's the fire, Joe?"

"Can't see it. Suppose we go out, Father, and take a look."

"Agreed."

So we sallied forth, got into the Market House, walked nearly down to the river and back. Cool breeze sprang up. Returned to our room. John brought a pitcher of iced water. We had worship. Much refreshed. Went to bed; slept well; dreamed of my sweet wife. And so the troubles went away. Took out your miniature this morning and kissed it: felt better.

Our report is finally out: handsomely printed. Sent you a copy. You can now read it in print. Have sent you the papers to amuse you.

Rev. Dr. W. C. Matthews of Kentucky, brother to Dr. John Matthews whom you know, called to see me this morning. My old classmate in Princeton; have not seen him since October 1830; did not know him. Most pleasant interview. Said "he would not have known me unless expecting to see me; that I was stouter than when in Princeton; that in Princeton I was thin and worked very hard." That is good testimony.

My dear Mary, much as I miss you and *all your love,* and much as I desire to see you, yet you must not come back until you choose to do so. If you stay out all August, no matter: you and my dear daughter will be gaining in health and strength. I hope to have our winter's arrangements made before you return. Tell Charles his letter gave me great satisfaction, and I will answer it as soon as possible. Hope he and Mary Sharpe are getting as hearty as possible. Joe wrote you day before yesterday; sends love to you—to Mother, Brother, and Sister. The Lord be with you and bless you all!

Your ever affectionate husband,

C. C. Jones.

My dear Parents,

It is a most beautiful night. The moon is shedding her silvery rays on all beneath; a delightful breeze is fanning the brows warmed by the heat of an August sun; all nature in silence seeks quiet repose, as if anticipating the calm of a Sabbath morning; and naught interrupts the stillness of the hour save the song of some late rambler or the occasional chirp of the watchful insect.

I have just returned from a pleasant visit to Mr. and Mrs. McCulloh. Found them viewing Jupiter through a telescope. Three of his moons were distinctly visible, and he presented quite an interesting appearance. We also obtained a fine sight of the moon. If those noble ancient astronomers, who labored and toiled to investigate the laws of other worlds, had only have possessed the means which we enjoy for investigating the same, what would they not with their minds and perseverance have accomplished? Yet obstacles did not intimidate them, labor weary, nor drudgery disgust; and we reap the rewards of their protracted and successful exertions. They were very glad to hear from you, and inquired particularly after your health, etc., regretting that they did not have an opportunity of seeing you again before your return to Philadelphia. They were much pleased with the remembrance of their little daughter, and thanked me for it in her behalf, she having (as all little children should by eight o'clock) retired to her crib. This is a pleasant family, and it gives me pleasure to cultivate their acquaintance.

We reached Princeton in safety after bidding you farewell, and have now fairly entered upon the duties of another college term. May good resolutions be carefully kept!

Already have we attended three lectures on mechanics. Find them deeply interesting, and hope to have them neatly and carefully noted. Mr. McCulloh is a fine lecturer, and by many happy and practical illustrations enlists the sympathy and engages the attention of the class, as well as adapts the truths theoretically stated to practical purposes.

Our ride to Princeton from the depot was somewhat novel. There was a fair race between our hack and another as to which should reach the town first. It was indeed not quite so exciting as a contest between two large boats on the North River; still it was not without its interest, and we participated respectively in the feelings of the drivers. I am proud to state that we came off conquerors; and although it brought not its laurel wreath, or the applause of a crowded amphitheater, still as winners we united in a hearty laugh and mutual congratulations.

An unusually large number of students have arrived this week. Sixty have already been examined and admitted. Among this number you will be pleased to know that there are four *native regular Georgians:* Roll, Simpson, Reid, and Clarke. Two of these are pious—viz., Messrs. Simpson and Clarke. They came on in company with a Mr. Reid (father of one of the boys), a minister, who has a male academy at Woodstock, near Augusta. He is well acquainted with you, Father, and says that he will call and see you on his return. I soon got on the right side of the old gentleman, and then of the young men, stated the case as it stood, and before two hours had elapsed had persuaded them all to enter the Cliosophic Society. Judge Berrien's son also will be introduced at the same time, so that we will have five from Georgia entering our hall at the same time. *Very good* for the *Empire State of the South*. . . . Do say to Mr. Alexander that Mr. Walworth has had all of his notions regarding Whig Hall reversed, and has concluded to become a good Cliosophian. We have established a Georgia table in the refectory, and enjoy a sociable meal among ourselves, served à la mode Jersey but eaten Georgia fashion, spiced with Georgia interchange of feeling. This is pleasant, and I hope will continue to be so.

In regard to my change of location, I have determined *to remain in college*. Our room is pleasant now. My friend Lee has left college this session, and accommodations in town are rather few—and poor, as most of the best rooms have been previously engaged by seniors. These considerations have induced me to remain where I am; and as they have raised the board in the refectory to $2.50 per week, we are looking forward to better board.

Our members have been very active in their endeavors after new members for the hall, and we hope to have about two-thirds of the "newees." (College term: excuse it, but it is very significant; or you may take another: "greenuns.") It would amuse you to see how very green some of them are: now trying to employ the high-flown language of a metaphor, again perpetrating some miserable pun or piece of worn-out wit current with them, and then afraid to laugh until they see if it will be reciprocated; now strutting through the campus as pompously as the nabob of Arcot, with standers so stiff that to encounter a point would be almost to endanger a jugular vein, again trying to use college phrases and almost invariably applying them inappropriately. For one I have been very assiduous in my attentions to Muse Clio's prosperity—not in electioneering or hoaxing, but flattering myself that by simply stating the facts as they are, no one with his eyes thus opened will choose the wrong road.

Our gain over the Whigs reminds me of my visit to Mrs. Hope, during which she took me to task for this. She is very well, and desires many remembrances. The doctor is now in Philadelphia, and will preach for Mr. Wadsworth on Sabbath.

Have handed the professors their reports, and will take an early opportunity of distributing the remainder.

I have, I believe, given you all the items of interest in my possession, and shall now close with warmest love to you, my dear father and mother, and my sister, in which Brother unites. Hope that you have before this succeeded in fitting up your little parlor and are quite comfortable. I remain, as ever,

Your affectionate son,
Charles C. Jones, Jr.

Mrs. MARY JONES *to* MESSRS. CHARLES C. JONES, JR., *and* JOSEPH JONES[g]
Philadelphia, *Tuesday,* August 12th, 1851

My dear Sons,

We were very happy to hear from you last evening, and trust you have re-sumed your college duties with renewed vigor of mind and body, and resolu-tions to be faithful in the improvement of your time and opportunities. May the Lord bless you, my dear children, and enable you to persevere in the right way, and preserve you from the snares and temptations that surround you!

I have only time to inform you that our valued friend Dr. Howe of Columbia is now with us at the Markoe, and will probably stop at Princeton on his way to New York either this evening for the night or tomorrow for a few hours, coming in the morning and departing in the evening train. I know you will be delighted to see him and render him every attention that lies in your power.

Not a line from home since you left. Will write you both shortly. Let us hear from you often and particularly. With love from Father and Sister, and the same from

Your ever affectionate mother,
Mary Jones.

In haste.

REV. C. C. JONES *to* MESSRS. CHARLES C. JONES, JR., *and* JOSEPH JONES[t]
Philadelphia, *Tuesday,* August 19th, 1851

My very dear Sons,

Your two affectionate letters to your dear mother and myself have been received, and it afforded us pleasure to hear of your safe arrival and of the commencement of your college duties once more. Our best wishes and prayers and hopes attend you. Let us know your wants, whatever they may be, at any and at all times. I saw Professor Hope in Tacony, and he reported you both well.

Dr. Howe's visit to us was most unexpected and delightful. He stayed at the Markoe, and reported Columbia to be in a prosperous condition. But he gave you all the news himself. We begged him to stop at Princeton, and one special object on our part was that you might see him. We must never forget his generous hospitality and Mrs. Howe's to us after our severe afflic-tions in Columbia, nor their constant and sincere friendship. Gratitude and friendship are virtues which should adorn the character. "Thine own friend, and thy father's friend, forsake not" (Proverbs 27:10).

Since you left we have had our old chamber fitted up for a little parlor, and you know what a comfort it is to us. Old Dembry the drunkard painted it, and we had it handsomely papered at our own expense. Mrs. Watson gave us a sofa, and Mr. Watson a better carpet; and we had the rocking chair painted over and a half-dozen chairs varnished up, and shades to the windows, and the fireplace painted (as John said, "with black varnish"); and so we look uncommon.

But the crowning piece of new furniture is your sister's *elegant new rosewood piano*. Your mother after looking over all the city finally made selection of one at *Mr. Schomacker's;* and we think it is a sweet-toned and remarkably fine instrument, having all the modern improvements and some others beside. Now Mr. Cross can give her lessons in our parlor, and she can practice at any and at all times; and I hope her improvement will be rapid. Mother also plays, and plays some of our early love tunes, and reminds me of our courting days. We wish you were with us, my son, to play your flute and accompany your sister in her music, and Joe to sing. Then we would have you all at work.

While the room was fixing, your mother put the portmanteau in a chair and stood upon it to put things to rights on the shelf in the closet; and when she finished, forgetting she stood on the portmanteau, she stepped as from the chair alone; and she had a severe fall, bruising herself and feeling it for several days. But she is now quite recovered from it.

Mr. Alexander desires his best respects to you, and says he is glad his young friend has joined your society, and hopes he may be a good student and do well in all respects. He came and sat an hour with me at the office, and is a very pleasant man. Do your best to exert a good influence on all your collegemates, especially the more young and inexperienced who have just arrived—and some from your own state.

We have had letters within a few days from Montevideo and Maybank and Arcadia. Our old friend and servant *Mom Flora* at Montevideo is dead. Mr. Shepard says after being taken sick he thought she would recover; but she died in the faith of a Christian. It makes us feel very bad to have our people sicken and die, and we away from them. All the rest well at Montevideo and Arcadia. Crops of cotton injured by rains. Provisions they hope to make. County generally healthy. I enclose you Andrew's letter, which will let him speak for himself and interest you much.

Your Cousin Laura writes in excellent health and spirits, and reports your aunt and uncle well and all at Woodville. Miley had lost the sight of one eye, and your Aunt Betsy carried her up to Dorchester, and there she received a blow in the other and has been blind ever since! They hope she may recover, but they fear it may not be so. There is some mystery about the blow. Your cousin intimates her husband, who is an unprincipled fellow, may have done it! Time will show.

We are all well today, through a kind Providence. Mother and Sister unite in much love to you, and will write soon. Mother has just called at the office to walk down to the post office with me, and it is growing late. The Lord be with and bless you, my dear sons!

Your ever affectionate father,

C. C. Jones.

Mr. CHARLES C. JONES, JR., *to* REV. *and* MRS. C. C. JONES[t]

Princeton, *Tuesday,* August 19th, 1851

My very dear Parents,

Many engagements have until this hour prevented me from corresponding with you so often as I might have desired. Lecture has succeeded lecture in quick succession, and it affords me as much business to write them up as I can well attend to. Professor McCulloh is very interesting indeed, and for one I feel myself totally carried away in the pursuit of those enticing truths which are every day opening fresh and harmonious to our view. It is no wonder that the philosopher should become an enthusiast. Theories new and flattering, the result of close application and deep thought; hypotheses, perchance suggested by some fortuitous experiment or accidental observation—all these fill his mind with longing desires to test their applications; while the numberless phenomena of the natural world, like a mighty sea, are everywhere calling loudly for renewed investigation.

The man of science in the present day occupies a position superior to that of any that preceded him. The alchemist of old groped in darkness, and the knowledge which he gathered was but the result of chance experiment, unenlightened by theories worthy the name. The stores of ages which were deemed at first intricate and perplexing, the laws which baffled the research of many a lover of nature—almost all of these he with ready eye perceives, understands their operations, and presses onward to the examination of others which have as yet defied the explanations of human ingenuity. Though the ancients may have stumbled in the darkness with which they were surrounded, yet many were the truths which they discovered, many the laws regulating the operations of the physical world which they either explained or left a clue sufficient to lead those of after years to a full understanding of their principles. Add to these the acquisition of later days, and we at once have laid before us a field already known that requires the attention of an entire lifetime to understand but in general.

One in order to excel must devote himself to one particular branch, and that with a zeal and perseverance seldom to be met with. It has been well remarked that vague generalities are at best worth but little, and that microscopic visions of truth are the most permanent and valuable. Yet one in order to be a scholar now must acquaint himself with as many of these general truths as he is able, and devote his undivided attention to that pursuit which forms the aim of his life, which shapes the character of his efforts.

Behind this curtain of high-wrought interest which folds itself around the natural sciences there appears to me to be rather a void. Though a man might find out all the minerals of creation; though he explore the "unfathomed caves of ocean," and from the depth of the sea bring to light things which have for centuries lain unseen save by Him who formed the "depths unknown"; though he search the forests of Africa and tell of birds and beasts unknown—yet, considered abstractly, to what does all this amount? Simply the advancement of science, an increase of knowledge which few have the means to obtain, and perchance the honor of being a distinguished naturalist.

We may view the subject, however, in a more enlarged light. We may trace the grand operations of the philosopher as, with telescope in hand, he tracks the planets as they roll along in the immensity of space, watches with steady eye their revolutions in their unchanging orbits; as he generalizes those universal laws pervading all matter, working out problems momentous in their results, and worthy the mind of one who feels himself the handiwork of his Creator and appreciates the talents committed to his care; as he discovers principles which affect the welfare of mankind in general and lays down rules which the mechanic, the gardener, and the workingman in general follows—although ignorant of their high origin and the toilsome investigations through which the mightiest of earth's intellects have passed ere these same principles were simplified and brought down to the level of everyone's comprehension.

Yet how few ever attain to such an eminence! While we find a Newton or a Galileo, how many do we see, like so many lesser stars, borrowing the only ray which they reflect from the bright diadem which encircles their brows. What an enlarged view is one in view of these things led to entertain respecting the majesty of Him whose glory fills heaven and earth, respecting the boundless stores of wisdom yet unrevealed upon this our little globe, and the powers of that emanation of the Deity which He himself has formed and implanted within the breast of man to be expanded, cherished, improved. Though much has been done, how much yet remains, and how loud the call for men of decision, of prompt action and persevering industry. Better be a first-rate bootmaker than a groveling pettifogger at the law, respected by no one, distinguished for naught. The one lives honestly, acts his part well, and receives the reward due his performances; the other misuses the confidence of his fellows, is a dead weight to society, a dishonor to his profession. Honesty and close application, then, with a fixed purpose in view and strenuous efforts to attain the desired end, all controlled by the fear of the Lord and a due regard to one's neighbor, seem the only ways by which one may expect to attain a permanent, deserved, and proper estimation among his fellows.

I am afraid that I have been indulging in rather a prosaic, long, and dull kind of reverie. In fact, I have almost forgotten what I have been saying, having commenced this letter rather late, after laying aside my lecture book, and desiring to hold a few moments' pleasant conversation with you.

We were much delighted at seeing Dr. Howe from Columbia. He appeared very well, and was much pleased with his visit to Princeton—or to particularize a little, with the appearance of our neat chapel, things around college, with his visit to the theological professors, sight of their library, and walk in the graveyard, where we went through in critical style, with the long Latin inscriptions graven on the tombs of the great and of the good of the land who lie entombed there.

A week ago I received one of the severest falls I ever experienced. On this wise happened the affair. It was very dark, and I was moving at a rapid rate through the second entry of Nassau. All of a sudden I found myself deprived of that equilibrium which it behooveth everyone to employ his utmost to preserve, and was pitched head foremost on my head and eye upon the hard and veteran bricks beneath—bricks which have withstood the lofty tread of dignified seniors, puffed-up juniors, impertinent sophs, and green little freshmen. The servants had very carelessly left a whole pile of old furniture (bedsteads, etc.) in the entry; and in the dark I was thus precipitated over a table, the inertia of my body being in quick motion, not permitting me to cease in speed until the electric spark had been struck from the hardened clay. We often hear of the fulminations of great intellects. Not wishing, however, to appear boastful at all, or to assume anything to myself which is not properly belonging, I will cease, only remarking by way of a winding up that a kind of fire flashing was very remarkable just at the moment when head and brick came in contact. The blood flowed freely from the temple and eye, and seeing that the cut over the eye was quite deep, I went down to Dr. Schanck and got him to close it for me. I hope that no scar will remain, and am unable as yet to tell what will be the issue in that respect. The wound is healing very fast, and all swelling subsided several days since. Told Dr. Maclean about the position of the furniture, and for about fifteen minutes he had a regular war with the servants. I almost expected that the old gentleman was about to inflict not capital but corporal punishment upon the negligents.

August 20th. I began this epistle rather too late to complete it, and upon going to the post this morning was very much pleased to find C. C. Jones among the happy few who were favored with letters. Yours, my dear father, has been duly perused, and let me return my sincere thanks for its receipt. Had no idea that my dear mother had suffered from the same cause that I did. Hope, however, that she will speedily recover. Your little parlor, so nicely fitted up, must present a pleasing and attractive appearance, and necessarily adds much to the comfort and quiet of your abode. And Sister— what shall I say to her on the receipt of so handsome a present? Surely she should become quite a proficient in that sweet and lovely science. May Calliope impart some of her mildest tones, and Euterpe guide the pliant finger and teach it to call forth notes of harmony!

Andrew's letter is characteristic, though refined with the taste of another. It seems rather an anomaly, when considered in the abstract, that a hand used to labor should wield the pen of so ready a writer, or the mind practiced in daily commonalities clothe its expressions in rhetorical form.

Received also a letter from my friend Lee. He is now in Wyoming Valley on a visit to Baker.

We have this morning commenced the study of Locke, and I was called up first recitation. These are the studies which please me most, and I expect to be deeply interested in its perusal and study.

We are all quite well, and hope that you are all in the enjoyment of similar blessings. Excuse this long epistle—if it be too long and pedantic. Brother unites with me in best love to you both, my dear parents, and Sister. I remain, as ever,

Your affectionate son,
Charles C. Jones, Jr.

Rev. C. C. Jones *to* Mr. Charles C. Jones, Jr.*ᵍ*

Philadelphia, *Tuesday,* August 26th, 1851

My dear Son,

Enclosed you find a very affectionate and handsomely written letter from your Uncle Charles Berrien. Without observing the direction I opened it with other letters in the office, and seeing from whom it was, read it—and your mother and sister also. And it was much pleasure to us to do so. We wish you and your brother to keep up a correspondence with all your uncles, and I would wish you to write to your Uncle James if you have not done so.

Mr. and Mrs. John B. Barnard passed through Philadelphia last week. We were very happy to see them. *Nat* graduated with the third honor—good for the old field school; and his father thinks of taking him to assist him in business. . . . Mr. and Mrs. Barnard have gone on to Saratoga. His health not very good.

My dear son Joe, I have very bad news for you. Miss Houstoun has written home to her niece about you; and her niece has "requested her not to negotiate any marriage for her, since she is very fond of dancing and enjoying herself, and she knows *you* will be a *minister.*" So you must console yourself under the impression that you have time enough yet, and there are as many good fish in the sea as ever were caught out of it; and as the world is unquestionably improving, the good ones are increasing.

We have had a most pleasant visit from Mr. and Mrs. Alberti: traveling for health. They just left us this morning; to return in a few weeks.

No news but Cuba news, which you see in the papers. However much we may sympathize with the Cubans in their oppression and desire and right to deliver themselves from a tyrannical and bloody military despotism, yet our government cannot countenance any hostile preparations on the part of our citizens, nor allow armaments to be fitted out against a friendly power. Individual citizens cannot be prevented going where they please; but they bear the responsibility, and throw themselves beyond the patriotism of our flag, when they enter Lopez' service. There is no telling where the matter will end. Our people are becoming highly excited. In New Orleans the excitement has been tremendous. But if Cuba be overthrown, then under the hand of Providence it is one of *the strongholds of popery cast down.* Liberty of conscience must follow, and Protestantism will advance. And in this result we will all rejoice.

On coming into the office this morning whom should I see but our old friend Mr. *Watson* from the seminary in Columbia. He is looking remarkably well, and has just returned from New York, where he has been to receive his appointment from the Board of Foreign Missions. He is assigned to the *Chickasaw Mission,* and consequently will not leave the United States. He sends his kind regards to you both, and regrets not seeing you here.

Your sister has just received a letter from your Aunt Betsy dated the 19th. All well, and send love to all. Write soon. Mother and Sister send much love. I am, my dear sons,

Your ever affectionate father,

C. C. Jones.

Mr. CHARLES C. JONES, JR., *to* REV. *and* MRS. C. C. JONES[t]

Princeton, *Thursday,* August 28th, 1851*

My dear Parents,

Your letter, Father, was duly received, and permit me in reply to return my thanks for the same as well as for that forwarded within. Uncle Berrien writes in good spirit and very affectionately, and I shall take an early opportunity of continuing the correspondence.

Even in this quiet little town did the recent news from Cuba create some excitement, although in an incidental way. Several of the boys have openly expressed a desire to join the side of the republicans and aid in the deliverance of that island from the oppressive yoke of degenerate Spain—yet I rather expect with the tacit assurance that circumstances will not permit. With many, an extra jet of courage is apt to burst forth the farther we are removed from the scene of danger. We cannot, it is true, in the capacity of a nation interfere with the domains of other nations without just cause, or aid in any revolution which would result in the injury of any foreign power. Yet we can demand reparation when our honor has been insulted, when a stigma of contempt has been cast upon the Stars and Stripes of our country, and the mail steamer of these United States, with her colors at her head, forced to round to before a miserable little Spanish armed vessel. No wonder that the people of New Orleans should have been greatly excited at the murder of the fifty Americans. Many of them were from that city, and the manner in which they were put to death, as well as the subsequent mode of treatment, was atrocious to such a degree that we might in vain search for a parallel even amid the benighted regions of heathenism. I hope in my heart that Lopez may be victorious, that the friends of liberty may flock to his standard, and Cuba be delivered from those chains which tyranny and oppression have thrown around her, from that iron rule which retards all advancement in religion, morality, intellectual culture, and national distinction.

A state of liberty is the prerogative of man. Each day are nations awakening more and more to a sense of this fact. Hungary struggled for it;

and although for the present she seems unsuccessful, yet there are hearts there still which long earnestly for the pure atmosphere of freedom. The Queen of England is obliged to yield in a measure to this prevailing disposition to demand and obtain natural rights, and is granting privileges and performing deeds which the iron-hearted spirits of former years would never have conceived of. It is only a month or two since that she attended the parties of a wealthy merchant of London—no nobility about him except such as his wealth and attainments may have imparted.

Saw the notices of the recent meetings in Philadelphia and New York. Tonight they expect another in the latter of these places. It must require a good deal of self-possession and calmness to address an assemblage of this character. The people who compose it are in all probability much excited, and unless the speaker exercises due caution in his sentiments he will but add fuel to the flame, propose measures which are either impracticable or merely evince the hand of a braggadocio.

Again has a great man fallen among us. It is surprising what a number of prominent individuals—persons full of attainments and their country's honors—have deceased within the last few years. Ex-Governor McDonald was, I believe, considered one of the finest orators in the Southern states— at least in Virginia.

Am very much interested in the study of Locke's *Essays*. Such studies particularly please me. Today we were examined upon that branch.

Dr. Torrey is now giving us lectures on chemistry. He is certainly a beautiful experimenter, and seems entirely at home in his department, which is highly entertaining yet quite hard to remember accurately. He teaches only the gases, metals, acids, etc., and their compounds. Professor McCulloh lectures on heat, light, electricity.

Dr. Carnahan preached a very fine sermon two Sabbaths since on swearing, and Dr. Maclean followed on the next in a tirade on dueling.

Received a letter from Lee this morning. He has given up the idea of returning to college, and intends teaching in Georgetown, D.C. He is fond of change; and it is only in this way that one can account for this disposition of himself, although other causes may operate.

I am now very busy. In four weeks I will have to deliver my senior speech on the stage, and have not completed its composition yet. We have so much lecture-writing to attend to that our time is much occupied—that is, if one will only attend faithfully to his obligations. This, however, is a most improving exercise, not only tending to impress the subjects more forcibly upon the mind, but also giving one a freedom of expression in committing his ideas to paper. Clio Hall is in a prosperous condition, and I think that I have made some progress, at least, in the line of extemporaneous debate. Here we have a fine field for such exercises, and it rests with the individual to improve or misuse these advantages.

Several students are on the point of being dismissed for gambling, drunkenness, firing torpedoes in recitation room, and similar offenses of that character. They will probably be graduated before their time this evening.

Father, I am sorry that I will have to ask you for more funds, but those given me in Philadelphia were not sufficient. If it be not convenient I can wait a while longer. Here you will see an account of the manner in which they were expended:

To board at Joline's, before session term, two days	$1.12½
To a bedstead	3.00
To a notebook	.87½
Paid into the college treasury	104.00
To subscription to *The Nassau Monthly*	2.00
To subscription to erecting a monument to William H. Timlow, a deceased classmate	4.00
Paid regular dues to Clio Hall	2.75
To a copy of Locke's *Essays*	2.00
	119.75

The board has this session been raised considerably, and they make the seniors pay several dollars more for the purchasing of chemicals, etc. I now owe $6 for instruction this session in Italian, $2 for a chemistry, and will have to get one or two more lecture books. Besides this, in three or four weeks we will speak on the stage, and each division has to defray its own expenses in the way of music and printing of handbills, which is always done. I also owe Dr. Schanck something for curing my sore throat, and for closing the cut over my eye, which I told you about in a previous letter. I regret that I have to ask you for more money, but I feel assured that you will see that the expenses incurred were necessary. I expect that $20 will be sufficient.

Hoping that you are all well, I remain, with much love, in which Brother unites,

Your ever affectionate son,
Charles C. Jones, Jr.

We have established a senior debating club, and the members seem to take quite an interest in the performances. This is free from all fines and designed solely for improvement. A member is requested to leave if he conducts himself in the least ungentlemanly or fails to perform his appointed part. It is, moreover, arranged so as not to interfere with our other duties.

REV. C. C. JONES *to* MR. CHARLES C. JONES, JR.[g]

Philadelphia, *Saturday,* August 30th, 1851

My dear Son,

Your very pleasant and interesting letter was received this morning, and we were glad to hear of your own and your brother's health.

The climate for some days past has been delightful, and they tell us we shall have no more oppressive days. I have begun my walks before breakfast again, and your mother has provided a tonic of the cherry bark for me to take twice a day. Between that and the walk I ought to grow stronger.

Your dear mother and sister are quite well, and are now busily employed doing up muslins.

We have had no letters from home since I last wrote you, and no news from Cuba. The probability is that Lopez has failed!

I enclose you a check on the Philadelphia bank for $50, which you can get cashed at the Princeton bank, and with it pay up all your dues, and all that your brother may owe. I have reason to praise you both for your carefulness and economy; and it is always a pleasure to your mother and myself to supply all your wants and to contribute in every way to your comfort and welfare.

Our heart's desire and constant prayer for you both is that you *may be saved;* nor can we ever feel at rest concerning you until you have both made your peace with God through our Lord Jesus Christ.

Mr. Powel is in a hurry to go to the post office, and I must close. Mother and Sister unite with me in much love to you both.

Your ever affectionate father,
C. C. Jones.

Mr. Charles C. Jones, Jr., *to* Rev. *and* Mrs. C. C. Jones[t]

Princeton, *Tuesday,* September 9th, 1851*

My very dear Parents,

This is rather an unpleasant morning with us. The atmosphere is damp and chilly. Nature seems to participate in the feeling, and the trees appear aware of the change which will soon rob them of their verdant foliage and leave naked trunks to withstand the frost and storms of winter. Man alone doubts his frailty, and although in all nature he views the hand of time, still he imagines his person free from that change which "sweepeth over all."

The package conveyed by Mr. Williams was duly received, for which let us thank you.

On last Saturday we spent a pleasant evening with the Misses Brearley. One of their nieces was with them—a very good-looking lady, although from her appearance I would rather judge her just out of boarding school and consequently unskilled in the arts of polished life. Beauty is captivating, but there is no object in this world that I dislike more than a lady who, though pretty, has not the common sense to carry on a respectable conversation or to show by her conduct that she has refinement and intelligence. Next to religion a mother should be possessed of a polished and substantial education—not one of these in the present day deemed by many fashionable; for these if analyzed will in the main be found to consist in a smattering of French, a regular graduation in the line of novel-reading, some music, and only a bare outline of history. No wonder that we find such a number of affected little beings—inert, with morbid sensibilities, the only excitement to obtain the last novel, the acme of their aspirations to flirt with some poor fool who can be duped by their artifices. Formerly I used to think every lady "almost divine," but now I do candidly believe that they are not one whit behind young men of equal ages in every sort of improprieties. At least, such is the case with the majority of instances in this place and Philadelphia, if general consent be true. Nothing could induce me to be yoked with one of these, even though she should hold the purse of Fortuna and be a grand-daughter of the nabob of Arcot. Give me a regular Southern lady with a warm heart, a true hand; and if she carry a horn of plenty with her, so much the better. However, I have any quantity of work before me, and until that is in part accomplished, let all concerns of that nature be banished. Tupper makes the following remark:

> If thou art to have a wife of thy youth, she is now living on
> the earth;
> Therefore think of her, and pray for her weal: yea, though
> thou hast not seen her;
> They that love early become like-minded, and the tempter
> toucheth them not.
> They grow up leaning on each other as the olive and the vine.

However true this may appear in poetry, I am rather disposed to question its bearings in real life.

The end of the college course is but the beginning of sober study. 'Tis then that one has a fixed end in view (or certainly should have), and to the attainment of this every effort of the mind should be directed.

We are at present all well. The college is quite full, and a plenty of oc-cupation. Three weeks from next Saturday our division speaks on the college stage.

We are very much obliged to you for the enclosed in your last letter, and will try and make a judicious disposal of it.

One of our students left this morning for Mississippi, and manifests a dis-position to join in the Cuban expedition if a suitable occasion offered. Am rather inclined to believe, however, that this was only spoken—not meant.

We as a class have extended an invitation to Dr. Henry of the Smith-sonian Institute to deliver a course of lectures to us. As yet, however, we have not heard his decision.

Hoping to see you here shortly, as well as to hear from you frequently, I remain, my dear parents, with much love to you both and Sister, in which Brother unites,

Your ever affectionate son,
Charles C. Jones, Jr.

Mr. Baldassair has been having his love letters to Baltimore corrected by the subscriber. Most amusing to read them.

Rev. C. C. Jones *to* Messrs. Charles C. Jones, Jr., *and* Joseph Jones[g]
Philadelphia, *Tuesday,* September 16th, 1851

My dear Sons,

I write principally to say that your mother and I will pay you a visit *on this coming Saturday,* God willing. We shall leave here in the nine o'clock train, and you will oblige me by telling Dr. Maclean that we shall avail ourselves of his invitation and stay with him in his hospitable mansion. I wish you also to see Mr. Ross and engage him to send me over in a conveyance *with a gentle horse* on Sabbath morning to Lawrenceville, where I have an appointment to preach, and to return in the evening. Would like him to send someone with me to take care of horse and conveyance: everything to be ready immediately after breakfast at Dr. Maclean's door, that I may reach Lawrenceville in due time.

We think of going on from Princeton on Monday as far as New Haven to pay a brief visit to Mrs. and Miss Clay.

We have heard from home this week. All our relatives and friends and people generally well, but the county rather sickly at present. Your mother and sister unite in affectionate remembrance to you both. May God's presence and blessing ever attend you!

Your affectionate father,
C. C. Jones.

Mr. Charles C. Jones, Jr., *to* Rev. C. C. Jones[g]
Princeton, *Wednesday,* September 17th, 1851*

My esteemed Father,

It afforded me much pleasure, upon opening your favor of the 16th, to find that you and dear Mother will be in this place on Saturday. I this day acquainted Dr. Maclean with your acceptance of his kind offer, at which he expressed his satisfaction and replied that he would be very happy to see you both. Will have the necessary arrangements made in regard to your passage to Lawrenceville on Sabbath. I am very glad that Mother and yourself intend leaving the city (although it be but for a few days) and paying a visit to esteemed friends. The vacation will be pleasant, and the friendly intercourse and social interchange of sentiment delightful, calling up associations of other days of the companion with whom mutual attachment has given and reciprocated.

Have been for some time attending to a sick young man from Georgia (Oscar Lewis), formerly of my class. His indisposition was caused solely by excess. For the last eight days he has been drunk, having during that time taken about four hundred drinks, or about fifty quarts. You may well imagine in what a condition he is. Has had *mania a potu,* and even now is in danger, and will be for many days, although the chance for his living is much better. The first night that I sat up with him, he would spring from the bed, roll and toss, call upon us for "only one more drink," adjuring by

227

all the powers of heaven and hell. It was certainly one of the most awful sights I have ever seen.

For further news I will await your arrival. With best love to self, dear Mother, and Sister, I remain, in haste,

Your affectionate son,
Charles C. Jones, Jr.

MR. CHARLES C. JONES, JR., *to* REV. C. C. JONES[t]
Princeton, *Thursday,* September 18th, 1851

My dear Father,

This will introduce to you my friend Mr. R. C. Clarke, of Augusta, Georgia. He is a member of the sophomore class, connected with the Presbyterian Church. You will find him a very pleasant and gentlemanly young man, and I know that you will be pleased with him; and as he is recently from home you may hear from some friends in that part of the state. He wishes to make some purchases in town, and see some of his acquaintances in Philadelphia.

I wrote you yesterday, and have made all necessary arrangements for your plans while in Princeton. Hoping to see Mother and yourself on Saturday, I remain, with much love,

Your affectionate son,
Charles C. Jones, Jr.

MR. CHARLES C. JONES, JR., *to* REV. *and* MRS. C. C. JONES[t]
Princeton, *Tuesday,* September 30th, 1851

My dear Parents,

You have again returned to Philadelphia, and I trust feel yourselves refreshed by that interchange of friendly sentiment in New Haven. I omitted writing last week, not knowing whether or no you had prolonged your stay beyond the anticipated period. This morning, however, I met Mr. Ross upon the street, and received from him my overcoat, this affording proof positive that you were once more in the City of Brotherly Love.

Since you left us we have been subject to a disagreeable change of weather, but are now blessed with the light of a beautiful sun—an atmosphere as pure as that which we are told is wont to settle upon the fair land of Italy, and a sky so blue and cloudless that a Thomson might have tasked his powers to tell its loveliness. The heavens above seem as if gathering new beauties, while the fall of the leaf and the golden tinge upon the grove betoken the changes of the seasons. Seemingly immutable, it heeds not the varied scenes of earth, but still unfolds itself, a mighty canopy, above the face of creation.

Last evening we beheld one of the most beautiful sights I ever witnessed. Just over our heads a bright halo of light seemed circling the zenith, ever changing yet always forming anew, assuming varied shapes as if to call forth renewed exclamations of admiration; while ever and anon bright coruscations of light were seen glancing along the north, then shooting athwart the azure vault of heaven, as if the attendants of Aurora, thinking their mistress slept, were toying with a sleeping world, and bright fairies, stealing rays from her radiant car, were sporting with each other in festive joy. It was the aurora borealis—the first I ever witnessed. The cry of "Heads out!" was echoed and reechoed through the campus, and soon the ground was crowded with numbers—some just from the arms of Morpheus, others quitting the student's desk to gaze upon the loveliness of nature. Gladly did I drop my pen and move out to admire this singularly attractive phenomenon. If such be its appearance at this place, what must it be in those polar regions where every ray darts fresh from its source and finds a thousand images in every iceberg reflecting back with undiminished luster its bright counterpart! Often had I heard of these, and listened to the traveler as he recounted its glories. Yet the impression fell as far short of the reality as this reflection here must of its original. I conversed with Professor Alexander a short time this morning in regard to it. He was very happy to elucidate anything which appeared enigmatical, and was just explaining the manner of its operation and the several observations he had taken during the night, when suddenly we were stopped by a stranger, and there the matter ended. I intend, however, to see him again and become further acquainted with the principles and operations of this highly interesting phenomenon.

This afternoon Mr. Green delivers his initial sermon, and Dr. Jones preaches also.

Saturday our division speaks. We are preparing for the debut, and hope not to disgrace ourselves. We would be very glad on many accounts to see you here at that time, and the only objection would be that in case of a failure the disgrace will be doubly felt. However, "they best succeed who dare" is an ancient proverb, and upon this principle we will proceed. Will expect you at that time, and also Sister if engagements will permit. The ladies have become disgusted with the performance of last Saturday, due to the ridiculous and indecent manner and matter of one speaker (Stavely) who pronounced upon the bloomer costume. It was a ridiculous and disgraceful performance, and he merits disapprobation. For this reason we will probably have but few present on the 4th of October.

Everything is moving on very smoothly. A plenty to do in the line of lecture-writing. Professor Henry has delivered a few lectures on true science. They were admirable, and in every sentence you could trace the workings of a powerful mind.

Hoping to see you all on Saturday, I will close, as nothing further of note remains to be conveyed. Brother unites with me in sincere love to you both, my dear parents, and Sister. I remain, as ever,

Your affectionate son,
Charles C. Jones, Jr.

Philadelphia, *Wednesday,* October 1st, 1851

My dear Brother Charlie,

Father received your interesting letter this morning, and we all thank you for your graphical description of the aurora borealis. I wish very much I could have enjoyed the view with you, for it is something which I have a great desire to see.

I think that some of us will come on Saturday to hear you speak, and I am glad to hear that you have a finely written piece, and hope you may do as well as you did the day before commencement.

Yesterday I witnessed the funeral procession of Stephen Girard. It was composed of masons and the city council. His body was removed some months ago to the college, and yesterday the masons went out to perform the burial services. I was very much disappointed in the procession, for I had anticipated seeing some pompous parade, and I believe that it was the general impression that it would be something quite impressive. But instead of this there were about fifteen hundred masons adorned with blue scarfs and aprons who marched on the sidewalks out to the college. The most striking thing in the procession was the music, which I think was unusually good.

I have just seen Miss Clayter, and she says that the aurora you saw was visible here also. Her uncle saw it about eleven o'clock on Monday night. I wish I had known it.

Tell Brother Joe that his friend Mrs. McDonald left this morning, and sends her love to him. Miss Houstoun will remain some time longer.

Mother saw Grandmother, Uncle Joe, Miss Newell, and the children in New York; also Mr. and Mrs. Gracey and Belle of Columbia. She met Mrs. Baldwin in one of the stores, and says she came up and spoke to her very warmly indeed. I should like very much to see her again, and I am pretty sure you would like to do the same.

I was very lonely indeed while Mother and Father were absent, although I had a very kind friend in Mrs. Blamyer of Charleston, who took care of me during their absence. She is a very pious lady, and I do not think that I have ever seen more sweetness and dignity combined. I am sorry to say that she left this morning for Charleston.

Mother received a note from Cousin Marion Erwin this morning; she sends her love to Brother Joe and yourself, and says that her wedding will take place on the 4th of November. Mother is very busy purchasing and having made her wedding outfit.

Father received letters from Mr. Shepard and Mr. Rahn; they mention that there has been a great deal of sickness in the county and some deaths. James Somersall is dead. As Mother wishes to add a few lines, I must finish. With best love to Brother Joe and yourself, I remain

Your ever affectionate sister,

Mary S. Jones.

Philadelphia, *Wednesday,* October 1st, 1851

I have been intending, my dear son, to write you every day since our return from New Haven, but from constant shopping during the day am so tired at night that I am glad to lie down and rest. I am making an effort to have all the wedding things ready for the next steamer, but it will require constant work to do so.

Our visit was very pleasant, and your sister, brother, and self have invitations from Dr. and Mrs. Wells and Mrs. Clay to visit them if your lives are spared next summer and attend the commencement of Yale College. We found Willie quite grown. He is as tall but I do not think as stout as Joseph. Has entered the freshman class, and hope he will do well.

Your father and sister hope to be with you on next Saturday, Providence permitting, and if I can, will come too. I trust, my dear boy, you will do yourself credit upon the occasion, as I believe that you will. Your college course is rapidly drawing to a close, and soon life with its realities, its cares, and its duties will press you into the field of action. May you, my beloved child, have the peace of God in your heart and wisdom from on high to direct your steps aright!

I have not time to write more. Father and Sister unite with me in fondest affection to your dear brother and yourself. Why does he not write us?

Ever your own affectionate mother,
Mary Jones.

MR. CHARLES C. JONES, JR., *to* REV. *and* MRS. C. C. JONES^g

Princeton, *Thursday,* October 9th, 1851

My very dear Parents,

In compliance with a sense of duty, pleasure, and habit I have now my pen in hand to discharge an obligation which should be met at least once a week. Those are always pleasant moments to me which are spent in communing with absent friends, and above all with you, my esteemed parents. We regretted, Mother, that your engagements were such as to prevent a visit to Princeton. Although Father and Sister were with us, still we felt that one was absent from the entire group.

In early youth when in the bosom of family, affected with all the tenderness and guarded with all that care which a parent can alone bestow, the young heart, alike regardless and ignorant of its true welfare, often wishes to throw off restraint, and like the prodigal esteems it of manly independence to leave the warm hearthstone of his native place and be partially, at least, removed from the benign influence of those towards whom every living love of his heart should be turned. After years, however, when circumstances determine that separations must be made, when with his increasing days he has gathered some few lessons from the book of experience, then does he in

231

reality long for childhood, that he may improve his advantages in a better manner, that he might dwell upon with greater delight, and cherish with warmer emotions, the wholesome admonitions and instructions, the general influence and moral training of the family circle. There are ten thousand charms we feel not which cling around a family altar, family friendships, family claims. He who deliberately or wantonly refuses to answer to such calls must possess a heart more barren than Sombrero's rocky isle. Yet how heedless of these we are until reflection and a removal from them convince us of their value!

The questions, What shall I do in this world? What station shall I occupy? What good perform? What benefit be to the human race? are of vast importance to a young man just entering upon life, and involve in their answers decisions second alone to that great first question, Whom will ye serve, God or Mammon? Lately the choice of a profession has been constantly before my eyes, and every time that it is presented comes along with it that empty void, that rudderless feeling, that conscious want of some great touchstone for the trial of motives and actions, devoid of which man is but at best the creature of fancy, change, caprice, and sin. I believe that it is well that one should keep revolving the subject in his mind. The great difficulty with most young men seems to be this—viz., they hope to do great deeds, hold important trusts, and become the chief of the land; and yet they seem unwilling, like the young Corsican at Brienne, to labor and toil while others slept, imagining that favors and promotion will spring up as if elicited by some magic wand. Fortunately a stern reality dissipates these idle dreams of the mind. In whatever vocation I may be called to act, I do hope the perseverance and application may be granted—not to say anything of probity and enlightened religious views.

Last evening our division of speakers was invited over by the hospitable old Dr. Maclean to partake of a supper. There we met Professors Forsyth and Hope. The time was very pleasantly spent in good conversation, intellectual and entertaining. The old doctor's fine engravings and book of Shakespeare illustrated were exposed, spiced with anecdotes of a recent visit to Scotland; and in conclusion, you may depend, the chicken salad, ice creams, and cakes were not lost upon refec boys used to "light bread and beef." Dr. Maclean reminds me more of one of our regular hospitable Southern gentlemen than almost any other person with whom I have met. You have experienced his kindness and will allow that I speak not with a biased view, although the presumption lies on the part of the pies, etc., of last night.

Just before retiring to bed several of my friends mentioned that they were going upon a serenade and requested my presence. The night was lovely: all nature in quiet repose, even the zephyrs forgetting to breathe, while the moon was beaming with an effulgence soft yet beautiful. Delightfully did the strains of music float upon the midnight air—soft, harmonious, well calculated to break the calm slumbers of fair maidens and awaken the poetic emotions of the soul. The young gentleman who sung and accompanied on the guitar has one of the sweetest voices I ever heard. A beautiful nosegay was thrown from one of the windows.

I suppose you have examined with great pleasure and interest the partial notices of the Georgia election. It appears well established, or rather confirmed, that Hon. Mr. Cobb will be elected by a large majority. Senator Foote has no opposition; and probably Mr. Bigler will be the successful candidate in Pennsylvania. So that the Union party will be very generally successful.

Just at this moment I heard a cry of "Heads out! Fire! Fire!" and upon going to the rear of North College found quite a large fire, the boys having set certain little unmentionables on fire.

We are both quite well, and will be very busy for a week, the quarterly examination beginning on next Tuesday. With much love to you both, my dear parents, and to my sister, in which Brother unites, I remain

Your affectionate son,
Charles C. Jones, Jr.

Mrs. Mary Jones *to* Mr. Charles C. Jones, Jr.ᵍ

Philadelphia, *Saturday,* October 11th, 1851

My very dear Son,

Your dear father left us this evening at six o'clock for Wilmington, Delaware, where he expects to preach tomorrow and return on Monday morning; and as I have the prospect of an uninterrupted hour, will devote it to my dear absent boys.

Mr. Snowden came and took tea with us, and we have just parted with him. He expressed the sincerest interest in you both, and best wishes for your prosperity in this life and the life to come. Says Miss Ruth King is to be one of Cousin Marion Erwin's bridesmaids.

Much to my satisfaction I succeeded on Wednesday in forwarding her whole wedding outfit from tip to toe. She is to be married on the 6th of November.

And on the same night your Uncle James expects to be married. He wrote your father a very affectionate letter this week inviting us all to his wedding. I should be happy to accept, but it will be rather early for my plans of departure, although your father urges me to go early; and as my great object in going—after the pleasure of seeing friends—is to benefit our servants, perhaps I should not delay. I have hesitated on account of your father's health, but he has improved very much recently. The interest of plantation and people certainly demands that some of us should visit our *home—spot doubly precious* in this cold land of strangers! If I dared anticipate the future, how cheering would the prospect be of gathering again around our own hearthstone, kindling once more the spirit of love and devotion at our family altar, and enjoying the sweets of friendship around the social board!

Much was given us of happiness and enjoyment in that dear old home. I do not repine that our Heavenly Father has now withdrawn them all. He has His own purposes to fulfill. We perhaps were ungrateful of our mercies and blessings and misimproved our privileges. We cannot receive any punishment or affliction beyond or in any degree equal to our deserts. The only wonder, when we reflect upon our sin and rebellion, is that we are not destroyed and consigned to endless woe. This turning away of God's wrath, this long-suffering and tender mercy, comes to us alone through the abounding love, the atoning Blood, the all-sufficient righteousness of Jesus Christ our adorable Redeemer. Oh, that God would send His Blessed Spirit to take away our hearts of stone and give us hearts of flesh, that we might be melted down before the Cross!

You, my precious child, must feel your need of this Saviour, your utterly lost and ruined condition, ere you can be saved. There is no other name under heaven given among men whereby we can be saved. Oh, believe it that you may have *life*—yes, *life for your precious soul!* On last Sabbath Day a noble-looking and healthy young man worshiped in Dr. Boardman's congregation. On Monday he was unwell; it proved to be inflammation of the bowels; he was in agony. Dr. Boardman was frequently with him. Every breath was an exhortation to the young men around him not to delay repentance to a dying hour. He had to struggle with his sins and grapple with the monster death. The strife was terrific. Before his decease he expressed a hope that he had received pardon through the merits of Christ; and living or dying he desired to be consecrated to God's service. Saturday afternoon found him laid away in his silent grave. Such is life! And such are we in the hands of the Almighty.

Mr. Peace came very unexpectedly to see us this afternoon, having recently returned from Virginia; looks remarkably well, and expects to go South this winter again. He will have to abandon all thoughts of preaching from the state of his health and seek some other field of usefulness.

Lewis Pynchon has returned, and we are looking for your Cousin Charlie every day. Major and Mrs. Porter and Miss Clifford Alexander spent two days in Philadelphia this week. Your friends always inquire particularly after you both.

Your affectionate and interesting letter, my dear son, was received yesterday, and your brother's today. You are a dear good child in your love and attention to us. At times I have felt quite grieved that Joseph forgets us. It was a great piece of self-denial to me in not accompanying your father and sister to hear you speak, but I was entirely gratified by the commendations they bestowed upon you on their return. Your dear father was very much pleased. My greatest earthly joy is to hear that my children acquit themselves with fidelity and honor in all things. I shall look with interest for the quarterly report. Dr. Maclean is truly a noble and generous-hearted being. Every time I see him these traits of character are more and more impressed upon me.

I will now close for the night. May you have hours of peaceful slumber, and be prepared in body and spirit to enjoy the heavenly rest of the holy Sabbath Day! *Then* especially are my thoughts with and around you!

Monday Morning. We had, my dear son, a pleasant Sabbath yesterday, although the day was rainy. Mr. Henry of Cranberry preached twice in the Central Church; "The Sabbath was made for man" and "Keep thy heart with all diligence, for out of it are the issues of life" were his texts. Both practical and excellent sermons.

Your father has just returned from Wilmington, taken a cup of coffee, and is off for the office. Your sister is unwell from a cold. Colds are prevailing almost like influenza, I am told; be careful of yourselves. I will send your other flannels by the first opportunity; and write me if there is anything you may want before I leave. Your father desires me to go early in November. I shall want to see you both before I do. We are expecting your Cousin Charlie every day. Our house is now very full, and I fear he may find difficulty in obtaining a room at the Markoe. I will write Joseph soon. Mr. Green was in Philadelphia yesterday; hope you will call to see him. Father and Sister desire best love to you both, with the tenderest affection of

Your mother,
Mary Jones.

Mr. Charles C. Jones, Jr., *to* Rev. *and* Mrs. C. C. Jones[t]

Princeton, *Thursday,* October 16th, 1851

My dear Parents,

Your letter, Mother, was duly received, and let me thank you for it. It is needless to affirm that all such are highly prized; and may I profit by the wholesome truths and admonitions therein contained!

Having just completed our examination, I feel more at leisure, and will devote a few moments to a transmission of such items of news as may be floating in my memory. I fear, however, that all have been displaced by recent "pollings," and that a cohesion of ideas can nowhere be found. Locke, you know, attributes to the memory two facets: *slowness* and *oblivion.* These are, I am afraid, my besetting sins; and I hope that if the thoughts conveyed prove incoherent that you will find a reason for this in the fact that the subscriber has recently been so much busied with metaphysical disquisitions and philosophical inquiries that it is a hard matter to recall the mind wandering after abstract theories to the realities of converse with existing beings.

Have recently been diving into the depths of "complex ideas," "mixed modes," "relations," etc. Although it is a hard matter for light to shine out of darkness and the rude beginner to comprehend the workings of a master mind, and with his weak eyes regard with intelligence the scintillations of a brilliant genius, yet may we hope that in this tremendous plunge bottom has been found here and there, and that amid the vast array of complex ideas, mixed modes, and substances, some stray, simple ideas may have been conceived and lately expressed. At least, let Dr. Carnahan's report so declare.

Professor McCulloh has taken us at one time amid the noise of steam engines, again beside the rattlings of machinery taught to trace the bomb in its airy flight, to search within the arcana of nature for those principles of science and gleanings of knowledge which seem securely entrusted to darkness until thence unveiled by that wonder-working animal man—now calling from honored tomb the noble shades of Newton, and bidding them explain the philosophy of the fact that an apple will fall to the ground, and a planet preserve a course unchanged despite the revolutions of centuries; of a Bendetti, who in the fair skies of Italy was wont to trace the paths of warlike missiles, adapt a parabola to the curve of a swift cannonball, and thence argue the effect of gravitation; of a Galileo, who in the consciousness of right opposes the prejudices and ignorance of a benighted world, inventing telescopes, revealing to all what the mind of man had never conceived, and contending manfully for the Copernican system, firmly supporting the cause of truth. Professor McCulloh is in the main a fine lecturer, although sometimes rather desultory in his remarks. He certainly possesses a very large fund of general information, and appears at home in almost any subject.

In fact, the faculty here are a very gentlemanly set, and in by far the majority of cases it is a student's own fault if he does not improve and get along smoothly. Just abstract Professor Alexander and let him wander alone amid his labyrinths of hyperbolas, asymptotes, returning curves, cycloids, etc. I will stand with anyone in the other branches; but when he enters in, the heart goes faint, the memory sinks into oblivion, and the whole man shivers before his doleful board, as one shrinking from a grapple with "airy nothing," or rather "the little end of nothing whittled to a point, having neither length nor breadth but merely position." I like to study mathematics, but can never bring myself to "poll up" on it solely for the sake of taking a grade. If the object be the discipline of the mind, you will have acquired this, if at all, when regularly studying; and if we look to the ultimate fact of the case, very little else can be obtained, for few will become professors in that line. The knowledge of such intricate abstract reasoning is soon lost; and if one has not improved his mind, then no good has been derived from such a course. This year we are engaged in studying an astronomy composed by the right honorable gentleman, which he was pleased to term the other day "the skeleton" of that study; and I thought that with a good deal of propriety the appellation of "purely mathematical" might have been prefixed. Instead of attempting, in some measure at least, an outline of the poetry and beauty of the science, our professorial author, in compliance with his own inclinations and fancy, prefers giving only the abstruse formulas and dry mathematical investigations, thus presenting a view enough to chill the blood in the bosom of any but an abstract being, which by right should be excited into a genial warmth of admiration.

Last evening a cry of "North College on fire!" was heard, and upon rushing with the crowd into the campus we found one of the chimneys in a large blaze, which lighted up the objects around. Fortunately, however, it gradually disappeared, causing no injury to this time-honored building.

Dr. Torrey has been absent from Princeton during the past week, and we have had no examination with him, and now flatter ourselves that we will escape his sarcastic queries. He has very little respect for a student's knowledge, possesses a fine command of ready wit, and generally expends it upon the heads of those on trial.

Hoping that you are all well, and enjoying this fine weather, I remain, with best love to you both, my dear parents, and my sister, in which Brother unites,

Your affectionate son,
Charles C. Jones, Jr.

P.S. You will probably receive our circulars by the end of next week or the first of the next.

Hurrah for *Bigler*—but *Cobb first!*

Mr. CHARLES C. JONES, JR., *to* REV. *and* MRS. C. C. JONES[t]

Princeton, *Saturday,* October 25th, 1851

My dear Parents and Sister,

As you doubtless feel much interest in the proceedings of yesterday, and were denied the privilege of being present at so solemn and imposing a ceremony, I have determined to repair the loss as much as possible by attempting a short, yet I trust faithful, description of the events that then transpired.

The poor and ordinary man dies: without parade is wrapped in his winding sheet and silently laid away in his cold and cheerless grave. The multitude look but for a moment, pass on, and the person of yesterday rests now unnoticed, forgotten and perchance unepitaphed. Death quietly marks his victim. The land hears not the tread of the last enemy, for he has singled out one upon whom no distinction has been lavished, who lived and died unknown save to a chosen few. Yet there are times when the great, the good, the learned, the honored are called away, when he to whom multitudes have pointed as a "father in Israel," at whose feet numbers have sat and drunk deep of the sage counsels and profound reasonings of his mighty mind, is now required to render an account of the ten talents committed to his care, and rest from his important labors. Far be it from me to attempt any eulogy upon the character and attainments of him who so recently has been taken from our midst. Youth, inexperience forbid; and you well know that to enumerate his virtues were but to dishonor them.

I promised a description of the funeral ceremonies and have wandered. At half-past two the students of the college met in the chapel. We had our respective badges of the two literary societies; and these veiled in mourning, with our professors at the head (Messrs. Carnahan and Hope excluded), we marched four deep to the church, the members of Clio Hall being first in procession. Breaking into double file we entered the church, passing up into the west gallery, the Clios occupying the seats nearest the pulpit, and the Whigs the remaining pews on that side and about one-fourth of those on the northeast end of the opposite gallery. The seminary students took up the rest on that side. The body of the church was reserved for the members of Synod and other clergymen who might be present. Upon either hand the ladies sat, leaving but little room for gentlemen, who as many as could filled the aisles.

The corpse was brought in and deposited in front of the pulpit. Just before it sat four of Dr. Alexander's sons—Dr. James and Addison, Hon. Mr. William Alexander, and the physician. Calm and motionless they remained. As I looked upon their massive brows, bearing the impress of mind cultivated and enlarged, while just behind were many of the synod, some of them hoary with declining age, others in the vigor of manhood, the thought was forcibly impressed upon me: How soon must all this talent lie dormant on earth? Save the savor of life, and the sweet perfume of good works which the good man leaves behind, the wise, the learned perish; and if they look not for a reward beyond the tomb, still are they, like all others beside, most miserable. In the pulpit sat the venerable Dr. McDowell, and on either hand Drs. Murray and Plumer. A stillness reigned through the large assembly, and as the hymn was read by Dr. Murray, "Why do we mourn departed friends?" the choir echoed the sentiments in pleasant unison, and with much effect.

After prayer and another song Dr. McDowell arose—an aged brother officiating in the last services paid to the memory of his companion. He seemed to feel his own weight of years, and that for him too these obsequies must soon be performed, that with him "the silver cord would soon be loosed, and the golden bowl broken at the cistern." Calmly he announced the subject of his discourse, as contained in the 14th Chapter of Revelations and 13th verse: "And I heard a voice from heaven saying unto me, Write, Blessed are the dead which die in the Lord from henceforth: Yea, saith the Spirit, that they may rest from their labors; and their works do follow them." Beautifully did he enlarge upon the topics contained in this portion of Scripture, with a perspicuity and force which must have commended them to the consideration of everyone present.

His concluding remarks were employed in giving a brief account of the prominent positions occupied by the deceased, together with the place of his birth, childhood, collegiate course, and the confidence reposed in him, as well as his fidelity in the discharge of every trust. He mentioned that Dr. Alexander requested two or three days previous to his death that no eulogium or encomiums of any kind should be pronounced, but that only a simple statement of facts should be made, and this only so far as might seem indispensable. From this account it appears that the venerated and departed dead was a native of Rockbridge, Virginia, graduated at Lexington in the same state, acted subsequently as a missionary, at a later period presided as president of Hampden and Sydney College, and for the last thirty-nine years of his life was a professor of the Princeton Theological Seminary. All his associates have died except two: the speaker and a Rev. Mr. Milledoler. It was by the special request of the deceased that Dr. McDowell delivered his funeral sermon, and ably did that aged servant of the Most High discharge the important duty assigned.

The services in the church were concluded by Dr. Plumer, who read a psalm and prayed. The congregation remained seated, and the order of procession was announced. Dr. Alexander was an honorary member of the American Whig Society, and the members of that hall formed the head, Cliosophians next, then the clergy, corpse, family and friends of the deceased, theological students, and lastly the inhabitants and strangers of Princeton.

The procession extended from the First Presbyterian Church very nearly to the graveyard. Arrived there, the college students filed to the right, forming on the east, the clergy on the north, seminarians on the west, ladies and others on the south, while in the center was the grave, near which the doctor's sons stood with other relatives. After the coffin was lowered Dr. Magie spoke for a few minutes in a mild and touching manner. Mr. Umsted, Dr. Maclean, and another person (whose name I did not learn) directed matters and acted as marshals. I did not see Mrs. Alexander or her daughter, although I presume they were in attendance, for three or four carriages followed immediately behind the corpse.

It was one of the largest funerals I have ever witnessed. The strictest decorum and propriety were maintained throughout the entire exercise. The college students in their best suits and with badges and crepe, the uniform black of the clergy and seminarians, all conspired to render the scene very impressive, solemn, and becoming.

He is buried near Dr. Hodge's wife—at least in that part of the graveyard: a central spot and eligible in location. Another distinguished man lies in that enclosure which already contains a long list of illustrious persons—men of worldwide reputation who, although sleeping still, are awake through the living name and the many good deeds left behind them.

What a wide difference exists between the obsequies of this good man and those of Aaron Burr! Though the latter was possessed of a mind and talents which if well directed might have redounded to the glory of a nation or the welfare of the church, still his heart was rotten to the core. The voice of ambition and lofty aspirations was to him louder than the call of God. To gratify such motives seemed his highest aim, for the attainment of which he shrank not from plunging the dagger into the soul of domestic happiness, from proving traitor to the land which gave him birth, from reducing to ignominy and shame the confiding hearts which had entrusted their keeping into his hands. And as a natural consequence of all these crimes he lies lamented by none—unepitaphed, unwept.

How opposite the character and end of him whom so lately we have lain in the silent tomb, knowing that the gates of death are to him but the portals of that heaven where joy, peace, and love forever reign! Early a servant of

God, long has he remained a faithful high priest, a benefactor to the community in which he lived, an ornament to the church, a Gamaliel in the holy law. Many there are who shed tears—copious, gushing tears—not of sorrow and distress but of exaltation and pious joy, who, though they mourn his absence, still rest assured that they will go to him "seated in Abraham's bosom" —a bright jewel in the crown of Him who shall finally come to judge the world. While many will in that day curse the former, while the remembrance of his many evil deeds shall crush that heart once so eager in the pursuit of worldly honors, to the exclusion of everything that was good and holy, and the perpetration of sins innumerable, thousands will rise up and call the latter blessed. Souls redeemed through his instrumentality shall shine as stars in his crown of glory, and the holy views inculcated into the breasts of many call forth witnesses in testimony of his faithful and Christian walk. Filial love will raise a monumental stone; yet his memory is embalmed in the remembrance of multitudes who will delight to cherish it and do him honor.

It was a privilege to be present on such an occasion. And may his example prove a guide to erring, sinning men! The remembrances of this scene will never be blotted from my memory, and I regretted, my dear parents and sister, that you were not allowed to participate in those last tokens of respect.

I fear that you are already tired with this protracted epistle; yet thinking and knowing that you would feel a deep interest, I have been thus imperceptibly led into somewhat minute detail.

We have completed our examination, and you will doubtless receive the circulars in a few days. Brother has left this evening upon a voyage of discovery in the neighborhood of the canal.

When do you expect to visit the South? Hope that you will leave early, and enjoy a long and happy renewal of friendships and associations existing in that land of childhood and riper years. Will you not be in Princeton for a few hours and let us bid you farewell? I wish that you all could go down together, for in proportion would the enjoyment of such a trip be enhanced. In regard to our visit to Liberty next December, we are both at your disposal, and will be happy to comply with your wishes in every particular. I ought by rights during the next vacation to review for the approaching examination and prepare two speeches; yet these are but secondary considerations, for I will get an appointment at any rate, if nothing prevent at the coming commencement.

The doctor is now with you, and I presume is once more applying himself with diligence to his Aesculapian doctrines. May he grow wiser than his teachers are! I feel indebted to him for the interest taken in the sale of my pony, and would like to make him a present of some kind or other.

Have received no letter from home for some time. Wrote a joint letter to all relatives on the Island last Thursday; hope that it will find them all well and in fine spirits.

I believe that I have communicated whatever of interest has recently transpired, and will therefore close with warmest love to you both, my dear parents, my sister and cousin. Brother unites in same.

Your ever affectionate son and brother,

Charles C. Jones, Jr.

Rev. C. C. Jones *to* Mr. Charles C. Jones, Jr.[g]

Philadelphia, *Tuesday,* October 28th, 1851

My dear Son,

Your most interesting and well-written letter describing the solemnities of the funeral of the venerable Dr. Alexander on the 24th inst. was received yesterday, and afforded us great satisfaction. An unusual pressure of business, but more especially the indisposition of your dear mother, prevented my attendance. It was my wish to have taken her up to Princeton on that occasion. She is, I am happy to say, up again, and hope will have no more return of it.

You are this day, my dear son, through the kind providence of God, twenty years old. I can hardly realize it, and yet it is so. To say to you that your parents feel the most constant and earnest solicitude for your temporal and eternal welfare, and that there is nothing which they would not cheerfully do for the promotion of that welfare, would be to repeat what you have heard from our lips times without number, and which we trust our whole lives as parents has demonstrated to you. We have through much imperfection (at least on my part) dedicated you to the service of God and brought you up in His fear; and the all-absorbing desire and earnest prayer of our hearts has been that you might be made a partaker of His grace, a believer in His Son our Redeemer, and an instrument for His glory on earth. This will compass the chief end of your existence, and nothing else will. Your own conscience and judgment, the Word and providence of God, impress this upon you.

We have been grateful for your growth into manhood, for the remarkable health you have enjoyed, for your intellectual development, for your studious and industrious habits and the improvement you have made of your advantages; and we have been particularly grateful for your affection as a son, your dutifulness and endeavors to please your parents and accomplish all their desires concerning you, and for your affection to your dear brother and sister, and for your increasing sobriety and the correctness of your principles and deportment. All these things are very sweet and pleasant to us, my dear son, and we hope you may continue to advance in everything that is lovely and of good report.

But what will intelligence, virtue, sobriety, amiability, accomplishments, learning, standing, respectability, and influence and the honor of the world avail if you have *no religion!* Consider this momentous question. While you remain unreconciled to God by the precious Blood of His Son, your soul is in danger of eternal death! We never can have peace of mind concerning you until you have passed the great and necessary change. It is a most proper time for you to turn your thoughts to the salvation of your soul. You have

241

gone three years beyond your mother and two beyond your father in their profession of religion; the one professed religion at seventeen and the other in the eighteenth year. We can through divine mercy say: "Hitherto hath the Lord helped us." And we would commend the service of so good and glorious a Redeemer to you, and urge you to an immediate approach to Him, that you may obtain the pardon of your many sins, and life everlasting in His name. For this we daily and earnestly pray; and at whatever time you may remember our secret or social hours of prayer morning and evening, you may rest assured that you are mentioned before God, and His mercy and grace and salvation invoked for you. Would that we could hear the glad tidings that you have found peace with God!

I send you by mail a certificate of honorary membership of the Board of Missions upon your birthday as a birthday present and memorial of your parents' love. My love to my dear son Joseph. Mother wishes to add a postscript. Sister sends love.

Your ever affectionate father,
C. C. Jones.

MRS. MARY JONES *to* MR. CHARLES C. JONES, JR.[g]

Philadelphia, *Tuesday,* October 28th, 1851

My very dear Son,

I have had time for little else than to think of and pray for you today. May the best blessings abide with you, and if it be the divine will, many many years of happiness and usefulness!

Your dear father has expressed fully our hearts' love and desires for you. He is now waiting, and I have not time for more. With best love to you both,

Your affectionate and devoted
Mother.

Take care of your certificate, and we will have it framed to hang in your study.

MR. CHARLES C. JONES, JR., *to* REV. *and* MRS. C. C. JONES[t]

Princeton, *Thursday,* October 30th, 1851

My dear Father and Mother,

Your highly esteemed letter, with the accompanying certificate of honorary membership of the Board of Domestic Missions, was duly received and would have been answered yesterday had not a necessary engagement in lecture-writing prevented. It would be useless for me to attempt in terms of conventionality to return you, my beloved parents, the sincere thanks and heartfelt obligations which I experienced for the great honor conferred upon so unworthy a recipient. In fact, this is but one of those innumerable acts of parental kindness and tender regard which have all my life been bestowed with

242

such lavish bounty. Never was there a son who had greater cause of thankfulness, who should bless God with more fervency of soul for the kind and religious parents which He in His goodness has granted, or who ought more to reverence, obey, and put forth every effort to honor and comply with their wishes. When I look back upon the past and consider the present, all, all is but one continued scene of repeated love, even where childish folly should have provoked displeasure: letter upon letter of holy teachings, prayer after prayer for divine blessing, watchful care and anxious solicitude, gratifications of such desires as might tend to real happiness and good—all conducted in that manner and with such motives as parental hearts alone know and feel. For all these, my dear father and mother, I thank you, and feel myself under eternal obligations.

May time show that these have not been exerted wholly in vain! Not that I would in the least hint at or intimate a future return for these many favors, for a hoary head would yet be wanting in years ere a proper conception of these obligations had been formed. Yet it is too true: twenty years of my life have passed away, and how little has been done; yea, truly nothing is accomplished. Imperceptibly the years roll by, and we suffer their escape unimproved. What a thought it is that in the Day of Judgment each misspent moment will rise up as a witness and condemn the ungodly! What a number are now enrolled against me, and there they will remain unless removed by the atoning merit of the Prince of Peace. Solemn thought! May the goodness, long-suffering, and forbearance of God lead the erring feet into the paths of virtue and rectitude!

Always will I prize and esteem this distinguished favor, and preserve it as a mark of my father's and mother's love; and may the unworthy recipient in after years cherish a sincere regard for that noble association, and in the good providence of God be enabled to contribute to its support and advancement! I have always esteemed this, ever since I knew anything of its nature, as one of the most philanthropic and useful institutions ever planned, founded, and sustained by Christian effort. Now it possesses triple attractions: you, Father, being one of its chief supporters, Mother a zealous advocate, and your son through your united kindness one of its members. May I never prove either in action or word unworthy this honor! Let me again thank you for this distinguished gift and assure you that I will retain it in lively remembrance. It shall be carefully preserved, and this certificate shown to after generations.

Yesterday I received a letter from Cousin Laura mentioning the death of Mr. Louis LeConte. As you will be much interested in the details, which are very painful, I will forbear any rehearsal of them and enclose you the account as given by her.

Heard also from Roswell—that is, only so far as an invitation to a wedding goes. Hope that the parties will enjoy themselves, and that the union will result in mutual satisfaction and good. Is it usual for one invited who is un-

243

able to attend to notice the invitation and return his acknowledgment? If so, I shall do it, but will suspend operation until I hear from you.

Have been very much interested lately in the perusal of Ovid's *Metamorphoses,* or, as the Latins would term the work, *Ovidii Metamorphoseon.* His fancy is exuberant, his colorings many of them vivid, and the style clear and forcible, bordering often upon the sublime. In proof of this, take his description of the creation of the world, beginning thus:

> *Ante mare et tellus et quod tegit omnia, coelum*
> *Unus erat toto naturae vultus in orbe,*
> *Quem dixere chaos: rudis indigestaque moles,* etc.

In this we have the embodiment of those opinions concerning our origin, and that of the globe, entertained by the ancient Romans. It is an easy matter to trace the rays of truth which, despite the clouds of superstition and error, now and then beamed in their souls; for in many respects this description bears a close resemblance to that given by the sacred historian. His primitive pair after the flood (viz., Deucalion and Pyrrha), their salvation, the wrath of Heaven upon beholding the sins of the fourth age, and the submersion of the earth, as well as the first state of man, all agree very nearly with the Mosaic account—at least so closely as we have any reason to suppose when the sun of truth had been eclipsed, and even those rays which illumined the minds of the wisest sages were shorn of their luster, and proved but dimly reflecting the image of the great First Cause and His wonderful works among the children of men.

Again, take Phaëthon's request in the second book, beginning with the 35th line—the description of the passage of the chariot of the sun as guided by this youthful boy. It is drawn hither and thither by the celestial horses—now wandering amid those regions where Scorpio stretches out his curved arms, threatening to seize the timid boy; now frightened by the headlong steeds, who, observant of the fact that their wonted master no longer held the reins, ran riot in their liberty; again descending near the earth, wrapping it in flames and causing the heavens to assume a lurid glare from the sparks and fire generated by the swiftly rotating axles. When we read this, so vividly is the picture presented that it requires no stretch of the imagination to conceive the whole and regard it as true.

The piece has its moral. Sol was the progenitor of Phaëthon, and promised to grant any request which he might demand. Little did he imagine that the youth, enamored with that bright car with which he was wont to course the azure vault and chase dark Night from the face of nature, would demand a ride in this and vaunt that his puny arm could guide those steeds which often proved rebels against the arm of him who was himself the King of Day. Despite the warnings of Sol, he insists, the request is granted, and we see the result of his aspirations. After being lost amid the constellations of heaven, having set the world and all its great mountains on fire, with the seas, lakes, and rivers—looking down, his knees tremble, tremble with great fear. Darkness comes over his eyes. He wishes that he had never sought to touch his father's chariot or curb his frantic horses. But now Phaëthon, with the flames of the clouds kindling in his hair, falls from the car as a star seems in calm twilight to fall from the heavens, which Eridanus receives and washes its visage. The folly of youth is bound up in the bosom even of a god.

I have here sketched only a small part of the barest outline; and you know the original possesses a freshness and vigor, besides those beautiful shades of meanings and other advantages of a similar nature, which baffle all attempts at correct translation.

It is an endless source of pleasure to be able in this manner to converse with the shades of departed greatness, to mark the great conceptions of their minds; for thereby we are enabled to mark the changes of time, the differences which it has wrought in the conceptions of men; and therein we trace notions and feelings which, unlike the present, have passed through no editions but are the fresh productions of the minds by whom they were originated. It is surprising how much of the present is borrowed from the past. Even in my limited acquaintance with the classics, often am I surprised when I chance upon certain expressions and thoughts which previously I had deemed the property of some modern writer, whereas in reality the latter could lay no claim whatever to it or them, but should be classed in the category of Irving's bookmakers. It would afford me much pleasure if I only could enjoy more time for reading, but this is so much occupied with lecture-writing and other college duties that such employment must in a great measure be laid aside. However, everything in its season, and this is now the season for collegiate pursuits.

I have just stepped to Mr. Babbitt's room to see if our grades are out, and find that he is not in. They are tardy in making them out, yet I hope that you will receive them in a few days.

I was very sorry indeed, my dear mother, to hear of your indisposition, and hope that it will not prove serious.

Many have lately been sick in college from diarrhea—caused most probably by the bad water. We have had only one pump that will yield any at all, and that only periodically. Water has been brought from the canal for the use of those in town. Refreshing showers have, however, recently descended, relieving the wants of man and beast. Yes, while I now write, the cheerful patter of the raindrop may be heard—sweet to the ear in the silence of evening, suggestive of thought and meditation, congenial to study, and agreeable to the couch-seeker because inspiring a feeling of security. Ever since the time that Morpheus shook those drops from the branch above the head of Virgil's pilot have men delighted to hear the patter of the raindrop when snugly in bed. Thomson felt this pleasure; and many before and after him have without doubt experienced a similar delight.

We are progressing pretty well, I believe, and everything seems very quiet.

Hoping to hear from you so often as it may prove convenient, I remain, with the sincerest love to you both, my dear parents, sister, and cousin, in which Brother unites,

Your ever affectionate and grateful son,
Charles C. Jones, Jr.

MR. CHARLES C. JONES, JR., *to* REV. *and* MRS. C. C. JONES[t]

Princeton, *Thursday,* November 6th, 1851

My dear Parents,

Although nothing of immediate importance or attraction has recently transpired, yet here I am, in obedience to a well-established custom, penning you a letter, with scarce any object save that of conveying remembrances and informing you that we are still plodding along, endeavoring to meet our duties as they appear.

Have you received the circulars yet? If not, it is high time that they were sent. You will there see that upon two branches—viz., natural philosophy and Locke—I have taken first with a few others. Now for the chemical grade. It appears very small. Yet let me say that by far the majority are under that. Again Dr. Torrey did not call upon me to recite during the entire session, although every lesson was regularly prepared. The only recitation was that for examination. Then he took me not upon the textbook but upon some incidental remarks made in the beginning of the quarter. So you see, that is not the fairest possible estimate of one's proficiency. His grades are in general very uncertain. He seems to put down just the first number which enters his head. One great cause of this probably is that he cares rather little about the whole matter, is not acquainted with the students, has never given an opportunity to many of them to recite, and is engaged perchance in other occupations which are so much more attractive that his duties as professor in this respect are deemed trivial. In proof of this, the man who passed the best examination in the class, who had recited beautifully, received for a grade 70. Another of a similar stamp, who had made equal progress, 81. Others again, totally ignorant, were presented with 84 and 85; while others still, who had neither recited in class nor at examination, were graded as high as 90. These are facts. Yet far be it from me to attempt anything unfavorable to Dr. Torrey's abilities, or question his motives. He certainly is a beautiful lecturer, and never fails in perfectly illustrating his principles experimentally. We receive no more lectures from him until next session, as he has engagements in New York during the winter.

We are now studying logic and reading Aristotle's *Art of Poetry,* together with our astronomy, natural philosophy, etc. I hope to take a good stand at the end of this session, as it will be the last except that incident upon the final which I will have before graduation.

Lately I have perused with great pleasure a life of John Paul Jones, by Mac-

Kenzie, an officer in our navy. He was certainly a brave man, ambitious of distinction, and to all appearances zealously attached to his adopted country. Some of his exploits were as notorious for valor, cool and determined courage, masterly seamanship, and military skill as may be found in the annals of any nation. To launch upon the deep in a small bark in the face of an English squadron, devastate the coasts of Great Britain, burn her shipping, conquer her frigates of war, sack her towns, were deeds of no common stamp. Danger seemed invested in his eyes with peculiar charms; and when the battle raged long and loud, then did he appear to the best advantage, animated by the terrific nature of the scene. The first to hoist the American flag (then a pine tree with a rattlesnake coiled around its root in the attitude of defense) upon the ocean. The first to receive a salute from a foreign power in token of recognition as a free and independent nation. Long did he cherish that banner; often did his brave arm contend manfully in its cause. Let the flames of Whitehaven, the conquered *Serapis,* and the vanquished *Drake* show proof. As a proof of his valor, see the French king presenting him with a golden jewel-hilted sword and the epithet of Knight of Honor; Congress conferring a medal, Catherine of Russia the rank of rear admiral, and a nation its hearty returns of glad acknowledgments. He was very much given to admiring the female sex, writing verses, and often declaring in an open manner the secrets of his breast, fond of honors, always fortifying himself with certificates formed at his own instigation to prove the handsome manner in which every step had been taken. By the English he is denounced as a high-handed robber and pirate. This, however, seems very natural when we remember that he repeatedly defeated them upon an element the mastery of which they had long boasted.

Nothing has transpired during the past week. The gasworks are nearly completed, and we hope soon to enjoy the superior light. I will now bid you good night, hoping to hear from you as often as you may deem proper. Brother unites with me in warmest love to you both, my dear parents, sister, and cousin.

Your affectionate son,
Charles C. Jones, Jr.

P.S. Friday would be the day which above all others we could spare to pay you a visit. The rest of the week we are engaged in taking lectures, none of which I would wish to miss, for it would break in upon the uniformity of my lecture book. Any day, however, that pleases you will suit us.

REV. C. C. JONES *to* MESSRS. CHARLES C. JONES, JR., *and* JOSEPH JONES[g]

Philadelphia, *Thursday,* November 6th, 1851

My dear Sons,

I write now merely to request you both to come down to Philadelphia on Saturday morning—the early train. Your dear mother wishes to see you both before she leaves for home, which may be in the course of a few days. And it may so turn out that I shall go with her and, Providence permitting, see her safe there.

Ask your leave of absence until Monday evening, and give your professors the reason for it. Remember to give my sincere regards to Dr. Maclean. Mother and Sister and Cousin Charlie all join in love.

Your ever affectionate father,
C. C. Jones.

$5 enclosed.

Mr. Charles C. Jones, Jr., *to* Mrs. Mary Jones^g

Princeton, *Friday Morning,* November 7th, 1851

Dear Mother,

Yesterday I consigned an epistle destined for the City of Brotherly Love to the care of Uncle Sam, and hope that you have received it ere this. Now a postscript is simply added to inform you that Father's letter was received, and that we will gladly avail ourselves of the opportunity of being with you tomorrow.

Your son,
Charles C. Jones, Jr.

VII

Mrs. Mary Jones *to* Miss Mary Sharpe Jones[t]

National Hotel, Washington, D.C., *Wednesday,* November 12th, 1851

I hope, my darling daughter, that you find yourself comfortably and pleasantly situated, and that you will strive by your correct deportment to commend yourself to your teachers and all with whom you may be associated as a good scholar, a kind friend, and above all an humble and consistent Christian, letting your light shine to the praise and glory of God. You are old enough to discern characters: avoid all companionship with the irreligious, and be careful *how* and *with whom* you associate. If our Heavenly Father spares our lives and prospers our plans, we shall soon meet again; in the meantime you must be cheerful and happy and try to improve your time.

We have had a pleasant journey thus far, and met at Baltimore an interesting gentleman and lady just returned from England who entertained us with particular descriptions of the Crystal Palace and the present state of things in France. He thinks the moral degradation of the last-named place as great as in any other period of its history. They were English people, now living in Richmond and preferring America to their native land.

We had an unusual number of children in the cars who were rather troublesome at times, but not to ourselves. I always make allowances for them, and strive to remember the days when our own children were helpless infants—and we too ourselves—needing the watch and care of tender parents.

We arrived so late, and shall leave so early in the morning, that there will be no time for seeing the Capitol. The Monument is progressing finely. We may not be able to write you again until we arrive at Marietta.

We are now seated in a delightful room with an anthracite coal fire burning most cheerfully, looking like a wood fire. Your dear father is seated in the large rocking chair reading and meditating upon his little Testament whilst I write. I will leave the next page for him. Everything is so natural around us, a calm gentility pervading every department, it seems like home already.

If you have the time, be sure and call to see Miss Cunningham and your other kind friends. Give much love to Cousin Charlie for us, and present our kind regards to the Misses Gill. Your father left a note on the center table for them. And now good night, my dearest daughter. May the Lord bless you, ever prays

Your own affectionate mother,
Mary Jones.

Rev. C. C. Jones *to* Miss Mary Sharpe Jones[t]

Washington, D.C., *Wednesday,* November 12th, 1851

Your dear mother, my dear daughter, has left me this page. All she has said to you I would repeat over. We confidently expect that by the blessing of God you will in all things demean yourself as a lady and a Christian. We shall constantly remember and pray for you. Never forget that whoever may be separated from you, your Lord and Redeemer is always with you.

The day has been pleasant, and our journey prosperous. Mother was so sleepy this morning she could hardly keep her eyes open; in fact, she took a newspaper to read and fairly dozed and slept over it. And at dinner she had a great appetite and enjoyed one of her favorite dishes: *wild duck.* I saw hanging up in the yard of the hotel in Baltimore a haunch of venison (a saddle of it, I should say); a *raccoon* clear of his skin; wild ducks of different kinds; the real partridge; and a fine large wild turkey gobbler! So the guests cannot lack for good dishes.

Our English friends said the Crystal Palace would be *taken down;* the nobility around it do not like to be incommoded by so great a building and such crowds as must always be about it. The balance in hand after paying all expenses and for the building itself will be fully $500,000—a pretty good speculation for Johnnie Bull. He is a shrewd old fellow. Having lived long on the earth, he has a great deal of worldly wisdom. The expenses to those who *exhibited* articles is said to have been enormous. Our English friends gave Louis Napoleon a very bad *private* character. They characterized the present government of France as a military despotism, and not at all a republic. There are a hundred thousand men of all arms in the army in and around Paris. You go nowhere, said the lady, without meeting *soldiers, priests,* and *religious orders, male and female;* and the Roman Catholic religion is virtually the religion of the state, and governs all. Liberty of conscience is a name. There is much to be done in France yet before that nation will know the blessings of civil and religious liberty. We have reason to bless God for His mercies to us as a nation. It is He who has made us to differ and has exalted us unto heaven above other nations.

We hope, God willing, to leave in the morning after breakfast: half-past eight. Stopping the night here is much to Mother's comfort, and will ease off the fatigue of the journey. Give our love to the doctor. I feel troubled about his throat. Tell him he must take care of himself, and not go out much at night until he gets better. The Lord be with and bless you, my dear child!

Your ever affectionate father,
C. C. Jones.

Rev. C. C. Jones *to* Miss Mary Sharpe Jones[t]

Charleston, South Carolina, *Monday,* November 17th, 1851

My dear Daughter,

We arrived here in safety on Saturday afternoon at $2\frac{1}{2}$ o'clock. Your mother was deathly seasick: the wind was ahead, the sea rough, the passage protracted. We left Wilmington Friday at 1 P.M., so you see how long we were coming. But a kind Providence has brought us safe. Mother is quite well and bright, and says she can't go back to Philadelphia; she believes she will have to stay at home!

Our friends the Misses Jones received us most affectionately. I preached yesterday at Dr. Smyth's; had great difficulty in speaking, from hoarseness contracted on the journey.

Everything looks bright and natural. Clear sweet skies and spring weather. We leave for Marietta in about an hour. Have stolen a moment to write you. Love to Charlie, and kind remembrances to all friends. Your dear mother sends the greatest love to you. May God bless and keep you, my dear child!

Your ever affectionate father,
C. C. Jones.

Write your brothers.

MISS MARY SHARPE JONES *to* REV. *and* MRS. C. C. JONES[t]

Philadelphia, *Wednesday,* November 19th, 1851

My dear Father and Mother,

Many thanks to you for your kind letter, which was received with feelings of peculiar joy and gratitude.

The Misses Gill welcomed me on Wednesday in a very kind manner, and the girls have done much to make me happy. I have a bed to myself, and Miss Sidney and Miss Emily are my roommates. The girls think I occupy the most unenviable position in the house, but I think I am much more pleasantly situated than those who sleep in a room with five, beside a teacher. Miss Sidney is generally disliked, but she has always been a favorite with me.

I have received the letters which Brother Charlie through mistake carried to Princeton; also one from Aunt Mary Robarts and Mr. Shepard.

Cousin Charlie has been quite unwell, but is better now. He came to see me last night, and as I was going down Miss Sarah said very quickly: "Tell the *young man* that Friday and Saturday are the days for receiving visits."

On last Saturday Susan and Maggie Dixon invited me to come out and spend Saturday and Sabbath with them; but Miss Sarah told them that she never allowed her young ladies to spend a night out with anyone. Yesterday she called me and told me that I might take tea with them whenever I wished to do so.

On Sabbath I went with the ladies to Dr. Parker's church. He preached a very good sermon from Matthew 7:13—"Enter ye in at the strait gate," etc. I expect he is a very practical preacher.

On Sabbath Miss Mary gave me quite a new definition of the belief of the New School Presbyterians. She says that the Old School believe in the Confession of Faith and the Bible, but the New School believe in the Bible and Confession of Faith. I told her I did not believe a word of it. At first she said this in fun, but afterwards she said that she thought this was the difference, and thinks the New School are by far the best part of the church. I wish you could have heard her criticizing Mr. Cheeseman's book; and I was quite astonished and amused when she had finished to hear her say that she had never read it.

On Sabbath evening Mr. Packard has a Bible class here which he makes very interesting. After the class is over, the members of the church have a prayer meeting among themselves. Last Sabbath they invited me to unite with them. I did so, and hope these meetings may be profitable to me. The religious influence here is remarkably fine. Every evening from seven to half-past is devoted to private reading of the Scriptures and meditation. This is, I think, a very beneficial regulation.

The ladies are very kind to me, but still I am very lonely, and am anxiously waiting for the time when you shall return. I look at your likenesses two or three times every day. I have not as much time to study or practice as I had before I came here; I have about two hours to study and one hour to practice.

I am glad that you will be in time for Uncle James's wedding. Aunt Mary mentioned that he would be married on the 27th of this month.

Mrs. Roser has left Mrs. Harrison's boardinghouse, and is now staying at the Washington Hotel. She had some difficulty with Mrs. Harrison about her rice. I was told by one of the girls that she intends returning to the Markoe, but I cannot say anything about the truth of this last report.

Mr. and Mrs. Alberti spent last Saturday and Sabbath at the Markoe, and were very much surprised to find that you had left. Mr. Alberti's health is not very good.

You are no doubt enjoying the pleasures of home and the company of our dear relatives and friends. Please tell Cousin Laura that I will write her very soon. I have written this letter with four or five girls around me, and all of them talking to me. Do tell me all about home, and if any of my cats are alive. Please, my dear mother, give my love to Mrs. Harden and Matilda Jane.

And now, my dear father and mother, as the clock has struck nine some time ago, and I must be in bed before ten, I will bid you good night. Cousin Charlie unites with me in best love to yourselves, Aunt Betsy, Aunt Susan, Uncle William, and Aunt Julia's family; also Uncle Henry and Aunt Abby. Believe me, dear Father and Mother,

Your affectionate child,
Mary S. Jones.

Rev. C. C. Jones *to* Messrs. Charles C. Jones, Jr., *and* Joseph Jones[g]

Marietta, *Wednesday,* November 19th, 1851

My dear Sons,

We left Charleston on Monday at 11½ A.M., and had a prosperous journey to this place, which we reached Tuesday morning at seven. Your Uncle John and Dunwody and Cousin Louisa and Ellen and Joe were at the depot awaiting our arrival. Dunwody was most fearful that we might not go home to his mother's house. We found all our dear relatives well except some colds, and Aunt Eliza about in her usual health, although suffering from a cold. They were all as glad to see us as we were to see them, and it has been a most delightful and refreshing visit to us. They have all made a hundred inquiries after you both, and express great pleasure at hearing that you were sober and discreet and attentive to the improvement of your advantages, and say they expect much of you, and wish to see you very much. We have tried to persuade Aunt to go down the country with us, but she says she cannot go just yet: it will make her stay from home too long. No doubt she requires the change.

Marietta is improving in buildings and population. The removal of some excellent low-country families to the place will help out your Uncle John's church, being Presbyterians. They have $4,000 subscribed for the new house of worship, which is to be erected on a part of your Uncle John's lot, which he gives them for the purpose—the part of the lot in front of the stable, the best site in the village. The foundations are soon to be laid. The military institute is in operation—thirty-five cadets—and with encouraging prospects. The village is becoming a place of resort in the summer, and consequently all supplies and provisions have risen, and so living is expensive. Aunt has kept open house the past summer, and saw a world of company—old friends and new.

The children are all much grown. Mary Sophia is nearly as tall as your mother. Joe talks pretty well; is a chatterbox, and the most industrious fellow in these parts. Dunwody is growing, and retains his identity of character with much improvement. Little Mary is a sweet little thing; knew and came directly to me: full of life and at times full of fun. . . .

We spent yesterday and night at your Uncle John's. Today and night we are at Aunt's. Tomorrow, God willing, I go down to Griffin to attend our synod. Your mother remains till Monday, when she leaves, and I meet her at Atlanta. We then go to Macon, remain all night, and to Savannah on Tuesday and stay Wednesday in town, and Thursday out home.

Your dear mother says you must consider this letter from her too, and sends much love to you both. And Aunt and Cousins Mary and Lou send much love also. They say they wish to see you a great deal, and when you come out here you must follow your mother and father's example and *not pass them by.*

Joe West is studying medicine in Augusta, and they say he is engaged to be married! This is a bright scheme, as old Mr. Ferris used to say. I suppose it is a scandal upon our young kinsman. I think it just as well for a young man to complete his collegiate and professional education and have some prospect before him of making a living in life before he changes his state. I was twenty-six years of age before I ventured upon marriage. It was soon enough for me. I think you have both just views in relation to this matter. I wish you to cultivate the courteous, polite manners and graceful, manly bearing of gentlemen, and embrace the advantages and privilege of association with accomplished, intelligent, and refined ladies both married and single; but avoid foppishness and a foolish softness of impression from every attractive acquaintance.

Write your dear sister frequently. The Lord be with and bless you, my dear sons!

Your ever affectionate father,
C. C. Jones.

Rev. C. C. Jones *to* Messrs. Charles C. Jones, Jr., *and* Joseph Jones[g]

Snider's Store, Savannah, *Wednesday,* November 26th, 1851

My dear Sons,

We arrived here last evening by the Macon Railroad. I left Marietta on last Thursday afternoon and attended the sessions of the Synod of Georgia in Griffin. I was never received by my brethren with greater confidence and affection, and my intercourse with them was of the most delightful kind. They gave me an opportunity of addressing them on domestic missions on Friday morning, and appointed me to deliver the address at our season for the religious exercises of the synod on Saturday afternoon. Many desired me to suffer my name to be put in nomination for the professorship in Columbia again, with the promise and assurance of a unanimous election; and in fact my friend Mr. Mitchel actually made the nomination and supported it in a speech of near half an hour. Of course I could do nothing but decline, expressing my sincere gratitude for this renewed expression of the confidence and favor of the synod. After much canvassing, with several nominations, the synod finally fell back upon Dr. McGill, and that on account of the impossibility of an election of any name proposed, and some intimation of Dr. McGill in recent letters that he might come in March.

Monday I returned to Atlanta, and there met Mother, and we came back and proceeded to Macon, where we stayed all night, and then here Tuesday. Your Uncle John was to have come down with us, but your Aunt Jane was taken sick, and he deemed it advisable to return to Marietta—a great disappointment to him and to us; and we regretted it much on account of the cause. We trust, however, your Aunt Jane's sickness will be but temporary. Dunwody is much grown—full of life as ever; and little Mary is a most interesting little thing, and became exceedingly attached to your mother, and insisted upon coming down the country with her. Aunt Eliza's health is far from being good: climate too severe for her.

We are met by the smiling faces and open hands of our friends here. The bad weather has passed off, and we have a most delightful day. I am writing in Mr. Snider's store, where your dear mother, who is quite well, is doing some shopping.

Cousin Joseph Robarts looks remarkably well, and is packing up *celery* and other matters for your Uncle James's wedding tomorrow evening. He and Mr. Wallace Cumming go out this afternoon to the wedding. Mr. Cumming is to be one of the groomsmen, and by all accounts it is to be quite an affair. If we get out in time, we hope to go up to it.

My dear son, if you feel desirous of coming on with your brother to pay a visit to your home and relatives and return with your mother, *do so* without hesitation. I left a check for $40 to pay Joe's expenses on—more than enough—and you can just call on Mr. Powel to advance you some $15 or $20 more. It will take about $30 each to land you in Liberty. If you run out, call on Mr. Montgomery Cumming in Savannah for what you may need.

I may remain a fortnight in Liberty. If so, you may be out before I leave. Mother sends much love to you. Be good boys. She will write your sister to-day. Have just seen our friend Miss Clay. The Lord be with and bless you, my dear sons! Mother is waiting.

Your affectionate father,
C. C. Jones.

REV. C. C. JONES *to* MISS MARY SHARPE JONES[t]
Pavilion Hotel, Savannah, Wednesday, November 26th, 1851
My dear Daughter,

We arrived here last evening in the cars from Macon. I left Marietta last Thursday and attended the Synod of Georgia at Griffin. Was never received and treated with more confidence and affection by my brethren. Had an opportunity of presenting the domestic missionary operations of the church before them, and was appointed to make the address at the religious exercises of Synod. Many wished me to let my name be put in nomination for the professorship in Columbia again, saying the election would be unanimous; and I was actually *nominated,* but of course declined, expressing my sincere gratitude for this renewed expression of the confidence and favor of Synod. Dr. McGill was elected.

I went up to Atlanta on Monday and met your dear mother, who stayed in Marietta with Aunt and your Aunt Jane. Aunty's health is far from being good (climate too severe), but would not come down *now* with us; said she could not leave home for so long a time, but may sometime during the winter. Little Joe had wood and lightwood cut up and put away in the room all ready for us, and said as I had sent word to kill something, so they had killed the turkey and the duck for us. I hope Lilla is truly a converted child; had a long and very satisfactory conversation with her. Mary Sophia has grown a great deal, and is nearly as tall as your mother. Ellen is quite a lady. Dunwody is grown, and little Mary a most interesting little thing: became exceedingly attached to your mother, and insisted upon coming down the country with her. Your mother left her with her old mama, busily packing up her clothes to be off in the cars.

Who should be in the cars on her way down to her new home in Charleston but *Mrs. Glen*—with her husband and his niece and nephew: the happiest and most delighted being you can imagine. I looked at her with wonder, and sincerely hope all her anticipations, bright as they are, may be realized. But in my judgment a professor of religion runs a fearful risk to marry a man of the world!

When we came down to Griffin from Atlanta it was rainy, dark, muddy, and cold, and we concluded to put off our supper until we reached Macon. We reached Macon at twelve at night, and could get not even a cup of tea at the Lanier House; and we went supperless to bed, Mother with a dreadful headache. Our ride down from Macon was in a new car, and the pleasantest railroad ride we remember to have had.

We are staying at the Pavilion Hotel, kept by Mr. Clark, opposite the Independent Church. Our friends have met us with smiling faces and open arms. The bad weather has gone, and it is a delightful day. We walked out to shop a little, and we met Mrs. McAllister *and Miss Eliza Clay,* and have seen Mrs. Porter and other friends. Miss Eliza came in the steamer from New York *alone;* is looking remarkably well. It is so pleasant here. We just passed out of the gate this morning when we heard: "Oh, Marse Charlie—look yonder!" And here came running across the street one of Cousin Harriet Handley's women to speak to us—as glad to see us as if we were relatives.

Cousin Joseph Robarts and Mr. Wallace Cumming go out this afternoon at three to attend your Uncle James's wedding tomorrow evening. If we get out in the stage in time, we will try and go too. Mr. Cumming is to be one of the groomsmen; and from all we can learn it is to be quite an affair. They sent to *New York* for their cake and so on! It is my impression we can make cake in Georgia as good as they can make it in New York. Folks must please themselves if they can; no doubt all friends present will rejoice and do justice to the wedding feast.

Have seen Mr. Roser: quite hearty. He tells me Mrs. Roser has gone back to the *Markoe.* This will add to our circle there. Tell Charlie howdy for us; will write him from Liberty. Love to him. *Monty* says "he is going to make a doctor, and Savannah is the place for him to settle." Mother wants to add a word. The Lord be with and bless you, my dear child! Take good care of yourself; exercise all you can. And never forget the care of your immortal soul.

Your affectionate father,

C. C. Jones.

MRS. MARY JONES *to* MISS MARY SHARPE JONES[t]
Savannah, Wednesday, November 26th, 1851

I must add one word to you, my beloved child. I have thought of you constantly, and often wished that you were with us, but feel that it would have been wrong for you to leave your studies.

Present our respects to your teachers, and ask Miss Gill if you cannot complete your English course all to *Wayland* this year. If God spares your life and health, I want you to devote the next to something else. Try and improve in your music. Miss Jones says you can overcome the difficulty in your hands if you will persevere; and Miss Cunningham says she used when learning sometimes to practice one bar a hundred times until she mastered it.

My old bonnet has become so shabby that I want you to go to the Markoe and make room in the trunk that has the things for Joe to bring on and pack in my straw bonnet with the blue ribbon. Do be careful that it is not mashed.

A call downstairs, and I must stop. Love to your brothers and cousin.

Ever, my own dear daughter, your affectionate mother,
Mary Jones.

Mr. Charles C. Jones, Jr., *to* Rev. *and* Mrs. C. C. Jones[t]
Princeton, *Thursday,* November 27th, 1851

My beloved Parents,

Your valued letters have been duly received, and it is with no ordinary interest that I peruse lines penned by your hands amid the familiar scenes of Georgia. The soul naturally turns to the mecca of its affections, and easy is the task for memory to revert to joys that are past and revel in pleasant pastures, sighing for another realization. It demands no extraordinary gift of fancy to portray to myself the happy picture of friends long separated, now united in voice and hand, engaged in mutual and unrestrained interchange of feelings, sentiments, and affections, reviewing the past with satisfactions, enjoying the present as golden moments because spent in the hallowed exercise of social and family friendship.

While you are thus in the midst of such delights, enjoying the mildness and uniformity characteristic of the Southern winter, imagine us in Princeton with a sheet of snow covering everything, while the loud bleak blasts of Boreas, mingled with sleet, are howling around the stern walls of Old North. Yet to the student snugly housed such weather is delightful. The farther one is removed from those allurements which would lead to trifling recreations the nearer is he to the attainment of knowledge. I know of nothing that pleases me better than to sit by a fine fire a stormy night, with everything quiet—with no returning tippler hammering at the door, or loafer crying from the entry "Hello, Charlie!"—and there devote myself to study or reading. Often have I been almost tempted to pronounce happy the lot of him who, sequestered within his retired cloister, spends his time in the pursuit of science with no friends but his volumes, no lifelike images save the imaginings of his own active mind. Yet such a manner of living would militate with the social nature of man, and were the world a mere collection of monks, hermits, and abstract literati, what a doleful time we would have! Man is in one sense a bookworm, yet in another he is not.

The day of thanksgiving was duly regarded in this village, the stores being shut, the churches open, and—by no means the least cause of rejoicing to many—a turkey prepared in the refectory. *O mensae O lurcones gallorum in-*

dicorum! Professor Green delivered a very fine sermon in the chapel, the attendance being large and the attention good. I presume that you observed the same season in Georgia.

Before this reaches you Brother will doubtless be with you all. He certainly has before him a pleasant vacation, and I hope that he will improve his liberty. Several other of the Georgia students here have left for their respective homes, all buoyant with pleasing anticipations which yearn for a full realization.

A day subsequent to that upon which you left Philadelphia the forefinger of my right hand was knocked out of joint by a blow from a shinny stick. It was, however, soon restored to its former position and is now much better, although my hand will not bear squeezing.

Dr. Carnahan is delivering a short course of lectures in Mercer Hall, the proceeds of which are designed to assist in defraying the debts contracted in erecting the Second Presbyterian Church. Being closely engaged in lecture-writing, I did not attend, although I have understood that the venerable doctor was very happy both in subject and delivery.

Have written to Sister, but as yet no answer has been received. She is, I presume, busily engaged in her studies.

Our examination is rapidly approaching, and it becomes the student to re-trim his midnight lamp long after the nightingale "hymns his last music to the moon."

We have been very quiet, with the exception of several petty little sprees—probably the concoctions of minds large enough to fill the breasts of fresh and sophs aspiring after immortality in this line. A few nights since, such honorable gentlemen displayed immense courage and extraordinary daring by setting on fire the entry windows of East and West Colleges. I always wish that such worthless fellows could all of them be sent off to Botany Bay and there be made to heat fire engines, burn tar kilns, etc., that they might enjoy full scope for the gratification of their fiery propensities. It is strange indeed how many boys, the moment they enter within college walls, take entire leave of their senses, virtually renouncing all pretensions to decency, propriety, and everything else that pertains to law and order. Boys are here sent to college so young that instead of being absent from home they should be just where Solomon's prime law might be soundly administered at least twice during the day—and that with the most salutary effect. One good paddling would do Judge Berrien's little son, now in the sophomore class, more good than all the studying nominally performed in a week. I am provoked more and more every day, and feel almost like administering the law myself in want of some other sober friend.

Heard from Cousin Charlie; he is well. With all love to you both, my dear parents, uncle, aunts, cousin, brother, and all other loved relatives and friends, I remain

Your ever affectionate son,
Charles C. Jones, Jr.

258

Montevideo, *Monday,* December 1st, 1851

My dear Daughter,

We left Savannah last week in the stage on Thursday, having Mrs. Harden and Matilda Jane, Mrs. Judge Fleming and little daughter, Mrs. John Stevens Maxwell and two little daughters from Florida, Mr. G. W. Walthour, Rev. T. S. Winn, Mr. Bennet, and a strange gentleman fellow passengers. We were happy to meet old friends and acquaintances. Much and pleasant conversation of things and persons past, present, and future. Matilda Jane much grown. Mrs. Harden since the death of her brother, Mr. Louis LeConte, undecided whether to remain in Liberty or to remove. Mr. Walthour down from the legislature on a visit to his family. Mr. Bennet just from England, and looking well and doing well. Mrs. J. S. Maxwell says Dr. Troup Maxwell and your Aunt Augusta are satisfied in Florida and prospering in their settlement there. She left the stage at Bailey's; Mrs. Fleming, Messrs. Walthour and Winn at Midway. We parted with Mrs. Harden at the Boro.

Your Uncle James sent his carriage to take us up to his wedding. Mother was too fatigued and unwell to go, and went home in our carriage to Montevideo. There Mrs. King and your Aunt Susan met and carried her over to South Hampton. I changed my coat at the Boro, dined, and went up to represent our branch of the family at the wedding. Passed through the estate of Anderson's; got out and walked to the private burying ground. Six graves of grown persons—all well known to me in life! The two last your Aunt Evelyn and Aunt Hetty. Opposite Brother Joe Anderson's on the Sand Hills, out he ran and brought the carriage to a halt, and would take no denial. So out I bundled. There was Sister Betsy and Brother William in the piazza. Brother Joe said they had been there two hours, looking for the carriage. Brother put his overcoat over his head to protect himself from the present rain, and gave me a welcome on the yard steps. Never saw him look better. Sister has been sick with phthisic, and looks badly. A joyous meeting. Bessie and Evelyn came running to meet me. But one whom I had always identified with the house, and had always welcomed me there, *was not!* I looked everywhere, but there was no form and no voice!

Soon the day shut in, and all were prepared for the wedding but Sister and myself. So we went upstairs and soon were ready. It was very dark. The carriage went for Laura at Mrs. Dr. Anderson's. Brother gave me the reins. Brother Joe Anderson went ahead. All I could see was the top of his buggy. We walked nearly all the way; and in like manner after the wedding about two o'clock in the morning! Fine hours for this region! But folks are not married but once in a while.

There were three bridesmaids: Misses Handley, Baker, and Quarterman; the groomsmen: Messrs. W. Cumming, Maybank, and Alexander Quarterman. The bride and groom looked remarkably well. The bride wore a veil falling from the head but not over the face; high-neck dress of satin (I believe) with a lace deep over it. Very becoming and genteel. Her maids were similarly dressed, with silk bodices; and the whole appearance of the bridal array was in good taste and pleasing to all. The room was crowded. Conceive a room entirely occupied all around with seats, and then as many persons as could be crowded into the center space, and you have an idea of our condition. And everybody engaged in the most animated conversation. The opposite room was a retreat for the gentlemen when they retired from the ladies' society. The troop fired salutes, to the consternation of some of the little children, and the great delight of others. The young ladies played on the piano and sang. The supper was served at eleven o'clock, and was very handsome. The company began to disperse about one o'clock. The whole evening passed off most agreeably, and the wedding was such an one as you ordinarily attend in our county. Your Uncle James was specially happy. He is thought to have made a prudent choice.

I came to Montevideo on Friday, and found Mother returned from Mrs. King's, and Aunt Susan with her. (I forgot to say Mr. Axson performed the ceremony.) We have been marooning, and have enjoyed our return home exceedingly. The people were joyful at our return. The quiet is refreshing. Mother has filled the parlor with the sweet perfume of flowers, which are yet blooming in the garden. We have received visits already. Mrs. Barnard was here this afternoon, and Nat. Yesterday we could not go to Midway, and so we spent our day profitably with the people in our little chapel.

This afternoon, while Mr. Shepard and I were walking, we saw two gentlemen walking in the road from the Boro! Mr. Shepard said: "One is *your son Joseph*." "No, it cannot be!" *Sure* enough, it was Joe—and Mr. Peace—just arrived. And now while I write they are talking to Mother, who is making a flannel coat for Judith's baby. Joe says: "Mother, it looks like old times to see you working, and Father writing, and this bright fire in this old parlor." We were happy to see them in health and safety.

Mother received your letter, and will answer it soon. I do not suppose Miss Gill will make much impression upon you with her New School notions. Mother and Brother Joe send much love to you, and Mr. Peace his respects. We are sorry to hear that Charlie is so unwell; hope it may be temporary. Respects to Mr. Happersett when you see him. The Lord be with you, my dear child!

Your ever affectionate father,
C. C. Jones.

REV. C. C. JONES *to* MR. CHARLES C. JONES, JR.[g]

Montevideo, *Monday,* December 1st, 1851

My dear Son,

Who should make their appearance this afternoon at two but Mr. Peace and your brother! Both well—after a prosperous journey. Joe tells me my letters from Marietta and Savannah had not reached Princeton before he left. I presume you have done right not to come home now, and your mother and I are satisfied with your determination. Am glad Joe has reached home before I left.

We had a delightful visit up the country. Left your Aunt Jane quite unwell, which prevented your Uncle John from coming down with us. Arrived in Savannah last Tuesday. Out in stage on Thursday. Mother came on to Montevideo, and I went up to attend your Uncle Jimma's wedding. An interesting and pleasant wedding. Mr. Axson performed the ceremony. A large company of the youth of the county—and some beauty. An elegant supper. Banky second groomsman, and he and West in the finest spirits. We did not reach Mr. Joseph Anderson's, where we stayed, until 2 A.M. The hour must be excused, as weddings do not happen every day. Your Uncle Jimma in the finest humor, and has by all accounts made a prudent choice. We dine by invitation at your Uncle Henry's with the bride and groom on Friday, D.V.

Returned to Montevideo on Friday. The people much rejoiced to see us. Yesterday too rainy to go out, and so stayed at home and spent the day profitably, I trust, with our own people.

Mr. King's family all well. . . . Your Aunt Susan and Uncle William and Cousin Laura looking remarkably well. Your Aunt Betsy looking badly: her phthisic has afflicted her lately. All our relatives well. County generally healthy now. . . . Shall remain a week or ten days longer, as my business requires it; and I think it will help my health.

Mother sends abundance of love to you, and will write you soon; says I give her no chance. Your brother sends love, and Mr. Peace his kind regards. He says he is going to kill all the deer around here if possible. He and Joe have been rigging out their hunting tackle all evening. They are now waiting for the candle to go to bed. The Lord be with and bless you, my dear son!

Your ever affectionate father,
C. C. Jones.

The people have made many inquiries after you, and say they are glad to hear you will finish your studies soon, and then expect you to return home.

Mr. Charles C. Jones, Jr., *to* Rev. *and* Mrs. C. C. Jones[t]

Princeton, *Saturday,* December 6th, 1851

My dear Father and Mother,

In my last letter I pled a scarcity of news and a lack of excitement. Now, however the tables are completely turned, and we are living amid robbery and confusion. That celestial spark which Prometheus secretly withdrew from heaven and placed within the breast of man has not always been fanned into a pure flame by the breath of love and kindness. Although the creator lay bound in iron chains upon the stern rock, still many of his descendants, imbibing the furtive spirit of their great ancestor, even now stalk the land, a terror to hen roosts—burglars in very deed.

This quiet little town has lately been thrown into much trepidation because of the appearance of several robbers who nightly disturb the repose of tea sets, the money drawers, etc. Various houses have been opened while the inmates, wrapped in the slumbers of midnight, knew not their coming until some broken window or bored door revealed in the morning the character of the nocturnal vistors. One of the students a few nights since was at Captain Crabbe's. About ten in the evening they heard a noise at the front door, and suspecting the cause, the student was commissioned to ascertain the nature of the disturbance, he being the only gentleman in the house. Upon opening the door he was grasped by a suspicious-looking personage; but upon his presentation of a formidable stiletto, the individual immediately relaxed his hold, making, together with a companion, a speedy retreat over the enclosure. Several students have been requested by families of ladies to serve as bodyguards—or perhaps more properly houseguards—during the night until these unwelcome guests shall have left these peaceful domains. They use sharp whistles, and may sometimes be heard communicating with each other in this manner at a late hour. No one has been injured, and they appear to be a timid set, easily frightened yet eager for booty. The people are alarmed, yet no attempts have been made to arrest them; nor is any knowledge of their character, place of abode, or plans possessed. The effects indicate causes, yet these are unknown.

Upon the evening of the 4th we had a general outbreak. While the tutors were all in the refectory, some forty or fifty students (all the measures being previously concerted) barricaded the third entry of North with boards, posts, wood, etc. Just as they had completed their operations, were beginning to tune up the fiddles, strike the banjos, rattle the bones, and pull the bell (the bottle having already passed freely around), who should step in their very midst but the real Dr. Johnnie! Having in some way or other received an intimation of the spree, he had about a half of an hour previous, unseen by any, entered the room of the tutor which is upon the third entry, and remained there quietly, sending the tutors into the refectory, until everything was completed and the barricade perfect, when, as we have said, he stepped out and detected the party. The presence of a hawk amid a flock of partridges in a pea field was never more unexpected or more unwelcome than the appearance of the doctor; and you may well imagine the smiting of knees, the dodging into rooms, the dropping of bottles, fiddles, etc., and the slamming of doors. Those, however, who were detected became very bold in action, and while Dr. Maclean was chasing others they chased him, hitting him with pieces of wood, shouting, and jerking him around with a rope to prevent his taking off the wood, which was immediately replaced so often as disturbed. He finally declared that he would go down if they would remove the wood, and that none of them should be reported provided they would cease operations and retire to their rooms. To this, however, they would by no means assent, and after the doctor had descended again piled on the wood, passed the bottle around freely, danced until so drunk that they could stand no longer, pulled the bell until perfectly tired out, then emptied a keg of tar over it, and then fell asleep.

The consequence of this ridiculous course is that twenty have already received permission for absence, with a probability that some ten or fifteen more will be granted the same liberty. The treatment of Dr. Maclean was very disgraceful. All law, order, and regard for college authority were totally disregarded, and the whole affair was one disreputable, not only because of the present influence but also by reason of the loss of reputation which the institution must sustain abroad in consequence of these repeated acts of riot. The offenders will be severely dealt with by the faculty—the only method for securing quiet in future. The doctor, although happy in the detection of the boys, was still unable to arrest the progress of affairs, for what could one do with a set of thirty "corned" and excited students? There is certainly no sense in such sprees—much nonsense and poor pay.

Next week our examination commences, the term closing on the 16th or 17th. Heard from Philadelphia last week; all friends there well. The arrival of Kossuth creates an interesting excitement in New York, although I do not think that the course of our national assembly has been very flattering. I need not embody any wish for your enjoyment, for doubtless your cup is running over. Excuse this desultory epistle, for we are all very busy. With warmest love to you both, my dear parents, aunts, cousin, uncle, brother, and all friends, I remain

Your affectionate son,
Charles C. Jones, Jr.

Will write Brother soon.

Miss Mary Sharpe Jones *to* Mrs. Mary Jones[t]

Philadelphia, *Saturday,* December 6th, 1851

My dear Mother,

I intended to have written you some days ago, but have been quite unwell, having had a very sore throat and some fever. I am much better now, although my throat is still inflamed. I received your letter two days ago, and am very sorry that Brother Joe had left before its reception, and so I cannot send the bonnet.

On Thanksgiving Day I attended Dr. Parker's church in the morning, and after service went with Miss Hoops (one of the teachers) and spent the day with Mrs. Mitchell. I enjoyed myself very much, and found her daughter a very pleasant girl. Mrs. Ambrose White and Susan Dickson invited me to dine with them, but I declined, as I had previously engaged to go to the Mitchells'.

Last Saturday evening I took tea with Mrs. Colwell, and there met Mr. Green, who had nothing special to call him to Philadelphia excepting that he had a few moments of leisure, and he thought he would come down and see how Mrs. C. and her family were. But unfortunately Miss Colwell had left for the South, and he had scarcely anything to say to anyone excepting occasionally a confidential conversation between Mrs. C. and himself.

Dr. Hodge of Princeton is really to be married to Mrs. Stockton. He has intimated to several of his friends that a change would very soon take place in his family.

I was told the other day that Father and Dr. Boardman were both very much spoken of as candidates for the professorship in Princeton. How strange it would be if Father should be elected!

Miss Mary Gill says that she has no doubt but that I shall be so much delighted with them and boarding here that I shall not want to go with Father when he comes; and besides, she does not think it safe that such a wild, flirting, talkative girl should be trusted alone at a boardinghouse. I told her that I hoped sincerely that I would go with Father. I asked her if I could not take up mental philosophy after Christmas, as you wished me to do so. She said that if I studied that next, she did not know when I would study moral science; and besides, *my class* would not pursue that branch until next term. I think I would rather study mental philosophy even if my class does not. I can go into the class that will study it.

I received a letter from Julia Fisher today in which she mentions that Mrs. Shelton has twins—two little girls. She says that Mrs. Thompson is so very proud of them; she has now four grandchildren. Julia begs to be remembered to you, and hopes you will come to Columbia before you return to Philadelphia.

Last evening Miss Gill invited her youngest scholars to spend the evening with her; most of them were between eight and twelve. For their amusement Misses Mary and Emily dressed them in various costumes. First one of the girls appeared as a French peasant, and after we had much amusement with her, in came Maggie Dickson dressed as a gypsy with a stolen child. I think that anyone in the world would have thought her a real gypsy, for she acted her part so well; she was also a fortune-teller. After the excitement of having our fortunes told had worn off in some measure, Fanny Evans of Georgia was introduced as a Dutch girl; and I think you may imagine how she looked, for she is very broad and fat. Then came in two little girls dressed as the Swiss sisters; and then a nun was very unexpectedly introduced to the company. And then came some ice cream and fruitcake and little sugar puffs! While we were partaking of these things in came an old woman with a basket on one arm and a stick in her other hand. Very soon we discovered the contents of her basket, which was half full of candies, and then there was a game of scrambles for them. At first we did not recognize this old woman, but soon saw that it was one of our wildest-looking girls, whose name is Lilly Skull. The entertainment of this evening was entirely unexpected, for Miss Gill told none of the girls excepting those whom she wished to be dressed, and it made it more amusing. She says that she did it solely for the amusement of the little girls.

I received an invitation for you and Father to Uncle James's wedding, and Cousin Charlie sent one to Brother Charlie. They did not invite me, or if they did I did not receive the invitation; so I think to make up for it they ought to send me a large slice of fruitcake. I am glad you reached Liberty in time to attend it. Cousin Charlie received a letter from Mr. Wallace Cumming in which he mentioned having seen you there.

Please give a great deal of love to Aunt Betsy, Uncle William, Aunt Susan, Cousin Laura, and Aunt Julia. Is little Johnnie as interesting as ever? I wish I could see them all. Do give my love to Uncle Henry and Aunt Abby, and kiss his little children for me. How is little Dove and Miss Jenny Lind? When will Father come back? Although it is selfish, yet I *do want* him to come soon, for I am more lonely than when you first left. I will soon have vacation. And now, my dear mother, I must bid you farewell. And accept for dear Father and yourself my warmest love; also Brother Joe.

Your affectionate daughter,
M. S. Jones.

REV. C. C. JONES *to* MRS. MARY JONES[t]

Savannah, *Saturday Afternoon,* December 13th, 1851
Six o'clock

My dear Mary,

On arriving at the Boro yesterday I found that the stage would not leave until eleven; so we lost one hour of life together, which is a great deal. We passed Midway while you were all engaged in divine worship, and my heart was with you; nor have I ceased to remember the meeting in its progress. Our dear son Joseph has been much on my mind. Who can tell but he has been brought home for special mercy to his immortal soul? May it prove to be so!

We had Miss Houstoun and Mr. Cook as fellow passengers only, which made our ride in very pleasant. Was highly honored in having our friend Miss Clay ride down to the seventeen-mile house to see me. She is remarkably well: in excellent spirits; had received my letter the day before; and from the favorable appearance and prospects of all things will perhaps make no changes at all. She says she must exchange visits with you *certainly* before you return. Mrs. Hardy and one of the Miss McAllisters rode down also, and made me bearer of a package of finery to some ladies who were to make an appearance at the legislative ball in the evening. The city has been all alive with the visit of the governor and legislature, receiving, mustering, feasting, steamboating, and so on. Will cost the city some $6,000; but will help the seaport and commercial emporium of the state. Took up our old acquaintance Mr. William King at the ferry.

Am staying with Major Porter. They gave me a most friendly and hospitable reception. Mrs. Porter hopes that you will pay her a visit on passing through. Mr. and Mrs. Gilmer quite well. Mr. and Mrs. Lawton dined with us today.

I send by the stage the carpetbag, and the canton flannel within; also six copies of *The Religious Instruction of the Negroes,* which you can deposit in the library at Maybank. I will have a copy bound for yourself and each of the children out of the number of copies I am taking on North with me. Also one dozen *Catechisms,* of which you will supply yourself and any others who may need; but deposit a few copies in the library at Maybank. Give Mr. Shepard and Mr. Rahn a copy. Mrs. Rahn will need one for teaching the children. The balance of them in Mr. Cooper's hands I take on with me. The board will buy the plates and hereafter issue the work. You will find also in the bag something for you to keep me for a short time in *sweet* remembrance.

The locks for the double-barreled gun I have had well repaired; and two chimneys are put with them, and the screw. Joe will find all in a little paper bundle. Should the *new* cock not strike the nipple of the chimney *"plumb,"* Joe can get Audley to take it off and put it into his vise and give it a slight inclination whichever way it may need it to set it right. Any deviation may shatter the nipple. He might use one of the new chimneys for his own gun and see if the cock strikes right. This may be the reason why the nipple is shattered to his gun. If the chimneys are too small, do not put them in at all; if too large, the thread may be reduced by Mr. Parks and then put in.

Tied on to the handles of the carpetbag are the trimming shears—the kind that will suit you best. They need cleaning and a little oil in the screen where they work. Also tied up with them a small, good lock for the paper canister as soon as it is fixed.

Saw Dr. Preston today, and expect to preach for him tomorrow afternoon and take up a collection for the board. You must write me soon the result of the meeting at Midway. Shall leave here Monday night, or rather Tuesday morning: four o'clock, God willing. Think of me as gone on the Lord's business and you will feel better. This consideration quiets my mind, but I feel our separation most keenly. Love to my dear son. Have left you in his care, as I am away. Love to my dear sisters and Laura and Brother. Hope Sister was not made sick by her going to Midway. The good Lord be with and bless you, my own dearest wife!

Your affectionate husband,
C. C. Jones.

Howdy for all the people and Cato.

Enclosed is the key to the carpetbag. The carpetbag comes out in the stage Monday.

Mrs. Mary Jones *to* Miss Mary Sharpe Jones[t]
Montevideo, *Monday,* December 15th, 1851

My dear Daughter,

I have been most anxiously looking for a letter from you, and today your affectionate favor was received. It distresses me to know that you have suffered from fever and sore throat, and that you are not entirely relieved. I feel happy in the reflection that your dear father will so soon be with you.

Do, my dear child, be careful of your precious health. Bathe your feet and neck daily in cold water, and use the green tea and alum gargle. If your *undervests* are not thick enough, get some flannel and have them made with longer sleeves. I feel grateful to your teachers for all their kindness to you, and beg that you will express the same to them for me. They must exert themselves very much for the happiness and entertainment of their scholars. You have also received much attention from friends. I wish you to cultivate the acquaintance of the Misses Dickson; and when the oranges arrive, you had best present Mr. D. with some; also the Misses Gill, if you please.

Your Aunt Susan and Cousin Laura are now both staying with me. We have returned this evening from the closing exercises of a four days' meeting held at our dear old church, Midway. On Friday Mr. Axson opened the meeting with a most solemn discourse to Christians founded on Esther's plea to the king in behalf of her people and her kindred. Most fervently did he exhort professors of religion to awake to the duty of feeling, praying, and laboring for the conversion of our own beloved kindred and all perishing sinners in our midst, and for the special descent of the Holy Spirit at this time, that the church might be revived and many souls converted to God. In the afternoon Don Fraser gave an excellent sermon from Hosea: "Ephraim is joined to idols." On Saturday Mr. Pratt preached first in the morning from Psalm 106:23 on the encouragements to prayer; it was a precious discourse, and followed up Mr. Axson's sermon on the duty of prayer. In the afternoon Mr. John Winn preached a very argumentative and solemn discourse to sinners from these words: "Almost thou persuadest me to be a Christian," in which the impenitent was stripped of every plea. Sabbath was Communion. Mr. Pratt preached in the morning on the Christian's love to Zion. It was a precious season, and many souls I doubt not were refreshed by the presence of our gracious Saviour. Mr. Axson preached in the afternoon a most awakening sermon from this verse in the 1st Psalm: "Sinners shall not stand in the judgment." Wishing to test the interest, services were announced for today; and although the morning was most unpromising, a large number were present. Mr. Pratt preached from John 5:40: "And ye will not come unto me that ye might have life." Mr. Sumner Winn followed with: "And He looked upon them with anger, being grieved for the hardness of their hearts." Mr. Axson closed with a most solemn appeal to sinners. He pressed upon them their awful condition as already condemned under the wrath of God and exposed to eternal damnation. I never listened to a more stirring address. Oh, that some poor sinner might be led to the Cross! I know not if there is any special interest among the impenitent, but they have been most faithfully warned and entreated to come to the Saviour.

I wish that I could tell you that your brother Joseph manifested a special interest in these sacred services. He has been attentive, but I fear, alas, has had no moving of the gracious Spirit on his heart. Let us, my dear child, who hope that we have an interest at a throne of grace plead more constantly and more earnestly for our dear ones who are out of Christ and exposed to eternal death. I pray that God would bless you from day to day with the influence of His Holy Spirit, that you may grow in grace and be a burning and shining light in His Kingdom. Although conscious of much coldness and deadness in my own heart and much misimprovement, yet I bless my Heavenly Father for granting me these great spiritual privileges.

Your dear father will be with you probably as soon as this letter, and will give you all the news of the county. Everything at home looks pleasant and desirable to our eyes—the people, the garden, the lawn, the trees, everything. Old Daddy Tony has taken care of your cats, and says he will continue to do so. The old mother is alive, two grown ones, and a poor forlorn little kitten. Dove begins to look old, but Jenny Lind is a fine little colt, and shaped like her mother. When we went to the Island, Dove recognized my voice and came to me as soon as I called her to be fed at the foot of the front steps, whickering as she used to do in her low, gentle way.

I presume your dear brother Charlie will be with you ere this reaches you. His affectionate letter was received today. I am shocked to hear of such scandalous and disgraceful behavior in the college; such things must certainly affect its reputation. I hope his watch has been repaired. I fear it was most seriously injured by his fall. *He did not tell us anything about it.* And his finger I trust is quite restored; if it is not, he must get the doctor to examine it in Philadelphia. So many tricks are said to be played upon watches, he ought to be careful with his, and get his father to go with him before it is removed from the hands of the jeweler.

Thank *dear Father* when he arrives for his kind letter and the carpetbag with its sweet contents. And ask him to write me immediately where the garden scissors were bought, as I shall have to return them. These are designed only for box and not for cutting limbs and shrubbery. I have already a pair for that purpose.

And now, my dear child, good night! Every eye in the house and probably on the place is sealed in sleep. Kiss your own dear father and brother many times for me, with much love to Cousin Charlie, in which Joseph and your aunt and Cousin Laura unite. I hope you will write Aunt Betsy soon. Remembrance to Mrs. Watson and the ladies of the house. The servants all send howdy. Write soon. Take care of Father! Believe me

Ever your affectionate mother,
Mary Jones.

Mr. Charles C. Jones, Jr., *to* Rev. *and* Mrs. C. C. Jones[t]
Princeton, *Monday,* December 15th, 1851[*]

My dear Parents,

Relieved in a measure from the pressing engagements of the late examination, my thoughts now turn towards family and home with more ease and satisfaction. Previously the words of recognition were few, and when the soul would indulge in the pleasing reveries of fancy and wander amid the sweet fields of love and friendship, behold in the very instant would arise the ghosts of departed shades. Aristotle, clad in sable mantle, with hollow voice would demand: "Son of man, knowest thou the distinctions of verse as contained in my *Art of Poetry?*" Hedge and Locke, with their silver locks and hoary beards, inquire: "Canst thou trace the sorites, retort the dilemma, or frame the epichirema? Canst thou state the workings of the mind and enter the secret chambers of the understanding?" Alarmed, I would drop my pen and hasten to repair as much as possible any neglect which might have offended these profound sages of yore. These are now, however, laid upon the shelf, and I am left to follow my own inclinations, untrammeled by any fears that my peaceful hours will again be disturbed by the dread forms and phantoms of bygone sages. The examination is over, and nearly one-half of the students have already left—many of them to enjoy the smiles and joys of the social circle, others to incur the displeasure and awaken sorrow in the breasts of those whose happiness depends upon their propriety of action.

In my last letter I mentioned the spree which lately occurred, and stated that some twenty of the principal offenders had been kindly presented with permission of absence previous to the closing of the term. It has always been a strange problem (although easily solved) that many boys, as soon as the threshold of their parents' residence is past, forgetting the sage counsels and warning voices of their best friends, prefer the ribaldries of the vicious and the language of the profane, plunging into a vortex more destructive, more terrible, than that which whirls in giddy circles around the rockbound shores of Norway. For while the latter shatters the outward man and dashes the frail creature man into a thousand fragments, the former saps the pure fountains of the soul with a pang more poisonous, and a mien no less subtle, than the vampire of Indian brake, withdraws every upright emotion and moral sentiment, leaving the victim with a heart as barren as the bosom of Sombrero's rocky isle, devoid of natural affections, transformed into a demon of darkness fit only for the black regions of Orcus, a chosen victim for the hate of the Furies.

However, let us change the subject and speak of matters at once more interesting and pleasing. What a matrimonial mania must be now pervading the quiet families of old Liberty! However, if we are to believe the testimony of many witnesses, such is most natural and becoming. Among the ancients Hymen was ever active, and even now he is weaving his indissoluble warp to unite the fair with the manly of earth in I trust happy union. I presume that each will have an eye to good suppers—a circumstance, by the way, never neglected in Liberty, where even "big pertaters" are "toted round" at agricultural fairs "by order of the chairman." Such considerations are, however, in these regions of vast importance, where "light bread and beef" are "all the go" and crackers only served up on Thanksgiving occasions. I fear, however, that I do injustice to our culinary department, for once within the memory of man we enjoyed the inexpressible pleasure of pulling at the tough sinews of a regular old *gander,* who, no longer able to afford a tolerable crop of feathers or pay for his meals, was beheaded to gratify the epicurean tastes of refec boys. The subject you have presented before you; the dissection, hauling, pulling, and jerking you may imagine.

Yesterday we had an interesting sermon from a Rev. Mr. Cook, corresponding secretary of the Board of Tract Society. He spoke in the First Presbyterian Church in the evening upon the cause in which he is engaged.

Brother and Mr. Peace are, I doubt not, safely with you, and enjoying themselves. Tell Brother to improve his liberty (no pun designed) and use his utmost in the exercise of field sports. Wish that I could be with you all for a short time.

Was very sorry to learn from your letter, Father, that Aunt Betsy was so unwell. Hope, however, that her indisposition may not prove serious.

Received a letter from Sister yesterday. She is very well, and seems to be enjoying herself. An invitation was therein couched for me to attend a party soon to be given at Miss Gill's School. If I reach Philadelphia in season I will probably accept, as I wish to see some pretty young ladies—at least now and then. Otherwise one must necessarily remain devoid of the finer polish; for it is the mild, attractive influence of woman which renders the man the gentleman.

With best love to aunts, uncle, cousin, brother, and all friends, I remain

Your attached son,

Charles C. Jones, Jr.

P.S. Tell Uncle Jimma that I congratulate him upon his change of state and new alliance, hoping that the pleasures of married life may prove more interesting than those of single blessedness.

Rev. C. C. Jones *to* Mrs. Mary Jones[t]

Wilmington, North Carolina, *Wednesday Morning,* December 17th, 1851

Through a kind Providence, my ever dear wife, I am thus far on my way. The passages by the boats, both from Savannah to Charleston and from Charleston to this place, were smooth and pleasant. Suffered only from sick headache. Hope you may have even a more pleasant time.

My stay in Savannah with our friends Major and Mrs. Porter was as agreeable as it possibly could have been, and they insist upon your staying with them when you come down; and I hope you will do so. I exacted a promise of them that they would not let you leave in the boat unless the weather was favorable.

Dined with Brother Adger yesterday, and called on the Misses Jones. They say you must stop with them as you pass through. All well. A good time on Sabbath in Dr. Preston's church: $117.37 contribution. Attended prayer meeting with them in the evening. Have very many pleasant associations with this church.

My heart was very heavy on leaving you, and when leaving Savannah; yet it is in obedience to the Lord's will, and that is our peace. The weather is very cold. The water on the wharf frozen thick. Shall have to get some thicker drawers. Embraced these few moments before the cars start to write you, having arrived here at $7\frac{1}{2}$ A.M. in the *Gladiator*. May you have a delightful sojourn at home! Would I could be with you! Love to my dear son, to Sister and Laura, Brother and Sister and all. Howdy for the servants. Write me as often as you can. Please send Dr. McWhir's papers carefully to Mr. Thomas Harden, Savannah; they were not put in the carriage and were left. Hope you received the carpetbag and contents and letter with key for mail safe. Look at my handwriting and see how *cold* it is! God be with and bless you, my dearest wife!

Your own affectionate husband,
C. C. Jones.

Rev. C. C. Jones *to* Mrs. Mary Jones[t]
Willard's Hotel, Washington, D.C., *Thursday,* December 18th, 1851

After closing my letter to you, my own dearest wife, on Tuesday morning —or Wednesday morning, I should say—we took the cars: all the passengers strangers. In half an hour the cars stopped, and who should come in but our friend Mr. Colwell of Philadelphia! The weather was so boisterous the day before, the boat arrived too late for the cars; he had to lay over for a day, and the cars left him, and he had to take the freight train and overtake us. We joined company instantly, and have been inseparable all the way. He has fixed his daughter most happily for the winter with Mrs. Anderson in St. Augustine. Did you know he was a Virginian by birth? We formed the acquaintance also of a very clever gentleman from London, Mr. Benson.

The weather has been excessively cold, and last night Mr. Colwell gave me the use of his cloak, which was a great comfort. All along we saw the waters frozen. As we crossed into Richmond the James River was frozen over except in the rapids. The streams frozen fast, and the Appomattox at Fredericksburg frozen fast. People walking on the ice. Had no idea it was so cold.

When we reached the Potomac, Aquia Creek (you know how broad it is) was frozen entirely over, and two shallops frozen in, the ice extending far out into the river itself. The poor ducks did not seem to know what to do with themselves, but flew about and sat along on the edge of the ice; and there was a raft of several hundreds alongside the ice opposite the steamboat landing. Here we waited and waited for the boat. Fears were entertained that she would not be able to come down on account of the ice. But at 4 P.M. she was seen in the distance, and at $5\frac{1}{2}$ we were all on board the iceboat *Powhatan,* to our great joy.

We left the landing and pushed on our way, now and then encountering ice, until we came opposite Mount Vernon; and from this point we beat through the ice several inches thick clear up to Washington. The noise of the boat, splitting, crashing, and plunging through the ice, and the sounding thumps of pieces flung by the wheels against the guards, and the roar of the wheels themselves, conveyed to you the impression as you stood on the deck of a fierce and heavy hailstorm. It was worth hearing. The head of the boat and the paddles are shielded with iron; otherwise the ice would damage the hull of the vessel and might cut through and sink her. A gentleman from Baltimore on board told me he had a vessel sunk by the cutting through of the ice in a very short time, she not being well defended against it.

Messrs. Caldwell and Benson and I put up at Willard's tonight, following Mr. Caldwell—or *Colwell*. Could not forbear writing you late, as it is now twelve midnight.

And now let me give you some directions for your journey which you must *by no means omit*. Get a thick pair of *woolen socks* to draw up high over your boots and all, to wear in and out of the cars should the weather be snow. Also a *large blanket shawl* to wrap around your feet and to cover all your person from the waist downwards while riding in the cars day and especially night if the weather be severe. You will need both these comforts, and it would be well for Joe to bring along one of those green or red blankets to wrap yourselves in. Be sure you make every provision *for warmth;* you will certainly require it. I fear you will suffer for want of your cloak. *You must be sure and substitute something for it.* I suffered some, and my friend's spare cloak saved me more. Was glad you were not along, for you would have felt the cold very much. Do let me beg you to remember this; I charge Joe to see that you do not forget it.

We arrived so late ($10\frac{1}{2}$ o'clock) that we could not go on to Philadelphia tonight. Indeed I had determined to stop anyhow either here or in Baltimore and not ride two nights in succession. We hope to leave at $8\frac{1}{2}$ in the morning and reach Philadelphia at 4 P.M.—through by daylight. This is the plan *you* must pursue.

Do write me, my dear wife, every week. I think of you all the time, and nothing in this world reconciles me to this separation from you but the conviction that we are both doing the will of our Father in Heaven. Tell my dear son I leave you in his care, and I know he will be wanting in no dutiful and affectionate and considerate attention to you and to all your desires and comfort. Love to him and to my sisters and brother and niece. Howdy for Cato, Stepney, Andrew, and all the people. Love to Henry and Sister Abby and to Jimma and Sister Sarah. Good night, my sweet wife. May the ever blessed God be with you!

Your affectionate and devoted husband,
C. C. Jones.

Miss Mary Sharpe Jones *to* Mrs. Mary Jones[t]

Philadelphia, *Thursday,* December 18th, 1851

My *very* dear Mother,

I am quite delighted! Brother Charlie has just been to see me, and has informed me that my dear father will be here next Saturday morning. I hope he will, and that nothing may prevent. Brother C. arrived last night, and I think looks as if he had been studying pretty hard.

I received Father's letter last week, and was very much interested in his account of Uncle Jimma's wedding. They must have received some very handsome presents.

Last week I went in company with Mrs. Roser, Mrs. Locke, Clara, and Cousin Charlie to a concert given by Catherine Hayes. She sings very well, but by no means equals Jenny Lind, who is now giving a few concerts here. Mrs. Locke (formerly Miss Laura Bulloch) thought I resembled you very much.

My vacation commences on next Monday, and then I hope Father will take me with him, for then I can have the use of my piano. I have made but little progress in my music since I have been staying here, although I have been for a week prevented by indisposition. I have had the prevailing influenza, and have been confined to my room for a week past. I am better now, and would have gone in school today had Miss Sarah not ordered me back to my room. Many of the girls have been unwell, and while I am writing there are three in the room all *coughing* and making *horrid faces* over *bowls of flax-seed tea* and bottles of squills, which Miss Sidney insists upon their taking. Strange to say, all the Georgians are sick at once.

Mrs. Roser came here last evening and brought some tissue papers, saying that Cousin Charlie had requested her to purchase them for Cousin Laura, who had written for them. She seemed to be very much perplexed, not knowing how many leaves or what colored floss or what colored paper to send. Little Frank is looking beautifully, and has committed many things to memory. Mrs. Roser told me to tell you that she hoped you would let me go to the Markoe, for she would take care of me.

Mrs. Smith came to see me last week. She desired a great deal of love to be given to Aunt Susan, Cousin Laura, and yourself. She invited me to come and spend an evening with her, and says that Mrs. Baird's little boy has grown so much and is so interesting.

Miss Cunningham wrote me a little note asking me to dine with her, but I have not been able to see her, as I have received it since my indisposition. I will go and see her as soon as I can go out. She begged me to say to you that she is much improved, having recovered from the injury she received, and several times walked into the parlor on her *"own feet,"* and now rides out whenever she feels inclined.

Mrs. Riesch called last Saturday, and sends much love to yourself, and hopes Cousin Laura will be persuaded to return with you. (I *hope so* too.)

The weather at this time is intensely cold—as cold, Miss Mary says, as they generally have here. I can only judge of the cold by what I see, as I have not been out for a week. For two days past there has been ice upon the inside of the window glasses all the time, notwithstanding a large fire has been burning in the room.

How is Aunt Susan? I hope she is quite well by this time and has not been very sick. Where do you spend the greater part of your time? Father in his letter described Montevideo parlor so naturally that I imagined that I could see you all seated around the fire. I can hardly believe it possible that the flowers are all in bloom at home, for everything is frozen here. I am sure that Uncle William would warm his overcoat and gloves before putting them on if he was here.

Miss Sarah has invited Cousin Charlie and Brother Charlie to spend to-morrow evening here, as she intends having her Christmas party then. I hope they will come, as she has invited them and seems to desire them to come. I do not know whether I shall be able to go down or not.

Please give a great deal of love to Aunt Abby and Uncle Henry. Has little Joe grown much? And now, dear Mother, I must bid you good-bye, as the girls are coming into my room. Brother Charlie unites with me in best love to Uncle William, Aunt Betsy, Aunt Susan, Cousin Laura, and Aunt Julia's family. Accept, dear Mother, the united love of Brother C. and

Your ever affectionate daughter,
Mary S. Jones.

VIII

Rev. C. C. Jones *to* Mrs. Mary Jones[t]

Philadelphia, *Saturday,* December 20th, 1851

My ever beloved Mary,

We left Washington at $8\frac{1}{2}$ A.M. yesterday, and after a prosperous journey reached here at 5 P.M. The Susquehanna at Havre de Grace was frozen over, and as far as we could see above and below resembled a mirror reflecting the heavens and earth. All the water courses were in like manner frozen over. The coldest weather since 1836. Thermometer has been down to 5° and 8°. But I have found the cold bracing and pleasant.

Saw an amusing scene at skating. Far out in the middle of the Susquehanna were two boys. One had his dog. He would lay hold of his dog's tail, and away he would start with his master, first a trot and then a gallop, his master drawn after on his skates! The dog and the boys were in the greatest glee. I laughed heartily at this new mode of locomotion.

On going up to our sitting room with faithful John, who greeted me at the Markoe door, and knocking, Charles called out: "Come in!" A surprise to him. He was sitting by a glowing grate of coal, reading Bancroft's *History of the United States:* improving his time. He is very hearty, and arrived from Princeton but two days ago. Our room wore the appearance of a medical studio. The doctor's books covered the center table, and in the midst of them, lying on some papers, was the skeleton of a very large hand! And one thing was here and another there. Soon Charles Edward came in, and we had a joyful time till the tea bell rang.

After tea we discoursed of friends and home until near eight, when we dressed up to attend the Misses Gill's *party,* given to the young ladies at the close of the session. The boys had received an invitation; I went without one. We were ushered into the receiving room upstairs and pulled off our overcoats. The young gentlemen put on their kid gloves! I put off my black ones and carried my hands dressed according to nature. The Brazilian young lady got a glimpse of me coming in, and ran and told Mary Sharpe "her father had come." The dear child ran upstairs and flew into my arms, without uttering a word, full of tears. She was full of joy and taken by surprise. Miss Gill told us she was the happiest-looking young lady in the room. She has been very unwell with the influenza; looks thin, and had not been down before for some days. Miss Sidney and herself are very fast friends. I asked her if she would prefer staying at Miss Gill's or coming home to the Markoe. She instantly replied: "I prefer coming to the Markoe." She will be with me today at eleven or twelve. Charles is to go for her; and as they both have vacation, they can take exercise together.

Am in the office a short time today. Brother Happersett and Mr. Powel and our new clerk, Mr. Bannister Hall, all well. *No relief from our debts yet!* Am engaged to preach and administer the Communion at Brother Ruffner's church tomorrow morning. He has an interesting state of things in his church. And in the afternoon to address the Sunday school at Dr. Jones's church. Here comes the harness!

Forty-seven years ago this day your husband was born! Years of boundless mercy! May grace abound and the sinner finally finish his course and be saved!

Tomorrow will be our *twenty-first wedding day.* Would that we could spend it together! You will not forget it; neither shall I. The good Lord pardon all that is past, and give us grace to love and be happy, and live more to His glory in time to come!

Charles and Mary Sharpe send much love to you, and Charles Edward sends love also. He has been quite sick, but is well again. Must now go home for the rest of the day. Write soon. Love to everybody and everything.

Your affectionate husband,
C. C. Jones.

There is nothing here but *Kossuth.* Have sent you two papers with his reception, speeches, etc. You will be interested.

I understand the steamers from *here* to Charleston *have been withdrawn.* When the oranges are sent, tell Mr. Cumming to send them by *Heron & Martin's line,* direct. (They run *sailing* vessels.)

The palings for the Island you can direct Mr. Rahn to make Robin and some other hand get out of the old heart cypress on the ground now and save the green cypress trees. They had better be full a half inch *or three-quarters of an inch thick;* and as soon as ready George and Little Andrew can haul them down, so that you can have them put up to your liking before you come away.

MRS. MARY JONES *to* REV. C. C. JONES[t]

Montevideo, *Saturday,* December 20th, 1851

Your birthday, my own beloved husband! May the best of Heaven's blessings rest upon you on this and all your coming years! And thanks—ten thousand thanks—for all your love and kindness, which dwells so gratefully in my fondest remembrance. Oh, that your valuable life may be long spared for usefulness in the Church of God, and to bless with happiness your own loved family and friends! I would gladly have spent today in sweet converse with you, but we have been visiting all day and returned late this evening. Sister S , Laura, and Joe are all asleep, and old Time is hastening on to the Holy Sabbath; but I could not lie down until I had given you assurance of my loving thought and kindest wishes. Tomorrow will be our wedding day! But good night until Monday!

22nd. Yesterday, my dear husband, was our twenty-first wedding day! Can you believe it? Oh, that I had the power to recall all the love and mercy that have crowned those departed years! I seem to have been dwelling in a land of receding shadows, and it is with wonder and astonishment that I stop to review the path by which we have been led. "Surely goodness and mercy have followed us all the days of our life"; and I trust we feel a desire to "dwell in the house of the Lord forever"! How much longer we shall be spared to each other is known only to Sovereign and Infinite Wisdom. I have no desire to rend the veil which obscures futurity! My husband, my children, my own soul, interests temporal and spiritual—I desire to place all in God's hand, to be guided and disposed of as His righteous will directs. May you, my beloved husband, enjoy more abundantly the Spirit's gracious influences and our Blessed Saviour's love and presence in your heart!

Dr. Talmage preached two excellent sermons yesterday at Midway. You cannot think how I have enjoyed the sermons and religious exercises since my return home. I know it is not another gospel, but oh, it seems as with peculiar unction that the Word is dispensed here. I wrote Mary an account of the meeting; have not heard of any special results.

I had hoped that our dear Joseph would not come away unblessed; but I fear, alas, that he has less personal interest on the subject of religion than he has ever had. I can mark but too plainly the effect of college life. I fear we have not been as anxious and as constant in prayer for this child as we should have been. We have relied with confidence upon his principles in some things, forgetting the subtle temptations that would beset him in others.

It is said that Mr. Axson will receive a call to the church in Charleston made vacant by Dr. Thornwell's election to the presidency of the South Carolina College. To lose him, so far as we can see, would be one of the greatest calamities Liberty County could sustain.

Everyone seemed to regret your leaving before the meeting.

Last Tuesday evening we rode over and called upon the family at the Retreat. James has had a likeness sent him from the North purporting to be that of our grandfather; but so far as my memory serves me of the old picture *(which has not been returned)*, it is a mere fancy sketch, and a pitiable one at that.

On Wednesday morning we were awakened by the rattling of sleet against our windows. It came on severely by eleven o'clock, and by night the ground and sheds were incrusted with ice. It fell in small globules, so round that it did not lodge on the trees to injure them. It collected in icicles five or six inches long from the eaves of the sheds and on the balustrades. On Thursday the sun broke forth, and everything shone with surpassing brilliancy. During all the storm Joseph went up on Wednesday to the Sand Hills on horseback, carrying two guns and an umbrella. I felt very unhappy after he left me, which he did at a time when the weather appeared to be clearing. He says by the time he reached the hills his overcoat, cap, gun, and horse were coated in ice. He had to stop at the Boro and warm, and then at Dr. Howe's plantation. He spent the night with Brother Joe Anderson, and had his guns fixed to his satisfaction. There are very few who would have persevered under such circumstances. Many persons think they have never experienced colder weather in this climate. I thought constantly of *you,* and felt rejoiced today when your affectionate letter informed me of your comfortable passage as far as Wilmington. I hope you will increase your clothing and not suffer yourself to want. Sister Susan is kindly assisting me to make you some nice warm drawers.

Whilst speaking on this subject let me remind you to make our dear boy Charles a present of a new and respectable-looking overcoat. As he will not be likely to outgrow it, it had best be an excellent article that will be serviceable. I think a blue broadcloth wears best, but you can judge best; only let it be good and genteel. They are good children, and whilst expending we must not overlook their dues, for they are never forward to exact from us.

Finding our servants so badly off for blankets, all things considered (time, expenses, etc., etc.), I have written Cousin Joseph to select them for us and send immediately out. The winter promises to be so severe I thought they had best have them at once. Those bought but two years since must have been very inferior, for they are all gone.

By the *Northern Belle* we shipped last week to Mr. M. Cumming *ten* bales of cotton from Montevideo. At the same time I sent a barrel of oranges *(sweet and sour)* to Aunt and Brother John; a barrel and trunk of sweet for yourself. A hundred of those in the trunk are from Charles's tree; it also contains those designed for Dr. Hodge. They are all that I will have to send on, as I fear those left on the trees were frozen, and but few at best. Please send half a dozen of the best to Miss Cunningham with my love; and if you choose you can keep a few until we return to enjoy them with you.

My dear son Charles's last letter was received today, and I will write him by the next mail. I hope he is with you by this time, and our dear daughter. Has she left Miss Gill? Sister Susan and Laura are with me, *L.* suffering from a severe cold; hope she will be better tomorrow. We are all invited to take Christmas dinner with Julia. Dr. Wells and Mary are with her; *M.* in very delicate health. Do, if you can obtain information about the expenses of a child at the Deaf and Dumb Asylum, send it to me for Mrs. Edward Quarterman. Mr. Shepard has left for Griffin. Sister Betsy has improved very much. Brother William well. They with Sister Susan, Laura, and Joseph join in much love to you and Charles Edward, Charles Colcock, and Mary. Kiss my dear children for me, and tell them to do the same to you.

Ever, my dear husband, your affectionate

Mary I.

Please make my kind regards to Messrs. Happersett and Powel and to all friends. Mr. *Peace* is quite well.

My dearest Mary,

Yesterday the Communion service was impressive in Mr. Ruffner's church; added eight on profession, twelve on certificate. They think there is some influence from on high with them. Addressed Dr. Jones's Sabbath school in the afternoon. Evening at home, and had our usual service with our dear children, and communed with you in spirit.

It was *our twenty-first wedding day.* I thought over all these years, and remembered the good hand of God upon us and our children and upon all we are permitted to call our own here below. Years of wonderful mercy are they. It fills me with wonder. I recalled all your kindness and love to me and mine, and prayed for every blessing for you, and for forgiveness for all my waywardness and shortcomings as your husband. What would I have given to have taken you into my arms and told you of all my esteem and love! This absence makes my heart as lead. The Lord can unite and separate us as He pleases, but were it left to my desire, the delight of my eyes should ever be before me. You are the best, the sweetest, the most loved of all beings on earth to me.

Dr. Hodge called to see Mary Sharpe before church at my request. She had fever on Saturday night. He made a prescription, and she is up and better today. She was up all day yesterday, but did not go to church, of course. Hope her cold will pass off in a few days.

It commenced snowing last night; 2 P.M. still continues, and the white sheet of winter covers all things. The snow is whirling from the roofs of the houses and drifting in the wind. The fire bell is tolling.

Will you copy the epitaph on Aunt Lee's headstone in Midway graveyard, and append to it the number of years she lived with Father, and whatever you know or can collect from Brother Axson of her deathbed exercises? Mr. J. P. Engles begged me for the information for a Rev. Mr. Allen. Please remember it.

Received a *confidential* letter from Dr. Foote of Romney, Virginia, inquiring if I am satisfied with my present position, and if *I would accept a call to Prince Edward, Union Theological Seminary, Virginia, as professor.* Our good friend Rev. Griffith Owen called to see me this morning, and a little quizzically in conversation said: "There are several candidates for Princeton: Dr. Boardman, Dr. Plumer, Dr. Hall of Trenton, and *yourself*—the last two the most prominent." I write these things for your *own eye,* and to interest you. We know there is One who orders all according to His will. It is our privilege to be without care.

Your letter to Mary Sharpe was received this morning, and we rejoiced to hear from you and of your health and happiness, and the enjoyment which you had at the meeting at Midway. I am glad you were there; and we must hope and pray that God will yet bless the seed so faithfully sown.

The shears were bought of McClesky & Norton; and I thought they would answer for shrubbery and limbs also. McClesky & Norton have but one of the other kind—for limbs: heavy, and too heavy for you. The pair was not a very good one, but perhaps a good pair might be had at *Weed's*. Cousin Joe will attend to it for you. You might keep the pair you have and write McClesky & Norton to send the other kind; and you can return one *or keep both,* which will be the better plan.

Charles says if Joe gets to Princeton by the 10th of February it will be time enough. He will write more particularly about it. So you may not hurry when you would like to be quiet.

The brethren of the committee received me this afternoon with great kindness, and heartily welcomed me back. Walking with Dr. Janeway after our meeting adjourned, on my return, the pavements covered with snow and ice, I put my foot on a dark spot; it slipped, and down I came—a solid fall. Caught on my hands. A severe jar, but thanks to a kind Providence, no injury. Irish John at the Markoe fell on the ice today and dislocated his arm at the shoulder: pulled in; sore and in a sling. John in describing his fall said: "I was capsized over upon my shoulder." The usual amount of broken limbs and bruises.

Dr. Hodge called after tea and prescribed a dose of Sampson for our dear child; ordered it given in *porter.* Pour in the tumbler a third full, then the oil, and add a little more; take it in the foam, and you taste porter alone. A perfect disguise. A great discovery.

December 23rd. Our dear child better—much better—today. The medicine needed, and hope she will be able to go out in a day or so. It is a protracted cold: no sore throat and no cough; more than a little hack now and then, as is usual in colds. Elizabeth is very attentive, and waits on us at all times cheerfully.

Clear day. Winter scenes without: sleighs running; sleigh bells; ladies with their muffs; everyone with red face and nose walking briskly; little boys pulling their sleds, etc. I enjoy it.

Everybody says I have *improved.* Do, my darling wife, write me frequently. I live upon your love. I enclose you a verse—and do not tell me *nay.* Love to Joe and everybody and everything.

Your own dear husband,
C. C. Jones.

To My Dear Mary
On Her Twenty-First Wedding Day

Years in their rapid flight have passed away,
And dawns our one and twentieth wedding day!
Cold were those wintry hours; cold are they now;
But fresh and warm, as then, my marriage vow
Earth has her spring; rough winter brings her snows;
The heart unchanged: that heart no winter knows.

Blest day that made thee mine! Another life
Breathed in me. Soft those thrilling words, *"My wife."*
Dost thou remember them? Moment of joy
That brought me happiness without alloy.
Hope realized; fears, disappointments flown:
She whom I loved as life—she, all my own!
Those early days! All nature bathed in light:
The brilliant sun, the paler moon more bright;
More soft the airs; clouds gently moved along;
More fresh the spring, more sweet the warbler's song.
The walk, the ride, the page, the social hour,
The quiet room, the Word, the fervent prayer.
Harmoniously our pure affections moved;
'Twas happiness enough to be beloved.
Sweet home, sweet friends, sweet children: bounteous store;
Sweet labors for our God: what could we more?
Oh, that these hearts with gratitude might break!
Oh, that these tongues His goodness e'er might speak!
Yet on our path the sunshine and the shade
His hand hath thrown; and by His teachings bade
Our hearts, through sorrows, *flames,* and trials rise
To that unfading rest beyond the skies.
Companions we have been in all these years
By day and night. In smiles we've shed our tears.
Yet for the joy that thou hast been to me,
Might I not live them o'er to be with thee.
These years have many, many changes brought,
But in my love I see no changes wrought.
That heart which thou alone in youth didst claim—
In riper age that heart is still the same.
Nay, nay: I love thee more—more sweet, more dear;
The maiden cannot with *the wife* compare!
Poor help I've been to thee. Perhaps a cross!
What was my gain perhaps has been thy loss!
Oh, could I pluck the shadows past, away,
Where sunlight only should have ruled the day!
The wrong do thou forgive as He forgives
Upon whose Word the trembling sinner lives.
Thou best of mothers, who with tender eye
Watchest thine own with ceaseless jealousy.
The best of wives, so modest, loving, neat,
So cheerful, frugal, generous, provident,
Discerning, prudent, active, happy, wise,
So gentle, just, and firm without disguise,
Charitable, magnanimous, and kind,

The heart improved, well disciplined the mind;
So fixed in faith, in piety sincere,
Benevolent and true, and free from fear.
Light of my home, thy virtues made that home
A seat of sweet repose to all who came.
Those better know who longest there have dwelt
Its order, quiet, happiness, content.
What have I, not thine own, since I am thine?
What need I more, since, Mary, thou art mine?
Not twain but one—one heart, one flesh, one soul.
What perfect union, and what strong control!
Thy countenance, thy footsteps, and thy form,
Thy voice, thy ways of love, thy every charm,
Imprinted deeply on my eye, my ear,
Enshrined within my heart, thy place is there.
Friends, absence, occupation, ne'er remove
The cherished image of the one I love.
Light of my life! my counselor, my aid,
My sweet companion, by kind Heaven made,
And prompt in duty, helper always true,
Always hast kept thy God and heaven in view.
I wish thee all that heaven and earth can yield
And God thy lasting portion and thy shield.
Next unto Him thyself on me bestow;
Thy husband seeks no happier lot below.
Time moves apace! And age is stealing on.
Our children to maturer years have come.
Blest be their life! Their happiness secured
In wisdom, piety, and heaven's award.
The vale of life, my love, before us lies!
Peaceful our walk! Our hope beyond the skies!
Oh blissful thought! The hearts united now
Forever shall before the Saviour bow!
Accept, my love, these fervent lines which love has penned
Of your devoted husband and your warmest friend.
                    C. C. Jones.
    December 21st, 1851.

Rev. C. C. Jones *to* Mrs. Mary Jones[t]
                    Philadelphia, *Wednesday,* December 24th, 1851
My darling Wife,
    Sent you a letter and a paper last evening. Charles and I went to hear
General Sam Houston lecture on the Indians. Cars did not connect: not
there! Rev. Mr. Willetts delivered an interesting *lecture* on "The Power and

Greatness of *Love*." Did not agree with some of his *ultra* peace principles. We walked home with Mr. and Mrs. Riesch. Mrs. and Miss Tate and Mrs. Roser have been quite kind to Mary Sharpe.

Today city all alive! Kossuth arrived! A grand procession. Streets crowded. An arch across Chestnut. "Hurrah for Kossuth! Push on, boys. Halloo! *My toes!* Get off my toes!" Our young clerk, Mr. Hall, says they cried out in the multitude as much for their *toes* as for *Kossuth*. The cannon are firing! But here he comes along Chestnut Street! Drums and bands; the military; numerous companies, but small: horse, foot, and cannon. The streets are lined; the windows above and below, the balconies, filled. The stream pours along the sidewalks. The crowd becomes more dense. The roar of the "hurrahs" increases. Here he comes in that barouche drawn by white horses plumed! The dense masses of men tumultuate: they roll onward. The noise deepens; the ladies wave their handkerchiefs; the banners bend. And see him! There he is, standing in the open barouche with a cloak on, bearded and moustached, a black beaver and feather on, turning and bowing gracefully as he passes! His countenance is calm, pensive, and bespeaking modesty. His stature medium. He is gone ere curiosity is satisfied. There follows the civic procession: carriages abreast, associations on foot. It is passed. The pageant is over.

Such a scene Philadelphia has not witnessed for many a year. There is sublimity in it: *a great people honoring in Kossuth the principle of freedom!* Charles and I looked from the windows of our office building. As he passed I gave three cheers for Kossuth. Charles said he cheered before. He went into the street at first and got 'most squeezed to death. He said he never smelt such a smell of onions in his life, mixed up with all the villainous smells imaginable, and was in distress for fresh air above all things. He was near, he says, being "smashed flat," and will keep clear of the crowd hereafter. Mary Sharpe saw all from Mrs. Roser's windows.

I do not agree with Mr. Kossuth's doctrine of *intervention* as he has broached it at his bar speech in New York. It is a departure from all the principles of Washington and the fathers of our country, which have governed and blessed us these sixty odd years. We are not called upon to fight the battles of the world! The people will not favor it.

Tell Joe his *beaver* is *à la Kossuth!* The very pink of fashion. A black ostrich feather would complete it. He may now give currency to that part of masculine wear.

Mary Sharpe received a Christmas present this evening of a pie and tumbler of jelly from Mrs. Newkirk and a copy of Nevin's *Biblical Antiquities* from Mrs. Colwell.

Please ask Mr. Shepard to set down the order of the carpenters' work: (1) Finish the ricehouse at Arcadia. (2) Finish the yard and garden at Montevideo, and the yard at Maybank, and anything else you wish done. (3) Build two new Negro houses at Arcadia: same size and material with the rest. (4) Put all the Negro houses and chapel at Montevideo *in complete repair.* (5) Shingle stable and Andrew's house, and do what repairs upon the cornhouse at Maybank may be necessary. And (6) then he can go on and complete his settlement on Carlawter hill.

Will it be too much trouble for you to bring *on the entire family records of both our branches as far back and as full as you can get them?* Sisters B. and S. will aid you. Leave a good copy at home.

December 25th. A Merry Christmas to you, my dearest one! A kind Providence ever be with and bless you and all yours! We all send our salutations and love to you and to all our dear relatives.

In the office till 12 M. Mr. Watson gave an elegant entertainment to his boarders. We sat down after four and got up after six. Called on Miss Cunningham: improved; sends much love to you. To my surprise, on coming out found the ground which had nearly thawed clear of snow covered near two inches, and a heavy snow falling!

At half-past nine a torchlight procession of great length and various banners passed the Markoe in honor of Kossuth. As we beheld the extended double lines of torches far up the street, the scene was brilliant. They pass by with music. The sidewalks are lined with dark forms, hats and umbrellas white with snow, and the exposed shoulders of men; the street and sidewalks white with snow, and the lights giving new brightness to the whole.

Today the streets (the 26th, Friday) present winter perfectly. The omnibuses are turned into great open sleighs, crowded, with bells on the horses; sleighs of all kinds passing and repassing; and no rumbling sounds, as the pavements are all underneath a bed of snow. The people are out enjoying the day.

Mary Sharpe walked out after dinner for the first time in a week. The weather has been very bad. She is pretty much relieved of her cold, and hope she will have no more of it. It has reduced her considerably. Enclosed is her circular for the last quarter. She thinks the six good lessons ought not to be there, but all perfect. The circular is a very satisfactory one. She and Charles and Lewis Pynchon and Brother Happersett are sitting by my desk as I write. All send love. Do, my darling, write me. Love to Joe and my sisters and brother and Laura and all others. Howdy for all the people.

Your own affectionate husband,
C. C. Jones.

Send you some stamps.

Mrs. Mary Jones *to* Mr. Charles C. Jones, Jr.[g]

Montevideo, Thursday, December 25th, 1851

A pleasant and happy Christmas to you, my very dear son! Brother is dozing on the couch, feeling drowsy from a very bad cold which has caused him some fever today. The chapel bell has rung, and the servants are at their evening prayers, and not a living sound falls upon my ear. Every now and then the fire blazes brightly up with a piece of fat lightwood, making every object in our little parlor cheerful and bright. I have never dreaded or avoided solitude; it has always been the natural element for my mental constitution. I love and crave to be *alone* as a kind of spiritual and intellectual feast.

But I must now tell you not of the ideal and visionary but the real and substantial. Your aunt and uncle and brother came up from the Island this morning; and your Aunt Susan, who has been staying with me ever since your father left, and myself all went over by invitation to South Hampton. When we arrived, besides the family were Dr. and Mrs. Wells, Miss Sanford and Edward Axson, your Cousin Laura, Augustus Fleming, and Mr. Peace. As usual your Aunt Julia spread out a most beautiful board: meats of various kinds, followed by puddings and pies, jellies and syllabubs, sweetmeats, nuts, and fruits of many kinds, to all of which there was great attention paid and ample justice done. In the evening your Cousin Laura, Audley, and your brother were invited to a party at Mr. Barnard's. Joseph was too unwell to attend, and so was Laura. I regretted this, as the Barnards have been quite attentive to him, and have one of Judge Lumpkin's sons with them, and young Screven.

They have all been over to see Joseph. Banky and West have not done so, although he has called at the Retreat and invited them to do so. But they have been engaged hunting, I presume. In consequence of the weather and the state of the guns he has not done as much in that line as he anticipated. The hunters visit our grounds so often that the deer and wild turkeys are very scarce, and ducks also, in consequence of the drought. I wish that you too were here with us, but you made the wiser choice in view of your present engagements.

Your Aunt Julia wished today for all the boys and your dear sister. Fred and Willie's daguerreotypes have just been received, and were in part a compensation for their absence. Your Cousin Mary Wells looks broken, and is in very delicate health; *Dr. Wells* a most gentlemanly and amiable person, and I doubt not an excellent *M.D.* Audley is quite an established planter, and fills admirably a useful position in the family, not only governing the plantation but all the little folks at home. His services could not well be dispensed with. To his mother especially he is a most dutiful and affectionate son.

Banky is said to be attentive to Miss Augusta Quarterman; how true I do not know. They would be a little couple.

Your Uncle James has, I trust, in all respects *done well*.

Should you see Mrs. White please say that Mr. Peace looks remarkably well, and will, I hope, be entirely restored to health.

Your father has told you of Dr. Thornwell's election to the presidency of the South Carolina College. The vote was unanimous when taken, although there was previously a division of feeling.

I received your dear father's affectionate letter this evening from Washington, and trust through a kind Providence he arrived safely in Philadelphia

285

on Saturday. You and Sister will, I know, take good care of him until I get back. I am happy to know that your Cousin Charles has quite recovered. I hope you will all enjoy the oranges. One hundred of those in the trunk were from *your own tree*.

It grieved me to hear of such disgraceful proceedings at Princeton; and from what your brother told me of Professor Hope's action, he has placed the *nine* who acted in fearless support of his requirements in a most unpleasant position. A regard to consistency and common honor should have led him to support his own words and their correct course. You, my beloved child, are nearly through this perilous period of your education. I bless God that, so far as I know and as I believe, you have been preserved thus far from the degrading vices and sins that ruin utterly for time and eternity so many promising young men. My constant prayer to my gracious Master and Saviour is that He would preserve you unto the end. Neglect not *your Bible, your closet, the Sabbath, the House of God, the prayer meeting;* and flee from the wicked, those who curse and blaspheme, who gamble and drink, who break the Sabbath and speak lightly of sacred things, or who practice any known wickedness. Added to all the claims of the Great Jehovah upon you, you are a baptized child of the covenant, and the son of a faithful minister of the Lord Jesus Christ. May God bless you, my dear child, and truly convert your soul! Then to whatever post or work you are assigned in life, *all will be well. This* is my chief—my great—anxiety!

All your friends and servants inquire affectionately after you and desire to be remembered. I saw the Miss McAllisters at Midway, and Miss Clem desired love to you. Kiss your dear father and dear sister for me. Brother unites with me in love to Cousin Charlie and to you all. My respects to Mrs. Roser, Mrs. and Miss Tate, and the ladies of the house. It is late, and I must close. Believe me ever

Your affectionate mother,

Mary Jones.

26th. Last night I gave your brother a dose of blue mass for his cold. Betimes this morning the servants were at him with a dose of oil as of yore; and he has been spouting in the shed room like a great whale. I have laughed heartily at the sounds that have arisen through the chimney to my room. *Mr. Bennet* and his cold is nothing to it.

Influenzas are prevailing, and measles in some parts of the county. Mr. Nat Way was buried on Monday; he took cold with the measles, and it terminated suddenly.

Mr. CHARLES C. JONES, JR., *to* Mrs. MARY JONES[t]

Philadelphia, *Saturday,* December 27th, 1851

My dear Mother,

Ever since my arrival in this place we have lived amidst excitement and ever varying scenes. The continued cry is: "They come! They come!" It would seem that the inhabitants of large cities above all others fully understand the ways by which daily occupations may be interspersed with novelties and the tediousness of accustomed routine relieved. The theater and circus both contribute their large "mite," catering to the tastes of certain classes, pleasing the eye, and captivating the souls of those who know not the tender sensibilities and refinements of heart. The opera again attracts those who, removed from the common herd—the self-styled "elite," can endure only the spasmodic effusions of Italian singers, regarding those lofty flights (which persons generally deem little less than mere shrieking) as the perfection of music. While orations and performances of other kinds also receive their appropriate degrees of attention from the crowd for whose benefit they are prepared.

The theme lately has, as you may well conjecture, been Kossuth, Hungary, and its claims. The people of New York gave the example, and to the letter has it been fulfilled by those of this city. Never perhaps since its foundation has this abode of brothers and sisters ever witnessed so moving a scene unless perchance in the case of General Lafayette. Could the strait-jacket soul of old Father Penn only have seen the uprising and unusual assemblages in his once quiet and economical domains, how would his Quaker heart have been completely "dumbfounded" within him! The procession was elegant in many respects, and exceedingly long. Never have I seen such honor paid to a single individual. The great Magyar is a fine-looking gentleman, and is possessed of a very kind and benevolent countenance. The clear blue eye, modest mien, and soft, tender sentiments breathed in his speeches, all conspire to render him a favorite in the popular mind; while his noble deeds and courageous actions in the cause of liberty have even now rendered him a hero and stamped him as the champion of Hungary.

He delivered several very interesting speeches while here, and certainly seems to possess a happy faculty of adapting his expressions to any occasion. Yesterday at three o'clock he met the Sunday school children in the Chinese Museum. In consequence of our not being aware of the meeting we were debarred the pleasure of hearing him. The occasion was an interesting one. Two of the little boys delivered handsome and patriotic addresses, which were beautifully and touchingly responded to by Kossuth, who cordially reciprocated their kind welcome and embraced them both. He must certainly be a man of the kindest affections and sincere attachments. Without any presumption or wish for display he modestly bears the honors conferred by an enthusiastic people, and when called upon replies in a calm and grateful manner.

Who would blame him when in the sincerity of his love for his country he comes to this land of civil and religious liberty to implore assistance and aid in the cause of the idol of his heart, now trampled upon by the Russian Bear and the Lion of St. Mark? Who regarding his situation, his feelings, and his aims can indulge towards him and his purposes other than honest motives? Yet while he demands our warmest sympathies, let us not forget that our first vows are to be paid to our country, that the land of our childhood claims the prime honors of her sons, and the sage counsels of a Washington, Jefferson, and Madison are by no means to be treated with neglect. The law of noninterference is one fundamental to the interests and perpetuity of our government; and if it be but once set aside, where will any limit be fixed? Let private contribution and individual enterprise minister to his necessities, but may the government stand aloof from all official intervention.

Father and myself enjoyed a fine view of Kossuth from the Mission rooms. Sister was similarly favored from a window in Mrs. Roser's room. I have refrained from attempting any description of the procession, banners, troops, etc., because you received papers from Father descriptive of the same.

The burning of our capitol and especially the library is truly a severe loss. Those ancient manuscripts with marginal notes by Washington, Jefferson, Adams, and others can never be replaced. The works of art may be reproduced, but the effusions of great minds, once gone, are gone forever.

A distressing fire occurred in Chestnut Street last evening. Hart's Buildings, the beautiful establishment of Schenck's Pulmonic Syrup, Johnson's law bookstore, with many others are reduced to a mass of ruins. Independence Hall and the theater were both in imminent danger of being destroyed. The saddest feature is that several lives were lost by the falling of walls. It has again broken out this evening.

Sister is again much better. She was this day presented with a beautiful canary bird from Cousin Charlie. Father's heart is with you, although his person is in Philadelphia. Hoping, dear Mother, that we shall hear often from you, I will close. Father, Sister, and the doctor unite with me in kindest love to self, aunts, uncle, cousin, brother, and all relatives and friends.

Your affectionate son,
Charles C. Jones, Jr.

The college term does not commence until the 5th of February. For the first week scarce anything is done save the appointment of recitations, so that if you return by the 10th or 12th little time will be lost. Ask Brother why he does not answer my letter and let me know "the spirit of the times."

Rev. C. C. Jones *to* Mrs. Mary Jones[t]

Philadelphia, *Wednesday,* December 31st, 1851

Your precious letter, my darling wife, came on Monday and filled us all with joy—especially your own dear husband. Thank you a thousand times for your kind and sincere wishes and prayers expressed on my birthday and on our wedding day. You have been to me all I could desire as a wife, and I pray that God may reward you abundantly for all your love to me and mine. His dealings towards us indeed have been wonderful. We can only wait upon Him in His appointed ways, and in the path of duty, and abide in quietness His will.

I forwarded to you yesterday an enclosure *of the heart* which I hope may reach you in safety. If you choose you can leave it at home, and I will prepare you one exactly like it and hand it to you on your return to Philadelphia.

Joe has peculiar and strongly marked traits of character, and we may have erred in the manner you indicate in our influence over him and earnest prayers for him. I sincerely rejoice that he is quietly at home with you, and trust that very special good to him will come of it.

How happy am I to hear of your enjoyment of the spiritual privileges in Midway! It is a place where God our Saviour has long recorded His name, and He records it there still. Large cities do not appear to me to be favorable to personal religion. At least, my experience is somewhat that way. It may be because I have long been used to a quiet and contemplative—though not inactive—life. It was a cross to bear in that I could not stay to the meeting. Tell my dear Brother Axson that Midway is better than Glebe Street Church. If he does not believe it, let them call him, and let him go and try it!

Right about the people's blankets: *exactly* and *promptly* right. The cold came to you after I left. Have sent you the papers which will tell you all about the *cold* and *Kossuth* and the *fires* here!

Tell Jimma to have *the likeness of Grandfather returned to him at all hazards.* If I can aid him any, will cheerfully do so.

Mr. Alberti has sent us a barrel of very fine oranges in excellent preservation. Fear you have robbed yourself to enrich us.

Friday night last when the fire occurred in 6th Street the thermometer was 3° below zero! The fireplugs had to be thawed out *by fire,* and much of the hose was frozen hard! Yet the brave firemen did all men could do battling the elements—hats, coats, whiskers, beards hanging in icicles! The loss of Mr. Haly the lawyer was deeply affecting. But six months married. His poor wife is said to be almost distracted! You will see by the papers how he was identified, and in what a state his poor body was found. *How merciful was God to us in our calamity!*

Sabbath a dreadful day of fog, damp, rain, and thawing: streets *"slush"* and flowed. Charles and I ventured out: Central in the morning, Mr. Barnes's afternoon. Exposure was too much for him. He was seized with fever at night, and it ran high, and his head was like to burst. In the morning (Monday) I gave him a large dose of oil. The medicine had the desired effect: in bed all day. Dr. Hodge saw him in the evening; prescribed for him. Fever has left him; he was up all day yesterday, and is up today; but his throat is very sore, and I have not allowed him to go out. Hope his throat will be better in a few days. These attacks of cold are very prevalent. Charles has a letter nearly ready to send you.

Mary Sharpe up and quite bright, and improving daily.

Will attend to your messages when the oranges come.

Last evening at half-past five o'clock Barnum's Museum took fire in the *"Lecture Room,"* as it is called. That is in the theater part (third or fourth story), and in two hours was a mass of ruins! The flames burnt immediately through and enveloped the entire roof, and then raged beyond control. The walls bent out of line, section after section, and down they came with a sound like stifled thunder and artillery; and every fall the ten thousand spectators sent their shouts up to heaven. Chiefly the boys. Such a crowd! No estimating the numbers! Much loss in stores below. No wind; and water in abundance, thanks to a kind Providence. Our good friend Mr. Colwell had no injury at all. Great difficulty in preventing the fire from crossing the streets. Thus Providence has placed His hand upon some buildings recently which have been of serious injury to the morals of the city. Barnum's Lecture Room is said to have been one of the worst places in the city. They say that a *hotel* will now go up there. The museum was sold out by Barnum some time since.

Mrs. Powel has been and still is quite sick. Mr. Powel feels concerned about her, and sends his kindest regards to you. Brother Happersett is very hearty.

Dr. Humphrey will not come to the Central Church. They are at sea again. I feel for them, and have their lectures on my hands this evening.

Send you some papers today. Charles and Mary Sharpe and Charles Edward send much love to you and to Sister and Laura and Brother and Sister and all friends, in which I join. Howdy for all the servants by name. I am counting the days of the return of my dear wife. Your miniature is a daily comfort to me. Will make inquiry about the Deaf and Dumb Asylum and let you know. Write every mail.

Your ever affectionate husband,
C. C. Jones.

REV. C. C. JONES *to* MRS. MARY JONES[t]

Philadelphia, *Thursday,* January 1st, 1852

My ever dearest Wife,

The first letter I write this new year shall be to you. A Happy New Year to you, my dear Mary! May the dew of heaven and the fatness of the earth be thine, and every spiritual blessing in Christ Jesus our Lord, with an everlasting inheritance for you and all yours when we have finished our course below! If it is God's will, may we be spared to each other—and that to serve Him more faithfully, and to love each other more heartily and tenderly, and be happier than ever before! And may we have the unspeakable joy of seeing both our sons converted, all our family in the ark, and religion flourishing in our household and family relations! May we be prepared for all the coming will of God, and be more and more prepared for His presence and glory! Pen and paper cannot convey the feelings of my heart to you.

Lectured last evening for the Central Church. Few out because of the present rain; but pleasant and hope profitable. Today we have a perfectly clear and brilliant sky and a calm, mild atmosphere. Snow and ice almost completely gone out of the streets. Roofs all clear. Such changes! Most trying to the constitution. Charles is out today; throat still sore. But Mary S. unwell again this morning; was remarkably well yesterday. She has taken a little magnesia, and hope she will be better. I had predicted this fine day and told her and Charles to make the most of it in exercise. The child is too much cooped up, and much of her indisposition is owing to a want of fresh air and exercise. Shall not send her back to school until she is in improved health. The acquisition of an education at the cost of health is not duty. Extend the term of study, and make the confinement less.

Shall answer Dr. Foote's kind letter today about the professorship in Union Theological Seminary, Virginia, in the *negative*. While all my tastes and inclinations are in favor of a professorship or pastoral or *missionary* charge over the post which I now occupy, and my thoughts do often run forward to a day of release into some such work, yet it does not seem that this is the time, nor *that* the place, so far as I can discern the leadings of Providence and His will. The affairs of the Board of Missions are in such a state as to require the closest attention; nor would I desire to leave them until they are more in order and in greater prosperity, if the Lord is pleased to have it so. We may enjoy a clearer sky and a more open sea before the meeting of the assembly. We ought to have learned by this time that the Lord reigneth and His will must rule His people; and we must not choose our own changes.

January 2nd, Friday. Good morning to you, my sweet one, this glorious, beautiful day! Thanks to the Father of Mercies, we are all up and doing well. Charles's sore throat much better; his sister put a mustard plaster on it last night. And she is quite bright. They are going out to walk.

Mary Sharpe sent Dr. Hodge some oranges yesterday, and he returned her a very kind note.

Charles Edward, Charles C., and I took a long walk yesterday afternoon. We called at the Deaf and Dumb Asylum. The charge for an inmate (boy or girl) is $160 *and everything found,* or $130 and the parents or guardians *find clothing.* If I mistake not, there is a deaf and dumb asylum in our *own state.* If not, I think the state makes provision for such cases as cannot be supported by their parents or guardians; *and our friends might avail themselves of this provision.*

Enclosed you have a check on the state bank in your favor; have left the sum *blank* for you to fill up with whatever amount you may wish to draw out for your expenses and for your own use here. You must also *include $400,* which we shall want for the college bills of the boys and for Mary Sharpe's tuition the coming terms in Princeton and in Philadelphia. Fill in the blank with the whole amount, and take what you need for traveling expenses in gold, and the balance in a check of the state bank on the Philadelphia bank here, which will be the easiest and safest mode of bringing it on. When you fill your check, endorse it *(write your name on the back of it);* and our good friend Major Porter will arrange it all for you and bring you the check for what you wish to bring on, and the ready money for your expenses by the way.

Mrs. Porter insists upon your staying a day or two with her as you pass through. If you come down to Savannah Tuesday, February 3rd *(God willing),* start on Wednesday evening by Charleston boat; next afternoon, Thursday 5th, leave Charleston for Wilmington; Friday morning leave Wilmington, and *be in Washington Saturday evening, February 7th, where,* God willing, *I will meet you;* stay over Sabbath in Washington; leave Monday or Tuesday morning as you may desire; and reach Philadelphia the same day at 5 P.M. This will be far better for you than to ride two nights in succession on the cars after two nights on the boats. *Let me know if this arrangement suits you.*

My whole heart and soul turn in earnest longings for my love, my dear, dear Mary. My loneliness without you at times is almost insupportable. I had sweet dreams and thoughts of you this morning.

The balance to my credit today in the state bank is $396.26. But hope Mr. Cumming will sell and make a deposit before you come on, which will then be enough for all purposes. Major P. can tell you this, if I do not in the meantime. *Love from us all to all.* You have good proof in my frequent letters that I am, as ever,

Your own true lover and most devoted husband,
C. C. Jones.

You may not spend so much, but take for your own and Joe's expenses *at least $80.*

REV. C. C. JONES *to* MRS. MARY JONES[t]

Philadelphia, Monday, January 5th, 1852

I have just returned, my dearest wife, from a visitation. Yesterday I preached three times—twice for the board and once to the children of a Sabbath school; twice at Frankford and once at Bridesburg. A pleasant day, but *snowy* and uncomfortable; hence congregations small. No collections taken up because so few people out; yet I worked as energetically as though I was addressing thousands. The Delaware opposite Bridesburg, six miles above Philadelphia, has been frozen over for two weeks; is still so, though we have had thaws, and it is now a mild beautiful day and thawing in the sun. When our two-horse stage got into Kensington, down slipped one of our Rosinantes; smash went our tongue! So we hurried out, as the other horse when his mate got up showed signs of a race. My own heels slid, and down I came catching on the tongue—under the heels of the horse! No walking on the sidewalks; the boys are skating there: all frozen glass.

Glad of the walk up; got to the Markoe steps as if walking on eggs, and found Charles and Mary Sharpe rejoicing over *Mother's letter* of Christmas

Day. Thanks to the Lord for His tender mercies to you, my dear wife, and to all around you. Hope my dear boy Joe will not be much sick. Tell him *the Sampson* is the thing. The death of Mr. Nat Way is sudden and affecting. Think he had married his second wife.

I wish I was with you to enjoy your solitude. I think you would sweeten my solitude. Home! Home! When shall I be permitted to dwell there again?

Charles and Mary S. play together very sweetly. While *shaving* just now they played "Twilight Dews" and some other tunes.

On Saturday Mr. Newkirk asked me privately and confidentially whether we liked our present position and would like to remain in it. Our reply was we came to it, as we believed, upon a call of duty, and did not desire to leave it without some intimations from Him with whom is our account. But the situation was too confining, and it was a question if my general health could stand it, and my tastes and inclinations were more for a pastoral or *missionary* charge, etc.

Said he: "If a suitable call came to you to leave your place, would you do it?"

I replied: "That would be determined only upon a due consideration of the call."

He remarked that "he only desired to know my feelings for his own satisfaction, for he meant to go in strong for me *for Princeton.*"

I mention these little things to amuse you. He said "a good brother was out as a candidate for Dr. A.'s place." I frankly told him I never had been and never would be a candidate for any place in the gift of the church. And so let the Lord order all things. I have never felt less moved to make arrangements for remaining in this place than at the present time. It may be the impress of Providence; we cannot tell. Let His will be done.

6th, Tuesday. Such a day! The morning ushered in with snow, sleet, hail, rain, and wind—all mixed up and coming down together! The pavements covered with soft, melting snow! Hope my love enjoys a milder and more cheerful sky.

Am reading *the Psalms* with more enjoyment than ever before. Oh, the wonderful love of God—the unfailing faith and hope in Him—therein displayed! Read some three, four, or five a day.

My heart rejoices to know that your visit home is so much a blessing to you spiritually. May your soul ever prosper and be full of the love of God our Saviour!

Mary Sharpe did not go to school yesterday, and by no means today. She says her cold seems to have settled in her bones, and complains of her right shoulder and arm, sometimes preventing sleep. We have made a bargain with Elizabeth to rub her arm every night and morning under promise of a present if it is cured. We shall try various schemes with it, and consider the affection temporary. I tell her she is getting old and rheumatic. She is improving fast again, and so is Charles Colcock.

Charles Edward says "he is much neglected by *Mother* and Sister! Three weeks and not a line! What a suitable occasion for fretting! But as he would have the fretting all to himself, he believes he will postpone it."

Brother J. P. Engles has just come in, and says that Dr. Van Rensselaer's wife (Mrs. V. R.) and their nurse have both *the smallpox or the varioloid*. It is in the city. May a kind Providence spare the family of our Christian brother! Brother Happersett went home to take physic yesterday; not down today—perhaps on account of the weather.

The children send a world of love to you and to Joseph and to all friends, and howdy for all the people. Tell my dear brother he must read Governor McDowell's speech (of Virginia) recently mailed to him. Love to him and to my dear sisters and niece. Say that my letters to you are designed for them too; and you must give them all the news you can out of them; and I shall write them as soon as possible.

Every morning I put on Uncle Maybank's spectacles and gaze on the face of my dear, dear absent wife. Oh, the world of love that will be poured into her bosom when we meet again—if it shall so please our Heavenly Father! I long, long to embrace my own dearest Mary, and am counting the days when we shall be united once more. Howdy for Cato and Stepney and Andrew and Patience and all the servants *by name,* little and big—and *Tony.* I remain, my dearest wife,

Your ever affectionate and devoted husband,

C. C. Jones.

Mrs. Mary Jones *to* Rev. C. C. Jones[t]

Montevideo, *Monday,* January 5th, 1852

Today's mail came richly freighted with the *precious* mementos of your devoted love, my own beloved husband. How I thank you for all—especially for those lines of tenderness and love upon our twenty-first wedding day. I feel humbled by such flattering expressions of your confidence and attachment, and am wholly undeserving of the compliments you are pleased to bestow. Of one thing only am I assured: that you alone possessed and now possess the first, the only, the undivided affection of my heart. My early love was all your own, and it will cease only with a pulseless bosom. I know that my married life has been marked with a thousand faults, which your loving charity has forgiven and forgotten; but in my own memory they are traced with sad regrets, and I trust with feelings of penitence before my Father in Heaven. As you permit me, I will leave the "lines" amongst my other treasures in the little worktable. How I dread to remove anything valuable from home! Keep the *copy,* that I may look at them when I come. How I have wished for a miniature of you that I might wear about my person! Will you not give me such an one?

Do, my dearest, do not reduce yourself by such constant labor. It is not right that you should be called upon to preach; it is unkind and inconsiderate in those who ask it; and you will thus incapacitate yourself for the duties of your office.

I am grieved to know that our dear son and daughter have both been sick with cold. They must not expose to the severity of the weather.

Old Winter has come upon you in earnest. I wish you were all here to enjoy the delightful sunny days of the week past. But we have also had much severe cold for this climate, and whilst I am writing, the wind is whistling sharply around the house. If *you* were not alluring me, I should shudder at the prospect of a journey North in February.

I have been as busy as a bee whenever the weather would allow me to work in the garden, and by trimming the trees the prospect has brightened all around. The carpenters commenced working here on last Friday. The first thing I made them attend to was flooring the back piazza, having had a tumble through in the dark which bruised my side and arm and strained the muscles of my right foot. But it is all over now, and I feel quite relieved. I found on examining the Negro houses at Arcadia that in consequence of the miserable way in which they had been blocked that several of them were down on the ground and careened aside, and bore evidence of great neglect. I pointed it out to Mr. Rahn; he said that work was done before he came on the place. I then called Sandy and told him before Mr. Rahn if any more houses were put up in that style, he and Porter's Saturdays were to be taken from them and spent in reblocking all they did improperly. And I shall say the same to Mr. Shepard.

I believe Mr. R. is an honest man, but he wants attention to matters about the place, and is ignorant in many things. There is one arrangement I should like to have altered: instead of increasing he has diminished in the number of hogs raised. Our object is to secure bacon to our people. I think it too much that he should be allowed half. Can we not for the future increase the stock of raising hogs and give him a proportion? James Newton kills this year for his people forty-five hogs of his own raising, and with our pasture and provisions at Arcadia we surely ought to raise over five.

It has been a source of satisfaction to me to be with our people to instruct them as far as I can and look after their comfort and the interests of the plantation; and I am thoroughly convinced of the necessity of doing so as long as your duties call you away. I am going to make Caesar and old Tony occupy poor Jack's house. This will be for the comfort of the old man and protection of the lot. Gilbert and Fanny will come into Elsie's house as soon as she is removed, and Lymus and John take the one next to Cato. It is a relief to my mind to have someone with old *T.;* and *C.* is his nephew and a single man. The Negro houses have all been cleaned around, and as Rose is perfectly able to do so, I shall insist upon Mr. Shepard's requiring her to keep them clean with the large girls who are nurses. This is necessary for their health. The blankets have arrived and been distributed here. I sleep much more comfortably these cold nights since *this has been done.*

Yesterday we went to Pleasant Grove and heard Mr. John Winn; but a slim turnout. Oh, how the past rushed over my mind! Many precious hours are associated with you and your ministry there, our departed friends, and the black people. They all inquired and sent unnumbered loves and messages. The long, long years of your toil and unwearied effort in the missionary field is ever present to my mind, especially on Sabbaths. May the Lord bless and reward you a thousandfold! Yesterday everything looked melancholy to me; but Mr. Winn is a most excellent man.

Mr. Law is actually going away to take charge of a church and school in the up country. One of his sons has recently been shot through the thigh by the accidental discharge of a pistol: *a flesh wound.*

What would you think of putting *William* to the carpenter's trade with Sandy? He thinks he would do well, and is the right age.

Tomorrow, Providence permitting, we hope to go down to the Island. I have not been down since you left. Sister Susan has been with me ever since you left, and will accompany us tomorrow. She has quite recovered, and gained three pounds since being at Montevideo. So much for *marooning; I* have *lost* that number. If you had been with me I should have gained: I miss you by day and by night. However, I ought to say the last time I weighed it was without my blanket shawl.

I will try to comply with your requests as far as I can about Mrs. Lee and the family records.

Last week we rode to see Charles Berrien and family; they have a sweet little girl two weeks old. James and his bride have been to see us; they are very handsomely fixed at the Retreat.

I desire to return in time to see my dear son C. before he leaves for Princeton. His affectionate letter was received today, and I will write him soon; also Charles Edward's to his mother. Kiss my dear children for me, and tell them to do the same to you. Sister S., Joseph, and all friends unite in love *to you all.* The servants send many howdies. Remember me to Mrs. Riesch, Mrs. Newkirk, and Mrs. Colwell, Miss Cunningham, Mrs. Smith, and the *ladies* of the Markoe, to *Irish John and Elizabeth.*

If Charles still talks of the law, ask him how he would like to study with Judge Charlton and Mr. Ward. He could make the acquaintance of the latter if he pleases, as he is now in Philadelphia. Brother William thinks him much changed for the better by affliction.

By the last vessel ten bales of cotton have been sent from Arcadia, and five from this place, making twenty-five now in Mr. Cumming's hands. I hope he will sell soon. I have written to Savannah for our supply of plantation medicines to avoid the extortion at the *Boro.* And now, my ever dear friend, good night!

Ever your affectionate and devoted

Mary.

Thank you for the stamps and Mary's report. It is excellent!

I looked at your sweet lines the last thing last night. How lover-like! Thank you! Thank you!

Mr. Charles C. Jones, Jr., *to* Mrs. Mary Jones[t]

My dear Mother,

A letter was yesterday received from Brother, with a postscript in your own well-known hand. Such epistles are eagerly looked for, and when received are hailed as welcome messengers from a loved land. This last contained good news, and on that account proved doubly gratifying. We can from experience testify to the joys and pleasures which now surround you, and hope that they may prove beneficial. The injunction of the old Latin poet was *Orandum est ut mens sana in corpore sane.* When therefore the physical man is engaged in active exercise, having full scope for the improvement of all its powers, then is a fit habitation prepared for the abode of the immaterial. Not that a stout frame always implies a vigorous mind, or that a diseased body necessarily argues a mental derangement; but in preserving the health of one we favor the action of the other.

Mr. John Ward of Savannah has for some time been in this city, suffering on account of an operation performed to relieve a complaint of long standing. Cousin Charlie has been very constant in his attentions, and the patient has almost entirely recovered.

Have of late been deeply interested in perusing *The History of Georgia,* by Captain Hugh McCall, in two volumes. The scenes where many of the events transpired are familiar, the actors known through their descendants; and giving as it does an outline of the prominent events, the transactions, struggles, and victories of that state which I am proud to own as my "father-land," every page is fraught with intense interest; and the account comes home to the soul with a truthfulness and propriety the counterpart of which few others can present. The author notices every place of note in our part of the state—now at Savannah, again at Sunbury, presenting the battle at Midway, that on St. Simons Island, Augusta, etc., while the Colonel's Island also comes in for her share in the story. The names of the heroes are also familiar. Among other things he describes the death of Great-Grandfather, killed near Spring Hill by a four-pound ball. The great trouble between the colony and directors in its early settlement seems to have been in consequence of the fact that the latter would not suffer the former to have *"rum and Negroes."* Now, however, everyone has the power to obtain as much of the first and as many of the second as his means will allow.

We have recently suffered much in this city from fire. Barnum's Museum, Hart's Buildings, Johnson's fine law bookstore, and many others on Chestnut Street have been consumed. Real estate is by no means secure in these large cities, but is subject to many dangers.

The new hotel near the office, alias Girard House, is very nearly completed, and will be duly opened on the 15th of the month, although already have all the rooms been engaged, with the exception of some single gentlemen's apartments in the fifth story. It will truly be a fine establishment, far surpassing any in this city as well as New York. The parlors are beautifully fitted up, and everything will be done calculated to please the eye and captivate the fashionable.

Spent a very pleasant evening at Miss Gill's, and enjoyed the privilege of conversing with several real Southern *girls*—or rather, *in propria lingua, young ladies*. Expect to call upon a fair one tomorrow evening. Her name is Miss Lizzie Trigg, from our sister state Tennessee. It really does the soul of man *good* to meet one from the sunny South in this land of snow, ice, and frozen hearts. Yet you cannot blame them, for in the first place they have no money, and then it is so cold that the external air has the tendency to chill the blood, which nature intended to flow fully and freely through the veins. Go to a warm clime if you would find open hands and lively affections. I am so much of a cosmopolite myself that I feel ready to live wherever I am left alone.

Mrs. Roser's daughters have been spending a week with her. She desires her kind regards to be presented.

You have doubtless regarded with interest these recent movements in France. Louis Napoleon evidently had perfectly matured his plans, and it is all in all one of the high-handed measures of the day. The procedure savors somewhat of the bold usurpation of Napoleon the Great, and his descendant appears to inherit some of the determination and boldness of conception which his ancestor possessed in so remarkable degree.

Tell Brother to write me and let me know the results of his hunting operations. My last grade on the average was 99 (100 being the maximum). Hoping that you will enjoy yourself, and thanking you for your letter and the golden counsels therein contained, I will close. Father, Sister, and the doctor unite with me in best love to self, my dear mother, uncle, aunts, cousin, and brother, and all other relations and friends.

Your own son,
Charles C. Jones, Jr.

REV. C. C. JONES *to* MRS. MARY JONES[t]

Philadelphia, *Thursday,* January 8th, 1852

My dear Wife,

It gave me great pleasure to recognize your well-known hand among the letters yesterday, and opening the seal found Joseph's letter and the last page filled up by you. I thank my son for his letter, and if I can find time to write anybody at home besides Mother, will try and write him. No doubt his relaxation and exercise will do him much good, and prepare him all the better for study the coming term.

Charles is spending the greatest part of his time in reading. His grade has just come, and 98.8 is his number—in 1.2 of the maximum: 100. Pretty fair. He has steadily gone up. Complains that Professor McCulloh has not graded him as high as he deserves. I tell him he must give the worthy professor a serious talk.

Mr. Kitzsing and Mr. James begged me to present their compliments to you. Mr. James, to his great grief, has just heard of the death of *a sister!*

The weather continues very changeable, and people say it is an old-fashioned winter. Mary S. called on Miss Cunningham today. Not so well, but rides out as usual. Have not sent Mary S. to school this week. The weather has been trying, and I wished her to improve more. She practices faithfully at her piano, and Mr. Cross promises to bring her some good pieces.

Mrs. Benson of the Markoe has had her trunk broken open and some $300 or $400 stolen, and a diamond ring or brooch given to her by *the doctor* worth $500, and her summer clothing stolen! When? Nobody knows. Nor by whom. This is interesting news to those who board in the same establishment.

January 9th, Friday. Brother Happersett has been very sick; is still sick. Feared an attack of *varioloid* or smallpox, but Brother Owen says it is not so. He saw him this morning; thinks the attack a kind of epidemic cold. He is better today. Mary S. sent him some oranges, which he received with great pleasure. He is rather desponding. Much sickness in town—said to be; and in New York.

We have nothing new. Through a kind Providence, all well. Charles Colcock is my *roommate*. He sleeps in a single bed by the side of ours, and lying in bed he is a great big man. Sometimes talks in his sleep. He is much company to me in my solitude.

Have sent you two papers today; and that I may not break my rule of writing you twice a week, must send this sheet not as full as common, as time is moving on. Do, my dear wife, write me of our affairs—how all things move on. Hope you are spending a happy time with relatives and friends, and doing good to our people, who I know must feel glad at your sojourn. Home —how sweet the sound! Would that I were with you!

The thief in the Markoe is found out! *A gentleman boarder*—young, modest, just from the Irving House, New York! Off this morning before day. Three trunks robbed—all for safekeeping put in the entry! Some of young Benson's clothes gone too. Police officers sent for! And so on.

The weather cloudy, raw, changeable, and trying. Mary S. says: "Give love to Mother, and tell her make haste and come back." She keeps house for me and mends up the rents. I long to see you, my dearest one. This day four weeks, God willing, I shall be starting on my way to Washington to meet my own sweet Mary. Love to my dear son. Love to my sisters and brother and Laura, and howdy for all the servants by name, and love to all my relatives in particular. Tell Cato I am sorry to hear of his child's death. He knows that death comes from the Lord, and I hope he may have a right spirit. As ever, my dear wife,

Your affectionate husband,

C. C. Jones.

Let me reciprocate the "Happy New Year" with you. I wish you every blessing from heaven above and from the earth beneath.

Mrs. Mary Jones *to* Rev. C. C. Jones[t]

Maybank, *Tuesday,* January 13th, 1852

My ever dear Husband,

Sister Susan, Laura, Joseph, and myself came down to Social Bluff on last Tuesday—*J.* driving, as Gilbert was escorting Patience and her household. They had in a young ox that failed near Dorchester, and they went up and spent the night at Henry's, and did not reach Maybank until the next night. Gilbert, returning the day after, did not get back until Friday evening—too late to write you by the last mail, bringing your affectionate favor containing your good wishes, which my heart most warmly reciprocates.

May the Lord ever bless you, my own beloved one! I sigh to be once more with you and our beloved children! Let us be more fervent in prayer, more earnest in exhortations and warnings and examples for and to and before them. Oh, that our gracious Saviour would draw them by His Holy Spirit unto Himself, and build up our dear daughter in every Christian grace! Nothing can supply the place of true and undefiled religion in the heart.

I hope our dear Charles and Mary are better of their colds. Joseph has quite recovered from his, and looks as rough as any old farmer.

We have just come in from trimming the circle of cedars, having left all well at Social Bluff this morning, where we spent the night, having gone over with them Saturday afternoon to assist them to church on Sabbath. I forgot to mention that they all came over and dined with us on that day. Sister Betsy had sent me a piece of nice corned beef; Joseph had killed a wild duck and several birds; Andrew had presented me with a fat young turkey; so with a dish of fried oysters, rice, potatoes, and turnips, with a dessert of oranges and sugared oranges, we had a very nice *maroon*. Sister Betsy says I must tell you I only call on her being so well pleased with marooning at home. Andrew and the people seem very much pleased to have us here, and have supplied us with fine oysters and fat lightwood. They have all had blankets but those at Arcadia.

I found Brother William so dissatisfied about the selection of lands at Maybank for planting that I told him, my dear, he had best use his own judgment and I would stand between himself and yourself. He seemed to feel that with the fields selected he would have no chance at all; but if he did as he pleased he would make as much next year as with all hands on the place. With this impression on his mind I really thought it wisest to let him have his own way. You will not be risking much anyway; and if you insist upon carrying out your own plan, in the event of failure it would be ascribed to his not being allowed to exercise his own judgment. I hope this will meet your approbation. *Do write me immediately* on the point.

I told him also there was no necessity—at least for the present—to send up any corn to Arcadia. Mr. Rahn might have enough, and that down here could be sold. There is also a plenty of fodder. Is it worth disposing of? Such are our expenses and the growing interest of our children that we should use all lawful economy. You have not sent me Mr. Winn's note for butter.

If the weather continues cold and inclement, would it not be for the best interest of Mary to board with Miss Gill for two or three months until it is milder?

I am perfectly charmed with your proposition to meet me at Washington. It was a scheme devised in my own heart even before your letter came. If our merciful Father spares our lives, oh, how happy we shall be! In my next will give you the exact arrangements for starting. Thank you for the check.

You had best write Mr. Cumming about our cotton. He has twenty-five bales on hand. Brother William makes eight bales here, and it will be ready for market next week.

I will now have to close, as Gilbert leaves to get to Montevideo before dark on account of the cold. He will come down early in the morning, and I hope bring letters. Mr. Shepard has returned, and Mrs. S. has sent you and I two beautiful wild turkey fans and Mary one of crane feathers. Mrs. Quarterman (*blind Robert's* wife) was buried on Saturday; he said "he wished he was to be laid in the same grave." Mrs. Charles Barnard Jones has also been called to her rest: a great loss to her family. Mr. Axson has been quite sick with influenza: much prevailing. I have been grateful for uninterrupted health; have lived in the open air, saw and nippers in hand; am scratched and burnt, and look as rough as Mrs. Anybody. Your sisters and brother and niece and son all unite with me in best love to yourself, Mary, Charles Edward, and Charles Colcock. Friends all inquire affectionately after you, and servants all send howdies. How can I stop with a blank space to you, my dearest?

Ever your own devotedly attached
Mary.

Make my respects to all the ladies in the house and all friends out of it.

Rev. C. C. Jones *to* Mrs. Mary Jones[t]

Philadelphia, *Tuesday,* January 13th, 1852

Your letter, my beloved wife, was received on Saturday, the fifth day after its date, and filled all our hearts with joy to hear of your continued health and that of all our relatives and people.

I expressed in the "lines" only and truly what was in my heart towards you, my dear Mary. I have often felt that language could not express my affection for you, and have wished for some way of making it all known to you.

The days seem long, and bear me slowly forward to the time when I hope in the mercy of our God once more to embrace you. Write me at once of your arrangements, and whether I shall meet you at the time appointed in my letter to you at Washington; or rather I will go down the river to Aquia Creek and meet you there instead of waiting until the evening for you in Washington. My friend Mr. Symington said today "that it was the greatest happiness permitted to man on earth to dwell in affection with the wife of his youth." He has been some years a *widower*. I feel it to be so. And how good has God been to spare my dear wife to me so many years! You shall have the miniature, Providence permitting. Do not have trouble at interest about your journey on in February. The heart of the winter I think will be well broken by that time, and you will find the cold agreeable and bracing. Only come prepared for your travel in the way I mentioned in one of my letters, that you may be comfortable on the way.

Your visit home I know is important, and will do great good. Am obliged to you for all the stirrings up to things and duty on the different places. We will have to let our contract with our manager at Arcadia alone for this year, as it is made, and consider upon it for another. We might go farther and fare much worse. He has excellent qualifications in many particulars: is honest, I believe interested in our affairs, and has on the whole done well. I like your arrangements about Tony and Caesar. William might do well; Sandy could give him a trial, although his association with Sandy's present apprentice would be no benefit to him. Have written Mr. M. Cumming requesting him to sell immediately. No answer as yet. I wish Prime, Fanny, and their family sent up to Arcadia: Prime, Fanny, Niger, and Harriet occupy Lymus' house; *Lymus remove to Montevideo.* Big Titus go with Stepney; and Little Titus with Agrippa and Bella; and Clarissa and Patrick take their house; and Phillis and her child take Clarissa's place in Silvia's house until we have two more houses built. When they are built, then Elsie can move with her family to Arcadia. This removal from Maybank had better be made at once, in order that the people may assist in preparing for the coming crop. Mr. Rahn needs them now. Please, my dear, speak to Brother about it. I made the arrangement for them to go as soon as the crop at Maybank was gotten out, which must be before this time. And when the people go up, write Mr. Rahn about fixing them in their houses. It was explained to him, but he may have forgotten it. Will endeavor to write Brother and Mr. Rahn in a few days, but am much driven with work just now. Let me know all your business operations when you write. You are a great hand for business.

Saturday Charles and I took a long walk, and we felt better for it. Sabbath preached in the evening for Brother John Miller; hope a profitable meeting. Charles slid down on the ice going. Walking very precarious. Came back in a snowstorm: small one. Had a very pleasant meeting both of our executive committee and of our board yesterday afternoon. Our affairs are brightening up a little, I hope.

Mary Sharpe commenced school again yesterday (*Monday* the 12th), and have substituted in her studies *mental* science (*Upham's*) for Wayland's *moral* science. Wrote Misses Gill a note that she must be considered somewhat in the light of an irregular scholar until her health is completely restored, God willing.

We are all well at present. Charles Edward has been suffering a little from a local affection, but is better, and always thrashing about. We try to keep our spirits up as well as we can under our circumstances. The block of buildings in which Mr. Schomacker has his piano factory and store took fire near

302

the roof last evening but was saved, the *tin* on the roof keeping the fire under. Charles and I called on our friend Mr. J. N. Dickson and spent an agreeable hour after tea. Brother Happersett has been very sick, and is still confined to his chamber. We shall call on Mr. Ward as soon as he receives company. The two Charleses and Mary Sharpe send love, love, love to you and to Aunt and Mother and Aunt Betsy and Uncle William and Laura, in which I join. And howdy for all the servants *by name*. My dear wife, we must never separate this way any more if we can possibly help it. I long, long to see and embrace my dearest wife, and am, as ever,

Your affectionate and devoted husband,

C. C. Jones.

Mrs. Mary Jones *to* Rev. C. C. Jones[t]

Maybank, *Wednesday,* January 14th, 1852

Oh, you dear naughty husband and naughty children! To think I sent up to the Boro on Monday and not one line did we receive—only a picture of Mr. Kossuth! Very fine, to be sure; but I would not give one letter from my own dear "governor" for even a sight of the famed Magyar chief. He is truly a man of noble spirit, and I honor him for his patriotic devotion to his country and the cause of civil and religious freedom, and hope he may receive the sympathy and succor which he so much craves for his oppressed country. But for our government to violate the wise law of neutrality and become the corrector of all abuses would, as Major Downing suggests, be taking the whole world under our control.

The people have just left; they came over for me "to have prayers," as they said. I made Gilbert bring the long benches into the drawing room, as it was too cold for me to expose to the night air. They all came in, large and small, and seated themselves around the room. I said a few words to them on the necessity of preparation for death, and told them of a melancholy providence that has recently occurred. The steamer *Magnolia* (Captain Blankenstein commander) in going from Savannah south blew up within twenty miles of Darien. The captain and twenty passengers were killed! They appeared to feel, and sang with solemnity: "Life is the time to serve the Lord." I then read them the 25th Chapter of Matthew, etc., etc. Paul says: "Suffer not a woman to teach." This surely does not include children and servants; if so, we are not accountable for their ignorance or their errors. Poor things, they always appear so grateful down here for any religious privileges. As they were going, Phillis and Dinah asked me for a pass to the church, which I will cheerfully give them, and trust they are united to the Saviour by a living faith.

As I wrote you, we came here on Monday. That night I slept but little, owing, as I thought, to a hearty supper of oysters. In reality it was the effect of cold. Early Tuesday morning Joseph called from his room: "Mother, look out the window." I did so—and what a sight for Southern eyes! The whole

303

earth covered with a white carpet of snow, which continued to fall in drifting showers until twelve o'clock. The ground was covered three or four inches, and even now on the tabby walk stands a pyramid three feet high, and was much higher at first on; so in each end of the piazza is a bank that has been swept together. Everything stood aghast! The Negroes could do nothing but make themselves comfortable in their houses. The redbirds and sparrows hopped around the steps; and the doves sat upon the banister rails of the piazza; and two or three times the birds darted against the window glasses. Joseph ran for his gun, but I forbade his taking an ungenerous advantage of even a dove that had fled to our roof for protection. Today he brought a fine trout for our dinner found frozen stiff; when thawed it came to life. And again this evening another large one. The thermometer at eight o'clock this morning in the sun in the front piazza stood at 21°—9° below freezing point. Andrew says it was the driest and coldest snow he ever felt. After it ceased, the wind would blow it like clouds of dust from the roof of the house. I asked Titus what he thought would become of them if the winter was all like this. He said *"it would froze we up."* Alas, for the poor orange trees!

Please remember me to Mrs. Newkirk, and say I fear it will not be in my power to fulfill my promise of a *myrtle orange* tree for her, as they appear to be dead. Do you know, I have at times felt very unhappy about her *velvet cloak,* which was borrowed to cut one by for Marion Erwin. It was returned by *Indian Andrew,* whom we afterwards had such strong reason to suspect of stealing Mary's dresses. Do tell her to inquire of Mrs. N. if it was safely returned, and tell her my reason for uneasiness.

How are you pleased at the Markoe, and have you made any inquiries at the Girard House?

Providence permitting, we expect to go up to Montevideo tomorrow, where I will close for the mail. Good night, my dearest! Good night, my daughter! Good night, my son! Good night, my nephew! Eleven o'clock p.m.

Montevideo, Thursday Night. We came up today, anticipating the pleasure which was fully realized in the receipt of your two dear letters, my dear husband, and one long one from my dear daughter, and one from my dear son. Thank you all. You can imagine the happiness conferred on your wife and mother. Tell my nephew Charlie I will scold them all for not writing him. They have no excuse for neglecting him.

I forgot in my former letter about the agricultural fair to say that Mr. Fleming paraded his Jack caparisoned with scarlet and the saddle he gave his little boy.

I have just been informed of very melancholy tidings concerning Mr. Fleming. Gilbert in returning from Arcadia met his driver Dembo, who told him that last night his master's dwelling and smokehouse with their meat was burned to the ground! The fire was from a spark that fell on the roof, and when discovered it was in a full blaze. They had time only to save a very few things. He had an ill servant—a young boy that *expired* this morning.

Oh, how deeply do I sympathize with them! I have felt like sitting down and writing and offering them a home here; but there is nothing to accommodate them; and they went immediately to Mr. Fleming's brother, Mr. P. W. Fleming. I give you the version as learned from Gilbert. Sandy saw the fire and said it was a house; and Cato says he saw it and heard the screams.

The carpenters are now at work on the palings, and they will look very nicely. Can you not draw me a picture of the manner you wish those done at Maybank? Cato will be through the cotton tomorrow: twenty-one packed bales in all, stained and white. The rice has been thrashed and measures 380 bushels. The people are cleaning new ground: fine work for the season. Our servants, I am thankful to say, are all well with the exception of mumps with the children. Andrew at the Island has had a violent *cold*, but is up and about, and bright as usual.

And now, dearest, for our future plans. With the blessing and permission of God our Heavenly Father, we propose leaving Liberty County on Wednesday the 28th for Bryan, tarrying there until Friday 30th, going to Savannah and leaving there as early the next week as possible. I am going to write and ask what time the boat leaves for Charleston, and will write you. Sister Betsy and Sister Susan will accompany us to Bryan on a visit, and Laura go with me to Savannah on a visit to Mrs. Porter, where I will stop at her kind invitation.

Joe has made himself a calabash mask, with a candle to light it, and is off scaring the people; I charged him not to be out a long time. Kiss my dear daughter and son, and give much love to Charlie, and accept, my own dear husband, the sincerest love of

Your own

Mary.

The servants all inquire constantly after you and the children, and send many howdies.

Tell my baby I used to have the pains just as she has them. They are neuralgic. When the weather gets milder she must try cold water. *The croton* on the spine would relieve.

My respects to Mr. Kitzsing and Mr. James, and kind regards to Mr. Happersett and Mr. Powel.

Rev. C. C. Jones *to* Mrs. Mary Jones[t]

Philadelphia, *Friday,* January 16th, 1852

My ever dearest Mary,

I do not think I can ever consent to such a separation from you again in this world if Providence does not positively order it. I cannot do anything to purpose. I cannot read, nor work, nor think, nor sleep, but am as one that is lost, or has lost some great treasure and is all the time longing after and looking for it. And then you visit me in sweet dreams, and I awake to my loneliness. What am I to do? If you accede to my proposition, then this day three weeks, if the Lord permit, my joyful steps will be turned southward to meet my love! Oh, the happiness of that meeting—if a kind Providence shall spare us to meet. We must say, even in our fondest anticipations, and with a spirit of submission: "If the Lord will, we shall live and do this or that." Husband and wife should never begin in the remotest degree to learn to live without each other; and many, contrary to all their strongest love and desires, learn to do it by long absences from each other! I do not wish to learn; I can't learn; I won't learn—as long as we are spared to each other here below. Do write me when I must come to meet you.

Have turned out a visitor. Charles and I went and took tea at Dr. Janeway's on Tuesday evening; and in Spring Garden, Market Street, down I came full length on my back, providentially catching on my hands—a severe jar but nothing more. The pavements have been coated with snow, worn smooth and iced over for some time. Now nearly gone; but you must be very careful yet.

Wednesday evening Rev. Mr. Ruffner was ordained and installed. Rev. Mr. Wadsworth preached the sermon—the first time I have had the pleasure of hearing him. Will not write you my impressions. He has striking peculiarities, and no doubt is doing his Master's work in this careless city. The church was very crowded.

One item of good news: a portion of the Old School ministers met for prayer on Monday morning in the large room adjoining Dr. Leyburn's office! Our own little prayer meeting goes on as usual Thursday morning at ten.

Thursday evening called at Dr. Mitchell's and spent an agreeable hour. Mrs. M. is an excellent lady. Then called on Brother Ruffner. *Out;* but saw his agreeable lady. They have moved into Chestnut, corner of Juniper.

Have been very busy up to this day. Brother Happersett better, but still confined to his chamber.

Charles Edward has a local affection which Dr. Norris says must confine him to the house for some days. He is embracing freedom from lectures in reading up and study. His life has been too sedentary.

Mary Sharpe has been regularly at school all the week, and is getting hearty again.

Charles Colcock quite well, and is spending most of his time reading. Is now captivated with Prescott's *Conquest of Peru*. I read the story in Robertson when about thirteen or fourteen.

Have received another letter from Dr. Foote about the professorship in Prince Edward; and a curious one from Brother Frank Goulding about the presidency of Oglethorpe. Of this we must say nothing—nor of the other.

Have bought a few books! The greatest wonder will be to be able to *read* them!

Dr. Curtis, the *old gentleman* from South Carolina, called on me this morning on his way back. Very hearty and full of spirits. Says in England they have two ways of burning a candle: the first to light one end and set it in a candlestick and let it burn naturally out; the other is to stick a fork into the middle and set the fork in the candlestick and then light *both ends!* This makes quick work with the candle. He recommended me in my office here not to burn my candle at both ends. I thanked him for his good advice. The difficulty is to follow it. Am getting on now pretty well, and will endeavor to gain all the time I can for exercise and relaxation of mind in study and reading.

You know how carefully I watch you about the fire. I needed your watch two evenings since. I threw my pantaloons over the chair as usual in undressing, and set the lamp in the bottom of the chair to put a new corn liquid on a late bruise of my boot—when lo, the lamp burnt a hole in the leg! Mary Sharpe took your place and mended the burn, and the pantaloons are trudging about as usual again. She sews on the little pearl buttons that drop off whenever they please. You must get me a set of sleeve and breast buttons when you come. Garrett says he has all kinds.

Do give love to all around you: my dear sisters and brother and Laura and my dear son. Tell Andrew and all the people howdy for us all by name. Hope you are enjoying your visit home. Oh, how I long, long to see you, my dear Mary! May the Lord be with and bless you in all things richly! The children and Charles Edward send much love. Believe me, my darling wife,

Your affectionate and devoted husband,

C. C. Jones.

MRS. MARY JONES *to* REV. C. C. JONES[t]

Maybank, *Friday,* January 16th, 1852

My dear Husband,

It was late this afternoon before Joseph and myself left Montevideo. As twilight came on about the new road, we commenced speaking of our afflictions in Columbia, and tried to recall every incident of the burning of the house: Mary's sickness and poor Jack and Marcia's death. Thus we conversed until the carriage drove through the gate near to the spot where it stops at the front yard—when looking out we saw fires burning low on the ground, and Gilbert exclaimed: "Aunt Patience's house is burned down!"

The carriage stopped, and not a living sound did we hear. My heart sank within me. I dreaded to look up. Soon two or three of Brother William's boys came up saying: "Oh, Miss Mary, my missis, the whole plantation ruined!" I walked through the house; and here where the kitchen stood, there where Patience's house stood, and the poultry yard and beyond the stable—all lay a heap of smoldering ruins. I felt awe-stricken and overawed, as in the presence of the Almighty Jehovah, who was displaying His power to save and His power to destroy; and even now my temples are beating as if all the arteries of my poor head were moving with terrific force.

Patience's account of the matter is this. About dinner time she had made up a fire (not large) to iron some things, and had just stepped into the dwelling house when Little Miley came running in to tell her she saw smoke on the top of the kitchen. She ran immediately out, and seeing it was so, hallooed for Dinah and Phillis, who were chopping cotton stalks nearby, and they assisted her to bring the ladder; but by the time they reached the kitchen the whole roof (which you know was made of pine shingles, very old and rotten, and was filled with early peas) was in a blaze from one end to the other. She sent Titus running off to call Andrew and the rest of the people, who were making up the line fence on the new road; and the poor little fellow went so fast that George says when he came to them he fell down with fatigue and fright. Patience, Phillis, and Dinah, seeing that they could not save the kitchen, went to work and removed almost everything. Beck in the meantime ran screaming to her mother to say her house was on fire. The wind was blowing very hard due west; the sparks lodged on the side next to the stable. About this time the people came up from the fields. Little Andrew started on Dove for Brother William, and he came over bringing all his men. The house, being old and very dry, was in a blaze in a few moments. They saved as much as possible of Patience's things. The flames swept on. A spark or something fell upon the stable loft, which had in fodder. It was like falling in a tinderbox. In one moment the flames rose in the skies and licked around. They now kept throwing water on the side of the carriage- and cornhouse. The roof caught! Andrew says the Lord helped him and gave him strength. He flew up like a squirrel (to use his own expression) and tore off the shingles. The flames flew on the wings of the wind—ran along the grass and fired the fence. They kept putting wet blankets on the cornhouse, and thus by the special and direct hand of our merciful God the fire was stopped. Had the wind varied, cotton house and all must have gone; and had it blown from any other quarter, our dwelling must certainly have been destroyed.

What shall we render unto God for all His mercy and goodness? Oh, that His repeated chastisements might make us more penitent, more humble, and more believing! I feel that it all comes from His immediate hand, and He has a right to dispose of us and all we have. I do entreat Him to save us and our dear children and our servants from the fire that never shall be quenched, and the worm that dieth not. Oh, if His judgments in this life are so terrible, what must it be to endure His eternal wrath and condemnation upon our guilty and unprotected souls! Perhaps all this is to remind me that I have been too much interested lately in my earthly home, too devoted to plans of improvement and making everything comfortable and neat.

Oh, that I were with you tonight! My heart leans perhaps too much upon you. I am sad and desolate, but I will strive to look unto my gracious Saviour, from whence cometh all my help. Joseph is asleep, and the stillness of death reigns around me. Were I to go to bed I could not sleep. Oh, that the distance

308

which separates us was passed! I dread the journey! But I am—and thankfully do I say it—not prone to anticipate evil. But I must not make you unnecessarily sad. So farewell for tonight!

One more word: Brother William and Mr. Peace rode over and stayed until near sunset; said to the servants if I came he would expect me there tonight. I could not go. Joseph wanted me to do so; but this solitude is most congenial to my feelings. I want to "be dumb and open not my mouth."

Monday Night at Montevideo. After writing the above, my dear husband, I read it to Joseph as we rode over the next day to Social Bluff. He said: "Mother, that will make Father feel very sadly." I fear I have written in too melancholy a strain. Do not think that I am unnecessarily depressed. We have reason to rejoice rather in the sparing mercy of God.

Brother William says no man in the world could have acted with more promptness or forethought than Andrew. Seeing there was danger of the cornhouse being consumed, he propped off a board on the side and commanded some of the people to commence throwing it out. Others he directed to dash on water and wet blankets and throw on whilst he rushed up on the roof and tore off the lighted shingles.

I am up here tonight to make arrangements for moving over the vacant house now occupied by the mill, which is good all to the sides and shingles, for Patience. It needs to be done immediately, as the lot will be left in a very unprotected state without it. We will locate it much farther back in the lot and beyond the range of any other building. Will have the shed back of the carriage- and cornhouse boarded up with the scaffold boards for a temporary stable; and if your life is spared, you can plan and locate one where you please when you come on in the spring. The cornhouse needs shingling entirely, and the cotton house much repairing. I thought it best not to touch Phillis and Fanny's houses; to remove them. They are good, and you might perhaps want to increase the force at some other time, and for servants' houses. Patience's house will answer also for a kitchen. She, poor thing, has lost many things, all of which I shall make up to her.

This has been one of the most windy Januarys I ever knew. Today and now it is *intensely* cold. We stopped and dined with Henry and Sister Abby; they sent the warmest love to you. Coming on, Joseph drove the carriage with the front seat thrown back; and three or four times he had to get out and thrash about as the sailors do to enable him to hold his reins. Such a winter has scarcely ever been known here—at least such a sleet and snowstorm. I trust the Potomac will not freeze up hard and fast ere I can reach my own dearest husband and dear children.

We attended Midway on Sabbath. Mr. Richard Baker preached. Mr. Axson was there, but too unwell to officiate: his throat affected, and something like rheumatism down his left limb, which caused him to limp and walk with a stick. He and Mrs. A. and Julia and all friends desired much love to you.

The past week has been unparalleled for fires: Mr. Fleming's house, of which I wrote you; our three buildings the next day; Brother Joseph Anderson's smokehouse containing $95 worth of bacon; a little daughter of Joseph Jackson so badly burnt that it was thought impossible for her to recover; and Mrs. Sumner Winn had her little son scalded.

The circumstances attending the burning of Mr. Fleming's house were very similar to ours in many respects. He had been watching his sick Negro for several nights. That day they had company, and the doctor came about tea-time. As soon as he left he had family worship; laid down for half an hour to prepare and refresh himself for sitting up. As he left the parlor he looked to see if the fire was extinguished, and said there were but a few coals remaining. Went into their chamber, locked the door; went then into the children's room and locked them in, as he came out saying to his house boy that he must stay in his mistress' room until he returned. On reaching the Negro house he found him declining, and remained until about three or four o'clock; and seeing him sinking fast, he roused up his family and went to prayer with the dying boy. A servant who had been sent out on some errand returned saying the house was on fire. He rushed out with indescribable feelings. The thought of the poor little ones he had locked in took possession of his mind. How he got to the house he knows not. When he arrived, the flames were rushing through; and huddled together in the yard stood his wife, his children, and the two Miss Quartermans. He said his feeling of gratitude to find them all there and alive was indescribable. He called them all by name, counted them over and over to see if it was indeed true. His little daughter said: "Yes, Father, we are all here; but your papers and your money are in the house." He rushed in and seized the portmanteau containing them, and two guns that stood by. The servants threw out five mattresses and some of their clothing, five or six chairs, their sugar and coffee; and their bacon was saved from the smokehouse; and an old mahogany table that no one could tell who brought it out. That table was the only piece of furniture saved from a two-story house belonging to his wife's parents which was burnt when she was six months old. When they married, Mr. James Wilson said to him: "Thomas, here is a table—the only thing saved to your wife that belonged to her parents of furniture. Take it and use it. Do not buy a new one." They did so. That night the cloth had been left on the table with three knives and forks and the same number of silver spoons. They were saved.

He and his family were all at church, and bear their loss with the most Christian cheerfulness. There is much sympathy expressed—and in the right way—for them: many individual contributions; and I am told the gentlemen propose raising a sum of money to be presented to him. It all reminded me so much of our own afflictions; and my feelings were so much interested in the recital that I went home with a severe nervous headache.

Joseph is writing a speech at my side. His cold was much better, but was slightly renewed by exposure in the snow. Kiss my dear daughter and son for me, and tell them to do the same to you for me. Much love to Charlie, and the same from Joseph and all relatives on the Bluff to you all. And howdies for the servants. Tell *Elizabeth* howdy for me. Providence permitting, we shall leave this Wednesday week for Bryan, and the following Friday for Savannah. Hoping soon to be with my dearest earthly friend, ever I remain

His own affectionate wife,
Mary.

I hope our good Brother Happersett and Mrs. Van Rensselaer have not indeed the smallpox. Would it not be well for you all to be vaccinated? *I think so!*

Respects to Mr. Happersett and Powel.

Rev. C. C. Jones *to* Mrs. Mary Jones[t]

Philadelphia, *Tuesday,* January 20th, 1852

My dear Wife,

Saturday morning was a busy morning. At half-past one I swallowed my dinner, and Charles and I set off at the top of our speed, walking to the Sheaf Hotel in 2nd above Race or Vine. Just in time: got stowed away in a closely packed stage; and taking leave of Charles, off we drove out to Abington to Dr. Steele's. The doctor and I took a walk, but it was a cold one to me, for he took my arm, and that prevented the swinging so necessary for comfort when it was freezing all the while. A clear evening that gave promise of a fine Sabbath. But lo, Sabbath morning a cold, heavy snowstorm which continued without intermission all the day and pretty much all Sabbath night. Yet the doctor said to church we must go; so his son-in-law drove a sleigh to the door, and in we gathered and drove in the face of cold and snow to the church. About twenty people, little and big: near a third of them from Dr. Steele's own family. Lectured; and it was so ordered in providence that the subject of the lecture was specially applicable to a member of the congregation then present. May the Lord bless the Word to him! Afternoon at home: no service. Evening just as the bell rang for family worship Mrs. Steele said: "We shall be very glad to have you lecture to the family!" I did the best I could. Monday morning took passage in an open sleigh: exceeding cold! And if Dr. Steele had not made me get a pair of India-rubber overshoes and wrapped me up in his big cloak and put Mrs. Steele's woolen concern around my neck, I should have run a risk of being frozen. Cold! Cold! Sat in the hotel above half an hour to thaw out before walking up to the Markoe.

All well except Charles Edward: still confined with his painful local affection, but better.

Today (Tuesday) the thermometer has been down *to zero!* And no colder winter has been experienced North since 1835–1836. Great complaints of cold and snow and ice. Mails balked and stopped everywhere. Five mails due from the South; and suppose your last letter is in one of them, for we have not heard from you for *ten days!* I wonder you cannot write at least once a week. But I suppose you are at home, quiet and happy, and have much to employ your time and amuse you.

My visit out to Abington to preach for the board has cured me of any further work of the kind during the severity of the winter. I do not think I shall go out again. I cannot stand it; the exposure to me is too much. It may do for people who have more vigor of constitution than I have. I am wearing down in this office, and ofttimes have serious thoughts of giving it up and returning home and trying to recover my lost energy.

So far as the pecuniary side of the question is concerned, it would not cost us a cent more to live at home and pay tuition, board, and everything else for our children abroad. We have spent over and above my salary since coming here $2,139.54. Miss Gill has just sent in her bill for Mary. Her board and other expenses while staying at the school amount to $28.19—about $1 per day. We must observe the leadings of Providence in these things. I desire to do that which is agreeable to His will. As to home feeling here, I cannot say that I have any to speak of.

Mr. Kitzsing says the thermometer was 7° below zero this morning! All complain of the cold. They are now running the locomotive, cars, and all right across the *Susquehanna on the ice!* People are walking across from Philadelphia to Camden. Streets nothing but sleighs: and no music but sleigh bells. Winter in earnest. Hope it may grow milder before you set out to come back.

Charles Edward and Charles Colcock and Mary Sharpe send a great deal of love. Mary went to school today; said her feet were very cold and painful. My love and the young people's to my sisters and brother and Laura and all our relatives. Tell all the servants howdy for me by name. Must close to be in time for the mail. Write you *regularly twice a week.* Love to my dear son. Hope he takes good care of Mother for me. I remain, my dear wife,

Your ever affectionate husband,
C. C. Jones.

REV. C. C. JONES *to* MRS. MARY JONES[t]
Philadelphia, *Wednesday,* January 21st, 1852
Your welcome letter of the 13th inst., my own dearest wife, came to hand this morning, and I give God thanks for His merciful care of you and all near and dear to me around you. I do not care how burnt you look, nor how scratched you may be from trimming trees, nor how rough from exercise, so long as you are strong and hearty. Health is my criterion for beauty. Am so glad of your enjoyment of home, and the happiness your presence gives to our people; though it is a sad privation to me to be deprived of your love and sweet society. Suppose you had seen your husband in his twenty-second married year kissing your letter; would you not call him your own true and devoted lover? I think you would. And such a refreshing dream of you last

night! It prepared me for your letter this morning. Be sure you write me in time of your time of setting out—that, Providence permitting, we may not be disappointed in meeting each other at Washington. Write some days—rather, two or three mails—beforehand, as the mails are often in these cold and stormy times stopped by snow and ice. Five mails were due this morning. The way is pretty clear from Savannah to Washington; after that comes snow and ice and so forth.

Mr. M. Cumming has sold ten bales cotton from Montevideo at $21\frac{1}{2}$¢; net proceeds: $647.61. This gives us to our credit in the state bank $1,043.87. So you can fill up your check for what you like. I wrote Mr. Cumming yesterday urging a *sale,* and this morning brought his letter: he sold on the 13th. Shall write him again today.

Do, my darling, tell Brother to plant anywhere and just what he pleases. I did not mean to confine him to any arrangement which he would not approve, and you did perfectly right to tell him to do as he judged best; for had he altered all without letting me know, I should have said nothing about it. I know he will do the best he can for us. *Only do not fall short in provisions. There is no necessity to send any provisions up to Arcadia for the people going up there.* Mr. Rahn must have enough for them. What fodder may not be needed can be sold—that is, *after the several places are supplied.* The old fodder at Maybank would be *well bestowed on the oxen and cattle in the months of February and March.* They need that help at *Maybank.* Montevideo and Arcadia have *straw.*

Will send Brother Winn's little bill to him from here, as I wish to write him a line.

Mary Sharpe and Charles are both quite well, and Mary S. has no notion of going back to Miss Gill's! Says she: "I have more time *here* to study, to practice, to be to myself; and if I go back, I shall surely be sick again." She goes well protected to school, and I tell her never to stay until the school closes unless she desires to do so. She is better here than at the boarding school; is my housekeeper and a great comfort and company to me when dear Mother is away. All she needs is more and regular exercise; but you know what a poor place a city is for such a thing, especially in the depth of winter, with ice and snow, and pavements so *"slippy"* that you are not sure one moment ahead whether you will be up or down!

Everybody cries out that it is a severe winter. The weather has moderated today somewhat: a very slight fall of snow, and clouds overhead. Have to keep all our fires in full operation.

Mr. Happersett is walking out again.

How sorry I am to hear of Mr. Robert Quarterman's loss of his excellent wife! Truly to him the greatest earthly affliction; and his wish was but the sincere expression of his broken heart!

My dear wife, these afflictions but call forth my sincere sympathy for the sufferers, and my gratitude to our most merciful God and Saviour that we are still spared to each other. How ought we to love each other, and do each other good all our days and not evil! I think I have tried to cherish your life, so precious to me, my own dear Mary; and if I know my own heart, there is nothing which I would not cheerfully do and suffer for your happiness. One of my greatest sorrows in life has been that I have not been a *perfect* husband, and so made my own dear wife *perfectly happy*. Those lines were penned to you in the sincerity of my heart:

> Oh, could I pluck the shadows past, away,
> Where sunlight only should have ruled the day!

Charles and Mary send love upon love to Mother and "Bubber Dodo" and to dear aunts and uncle and Cousin Laura and all our relatives, in which I join, soul and body. Glad to hear Joe looks rough and hardy; he will be able to do a good winter's study. A good constitution for this rough world is the greatest temporal blessing.

Tell Andrew I am much pleased that he is so attentive to all your wishes and commands, and to hear that all the people are well and doing well. I hope, God willing, we may see them again in May.

While I write, Mary Sharpe's little canary is chirping and singing away at the top of his voice. Charles let him out of his cage, and he flew about the room a while and amused himself and then went back, as he always does, into his cage. He is quite an item in the cares of the household; and when Mary practices he tunes up his little pipes all the time.

Charles Edward is much better today, and received his mother's letter this morning.

All in the Markoe well. A runaway match came here last week; and on Saturday the father of the *woman* came, and with constable and writ apprehended her first and the *man* next; and they have all marched back to where they came from—precious New England.

My own dear love to you, my own dear wife; and am, as ever,

Your affectionate and devoted husband,
C. C. Jones.

Rev. C. C. Jones *to* Mrs. Mary Jones[t]

Philadelphia, *Friday,* January 23rd, 1852

My dearest Mary,

Your welcome letter of 14th inst. was received last night, and made us all happy. The cold has been extensive, universal. A rare sight you enjoyed at Maybank. Teach and preach as much as you please in the mode you did. I give you leave. You are a minister. We are one flesh, you know. This will do for the occasion; but we *will not* carry the matter beyond the family and household. Would that all our people were united to the Lord by a true and living faith!

We will inquire about the cloak.

My dear, you forgot how long it takes to get a letter to Liberty. You will leave there the day *before* by any possibility this can reach you; and consequently I send it to meet you on your arrival in Savannah the day *after* you would have received it in Liberty. That is, barring all stoppages from ice and snow on the way. The steamers leave Savannah every morning (used to) at four; you will have to sleep on board to be in time. The Potomac is now closed with ice; but it is hoped and expected that the boat will be running to Aquia Creek in a week or ten days. The quantity and thickness of the ice is unprecedented. This is the 23rd; you will leave Savannah on Monday or Tuesday evening the 2nd or 3rd of February—ten days from this time. If you leave Savannah *Tuesday morning,* 4 A.M., *February 3rd, and the ice does not obstruct the boat in Potomac River,* Providence blessing your journey, you will be in Washington *Thursday evening.* If you leave Savannah *Wednesday morning,* 4 A.M., you will be in Washington *Friday evening.* And if you leave S. *Thursday morning,* 4 A.M., you will be in W. *Saturday evening.* Now, *immediately* as you reach Savannah and read this letter write me *precisely* the *day and hour in which you start from Savannah, that I may not be disappointed in meeting you. You can come on to Richmond;* and should the ice still obstruct navigation, you could stay at Richmond a few days until we see which way to turn. The route by Norfolk is now stopped by ice also! At Richmond you can telegraph me at Washington, if when you get there you learn that the Potomac is still closed. If possible will try and get to you. I will be at the *National Hotel.* At Richmond go to our old friend Mr. Caskie's; and be sure to see Mrs. Hutchison in Savannah. I will telegraph you to Savannah *on Saturday the 31st* to let you know how the Potomac is, and will write you also next week to meet you still in Savannah. You had better make your calculations—if the weather suits and all—to leave Savannah from the 2nd to the 4th, and come by the way of Richmond, *letting me know in time when you will start;* and we will hope the best for the river.

Will attend to the *palings* through Mr. Shepard if you have left no directions. Grieved to hear of Mr. Fleming's loss. We know how to sympathize for them. In much haste, my dear, for the mail,

Your affectionate husband,
C. C. Jones.

REV. C. C. JONES *to* MRS. MARY JONES[t]

Philadelphia, *Monday Evening,* January 26th, 1852

Your letter, my ever dear wife, commenced on the 16th and finished on the 19th, came to hand this evening. I thank you for the minute account which you have given me of another stroke of the hand of our Heavenly Father upon us, and in kind similar to the first. I see His great mercy mingling with it. It occurred not at night; the provisions of the plantation, and our dwelling with all our furniture, books, and papers, and the cotton house with the market crop were all spared; and *not an individual was so much as scorched with the flames!*

As I read your moving account I felt with you that it was of the Lord. We should ask wherefore hath He done it. No doubt to teach us over and in a milder form the lesson that all our earthly possessions are held by us at His pleasure; that they are ours to hold for necessary and charitable uses in His fear, but not to keep as an unchanging inheritance. Our removal to Philadelphia has not resulted thus far in our making any permanent fixtures for a home, nor in forming any attachments that would incline us to do so; and having a feeling of uncertainty, we have turned with fond remembrances to our old home, and looked forward to a return to it, where, freed from pressing cares and unending duties, we might repose in quietness and peace. There has been perhaps an uneasy bearing of His will which we thought indicated our coming to this city, and a secret idolatry of heart which still clings to earth for home and happiness. The Lord may be revealing our hearts to us, and teaching us that *our home* is in His hand; that He can take it all away in a moment of time; and therefore we must live upon Him, to Him, and for Him; and He and He alone be our portion and our inheritance. May it produce this fruit in us, to the praise and glory of His grace! So remarkable have been His dealings towards us, so wonderfully has He disposed our lot, that I have endeavored to learn *to live by the day;* to rely upon His infinite wisdom, justice, and mercy; and to learn, whatever may be His dispensation, however sudden, however great and affecting, *to rest in Him*—let Him do what seemeth good in His sight. All is and must and will be right; only let God sanctify all to me.

As I read your account my heart turned unto the Lord, and I felt quiet. Let us pray that we and our dear children and servants may be saved in *that day* when Christ Jesus cometh to judge the earth. *Extract good,* my dear wife, out of this. It comes to give you a good parting lesson from your home. Bless God for it. It comes, too, while you *are at home* to see *how it came, how it ended;* to see *the devotion* of our servants; and to *make provision for their losses* and for *their accommodation.* I feel happy that it was so ordered. So while there is a sadness at the loss, yet there is comfort in leaving after it, and leaving good and pleasant arrangements behind. Your suggestions are all good; and when we reach home in the spring, God willing, we will complete the necessary rebuilding.

We sympathize deeply with our friend Mr. Fleming; *we* should know how to feel for him.

I wrote you at the close of the last week, chiefly in relation to your journey back. The Potomac *is frozen fast.* But we have had several mild days; ice and snow are thawing here; and our hope is that in a few days we shall hear that the boat has resumed her trips to Aquia Creek. At any rate, the mail now runs from Washington to Aquia Creek *by land,* and a passage may be had in that way. As promised in my last, I will *telegraph you to Savannah on Saturday next, the 31st,* and let you know how the river is, D.V. If the Susquehanna at Havre de Grace is impassable, we can take the railroad from Baltimore to Columbia, in Pennsylvania, and thence to Philadelphia, and so *head* the difficulty. My heart yearns for you, my dearest wife. If ever spared to be united again, I think we must, Providence permitting, part no more. Where one goes the other must go too.

Mr. Happersett is pretty nearly well again. Mrs. Van Rensselaer has had smallpox; is well again. Mary Sharpe, Charles Colcock, and I have all been vaccinated. The children *twice: no effect whatever.* Dr. Hodge recommended it. The cases, I believe, are subsiding in town. Hear little of the disease this week.

We have had milder weather for three days: thawing, streets flooded, sleighing stopped, bad walking. Suspect you have suffered as much with cold in Georgia as you would have suffered had you been in Philadelphia. The cold has not been unpleasant to me at all, and have had since my return no sore throat whatever. In this respect this winter differs from the last, thanks to our merciful Parent.

Tuesday, 27th. Read with great interest this morning the *121st Psalm.* Read it: it will comfort and strengthen you. *"The Lord is our Keeper."* I praise Him for His merciful kindness to you. We all unite in love to you and Joseph and Laura. My kindest regards to Major and Mrs. Porter, and to Lieutenant and Mrs. Gilmer. I am counting the days when I shall set out to meet my love. *Wrote Brother* about the fire and the new house for Patience last night. God bless and be with you, my dear Mary!

Your affectionate husband,
C. C. Jones.

Mrs. Mary Jones *to* Rev. C. C. Jones[t]

Montevideo, *Monday,* January 26th, 1852

Thank you, my own darling husband, for your sweet letter this day received. My heart bounds with joyful anticipations at the prospect of so soon meeting you—if it be the will of our Heavenly Father! I never wish to be or can be happy away from you; and yet I feel it was my duty to submit to this separation, and hope it has accomplished good.

It is now near twelve o'clock at night, and yet not one moment have I had earlier to sit down and write you. Soon after breakfast Mr. Shepard came, and you know he can talk as well as write *long.* He had not left before my friend Mrs. Harden drove up and stayed until two o'clock. We had scarcely dined when Julia arrived, and soon after James and his wife and Mr. Peace; they remained until dark. And since tea I have been most diligent with Joseph's assistance parceling out medicines for the different places, the box having just arrived from Savannah.

317

And now for our journey. *God willing,* Sister Betsy, Sister Susan, Laura, and myself hope to leave day after tomorrow (Wednesday the 28th) for Bryan, tarry there Thursday, and take the stage on Friday, when Joseph will come on and meet us with the baggage. Laura goes on with me to Savannah, where we will remain until Tuesday morning; or rather we will go on board the boat at night and leave that morning at four o'clock. You can best judge of the journey thence northward. I trust a kind Providence will grant us milder skies.

The weather has been extremely cold: Miss Clay writes me down to 15° in Bryan; same day 12° in Midway. And James told me on last Tuesday Cousin Charles West, coming on in stage from Darien, called at the Retreat for breakfast; and the driver came in with his beard and moustache hoary with his frozen breath, and long icicles pendant from the hairs. I never heard of anything like it in this climate. We have been greatly blessed in the health of our servants.

Our good Mr. Axson is suffering from severe cold still. Joseph rode to see him this afternoon. His throat blistered; confined to his chamber; and rheumatic pains all over. *Mr. Law* preached at Midway on Sabbath. Not going away: Mr. Walthour has increased his salary, it is said.

Mrs. Howe writes me that Mr. Palmer has received a unanimous call to Mr. Jacobus' church, Brooklyn, New York, which she has no idea that he would accept; but says the Glebe Street Church had notified their session that they intended to call him, and she fears Presbytery will make it his duty to accept. To use her own words, this has thrown them into "a great ferment." She fears if he goes, it will result in much distraction and put a stop to their building. Thus you see the Central Church would certainly have been disappointed if they had called him. *Changes* are very questionable things. Good night, dearest!

27th. A charmingly bright, mild, and beautiful morning! Oh, if my lover were only here, we would live in the *sunshine* today! To *meet him will be* sunshine to my heart. Gilbert is waiting, and the mail will soon be gone. Kiss my dear children for me. Give love to Charlie. Much love from Joseph and all friends. May God ever lift upon you the light of His countenance!

Ever, my dear husband, your attached wife,
Mary Jones.

Rev. C. C. Jones *to* Mrs. Mary Jones[t]

Philadelphia, *Thursday,* January 29th, 1852

My dear Mary,

This is Thursday, the day you are at Richmond, God willing; and tomorrow you will be in Savannah. Dr. Leyburn *telegraphed Washington today, and received for answer that the boat was making her regular trips to Aquia Creek!* So in the kindness of Providence the way is opened from Savannah to Washington; and I write now to say, as you have written me *nothing definite of the day of your leaving Savannah* (forgetting that these arrangements should be made at least two weeks ahead on account of the distance between us and the failure of the mails)—I write now to say that, Providence permitting, I will be in Washington *on Thursday evening the 5th of February*, which place you will reach *at the same time* if you leave Savannah *at four o'clock Tuesday morning* or *anytime Monday night*, according as the boats run. If you do not leave until *Tuesday night*, you will be in Washington *Friday evening. I will remain in Washington until you arrive.* And if you do not meet me Thursday evening, *then I will go down in the boat Friday and meet you at Aquia Creek.*

The train from Baltimore may not reach Washington until *after the boat has arrived with you from Aquia Creek.* If I am not on the wharf to receive you, then take the hack up to the *National Hotel,* where we stayed before, and let Joseph enter our names and secure *good* rooms for us.

And once more: the Susquehanna may be impassable. In that case I will be obliged to go up through Pennsylvania and *head* the crossing, and so down to Baltimore, and on to Washington. In that case I may not reach Washington until Friday sometime. *Stay if you are there until I come; else we may miss each other on the way.* I state this as a *peradventure.* But I will endeavor *if possible to be in Washington Thursday night anyway.*

As the time draws near for your return, my dear wife, the days grow longer and my heart waits in suspense. I requested you to write me immediately on your arrival in Savannah Friday night and let me know the day of your leaving. If your letter is mailed Friday night, and no break in the connection on the route occur, that letter will reach Philadelphia *Tuesday or Wednesday morning,* February 3rd or 4th. This letter will reach you if successful Monday morning February 2nd or Monday evening when the Charleston boat gets in.

I trust we shall meet about the time appointed in Washington. I long, long to embrace my own dear Mary. How could I ever have consented to this separation? I desire to be separated from you no more. We are all quite well, and anticipating your arrival with joyous emotions. Tell my dear son he must take my place, and take the best care of you, and let you want for nothing. Be sure to make your arrangements so as to travel *warm.* The intense cold has passed away, and the snow and ice are going fast, and the weather is mild and pleasant; and my hope is that you will have a pleasant journey on. The Lord make your way prosperous!

Charles C., Mary S., and Charles E. send much love to you and to Joe. Our kindest remembrance to Major and Mrs. Porter and to Lieutenant and Mrs. Gilmer. Love to Laura. Her letter and her mother's came last night, and one from Mr. Shepard.

And now, my dear wife, this letter will close our correspondence for this long, long separation; and I have endeavored to be a faithful correspondent to you, and a loving one also. I will now live in the joyful hope of seeing and embracing your sweet and precious person in a few days, and once more hearing your sweet voice, and communing in heart and soul with you as my own loved and loving wife—more to me than all the world beside. I think then I shall never consent to let you go from me again. The Lord watch between us and suffer us to realize these happy anticipations! I remain, my darling wife,

Your ever affectionate and devoted husband,
C. C. Jones.

Mrs. Mary Jones *to* Rev. C. C. Jones[t]

Savannah, *Friday,* January 30th, 1852

Just arrived, my dearest husband, and your kind letter received. With our good friends Major and Mrs. Porter. Left all well; and will leave this, God willing, on the 3rd of February—say, go on board the steamer Monday night and leave four o'clock Tuesday morning. I hope the rivers will thaw out, and with the blessing of God that we shall meet in peace and safety. With tenderest love. I must close in time for the mail.

Your ever affectionate
Mary J.

IX

Rev. C. C. Jones *to* Mr. Charles C. Jones, Jr.[g]

Philadelphia, Friday, February 13th, 1852

Your Aunt Mary's letter was opened by mistake, my dear son, and we made ourselves acquainted with its pleasing contents. I wish you would write your Aunt Eliza.

We received your letter from Princeton yesterday, and were glad to learn of your safe arrival, and that you were both once more at study. Be careful now to exercise *regularly* and *abundantly*. I must compliment you on *the penmanship* of your letter—the best I have ever seen from you. Go on unto perfection.

Your Cousin Charles Edward has met with a severe affliction in *the death of Dr. Richardsone*. He died in Savannah Thursday week. He feels his death greatly. And we have met with a great loss in our board in the sudden death on Monday of Mr. Alexander Symington! Solemn warnings to us all to be ready for our summons.

Mother, Sister, and your cousin unite in love to you and your dear brother, in which I join.

Your ever affectionate father,
C. C. Jones.

Mr. Charles C. Jones, Jr., *to* Rev. *and* Mrs. C. C. Jones[t]

Princeton, Monday, February 16th, 1852

My dear Parents,

Your note, Father, with enclosed letter from Aunt Mary was duly received on Saturday, and perused with much pleasure.

I was very much surprised and grieved to hear of the death of Dr. Richardsone. His loss as a public benefactor and an eminent physician of Savannah is truly to be seriously deplored. Skill and proficiency in any branch of science are the result of long, patient investigation, labor, and research; and so frail and uncertain is the silken cord which unites us to earth that this is too often sundered and "the golden bowl broken at the cistern" just as we have begun to live aright, developing the powers implanted within us and acting such parts as befit high, moral, intellectual beings. It seems a comparatively trivial occurrence when the young and inexperienced are taken away; yet by no means is such the case when we are in a moment deprived of that mind which long experience, close application, and success had fitted to deal with those higher subjects and important interests which we dare not commit into the keeping of tyros or the unprepared. Cousin Charlie must indeed feel most sensibly his death. Strong is the attachment which exists between the zealous pupil and the ready instructor. Dr. Richardsone seems to have reposed an uncommon degree of confidence in him, and would, if report be true, have handsomely rewarded him for his continued attention and successful pursuit of medicine. He was, I have understood, one of the most influential and enterprising citizens of Savannah, being connected with several important associations, at the same time sustaining his reputation as a prominent physician.

This morning Dr. Schanck delivered a lecture to our class on comparative anatomy, which will be followed by several others. He appears acquainted with this subject, and having in his possession a very good manikin, besides specimens and drawings of the principal varieties of animals, he is enabled practically and in an interesting manner to show their distinguishing characteristics and elicit proper attention.

With Dr. Maclean we are now reading Longinus. This is truly interesting; and one of his chief excellencies, independent of his power of division and assigning proper subjects for the exercise of the sublime in composition, seems to be his extensive reading, whereby he shows a profound acquaintance with the authors who wrote before and as contemporaries with him, with freedom states their distinguishing features by clear analyses of their respective styles, and is thereby enabled to select the most appropriate illustrations of any point which he may be laboring to sustain. . . . One of the most interesting engagements, it seems to me, in which the student may employ his time is that of reading these old classics, where you find the ideas and impressions of the authors newborn, oftentimes derived solely from their personal observation, experience, and close communion with nature and their own minds. There is a freshness and vigor about their thoughts, as well as a power of direct unfolding and presentation, which may well laugh to scorn the circumlocutory phrases and borrowed notions of more modern times.

In fact, most writers of the present day are mere bookmakers, and the dream of Geoffrey Crayon, Gent., may no longer be regarded as truth in the garb of an allegory, but as out-and-out matter of fact. Those occupations which Goldsmith, Otway, and others were compelled to engage in, solely for the purpose of clothing their ragged persons or supplying the necessaries of life, form now the highest aspirations of the "would-be literati"; while they at the same time appear almost entirely destitute of that poetic love of learning and composition for improvement's sake, and the ability to execute, although placed in far better circumstances for the developing of whatever is lofty and interesting within their minds than those poverty-stricken yet truly great men ever were.

How the heart sickens often at the pitiful shifts which some of our most gifted poets were often compelled to make in order to keep soul and body together! And how gladly would we again call them from their tombs and place them in circumstances where, free from the depressing influences of pecuniary want, they could devote themselves solely to pursuits so congenial to their natural dispositions! Yet in such an event we would have no positive assurance that their fame would be exhausted by productions still more surprising, for a certain degree of disappointment and difficulty seems necessary in order to incite the mind to renewed exertions and more enlarged enterprises. If the mind be free from every trouble, and the person surrounded with all that pampers the tastes and gratifies every desire, then are we apt to remain in a state of inactivity, with morbid affections and sluggish souls. Many are the examples where genius, born amid oppression and nourished amidst unnumbered difficulties, has finally triumphed over all opposition, and like fine gold shone brightest having passed through the hottest fires.

It really does seem that the icy chain of winter is still more binding than ever. When we reached this place the ground was covered with snow. Scarcely had this begun to disappear when a new supply descended on Friday, and last night there was an additional fall of several inches. Such is the severity of the cold that although exposed to the action of the sun, its beams fall powerless upon this spotless mantle. The romance of snowstorms has long since died away with me, for while I admire its purity and beauty, my thoughts are apt to picture the after days when in its stead shall be found naught but a quagmire, which in this vicinity is magnified in truth to such a degree as to merit the appellation from the "exercise-taker" of "the Slough of Despond."

Saw Dr. and Mrs. Hope on last Friday evening. She is the same mild and pleasant lady as ever, but the professor is still self-sufficient and as eager after big words and Cowley metaphors as a long crane is after the small fry—with this difference, however, that the acquisitions in the latter case are more easily managed than in the former, although in both the *tortus cervicis* denote a severe effort. However, such similes ill become a pupil. Yet the analogy struck me forcibly in the main.

Hoping that this will find you all prospering in every respect, I remain, my dear parents, with much love to selves, Sister, and Cousin Charlie, in which Brother unites,

Your ever affectionate son,
Charles C. Jones, Jr.

MRS. MARY JONES *to* MR. CHARLES C. JONES, JR.[g]

Philadelphia, *Tuesday,* February 17th, 1852

My dear Son,

Your two interesting and affectionate letters have been received; also your brother's. This frequent intercourse and communication with you both is most gratifying to the feelings and affections of your parents. My thoughts are with you by day and by night, and often I wish that I could stretch out my arms and draw you both to me. We rejoice to find that you have entered upon your college duties with such cheerful spirits and good resolutions of improvement. May the divine blessing rest upon and enable you to perform every true and noble purpose of your soul!

Dr. Richardsone's death is indeed most afflictive—to the church of which he was not only a consistent member but firm supporter, to his desolated family, and to the whole community. His professional skill stood preeminent in Savannah. It has been a great stroke to your Cousin Charlie; for several days he did not leave his room. He had not only a strong personal affection for the doctor but great confidence in his integrity as a man and his sincerity as a Christian. He has written Mrs. Richardsone a beautiful letter of condolence and I may say consolation.

Have you seen young Berrien since his mother's death? If it lies in your power, show him kindness in his hour of sorrow. His mother and myself were schoolgirls together, and during that period entertained feelings of mutual friendship and affection for each other. Our pathway in life diverged widely. We seldom met, and never renewed our early intercourse, but I always retained an interest in her such as ever clings to the associations of our youth. In memory I often delight to recall and cherish the friends of early days. It would surprise you, were I to enumerate them, to see how many of my own age have gone to their rest, and how few remain to fight the battle of life. Their personal appearance, their peculiar characteristics, their mental and their moral traits often throng my vision with a living reality. Of most if not all I have the sweet assurance that "they sleep in Jesus and are blessed."

Last evening your dear father, sister, and myself attended at the Chinese Museum the lecture of General Sam Houston upon "The North American Indians," delivered to aid Mr. Owen for his church. It was an interesting defense and portraiture of the sons of the forest, and breathed the benevolent feelings of a noble mind. In appearance he is one of the most perfect and splendid-looking men I ever beheld. Wore a coat and vest (which was white) of Revolutionary cut, adding much to the dignity of his stout and manly form. In the progress of the speech we were greatly annoyed by a German masquerade ball going on in the room above us. Three thousand Germans were said to be present; and when they commenced waltzing, the whole building trembled, the glasses rattled, and chandeliers danced up and down in the center of the room. The noise, motion, and all together was like the raging of a tremendous storm at sea. It became impossible to hear. He remarked: "This is not an Indian war, but it seems to be a war of elephants" (or *elements*—we knew not which). His speech I doubt not was closed hastily on account of the overpowering noise.

Mr. Owen hopes to get Mr. Webster. He is to deliver an address on the character of Washington in Washington City, and he hopes to have it repeated here. If so, I wish that your brother and yourself could find time to attend.

Our long-looked-for trunk and barrel have come at last, and on Thursday we will send you some oranges. Some of them have rotted, but comparatively few considering it is two months since they left home.

Your cousin received a letter from his mother yesterday: staying at South Hampton; and your aunt and uncle on a visit to your Uncle Berrien, who had four children taken with measles. I dread their reaching the plantations, there are so many to have them. Mr. Axson has been very ill since we left, and the church are going to send him to Havana. His life and labors are beyond price to them.

Wednesday Morning. Bright and beautiful: how charming it would be in our sunny home today!

Your dear father passed Princeton on his return from Newark on Monday, having preached there twice on Sabbath, which exhausted him very much. His labors will never cease until the warfare of life is accomplished. With the exception of your dear and honored grandfather I never knew anyone so perfectly free from selfish considerations or regard to personal ease and comfort. Noble examples have they set those who are to come after them and labor for the good of mankind in their own day and generation.

I must now close to be in time for the eleven o'clock mail. Present our best regards to Dr. Maclean, with love to the Misses Brearley, and my respects to Mrs. Hope and Mrs. McCulloh. I hope Joseph and yourself will call to see Mr. Green; he was very polite to you here. I will write your brother next. Excuse my writing; my hand is very nervous for want of exercise. The fear of falling on the icy pavements keeps me within doors. Father, Sister, and Cousin unite with me in warmest love to yourself and brother. The gentlemen of your acquaintance in the Markoe inquire after and desire to be remembered to you.

Ever your own affectionate mother,
Mary Jones.

Rev. C. C. Jones *to* Mr. Charles C. Jones, Jr.^g

Philadelphia, *Friday,* February 27th, 1852

My dear Son,

Your last letter of 23rd inst. gave us great pleasure, and we are happy to observe your improvement in your handwriting, and also in the ease and correctness of your style of writing, and more particularly in the correctness of the sentiments you express. Open your letters in writing a little more; write a little heavier; and give strength to all the down strokes. It is one of the accomplishments of the highest value to the scholar and the gentleman to be able to write a fine, ready business hand and an accurate, well-composed letter. In this, as in 'most all things else, *"Practice makes perfect."* When I first began to write letters, my habit was to write them in full and then carefully correct the etymology, syntax, and prosody and copy off in as fair a hand as possible and send them. *All excellence is the fruit of careful, persevering labor.*

It is related of Mr. Burke that when he entered the door of his own house he left all the cares and anxieties of public business and of public life behind him, and became the life and happiness of his devoted wife and affectionate children, and exerted himself to please and to edify. Few public men are as considerate and as wise and indeed as economical of their own felicity. They ordinarily carry their public cares and anxieties into their own homes, with all the ruffled feelings incident to them; and hence the neglect of that faithful training of their children which you have observed in one instance before your eyes in Princeton. The due adjustment of public and social and private duties is a difficult task to poor, weak human nature. The prizes of ambition are too frequently paid for with unavailing tears and griefs that know no consolation. We have grasped the shadow and lost the substance of happiness.

You know, my dear son, what the all-prevalent desire of your parents has been in relation to yourself and your dear brother. Our affection for you both knows no bounds, and that desire is *your conversion to God.* Until *this event,* long labored for (it may be in weakness) and long prayed for (it may be in too little fervency of faith), takes place, we never can be at rest respecting either of you. You may be both men of probity, of honorable, virtuous character, of high intellectual attainments, of superior scholarship, and of distinction in society, and act well your part, and be blessed with competency by a kind Providence; yet if you neglect the interests of your immortal souls, if you live in rebellion against God and withhold your gratitude, your repentance, your love, and your obedience from your crucified Redeemer, what is it all worth? And alas, alas, *if either of you should die without hope, a cloud of sorrow would fall on us and cover us with its shade all our days upon the earth!*

You are both fast advancing to a choice in life of some calling; and we feel that ere you make this choice your eyes and your hearts should be lifted to God, and your prayer should be that God would be the Guide of your youth; and your *first* inquiry should be *to Him* who *made* you, who *redeemed* you, who *preserves* you: *Lord, what wouldst Thou have me to do?* This is your duty, this the gracious Being to whom you should go for direction above all others. You belong to Him soul and body, for time and for eternity, and are bound to consult His will; and it is your truest, highest interest to do so. Our wishes then in respect to your future plans are that you should first give yourself to God your Saviour; and then will you be able to see more clearly what course you should pursue in life, what profession you should choose. We do not interpose any objections to any purposes you may form, and whatever choice you make we will do all in our power to afford you means and opportunity and to aid you forward to success. Our happiness ever will be to contribute to the welfare and happiness of our dear children.

We shall be glad for you to write us your own views and wishes fully.

We are all well today, through God's mercy, and unite in love to you both. Mother sent you a box last week, care of Mr. Ross, of oranges, etc. Have you received it? Joe's letter about the aurora was very interesting, and Mother says she will answer it or I would do it. My love to him. I have bought Prichard's *Natural History of Man* and Cooper's *Naval History of the United States,* so you need not buy.

Your ever affectionate father,

C. C. Jones.

Mr. Charles C. Jones, Jr., *to* Rev. *and* Mrs. C. C. Jones[t]

Princeton, *Monday,* March 1st, 1852*

My dear Parents,

Your letter, Father, was duly received on Friday, and for the kind instructions therein contained I feel very much obliged to you, hoping that the precious advice so often repeated from your lips as well as those of my mother may not prove as "pearls cast before swine" but be cherished and regarded.

The box also with its interesting contents was safely deposited in our room by Mr. Ross, and I can assure you that its merits have been candidly as well as thoroughly discussed by dozens of admiring epicures. The oranges were pronounced by many to be the sweetest they had ever tasted; and you may depend, actions in such cases do emphatically speak louder than words.

Your present to our esteemed friend Dr. Maclean was promptly conveyed, and he desires me in return to tender his grateful acknowledgments. He has been appointed as a delegate from the Presbytery of New Jersey to attend the next General Assembly in Charleston, and anticipates leaving for that place in the spring. Several evenings since, he was conversing with me in regard to the miasma of the swamps around, and with reference to the prevailing fevers as well as the danger and risk incurred by one from the North spending a summer there. On these points I tried to give him all necessary information, for the subject was one with which I was somewhat familiar, having heard you speak many times with reference to it. He remarked that he would very gladly embrace the first opportunity offered of conferring with you, as your opinion would be "law and gospel." His desire for visiting that part of the South appears very strong, and I doubt not the hospitality of the inhabitants will produce a favorable impression on his mind. I hope, at least, that it will be found to be as generous as his own.

Never have I seen a more perfect model of a kind, benevolent, and tender-hearted professor. Is anyone sick or in distress? Is anyone depressed in spirits or under serious impressions? Anyone poor or deserving of sympathy? Dr. Maclean is ever ready to relieve his every necessity and administer that healing balm of consolation which only the troubled can best appreciate, which none save the kindhearted know how to bestow or are willing to impart. Long will I cherish his numerous good deeds, and ever hold his character in lively remembrance. It is truly astonishing what an influence a professor may deservedly obtain over the minds of students placed under his care, by a proper course of ascendancy which they shall always with pleasure acknowledge. Yet how frequently do we find persons occupying such positions reserved, abstract, cold, phlegmatic, surrounded with an artificial atmosphere of their own creation, tending but little to their exaltation and still less to the enjoyment of others. In such cases is it reasonable to expect that mutual regard and those sincere attachments which can exist only between spirits in some degree at least of a kindred nature?

Professor Hope has thrown himself quite on his dignity towards me this session, but his lady is still the same kind person. Not being very essentially dependent upon his exertions for the existence and accretion of my knowledge, I shall treat him respectfully and gentlemanly, minding my own business, yet not too obsequious an invoker of his smiles.

Professor McCulloh has not returned, although he will probably be with us this week. He has been engaged in making a series of experiments in the mint of Philadelphia with reference to a new method of refining gold.

And now, my dear father and mother, I must convey a piece of intelligence to you which I know will delight you much. Brother has been elected as a junior orator from Clio Hall for the ensuing commencement. His success was complete, for he appeared at the head of the four representatives, having received the largest number of votes (some ninety-six), which you see was very nearly a unanimous election. Another Georgian was also chosen; Fraley is his name, from the middle of the state. This appointment is deservedly considered, I think, the most honorable of those conferred while at college, because given by your associates and with a view to the honor of the hall. So you will have *two sons* speakers at the next commencement.

However, waiving particulars for the present, I will ask the acceptance of our united love for selves, Sister, and Cousin. Ever the same,

Your devoted son,
Charles C. Jones, Jr.

REV. C. C. JONES *to* MR. JOSEPH JONES[t]

Philadelphia, Tuesday, March 9th, 1852

My dear Son,

You cannot think how much gratified your dear mother and I were—and your sister and Cousin Charles Edward—to learn first from your brother and then from your last letter of your handsome election to the junior oratorship from the Clio Hall. We were gratified because we believe that your conduct, scholarship, and fidelity to the duties of the hall fully entitled you to it, without any disparagement of your fellow students. And now we trust that if spared in God's good providence you will prepare yourself and deliver a good and efficient oration. In casting about for a subject for you, as you requested, we could think of none which perhaps you could better handle than that of *the unity of the human race*. It is a fruitful subject, and you might give it a popular cast and strike a manly blow for the truth, seizing upon the most prominent, striking, and powerful arguments, especially bringing forward the *divinely inspired historical evidence in the Scriptures,* which the anti-unity men leave out. On this part of the subject you will find a fine article in *The Princeton Review*—some number of last year: 1851, I think. We only suggest it, and you can think of it.

Am very much pressed with business just now, and feel the want of exercise badly. Your mother and I are reading *Prichard*, and find him very interesting. Mother has been out day after day all last week shopping for our friends and relatives in Marietta. She is now through it all, and the beautiful articles were sent on Monday by Mr.—now *Dr.*—Lewis Pynchon.

I saw last week 228 doctors made by the Jefferson Medical College. It took one hour to distribute the sheepskins. Dr. Meigs said in his address about one-half who practiced medicine were quacks! So he left a wide margin for educated physicians.

Your Cousin Charles Edward's examinations commenced last night. He has been very unwell with a cold, and felt apprehensive he would have to lie up awhile; but he is out.

We hope to visit Princeton ere long and spend a Sabbath and preach for Dr. Maclean in the college chapel.

Professor Hope preached two excellent sermons at the Central Church on Sabbath. He told us you were better of your cold, which we were very happy to hear.

Our recent letters from home report the county *healthy, lively, dry;* and Mr. Leander Varnedoe, who married Miss Mallard, had his dwelling burnt down, and he and his family saved—*as we were,* in God's great mercy—in their nightdresses! Supposed to have been set on fire by a Negro belonging to Dr. Way! All our relations well except your Uncle Berrien's children, who had measles. All well also at Marietta. People at the different places all well, and busily preparing for the crop. Am trying to make arrangements to go home in April if I can, and want Mother to go with me.

Our united love to you and to your dear brother. Be good boys; and do not forget poor Jack's advice in Scripture to you both: "My son, if sinners entice thee, consent thou not." Mr. Cline from Columbia was here yesterday. *Old Mr. Law is dead!* The servant gone in his age to be ever with his Lord! Mr. Palmer stays with his people. Mr. Snowden has had an attack of dropsy: better. We received your brother's interesting letter last night. Excuse a weary and a trembling hand. The Lord be with and bless you evermore, my dear son!

Your affectionate father,
C. C. Jones.

Mrs. Mary Jones *to* Mr. Charles C. Jones, Jr.[g]

Philadelphia, *Friday,* March 12th, 1852

My dear Son,

It would cheer your mother's heart to hold converse with you every day of her life, but this may not be now, and she must at least write your brother or yourself once a week. Your last affectionate favor has been received and interested us very much, and we were especially pleased to see your views of the proper mode of preaching the gospel just such as we believe to be right and effective. We have endeavored to train our dear children according to our own conscientious belief of the truth, and when we see them embracing the same precious faith in any one particular, we rejoice with sincere happiness. May you, my beloved child, be not *almost* but *altogether* a follower and disciple of our Lord and Saviour Jesus Christ!

We have received letters from various friends since I wrote last to your brother. Through the goodness of God all our relatives are in health and prosperity, although some of our friends are beneath the rod of affliction. Mr. Palmer enclosed to your father a just and handsome obituary of our venerable friend Mr. Law, who has recently deceased in Columbia. His life and strength had been spent in the service of his Master, and his death was that of the righteous. Leander Varnedoe has had his house burnt in Liberty, himself and family barely escaping with their lives. What renders this particularly distressing, it is thought to be the work of an incendiary—a runaway servant belonging to Dr. Way. Rev. Richard Way and family are expected very soon to return from China. How sad it is that our missionaries have so often to return to this country at the very period when they are best prepared for usefulness!

A pleasing little incident occurred with your sister a few days since in Miss Gill's seminary. The Rev. Mr. Goodell, a returned missionary from Constantinople, was addressing the young ladies, and said one of their favorite and useful books was a catechism which had been prepared in this country by *the Rev. C. C. Jones*. After the address Mary says Miss Gill took her up and introduced her as a daughter of the author of the catechism. You know it has been translated into three foreign languages: Armenian, Turko-Armenian, and Chinese. Thus what was prepared with humble prayer and study in that little corner room at Montevideo, taught to and corrected from the schools of poor black children at home, has gone forth to the light of day, and is now conveying the knowledge of salvation to oriental nations now sitting in the region and shadow of death. What an honor it is thus to have your dear father's labors, which were undertaken only for the poor and humble and perishing of his own native land, owned and blessed of the Great Head of the Church!

In remembering the many precious things which lie in one common grave in Columbia there is nothing that I oftener think of with regret than your father's missionary journals. They would have been to his children an invaluable legacy of rich Christian experience—a record of toils and labors that I have never seen equaled by anyone and I presume have been surpassed by few, which have been valued and improved by the immediate recipients but which were but poorly appreciated at the time by the owners themselves. The reward of the good man must ever come from above. There is a line (I think

330

it is from Young) that was very early impressed on my memory: *He builds too low for happiness who builds below the skies.* Yes, when our motives for action spring from a desire of the divine approbation and are regulated and governed by the divine will, we may go boldly forward, leaving results with our Almighty Sovereign; and "He will make all things work together for good to them that love Him."

Last week I was as busy as I could well be shopping for Aunt and family in Marietta and for Mrs. and Misses Pynchon. On last Saturday Lewis Pynchon received the degree of *M.D.* There were over two hundred in the class, and your father says he was one of the finest-looking in it. He has improved very much in every respect, and has studied well this winter, and I doubt not will make a good physician.

Your Cousin Charlie has been very unwell, and still has a violent cold. He is undergoing his examination. I had no idea before what an anxious time it was. Everything seems to turn upon the examination, and they are very rigid in the university. I shall be glad when he has time for rest and exercise.

Do you, my dear boy, give that systematic attention to exercise and to your diet which your health demands and which you promised me to do? I hope my dear Joseph has recovered from his cold and sore throat. I have felt very uneasy about him, particularly as Professor Hope told me he looked thin.

When, where, and how is your vacation to be passed? What are your wishes about it?

I cannot and perhaps I ought not to express all the sense of gratification which your father and myself experience in anticipation of the next commencement at the thought of having our two sons appearing in such honorable positions. The subject of "The Unity of the Races" is so much in your brother's line of thought and of the popular interest that if he could handle it ably it would reflect great credit upon him. It is one which would admit of powerful reasoning and thrilling eloquence. What is to be the subject of your piece?

Your dear father insists that I must accompany him home in April, urging his lonely situation if I do not go, which I presume I will have to do. But I am painfully divided, not liking to leave your sister entirely with strangers. We could not return before the third week in May. He goes on to New York tomorrow in the evening train to present the cause of missions in Dr. Krebs's church on Sabbath. I will send a little parcel for you to be left at the depot by him. Today he has held three services for the Central Church. It has been a day of humiliation and prayer in view of their desolate state, and to ask direction in the choice of a pastor. Father, Sister, and Cousin send love to you both, and your friends in the Markoe desire remembrance. God bless and keep you, my dear sons!

Ever your affectionate mother,
Mary Jones.

Rev. C. C. Jones *to* Messrs. Charles C. Jones, Jr., *and* Joseph Jones[g]

Philadelphia, *Saturday,* March 13th, 1852

My dear Sons,

I find that it will be out of my power to spend a Sabbath in Princeton as I promised you and my kind friend Dr. Maclean, in consequence of engagements to preach for the board in the city, and my necessary confinement in preparing the annual report, which must be ready by the 12th of April; and there is much to be done. Please let Dr. Maclean know this, with my regrets that it is so. However, am going to New York to preach for Dr. Krebs this afternoon, God willing, and will be in Princeton *Monday noon,* and address the students of the seminary in the evening on domestic missions, and return to Philadelphia Tuesday morning. Say to Dr. Maclean that I will do myself the pleasure of staying with him.

Will see you then, my dear sons, on Monday, and will then talk over all your arrangements for commencement and vacation and for your visiting us in Philadelphia, as your mother wishes to fit you both out in the clothing line.

We are all well today, and unite in love to you both.

Your ever affectionate father,
C. C. Jones.

Mr. Charles C. Jones, Jr., *to* Miss Laura E. Maxwell[g]

Princeton, *Monday,* March 22nd, 1852

My very dear Cousin,

Judge of my pleasure and delight when I this morning traced upon the back of a letter the impress of your own beautiful hand! Yet how was that joy rendered tenfold more intense when upon opening it I was permitted to drink in its interesting intelligence and hold happy converse with one so sincerely loved! Highly do I appreciate the privilege of corresponding with you, and honored indeed do I feel when one of these paragons in "the world of letters" is received. Around me are lying differential and integral calculus, astronomy, ancient Roman and Greek authors—all calling upon me to turn and peruse, pointing with warning fingers to the final examination. Yet I must, my cousin, throw them aside, even though their specters in the still hours of midnight, like the birds of "Indian brake," should torment me, and engage in a far more delightful enjoyment—that of transmitting to you a few items of news and a deal of regard.

Would I possessed that magic power which you enjoy in so remarkable a degree of infusing a charm into every sentence and stamping the whole with an air of vivacity and due affection! However, although my pen flow not smoothly, and the ideas expressed seem abstract and devoid of warmth, remember that for several weeks I have been doomed to the acquisition of dry formulas and abstruse theories, which are by no means conducive to refinement of feeling or a cultivation of the tender sympathies of the soul. Were it not for the privilege of thus holding intercourse with my friends, I verily believe that I would daily become more and more assimilated to those old cloistered monks and pillar saints of the Dark Ages. Yet, however I may be attached to the pursuits of literature, I know of no opportunities which I more readily embrace than those which afford a chance of receiving that polish which is a concomitant of female society; for you know I feel highly honored when called a "ladies' man," and hope under your guidance and with your approbation one of these days to be indoctrinated in such arts as are calculated to win the smiles of the fair sex.

You must indeed be enjoying yourself very much in Savannah. The most delightful season of the year has now appeared, when all nature in her youthful garb invites her admirers to walk forth and admire her beauties; and many must be the pleasant evening rambles beyond the common in company with some fair companion or captivated gallant. Am glad to hear of the welfare of Miss Clem. She is a very pleasant young lady—one for whom I entertain feelings of sincere regard; and hope that you will present my best wishes when next you see her.

Speaking of the charming Southern climate, you can imagine our condition by picturing to yourself a country overspread by a sheet of dissolving snow, a soil as soft and muddy as the uncertain banks of the Styx, while not a verdant leaf is as yet visible to gladden the eye—sweet harbinger of returning spring.

We seniors are, however, so busily employed in preparing for our final examination that changes of weather pass unnoticed. Our class graduates on the 10th of May, and we shall then be released from those engagements which for several years have been engaging our attention; and a large number will be thrown upon the stage of action, each to maintain those principles and exemplify such virtues as shall in after life conduce either to his welfare or woe. The Latin proverb *Quisque suae fortunae faber* is in a great measure correct. It is by exertion, close severe application, and determinate perseverance that achievements are to be made and honors merited, and not through any falsely styled inspiration—a persuasion fatal to many. The commencement will take place on the 25th of June. Brother and myself will then in all probability appear in public. How we would be delighted, my dear cousin, if we could have the pleasure of seeing yourself and other relatives here at that occasion! Hope that we will not sadly disappoint the expectations of our friends.

You ask what are my future plans. At present they are not specifically entertained, although my expectation is to commence the study of law so soon as it may appear convenient and advisable. Will perhaps attend two courses of lectures at the Virginia University. So, Cousin, if you get into any troubles, or wish to call in the arm of the law to your assistance, the subscriber doth hereby tender his services, craving patronage and a good word.

I expect to remain in Princeton until the commencement is over, as a fine opportunity will be afforded from the early part of May to the 25th of June for reading and speech-making.

Since Dr. Alexander's death I have not visited Miss Alexander, thinking that my acquaintance was not of such a character as would justify me in calling upon the family while thus in the midst of a most severe affliction. She will be very happy to hear from you, for she has more than once inquired after you, and spoken in my presence of the high sense of regard and affection which she cherished for you.

Expect to visit Philadelphia on Monday in order to bid our dear parents farewell previous to their departure for Georgia.

Cousin Charlie is standing, I have understood, a superior examination, and there is every reason to expect that he will become a very prominent member of his profession.

Now, Cousin, although I might continue longer, yet I fear this letter is becoming tedious; and as it certainly is badly composed, I will bring it to a close, hoping that you will excuse the present delinquencies on the ground of engagements, forbidding that due attention which the subject demands. Better epistles from me in vacation when, delivered from this tumultuous round of engagements, I can at ease pen words more captivating—and with greater care. Brother unites with me in warmest love to you, my dear cousin; and believe me ever the same.

Your attached cousin,
Charles C. Jones, Jr.

Mrs. Mary Jones *to* Miss Laura E. Maxwell[t]
Philadelphia, *Tuesday,* March 23rd, 1852

Thank you, my ever dear Laura, for your affectionate letter received a week since. It was my intention to have written you whilst you were in Savannah, and through you to have acknowledged the gratitude I felt to Major and Mrs. Porter and their family for all their kind attentions to me. My visit to them was truly pleasant, and I shall long remember it. I feel very much concerned for the health of our good friend Mrs. P.; those headaches are most distressing.

Your uncle returned from New York on last Tuesday (this day week). That night we received a note from Miss Emma McAllister asking us to visit Mrs. Clay, who has been unwell all winter. We left at seven o'clock the next morning in a storm of wind and rain, which soon was converted into snow. We reached New York barely in time for the New Haven cars, which were so full I had to stand up until I nearly dropped, only one person offering his seat, until your uncle discovered that a *lady* was occupying a whole seat to herself by elongating her lower members and requested her to give me a place. He had to stand by my side almost the whole way. One *gentleman* did offer to *spell* him. The snow retarded the progress of the cars so much that we were three or four hours behind our time, and when within three miles of New Haven the wood gave out. The locomotive ceased to breathe, and we came to a hopeless halt. Being provoked previously to the

334

point of revenge, I said with the intention of being heard: "As we are in Connecticut, what a pity they had not thought of taking a barrel of nutmegs and hams on board! They would have kept us moving." It was really amusing to see the dilemma. After some delay a locomotive was sent out from New Haven and took us in. It was so late when we arrived that the hacks were all gone, and we trudged through the snow six inches deep under foot and falling in showers from above. Mrs. Clay looks very thin and reduced, and we entertain fearful anxieties for her health.

I have been very busy in divers manners since my return, and have now a long table to make out for Mr. J.'s report, which requires time and close attention.

Miss Canning has just sent home three of your dresses—the swiss, a green tissue, and an organdy, which is said to be the most fashionable article for summer. Tomorrow, if I am able (for I have been quite unwell since returning from New Haven), I will go out and get you another dress, as you desire through your last letter to Charles. You did not say anything about open fronts; consequently I had them all made as you usually wear them, and according to the dress you sent as a pattern. The lace mantles cost from $5 to $10; those at $5 are common. The best way of getting a good article would be to purchase a square of lace and cut it in two and put an edge around it. This would bring the half-shawl or mantle to about $6. They have usually to be lined with silk. *Write me immediately about this.* I have been so fearful of getting what Sister Susan might not like for a mantle (as she has given me no instructions about it) that I have had nothing but her bombazine made, and her boots. I hope she will write if she desires anything more. Winter lingers so long that it has been difficult to get at spring goods.

Please thank Sister Betsy for her kind letter, and say I will try and find the birds and butterflies for her quilt. And say to my good friend Julia that we saw Willie in New Haven; he looks remarkably well, and is encouraged in his studies, and was in fine spirits. Fred quite well. All anticipating with great pleasure seeing her this summer.

Charlie has passed his examinations! Saturday week will be the commencement in the university, and I rejoice in his prospect of release. He has been suffering from a severe cold and cough, and looks very thin. If possible he ought to recruit his health before he enters upon the active duties of his profession.

Your uncle is now very busy preparing his report for the assembly, and hoping to leave by the 12th of April for home, which will give him a little rest, which he needs above all things. *Mary* pleads so eloquently that, Providence permitting, you may look for us *three*. We have concluded that it would not do to leave her.

It will gratify you all at the Island to know that our dear boy Joe has had the same honor conferred on him by his society as Charles had last year, and he will represent them as *junior orator* at the next commencement. He obtained the appointment by far the largest vote of any of the candidates in the society, and I trust he will be enabled to acquit himself with credit to himself and to us all.

Your friends make many inquiries after you, and your Sunday school scholars have not forgotten you. Amelia Wohlgemuth has just left for St. Louis. She says she became interested in the Sunday school from your kindness to her; has been feeling deeply on the subject of religion, and now expresses a hope that her sins have been forgiven. I have had thirteen in my class—rather too many, as some of them are nearly grown; but it is a good work. I know you love it.

I hope my dear sisters will forgive me for not writing them. I have been so busy trying to get my work ready for spring, and shopping for various friends, that I have not had the time. Mr. Jones, Charles, and Mary unite with me in best love to them and yourself and Brother William, to your aunt and family, to Henry and family, and all friends. Write soon to

Your ever attached aunt,
Mary Jones.

Howdies for all the servants.

REV. C. C. JONES *to* MESSRS. CHARLES C. JONES, JR., *and* JOSEPH JONES[g]

Morristown, New Jersey, *Wednesday,* March 31st, 1852

My dear Sons,

We took a carriage at Elizabeth Town, and after a ride of eighteen miles reached here at one o'clock in the night, getting through the ride more comfortably than we anticipated. We found your dear cousin very ill—glad, glad to see us, as we to get to him. The attack has been exceedingly violent, and his situation is very critical, although we hope for the best. We sat up the remainder of the night with him, and this morning Dr. Stevenson and Dr. Kinnelly from New York (your cousin's old office friend in Savannah) think he is better. We have just changed all his clothes and bedding, and he is more comfortable. We cannot tell when we shall be able to return, as it will depend upon the sickness of your cousin, but will write you from time to time.

This sudden stroke of God, my dear sons, should seriously and solemnly impress you both. You see how uncertain is life, and how absolutely necessary is preparation for death. Your mother and I do earnestly entreat you not to put off your soul's salvation, but seek the Lord while He may be found and call upon Him while He is near.

Be careful of yourselves in this trying, trying weather. Hope you suffered nothing from exposure last night. Will write you of your cousin's case as often as possible, but hope it may please God to restore him to health soon. Mother unites in love to you both. Dr. K. takes this letter to New York to mail it for me. In haste, my dear sons,

Ever your affectionate father,
C. C. Jones.

Mr. Charles C. Jones, Jr., *to* Rev. *and* Mrs. C. C. Jones[t]
Princeton, *Thursday,* April 1st, 1852

My dear Father and Mother,

Your letter of yesterday reached us safely this morning, and I was glad to find that you reached Morristown with less difficulty and fatigue than might have been anticipated. Truly do I rejoice to learn that Cousin Charlie is somewhat relieved, and sincerely hope that his recovery may be as speedy as his attack was sudden and unexpected. We can appreciate the pleasure and satisfaction which your presence must afford him, giving him every assurance that all the relief which lies in mortal hands will be promptly administered—and that by those who are near and dear relatives. I hope that you will spare yourselves as much as possible, and not undergo too great exposure and deprivation of rest. Do, my dear parents, let me know immediately if I can render you or my sick cousin any service, and I will be with you at the spot.

We reached Princeton safely after parting with you at the depot, and are both of us today quite well. The pleasant change of weather is truly delightful, and this beautiful day contrasts sweetly with those dark and gloomy ones that have just preceded it. Every person and object in this little town seems instinct with new life and buoyant with delight. Hope that the temperature also may exert a favorable influence in restoring the doctor's health.

Today at twelve o'clock we looked at the spots on the sun through Professor Alexander's telescope. Three were seen—rather small, yet quite distinct. Our class is so large that each individual could only view them for a few seconds and then give place for another.

We are busily engaged once more in prosecuting our studies, and in preparation for the final examination. The senior class are sitting for their daguerreotypes, to be placed in the picture gallery. We sit two by two. As yet mine has not been taken.

Again, my dear parents, begging you to send for me if I can at all be of any aid to you, and hoping that Cousin Charlie may speedily and safely recover, and that you both will not suffer from overexertion, I remain, with much love to you and Cousin, in which Brother unites with me,

Your affectionate son,
Charles C. Jones, Jr.

P.S. Hope that you will write us as often as circumstances will allow, for we shall necessarily feel very solicitous until the crisis be past.

Rev. C. C. Jones *to* Messrs. Charles C. Jones, Jr., *and* Joseph Jones[t]
Morristown, *Thursday,* April 1st, 1852

Your cousin, my dear sons, had a bad night of it last night, and is not so well today. Have called in another physician to him this morning. So we have the two ablest in the town. Yet we must depend upon God's blessing. He has had a little sleep, and says he feels much better. But he is *critically ill,* and we know not how his case will terminate! We must pray and hope for the best. He sends love to you. And Mother sends love; she is quite well. It was ordered all right that we come. People very kind.

Be careful of your health. In haste for the mail,

Your ever affectionate father,
C. C. Jones.

REV. C. C. JONES *to* MESSRS. CHARLES C. JONES, JR., *and* JOSEPH JONES[t]

Morristown, *Friday,* April 2nd, 1852

My dear Sons,

Your cousin did not pass as bad a night as the one previous, and we hope he is better this morning. Says he feels better, but is by no means out of danger. Drs. Johnes and Stevenson think favorably of the case, but consider him still critically ill. We must use all the means in our power and leave him in the hands of God, whose mercies are great.

A deathbed, my dear sons, is no place for you to prepare to meet your God!

Mother sends much love to you both, and says you must be very careful of yourselves. In haste for the mail,

Your ever affectionate father,
C. C. Jones.

REV. C. C. JONES *to* MRS. SUSAN M. CUMMING[t]

Morristown, *Saturday,* April 3rd, 1852

Oh, my sister! My sister! How shall I speak? "The cup which my Father giveth me to drink, shall I not drink it?" Oh, this cup—so unexpected, so bitter, so deep! God writeth you *sonless!* Help her, O my God! Your help, my sister, must come from Him who made heaven and earth—the almighty and compassionate Saviour.

We are in sore dismay and distress beyond expression! Alas, how sudden, how violent past all remedies his disease! Nothing left unattempted, undone. We were with him day and night. He lacked for no attention. All skill was executed in his case. Dear child, his hour had come, and God has taken him. You were spared the agony of the eye and the ear. The kindness of the people is extraordinary. We will do all things the best we can. My dear wife and I are cast down and overborne. He was beloved as a child to us. He died this morning at ten minutes after five o'clock. God only can comfort you and our dear Laura! Pray for us as we do for you. Love, love to everyone.

Your ever affectionate and afflicted, distressed brother. Mary writes this letter with me.

C. C. Jones.

X

Princeton, *Friday,* April 23rd, 1852

My very dear Parents,

Your welcome note conveying your united love and signatures previous to your departure from Philadelphia, and also the letter from Wilmington, have both been received, and for them we feel deeply indebted to you. Happy are we that you are once more removed from the noise and confusion, the confinement and monotony of a large city, and have now entered a milder and more stable climate, where we hope your physical powers may be resuscitated, your health restored, and the mind, relieved from the pressure of engagements and the never-ceasing routine of fatiguing business, may for a time forget these cares and seek repose in pleasant communion with nature, with nature's God, and the kind relatives whom He has given here on earth.

Yet from amid that circle one is not. Snatched away just when the pride of manhood had fairly mantled his brow, when his mind, just trained with assiduous care and affections warmly cherished, gave promise of a noble and useful life, of a career distinguished and honorable, he now lies in a foreign land, still and motionless in the cold and silent grave. Already have the snows descended upon that consecrated spot, and stranger feet have paused around his tomb. Yet that voice so cheerful, so friendly, is heard no more; that bosom ever swelling with generous emotions and that heart which always felt for the ills of others and regarded with tenderest love his family and associates, that mind whose successful efforts in the acquisition of knowledge and truth might justly claim for him a station far, far above the multitude—all these are passed away; and naught else is left us save that sweet perfume of pleasant deeds, those endeared recollections of happy intercourse, of kindly affections and winning smiles, the knowledge of his high regard for morality, religion, honor, and truth, the repeated expressions of sympathies and regard from friends, and the little mementos which he has left to remind us of one who was very dear to us in life and whose recollection in death we delight to cherish. Truly God Almighty has been in our very midst, and from this family circle has singled one and borne him away upon whom we loved to look and from whom we anticipated increasing reputation and honor.

Heavy indeed is the stroke; yet it is the Lord alone who has directed it; and shall mortal man presume to rebel? Rather let him lay it to heart, search out and remember his own shortcomings, pray that it may be sanctified to the living, and endeavor to live a life of readiness, of faith, and of watchfulness.

339

Mournfully true is the shortness and uncertainty of our existence. Often when the brightest hopes are cherished, when the prospects of success seem most flattering, when every path seems open to favor and renown, then is that last enemy nearest to us; and while we are engaged in proposing plans for future conduction, He may that very instant be bending His bow and fitting that shaft which shall entirely thwart our own purposes, bearing us from time into eternity. If then there be no preparation, truly we are of all men most miserable. How vain then to neglect the eternal, striving to attain that only which perishes with the using and leaves naught but vanity. We pursue the enjoyments of this life, and seek for worldly honors with perseverance and sincere desire, while we are intellectually convinced that the true course of action calls for different efforts, that we are reaching forward to the secondary and at the same time neglecting the primary. How great the difference between mental and spiritual conviction! The former we possess in common with all enlightened men, while the latter is known only to the saint and the true believer. Human happiness is at best but relative, and yet how we attempt to realize that ideal notion of entire enjoyment which each one frames for himself! He alone attains this truly who uses the present as a preparatory state to the future.

> The flower that smiles today
>   Tomorrow dies;
> All that we wish to stay
>   Tempts and then flies.
> What is this world's delight?
> Lightning that mocks the night,
>   Brief even as bright.

Thus does Shelley express the changing nature of all things human; while the Ettrick Shepherd also unites in revealing a similar lesson:

> Fadin' as the forest roses,
> Transient as the radiant bow,
> Fleetin' as the shower that follows
> Is our happiness below.

I would have written my dear aunt and cousin, yet feared that anything which I could have said would have been rather useless in this our common affliction. May they and all our relatives find consolation in that Book of Life whose promises to believers are ever ready and suited to every case!

Miss Comfort passed through Princeton this morning, and will soon return, when we will try and render her some returns for the many kind obligations under which she has placed us. A noble lady indeed she is, and her kindness to our deceased relative knew no bounds in his last sickness, and was only surpassed by your devotion and unceasing attentions, my dear parents. We there met with sympathy and kindness even more than we had any reason to expect, for our only claim in a stranger-land was that founded upon a natural benevolence of soul which all men possess in a greater or less degree.

In about three weeks our final examination will commence, and we are excused from exercises on the 18th of May. This examination will be quite severe, and pretty extensive, for you know it includes all the studies which we have been over for four years, and consequently embraces some which I had not an opportunity of attending to in proper season, being away the fresh and soph years.

Dr. Maclean is pretty well, although his cough still lingers and troubles him considerably. The rest of our professors and the students generally are in fine health.

I hope, my dear parents and sister, that you will derive much benefit from this visit, and return refreshed in mind and body. Hope that you have found all of our dear relatives in the possession of health, and that everything at home is successfully progressing. Brother unites with me in warmest love to you both, my dear parents, Sister, Aunt Susan and Aunt Betsy, Cousin Laura, and Uncle, to all friends at South Hampton, and relatives in the county.

Your affectionate son,
Charles C. Jones, Jr.

Howdy for all the servants.

Mrs. Mary Jones *to* Messrs. Charles C. Jones, Jr., *and* Joseph Jones[g]

Montevideo, Monday, April 26th, 1852

My dear Sons,

I felt very much disappointed when little Tyrone came from the Boro today without a line from either of you; but upon consideration it was too early to expect a letter, and I will live in hopes of one by Thursday's mail.

Through the goodness and mercy of God we are once more at our own home. Your dear father wrote you from Wilmington, making you acquainted with our journey to that place, where we spent the Sabbath. Your sister was taken so unwell in the morning that I could not leave her for church, but administered a dose of magnesia, which was blessed to her relief; and I accompanied your father and Mr. Gibbs to church at night, hearing an excellent sermon from Mr. Grier on "Let me die the death of the righteous, and let my last end be like his." Do you remember Dr. Alexander's sermon on that text? Oh, how impressive—and filled with the rich experience of over three-score years and ten. We all must desire to die the death of the righteous, or say that we do; but if this desire does not lead us to repentance and faith in the Lord Jesus Christ, to newness of life and obedience to all God's commandments, we shall have nothing to support us in our dying hour, and only a fearful looking forward to judgment beyond the grave. From such an end may God in mercy deliver us, my beloved children! The first thing we saw on arriving at Wilmington was the coffin of a little girl whose parents had come on with their dead child from Savannah for interment there. Her death had been caused by a fall when at play on the back of her head.

Whilst coming down the Potomac on board the steamer *Baltimore* I was thrown in company with one of the most perfect devotees of fashion that I have ever met. She was young and beautiful, and seemed intoxicated with exhilarating draughts of worldly pleasure. As might be expected, a trifling novel was her traveling companion. She spoke of her past winter in Washington as spent in the ballroom, the theater, the opera, and the various sources of amusement to be found in fashionable life. To use her own expression, "She had now fairly learned the ways of the world; she hoped to spend the next winter in the same manner, and the next, and the next, and to drink in pleasure and enjoyment until she was *satiated,* and then—and then—she would retire in disgust from the world." Such were her plans for life! Gladly would I have lifted the veil from her deluded heart and shown her the true pathway to happiness. Oh, these calculations for life—*for life*—whilst death may be at the door!

We left Wilmington about twelve o'clock in the *Gladiator,* and a stiff breeze ahead gave us a rough passage, from which as usual we all suffered, and arrived at eight o'clock next morning in Charleston feeling sorry enough from seasickness. We went immediately to the Savannah boat, the *John C. Calhoun,* calling on our way for a moment to inquire after Mr. Adger. Whilst waiting in the upper saloon, who should come on board but the two Miss Percivals from Columbia, going on to attend the wedding of Miss Habersham. We were very happy to meet them, and to hear of all friends in Columbia. We arrived in Savannah about five o'clock, and went to the Pulaski House. As we went into the ordinary, saw Miss Colwell from Philadelphia and Mr. Roser.

Whilst at tea Mr. Wallace Cumming came in. I felt very much overcome at seeing him, and could scarcely command my feelings. He gave us a full account of his visit to Liberty. As we feared, none of our letters had reached your aunt. Major Porter received the sad tidings on the morning of the 7th, sent to the Cummings', and Wallace took the letter, and getting a private conveyance left about eleven o'clock, and did not reach the Island until dark. Stopping at the gate, he sent in for your uncle, to whom he made the first communication, and who was completely overwhelmed. Your aunts and cousin, hearing that a carriage had arrived and your uncle called out, concluded that your poor cousin had come and were meditating a surprise to them. Wallace walked in and spoke. They saw that all was not right from his countenance, and asked what was the matter. In the most gentle and collected manner he revealed the whole truth—and oh, then for three hours such a scene of agonizing grief as could not be described! You may strive to imagine it.

Your poor aunt's *heart is crushed.* Your Cousin Laura is but the shadow of what she was, and your aunty and uncle are bowed with sorrow. Your Aunt Susan says all she has left to comfort her is the evidence he gave in his life that he tried to serve God, that she never knew him to neglect his Bible, and has at all seasons gone unexpectedly into his room and found him on his knees. She says if she thought his *soul was lost* she would *go deranged;* she could not survive the blow. As it is, it would rend your heart to look upon her calm but utterly despairing and grief-stricken face. Nothing but the compassionate Redeemer's love and power can fill and sustain her heart.

Oh, my sons, my sons! Will you tempt God to forsake you utterly by delaying to embrace His offered salvation? I feel that if this warning *to you* from the deathbed of your beloved cousin—he who was unto you as an elder brother—as he stood almost at the Judgment Bar of God fails to affect your hearts, and to be the means of leading you to a decision on the subject of religion, that your state will be awful indeed. "He that, being often reproved, hardeneth his neck shall suddenly be destroyed, and that without remedy." My soul trembles before God for you. *Delay not* to make your peace with God. I do entreat you, my dear precious children, lest His wrath overtake you and you be sent away into everlasting burnings. These things are *true,* and I pray you to believe them ere it be forever too late.

Dr. Cumming came immediately down from Augusta and remained with your aunt until our arrival; and his presence, his conversation, reading of the Scriptures and prayers were very comforting to her. They have all acted the part of kind and sympathizing sons to her, and I hope God will reward them a thousandfold. As you may suppose, our meeting opened every fountain of grief. Your kind Aunt Julia, as soon as she received the tidings, went down with Audley in her large boat and brought them all up to South Hampton, and there they remained until we came. . . .

27th. A charming morning. We had a delightful shower last evening, and now all nature rejoices. I wish you could see and enjoy everything around us. Sky, earth, air, birds, trees, and flowers—all God's works do praise Him. After breakfast your aunt, cousin, and sister are to come over and remain with us whilst we are up here. Your dear father has much business to attend to, and it will be necessary for him to administer on your cousin's estate.

I have not written half I intended, but must close for the mail, and your father will add a postscript. The servants all send howdy to you.

Ever, my dear sons, your affectionate mother,
Mary Jones.

REV. C. C. JONES *to* MESSRS. CHARLES C. JONES, JR., *and* JOSEPH JONES[g]

Montevideo, *Tuesday,* April 27th, 1852

Your dear mother has given you all the news touching ourselves and others, and I add a brief postscript.

Your Aunt Susan and Cousin Laura will, according to present prospects, God willing, return with us to the North in June; and it is on many accounts desirable that our summer be spent *out* of Philadelphia. I wish you therefore to make inquiries *in Princeton* whether board can be obtained *for us all*—not in the hotels, as they appear not to be comfortable and are high in their charges; in some private establishments—and at what price per week. There will be a room needed for your Aunt Susan and Cousin Laura, and one for Mother and myself, and one for your sister, and one for you both should you remain in Princeton—although Mother thinks you had better make a trip somewhere. You need not *mention names,* but merely say *a family of friends from the South.* Inquire at the place where Mrs. and Dr. Chester boarded last summer. And let me hear from you as speedily as possible. We shall leave here about the middle of June—say, the 15th, and if quarters can be had in Princeton will go right on there. Do your best.

We shall write you every week, or try to do so. The season is beautiful, and the air of home refreshing; and hope by God's blessing to recruit. Let me beg you to listen to the exhortations of your mother. May God bless you both, my dear sons, and incline your hearts to Him!

Your ever affectionate father,
C. C. Jones.

A sweet rose apiece for you from Mother's garden. Remembrances to Dr. Maclean.

Mr. Charles C. Jones, Jr., *to* Rev. *and* Mrs. C. C. Jones[t]

Princeton, *Saturday,* May 8th, 1852

Although the week has passed unmarked by any event of consequence or interest, still I have taken my pen according to my usual custom in order at least to let you know that your son thinks often of you in your absence.

Have received two precious letters within the last few days, one from my sister and the other from my beloved Aunt Betsy. How I thank them both for such expressions of their interest in our spiritual welfare! Surely few—very few—enjoy the privilege of so many kind wishes and Christian prayers. May these never prove a source of deeper condemnation to those for whom they are offered, but may they pray also—and that unceasingly; for although "the prayer of the righteous man availeth much," still it cannot save a soul that refuses itself to accept of salvation freely offered, or that lives regardless of the counsels of pious parents and relatives, choosing death rather than life eternal.

Aunt gives a most heartrending account of the first intimation which they received of the decease of our dear departed relative. What anguish must have seized upon the souls of Aunt Susan and Cousin Laura when first they learned that their arm of support—their joy—was no more! Then the meeting of those who had but just left the dying couch and came as messengers to bear the last tokens of love and affection to such as felt deeply the common bereavement—who can describe or imagine save such as have themselves experienced pangs of woe and grief almost beyond what the human heart can bear?

My heart was sad as I perused the postscript to Sister's letter, announcing the death of Uncle John's little girl. She was, I believe, Mother, named after

344

you; and I remember hearing you both, my dear parents, speak of her subsequently to your return from Marietta last winter. The death of the infant, although painful indeed, is still divested of many sorrows that often attend the decease of those advanced in years. Yet it is at all times hard to part with those in whom our affection is bound with the tenderest earthly ties, from whom we anticipated increasing delight and the development of a lovely character. Milton thus beautifully speaks of the death of a fair infant:

> O fairest flower, no sooner blown but blasted,
> Soft silken primrose fading timelessly,
> Summer's chief honor, if thou hadst outlasted
> Bleak winter's force that made thy blossom dry:
> For he being amorous on that lovely dye
> That did thy cheek envermeil, thought to kiss,
> But killed alas, and then bewail'd his fatal bliss.
> But oh! why didst thou not stay here below,
> To bless us with thy heav'n-lov'd innocence.
> To slake his wrath whom sin hath made our foe,
> To turn swift-rushing black perdition hence,
> Or drive away the slaughtering pestilence,
> To stand 'twixt us and our deserved smart?
> But thou canst best perform that office where thou art.
> Then thou, the mother of so sweet a child,
> Her false imagin'd loss cease to lament,
> And wisely learn to curb thy sorrow wild;
> Think what a present thou to God hast sent,
> And render Him with patience what He lent;
> This if thou do, He will an offspring give
> That till the world's last end shall make thy name to live.

Far, far above the language of the poet is the kind invitation of Him who said: "Suffer little children to come unto me, and forbid them not, for of such is the Kingdom of Heaven."

I hope that Aunt Betsy and Sister will excuse me if I do not reply to their letters until after examination, as we are very much occupied. This final examination begins on Tuesday next (May 11th) and continues until the 18th, when we will be excused from further attendance until commencement.

In my last letter I gave you an account of a set of rooms in this town. Since then I have not seen any better or as good, but will look out for them still. Those I spoke of are perhaps the very best and most private that can be secured.

Wishing you both, my dear parents, every blessing, with warmest love to selves, Aunt Susan, Aunt Betsy, Cousin Laura, Sister, Uncle William, and all relatives and friends in the county, I remain

Your ever affectionate son,
Charles C. Jones, Jr.

Brother unites with me in the same.

Howdy to the servants.

MRS. MARY JONES *to* MR. CHARLES C. JONES, JR.ᵍ

Maybank, *Monday Morning,* May 17th, 1852

½ past 4 o'clock

My dear Son,

Since coming to the Island we have seen your Aunt Susan, and cannot under present circumstances send Mrs. Van Dyke a positive answer. Say to her if she has an advantageous offer to engage her rooms, to do so and not keep them for us. We may want them, but as there is uncertainty connected with our movements, we would not like to interfere with her interest in any way.

Your dear father was taken with fever this day week in consequence of exposure to the sun. It lasted several days, and has prostrated his strength very much. He is now taking tonics, and I trust with God's blessing on them and the change to this delightful atmosphere will do him good. He is completely worn down from the peculiar and exhausting nature of his situation in Philadelphia and the deep, deep sorrow through which we have and are now passing. May the Lord in mercy sanctify these afflictions to us all! Awful will it be if they pass unheeded and work not out the fruits of righteousness.

Should you see dear Miss Comfort give her our sincere love. I have desired to write her, but have been peculiarly situated for not doing so.

Your *Uncle Henry,* together with Messrs. John Ward and John Anderson of Savannah, have been elected delegates to the *Baltimore Convention,* which meets early in June to nominate a candidate from the Democratic party for the Presidency. This is a highly flattering appointment. He goes on next week in company with your Uncle Charles and Aunt Marion. They will proceed to Saratoga for a few weeks, and I suspect *attend your commencement to hear their nephews.* You must both try and do them credit.

I must close in haste to be in time for your uncle. With love from Father and Mother to their dear boys,

Ever your affectionate mother,

Mary Jones.

MR. CHARLES C. JONES, JR., *to* REV. *and* MRS. C. C. JONESᵗ

Princeton, *Tuesday,* May 18th, 1852

My dear Father and Mother,

Our final senior examination terminated yesterday, having continued from the 11th to the 18th of this month. It was protracted and on that account rather tedious, yet all college obligations have now ceased, and we are really graduates, although the degrees will not be officially conferred until the 25th of June.

The examining committee, appointed from the board of trustees, expressed themselves highly pleased with this our last examination—and very deservedly so, I am persuaded, although you may deem me presenting an interested opinion. The actual fact of the matter is, the members of our class are nearly all of them fine students, and grade high. In proof of this I need only tell you that over twenty of them have an average throughout the entire course over 96, and some seven or eight of these range between 99 and 100. It is a class, however, not as prolific in fine speakers as it is in good scholars. Yet even in this respect it will, I doubt not, compare favorably with an equal number chosen elsewhere.

This period of graduation forms an important and solemn era in the life of a young man. Hitherto his path has been clearly defined, his duties and obligations of a comparatively defined and limited nature, his plans all matured by wise and prudent minds, and the student himself engaged in bare preparation, often without any specific purpose save that of general improvement. Now, however, his college vows have been paid upon their appropriate altar, his apprenticeship is ended, and he feels that he has new responsibilities to meet, responsibilities that savor of manhood, that call for some determined choice, a specific aim for individual action. He has now to care for, and direct into a proper channel, the powers of this "intellectual being—these thoughts that wander through eternity," and see of what avail they may not become to his friends, his country, and his God.

In order to the right performance of this, self-study is indispensably necessary, that he may if practicable acquaint himself with his peculiar mental and physical abilities, his aptitude to a given end, discover his failings and thereby be saved from mistakes which many have made—namely, such as accrue from a profession illy chosen. It is at all times an arduous task to dwell upon the truly stable and valuable part of life, neglecting many of those fanciful notions and vain aspirations which, however pleasing they may be in the eye of fancy, will nevertheless appear like "the baseless fabric of a vision" before the scrutiny of bold impartial reason. Young men especially are too apt to look only at the wreath of victory, without inquiring into the efforts necessary to insure it, and the laborious preparation for the continued struggle to win a well-merited reward. Dazzled by the brilliant fame of some distinguished personage, they think to equal him, to shine with his luster; and like the peasants of Erin chasing the fleeing *ignis fatuus,* they are left amid disappointments, doubts, and darkness to lament their folly while yet there is room, or find perchance too late that all their hopes were deceitful and their aspirations vain, because the living rock of principle was wanting, because their attempts were not supported by those claims founded upon true merit, religion, and profound learning. Preparation is necessary in every undertaking, and who neglects this must expect to encounter many failures. Southey in a letter to one of his young friends thus speaks: "Read and write. Shoot at a high mark, and you will gain strength of arm. Precision of aim will come in its proper season." Labor is certainly the lot of man here below, and he who looks for happiness and profit elsewhere than in a life of activity and industry—and that in some noble cause—mistakes the nature of his being and the constitution of his frame. Milton has said:

> Man hath his daily work of body or mind
> Appointed, which declares his dignity
> And the regard of Heaven on all his ways;
> While other animals unactive range
> And of their doings, God takes no account.

As far as I know myself, I wish to be of some use in the world, and under the providence of God to be employed by Him for the promotion of His glory, the good of my fellow men, and, my dear parents, for your honor. This latter consideration weighs heavily upon my mind, has hitherto formed the incentive to action, and I hope will ever be cherished with increasing ardor. My highest hope and wish is that I may one of these days be able to give you, my parents, some substantial assurance that your many labors, cares, and anxieties, as well as boundless kindnesses, have not been entirely bestowed in vain. My mind is, you know, turned to the *law* as a profession. Could I become a minister I would esteem it the most exalted and noble office on earth. Yet in law a boundless field lies open for usefulness and honor to him who uses aright the opportunities therein contained. In regard to this matter, however, my views, although at present fixed, are open for advice and change.

Last Sabbath we spent an interesting season in the chapel. Dr. Carnahan delivered his baccalaureate to our class. His remarks were most touching regarding his own declining years; and his kind advice and fatherly counsel came with melting power from those venerable lips. Truly he is a great and good old gentleman. I feel much attached to the majority of the members of the faculty, and to many of the students; and the heart grows sad when it reflects that all these associations and friendships are so soon to be dissolved, nevermore to exist in the same capacity or be renewed save in an incidental manner. College attachments are very strong, and the recollections of them often prove in after life sources of much enjoyment.

Father, I presume you are about leaving for Charleston. I hope that you will there meet with the same cordial welcome, and that your report will command a like regard and consideration, as that which it received last season.

As I wish to write Aunt Betsy, Aunt Susan, Cousin Laura, and my sister, I must now bid you farewell. Brother unites with me in love to you both, dear parents, aunts, cousin, uncle, sister, and all relatives and friends.

Your ever affectionate son,
Charles C. Jones, Jr. (A.B.)

Brother has almost completed his junior orator speech, and I am busy reading. Will have to prepare a speech also for commencement, I presume, so soon as the grades are made out.

Howdy do for all the servants.

My dear Father,

Two weeks have elapsed since we enjoyed the pleasure of receiving a letter from you. Your many engagements of a professional nature as well as of a social are not unknown to us; and although at all times solicitous with reference to frequent communications, still we are fully aware of the responsible duties which at this particular season are incumbent upon you, and resort for comfort to the old motto: "No news, good news." The General Assembly is now in session, I presume; and as you see, I have directed this letter to Charleston, and hope that your report of the present year will command a like regard as that presented at St. Louis.

Our final senior examination is over, and the major part of the class have left Princeton, some for their homes, others for recreation in traveling, etc. This stay or rather vacation of five weeks affords a fine opportunity for reading and the preparation of a speech for commencement, and I purpose to improve the occasion.

American history and the lives of the great and good of this our favored land possess countless charms for me; and I have accordingly commenced the perusal of the biographies of the most prominent characters who have assisted in rearing this mighty republic, and have left their deeds and names everlastingly associated with all that is noble and praiseworthy. We possess not the long lines of regal potentates claimed by other people beyond the waters; our institutions and public places wear not that garb of venerable antiquity which they boast; yet the heroes we worship were men actuated by no love of kingly honors. They appeared not as claiming authority by virtue of hereditary rank or royal lineage, but they came forth as the peoples' representatives, pure in heart, with singleness of aim, relying upon the justice of their cause and their native talents for any and every promotion. Although our national history is thus comparatively limited, and our public characters few, still it and they form glorious exemplars for imitation, and subjects worthy the severe study and admiration of all their descendants.

Few appreciate aright or understand the comprehensive nature of our Constitution, and know the just applications of its regulations; hence the necessity for such as may not prove *confounders* but true *expounders* of its glorious principles. How can we in the smallest degree, or with the slightest propriety, lay claim to the office of such if we be not conversant with the lives and opinions of those who were the fathers of it? It is a pity and serious evil that its great principles have of late been so much prostituted to suit the ends of designing men and support the pretensions of those whose aims are really in direct opposition to its spirit.

I have just finished *The Life of William Wirt,* by Kennedy, in two volumes. Every young man who anticipates engaging in the study of law should read it carefully. His letters to Mr. Gilmer, who was under his care, are fraught with ennobling principles, and clearly point out to the young lawyer the only sure way whereby he may merit distinction and pursue his profession with assurance of success. Wirt certainly held the pen of a ready and gifted writer. His letters are model performances, evincing an extended knowledge of classical literature and a familiar acquaintance with standard authors. His versatility of talent is surprising; at one time he deals in the wise counsels of Latin sages, again treats of the engaging scenes of the day with the clear conceptions of a true philosopher; and again, dismissing all technicalities, he indulges in a freedom of intercourse, and with a youthful vivacity and kindness which shows how tenderly alive his heart was to every affection. Although too free in his company and not sufficiently guarded in his morals when a young man, still after his second marriage he became a devoted husband, one of the most loving fathers, and, as he himself hopes, a pious man. The fact of his being a poor boy and an orphan at an early age, together with the knowledge that severe application and merit alone raised him to that high and responsible station the duties of which he so long discharged—and that with such honor to himself and country—invests his every act and triumph with a charm; and at every step we feel desirous that he will bear off that palm which we know his due preparation and fine acquirements may justly claim. Effort—renewed effort—forms the burden of every hour. In one of his letters we find this sentiment, which I hope will not prove uninteresting to you, as it is frequently breathed in his correspondence with young men, whom he desired to stimulate to strenuous and continued exertions:

I have formed in my own imagination a model of professional greatness which I am far—very far—below, but to which I shall never cease to aspire. It is to this model that I compare myself whenever the world applauds, and the comparison humbles me to the dust. If ever I should rise to this imaginary prototype, I shall rest in peace. Herculean enterprise! But I will not despair, since it is only by aiming at perfection that a man can attain his highest practicable point.

Here, then, we find one great secret of his professional advancement and rapidly increasing fame. Again, we behold him in his letters to his children conveying advice and counsel in a beautiful manner. For example, in writing to his daughter he speaks thus:

The way to make yourself pleasing to others is to show that you care for them. The whole world is like the miller of Mansfield, "who cared for nobody—no, not he—because nobody cared for him." And the world will serve you so, if you give them the same cause. Let everyone, therefore, see that you care for them by showing them what Sterne so happily calls "the small, sweet courtesies of life"—those courtesies in which there is no parade; whose voice is too still to tease; and which manifest themselves by tender and affectionate looks, and little kind acts of attention, giving others the preference in every little enjoyment at the table, in the field, walking, sitting, or standing.

In such private interviews we trace the quiet, unostentatious communings of his mind; but it is in some important intricate case such as the trial of Aaron Burr, the Mandamus case, etc., where vigorous mental exertion, coupled with profound sagacity and an intimate acquaintance with the intricacies of law as a science, are required, that we must see and admire William Wirt as the attorney general of the United States. We need only see to praise. Never an office-seeker, he had always at his command high appointments, tendered by Presidents Monroe, Jefferson, and others high in authority. Did you know that the presidency of the Virginia University and the department of law were offered him by the latter of these distinguished statesmen?

Father, I could protract these remarks to an almost indefinite extent, yet I fear that I am trespassing upon your time and patience. If, however, they serve to beguile a few moments, they will have accomplished all I can desire.

It is Saturday evening, and I will leave my paper for a few moments, to be resumed so soon as I return from the post office, as I have a strong presentiment that there are some lines there from those whom we love best.

Agreeably to my expectations here comes a letter from my dear mother, bearing news at once welcome and sad. How I regret, my dear parent, that you have been laid upon a bed of sickness just at the season when I had hoped that you were in a measure at least regaining that strength and health which had been so seriously impaired by long confinement and continuous labor in Philadelphia. You are not now able to endure the heat of the sun or breathe the air of the ricefields with the same impunity with which you once could. The white and tender plant of the hothouse, reared and nourished by artificial means, cannot withstand the warm rays of midsummer, and pines away under influences which naturally would conduce to its growth and increase. Father, I wish that you would follow the advice of Dr. Jackson and dismiss for some length of time all care from your mind, husbanding the lamp of life in order that at some future day it may burn with a brighter and more enduring ray.

What do you think of my becoming a teacher for a year or so previous to entering upon a profession? It might be advantageous in some respects; and then it may be better to enter at once with assiduity and ardor upon the study of my profession, looking to God for help and instruction.

Father, your system requires rest; and that you are full well persuaded of, especially now when the physical man is not alone the affected part, but the whole soul is melted down with sorrow at this our recent affliction. How hard my heart is! I cannot feel it as I ought; yet I will pray the Lord to sanctify it to me, to impress it hourly upon my thoughts, to make me feel my own unworthiness and liability to death at any hour, in order that I may no longer put my trust in sublunary things, which pass away like the early dew and have no abiding inheritance, but be found trusting in Him who is the "Rock of Ages," the Ever-Living God, the Father of Abraham and all other Christians together with their seed. What is man in life devoid of a real, true religious principle? A ship without a rudder, tossed about by every wind of doctrine; and the worst is, that although good works may be on board, still there is no final haven where it may ride in safety when the voyage be run.

How necessary that a lawyer especially should be a devout follower of the Lord Jesus! He is apt, unless supported by divine help, to forget that nice perception of truth and duty, that conscientious regard for and scrupulous adherence to the requirements of religion and experimental Christianity; for at the present day there are so many pettifoggers and even men of talent who, judging by their actions, seem only intent upon making the wrong appear the better side, that it requires more than unaided human nature can give to preserve a mind uncontaminated and a "conscience void of offence" towards God and man. If I am ever permitted to be a lawyer, may I be a pious lawyer!

It was with great pleasure that I read your mention, Mother, of the very honorable appointment of Uncle Henry as a delegate to the Baltimore Convention. The choice could not have been wiser, and I hope that he will let us see honorable mention made of him, that he has shown himself a firm defender of the Democratic faith, etc., etc. Merit will meet its reward, although for a time party spirit and ungenerous chicanery prevail; for the principles of right and manly conduct are more lasting than the evanescent triumphs and boasts of the vulgar.

Miss Jane Comfort is not now in Princeton, yet it is probable that she will return in a few weeks; and then, Mother, I will comply with your request by the earliest opportunity. The presence of Uncle Berrien and Aunt Marion will add much to our enjoyment; and Brother and myself must try and not give you, my dear parents, and our relatives any cause to be ashamed of us. On Monday morning, if nothing prevents, I will see Mrs. Van Dyke and let her know your determination. I think it very probable that you will be able even after the lapse of several weeks to secure the same rooms, and will in the event again make application at any time that you may desire.

Our campus now looks beautifully. Summer has completely usurped the throne of spring, and the trees are already robed in their richest green.

Father, I addressed this letter to you intending to direct it to Charleston. Yet as I find that you are still in Liberty, I will change its place of destination. Mother, you and Father are "no more twain, but one flesh," and therefore it is needless for me to say that I now write to you both. Hoping that you will excuse the lengthened and wandering pen of your son, I remain, with dearest love to you both, my parents, aunts, cousin, sister, uncle and all relatives and friends, in which Brother unites,

Your affectionate son,
Charles C. Jones, Jr.

P.S. I hope that you received the *four* letters written last Tuesday. Howdy to all the servants.

REV. C. C. JONES *to* MRS. MARY JONES[t]

Charleston, *Saturday,* May 22nd, 1852

My dearest Wife,

We had a load down to Savannah yesterday: Mr. King and family, Mr. Axson and party, Dr. King and two others and myself. At Bailey's we had to refuse taking Miss Rosa McAllister and Miss Avery. However, a pleasant but dusty ride. At the Pulaski saw Miss Emma McAllister, just on from New Haven. Mrs. Clay *altogether better;* Miss Eliza with her, but still troubled to know *"what to do."* How this troubles many! They may put the boys to school somewhere and travel. But Mr. Miller's school seems "too strict." Mrs. Colonel McAllister and Joseph McA. back too.

Tell Sister Augustus is better. Went to see him. Cousin Joe Robarts will send your things out by Monday's stage, and also the likeness of little Mary from Brother John in the same package. All well at Major Porter's who are at home. Mrs. P. up the country. Took tea there. Had no chance of seeing Cousin Dr. West.

Came on board the *Metamora* and started at four this morning. Captain King came *inside,* to our great relief, as far as Port Royal; then when we put out to sea I went into my berth, and did not get up until we were inside Charleston bar, and so escaped seasickness altogether. Several sick on board, though sea not rough. Brother Axson improves, and they have gone up to the Charleston Hotel.

William met me on the wharf and shouldered my trunk. Miss Elizabeth only at home; the other ladies gone to a Sunday school celebration; gave me a most cordial welcome. Dr. Samuel Beach Jones here with crick in his back! Scarcely walks about. I tell him it is gout. Temporary affection, no doubt. Have come up into my pleasant third-story room, washed, dressed clean, got rid of the steamboat; and my first duty is to write to my dear wife. A fine sea breeze fans me while I write, looking over the tops of the houses: two church steeples before me, and all the rattle and noise of the city beneath.

A full assembly. Rev. J. C. Lord, D.D., of Buffalo, New York, moderator. Meet in Dr. Smyth's church. Weather delightful, but dusty. Hope great good will come of this meeting. My report is to be presented on *Tuesday,* 10 A.M.—the regular time. Foreign Missions on Monday; Board of Publication Wednesday.

Feel decidedly better. The sea air was refreshing. Will write you in time for Thursday's mail, God willing. Hope you may get this Monday; it ought to reach you on that day: mailed this afternoon. Kiss my dear child for me. She must take all the horseback exercise she can. Love to my dear sisters and Laura and to Brother. Wish I was with you all. Tell all the servants howdy for me. The Lord watch between us while we are separated the one from the other, and keep and bless you, my dear wife, evermore!

Your affectionate husband,

C. C. Jones.

353

Rev. C. C. Jones *to* Mrs. Mary Jones[t]

Yesterday, my dear wife, was a day of privilege. Heard Rev. S. Robinson of Frankfort, Kentucky, preach on "All things shall work together for good to them that love God," and wished my dear sister and indeed that you all had been here to hear it. It was addressed to the *afflicted*. In the afternoon a sermon from Rev. Drury Lacy of Raleigh on "Come, let us reason together," addressed with much feeling to the impenitent. And in the evening a sermon from Dr. Scott of New Orleans before the Board of Foreign Missions on the power of faith: excellent. I thought much of you and old Midway, and prayed and hoped that you all might have a precious and profitable Communion. Wish I could have been there. Remembered our usual hour and service in the evening.

This morning saw Mr. and Mrs. Newkirk, Mr. and Mrs. Colwell and daughter at the Charleston Hotel, where I called to see Dr. Humphrey on business. All inquired very particularly after you and Sister and Laura; glad to hear they were going back with us.

Have been all day occupied getting the report ready for tomorrow, God willing. Hope it may do good. Have seen very few of the brethren, as I have not been up to the assembly at all. It is said to be a fine assembly. All are delighted with Charleston. May it so continue unto the end! The migratory character of our meetings serves to unite the church and break up *sectionalism*. Have cast all cares upon the Lord, and will endeavor not to move them with one of my fingers. May His fear and glory be ever before my eyes!

Will leave my letter open until tomorrow, D.V.

Tuesday Afternoon. The report was delivered this morning at ten. It took one hour and a half in delivery, and was listened to with marked attention and approbation on the part of the assembly. Many of the brethren congratulated me upon it. My vest and *coat* were soaked through; and came home and changed everything, and lay down for an hour. It was an effort. I asked God's blessing before I went; I commended it to His blessing when I came back.

The assembly moves on pleasantly. Saw many dear friends, male and female; but little opportunity to speak with them in the house. Invited to dine with *Mr. and Mrs. Howe,* but was too tired to go. Defer accounts till we meet, God willing.

Must close, as am obliged to go up to the assembly on business. The ladies unite in much love to you. They are as kind as ever, and grow better with time. Love to my dear daughter. Howdy for all the servants. Love to my dear sisters and Laura and Brother. Hope to leave on Saturday for Savannah, and be out Monday

Your ever affectionate husband,
C. C. Jones.

Rev. C. C. Jones *to* Messrs. Charles C. Jones, Jr., *and* Joseph Jones^g

Charleston, *Friday,* May 28th, 1852

My dear Sons,

I have been in attendance upon the meeting of the General Assembly since Tuesday last. Arrived here Saturday afternoon, May 22nd, but was engaged Monday preparing report. Went up to the assembly Tuesday, and at 10 A.M. delivered our annual report—a portion of it *read*. It was received with marked attention, and so far as we have heard, with universal approbation; and the concluding resolution of the report of the committee to whom the annual report of the board was referred is in these words: "Resolved, That the warmest thanks of the assembly are due to the Rev. C. C. Jones and the Board of Missions for the energy and zeal and good judgment with which their whole work has been prosecuted during the past year. And the assembly would further express its special gratification with the enlarged and liberal views of this great subject presented in the annual report." Such a resolution is uncommon. It is a matter of thankfulness if we have been enabled to perform the duties assigned us successfully and to the satisfaction of the church.

The meeting of the assembly has been a pleasant one. Its composition unusually good. All the delegates from the *free* states *delighted*. The meeting of the assembly in the various sections of the United States has done a great deal to promote harmony, brotherly love, allay jealousies and prejudices, and promote the welfare not only of the church but of the whole country. We meet next year in Buffalo, New York: a long step off. Have seen a great many friends. People are in from all parts of the state to see the assembly: Dr. Leland and Dr. Howe and their families, all the seminary students. Many kind inquiries after you both. Mrs. Macfie and daughters down also. Much business has been done by the assembly. The citizens have attended all the meetings in considerable numbers. Dr. Maclean is a conspicuous and useful member. Says he is glad to see Joe stand so high in mental and moral science. Received the *circular* day before yesterday.

Mr. Dubuar is here, looking remarkably well, and says he has two daughters and one son. Family all well, and he has a good settlement in Michigan. Desires to be particularly remembered to you, and looked out at the Princeton depot to see you as he passed. I told him you were not often there unless it was to go on a journey somewhere.

Mr. King and all his family have sailed by this time for the North. Your aunt and uncle go up the country in July, and your Aunt Susan and Cousin Laura return with us, God willing. . . . We hope to be in time to hear you both speak. Your Uncle Henry has gone on to attend the Baltimore Democratic Convention, and says he means to call through Princeton and see you. It will be a pleasant meeting to you.

My visit to Liberty has been exceedingly agreeable. The people black and white all say: "Come back." But had a fever from overexercise and exposure that pulled me down. Am recruiting again. Hope to leave in the morning, spend Sabbath in Savannah, go out Monday and meet Mother at Montevideo. Our time for leaving Liberty is the 15th of June.

Mr. Peace has not acted very well in his attentions to a certain relative of ours. Wrote him a note on the subject.

Your aunt and cousin are greatly afflicted! They were much gratified with Joe's letter. We must do all we can for them. Have to administer on your cousin's estate.

Am staying with our old friends the Miss Jones, who are as kind as relatives, and have given me a fine airy room all alone. Charleston is decidedly improving.

Last Sabbath must have been a most interesting day at Midway. It was Communion, and *four young men* were received into the church: Mr. Quarterman Baker's two sons and Mr. Thomas Cassels' son and Robert Mallard. One or more of them will study for the ministry! The Lord guide you, my dear sons, into the way of life and usefulness! As ever,

Your affectionate father,
C. C. Jones.

Dr. E. P. Humphrey, of Louisville, Kentucky, moderator of the last assembly, has been elected to fill the professorship in Princeton Theological Seminary vacated by the death of Dr. Alexander. A very good choice, I imagine, on the whole.

C. C. J.

MR. CHARLES C. JONES, JR., *to* REV. *and* MRS. C. C. JONES[t]

Princeton, *Wednesday,* June 2nd, 1852

My dear Father,

Your kind and highly prized letter of May 28th came safely to hand, and for its receipt I feel much indebted to you. It was with great pleasure that we learned of the happy presentation of your report, and the honorable testimonials of regard and respect which it drew from the General Assembly. The resolution was couched in very flattering terms, and the entire reception must have proved highly gratifying to you after a year of so much care and responsibility. You speak of the kind attentions which have been universally paid to the delegates by the citizens of Charleston. It has always seemed a capital arrangement to me, this of convening the assembly in the several parts of our country alternately. Such a distribution tends to bind the whole church in a happy union, divests the members of many local prejudices, acquaints them with the excellencies of their neighbors, and opens a field more extended in its character both for the exercise of thought and action. I see from the newspapers that Dr. Maclean has had a good deal to say at this meeting, and I doubt not has enjoyed himself very much. This is his first visit South, and I hope he will be favorably impressed with the citizens, institutions, etc. It must be gratifying to you to meet many of your friends at this

356

time from distant portions of the country, some perhaps whom you would seldom see were it not for this assemblage. To see Mr. Dubuar would recall many pleasant recollections, and we are glad to learn that he is succeeding so well in his labors. Had I known that he was passing through Princeton, I would have tried and welcomed him.

Wrote Uncle Henry last evening, wishing him every success in the maintenance of Democratic principles, and urging upon him a fulfillment of the promise given in Liberty "to stop in Princeton and see the boys."

We regretted sincerely your late indisposition, Father, and hope that your recent exertions will not cause a relapse or prove productive of debility.

It was the opinion of many here that you would have been elected to fill the vacant chair in the seminary; yet I see that you early requested your name to be withdrawn and on that account forbade the votes of many. The professors here are, I have understood, very well pleased with the election of Dr. E. P. Humphrey, and have expressed themselves to that effect. Hope that he will have a little more care for the buildings and external appearance of the grounds than some others, for the whole establishment wears that aspect which was presented by the seminary in Columbia previous to your refittings and arrangements—"only a little more so."

Spent a pleasant afternoon with Miss Comfort yesterday, and spoke long of our deceased relative, recalling many pleasant recollections, reviewing all the scenes which transpired in Morristown. She and her father are both residing now in Princeton. They have a pleasant retired situation, a little removed from the town, on the Trenton road. Miss Comfort requests that you would remain with her during commencement, as she will be able to accommodate you very conveniently, and will be very happy if you comply with her invitation. A similar invitation is offered by Professor and Mrs. McCulloh.

Quite a difference of opinion prevails here with respect to the nomination of the Democratic Convention. Many think that the delegates will play the Polk game over again and bring forward some person who is at present little thought of. Whoever the successful nominee may be, I hope at all events that we will be able to elect him—and that triumphantly. The Democratic flag which has so often floated in victory must not now be suffered to droop in defeat, if wise counsels and strenuous efforts can insure success.

We were surprised to hear of Mr. Peace's renewed and ill-timed approaches, and hope that your "note" on the subject will cause a return of right reason, which apparently has quite deserted him.

Hoping to see you before many weeks elapse, I remain, with warmest love, in which Brother unites,

Your affectionate son,
Charles C. Jones, Jr.

Have not heard from Liberty for two weeks, although I wrote five letters there last week.

Princeton, *Friday,* June 4th, 1852

My dear Mother,

I this evening received the very interesting letters from Cousin Laura and Sister, with the note from my dear Aunt Susan. They were truly gratifying, and it will afford me much pleasure to return speedy answers.

A few days since I spent an hour or two with Miss Comfort, who you know is now a resident of Princeton with her venerable father. It was with sincere feeling that she conversed of our departed cousin, recalling all his virtues and noble traits, mentioning many personal acts, and reviewing again the mournful scenes of Morristown. Hers is a tender heart, and his image is tenderly as well as closely cherished in her memory. She showed me a likeness of Cousin Charlie which was given her by Father or yourself in Philadelphia and very highly prized. Mr. Comfort remarked: "That funeral was an uncommon one for Morristown. The people never saw so large a one before, or experienced such sympathies for a stranger." Miss Comfort wishes that you all would make her house your home at commencement. Mrs. McCulloh also extends to you a similar invitation.

On Wednesday a terrible storm passed over Princeton. The day had been very warm and sultry, and late in the evening the heat had abated but little, when a thundercloud arose, accompanied by much wind and charged heavily with electricity. The magnets and ends of the telegraphic wires at the depot were melted by the lightning; and in the campus several of our large and beautiful trees were seriously injured, some of them losing nearly every limb. The one just before our window had all its top and branches on one side twisted off, thus becoming little more than a mere trunk. I was watching the storm at the instant and happened to be looking at the tree, and the wind appeared to tear it apart as easily as we would a blade of grass. It is in such grand displays as this that man learns practically his own insignificance and the infinite power of Jehovah. I could but think as I sat alone in my room what a paradox man is—at once the creature of a moment, liable at any moment to be carried away by a thousand physical causes, and at the same time an heir of immortality, and by the exercise of his mental faculties the controller in a measure of the rest of creation.

Have been much interested in the proceedings of the Baltimore Convention. It seems impossible to conjecture with any degree of certainty who the successful candidate will be. Before this reaches you I presume the choice will be made, and I hope that the victory of the Democratic party will be certain and glorious. Mr. Buchanan is my choice, and Mr. Douglas next. It was with much pleasure that we learned from your letter that Uncle Henry was one of the delegates. My wish for him is that this may only prove an earnest of future preferment. Judge Charlton's appointment was a wise choice, for he has as sound a head and as firm a character, as well as devotion to true Democratic principles, as any person in the state whom we could honor with a seat in our high national convention.

Have lately been perusing the lives of the orators of the American Revolution. Seldom do we find at any one period such an array of talent, such intrepid action, or such precious models for the imitation of the young, as were then presented. What an example of stern true patriotism and devotion to the calls of country does the life of P. Henry exhibit! We should have seen him when he knew that he spoke under the scaffold, when British cannon were booming in the North, and standing in the outlawed Assembly of Virginia, like a lion at bay, he caught the first cry of distress from Lexington and Bunker Hill. With a generous devotion that made no reserve and knew no fear; with a voice solemn, tremulous with patriotic rage, and "swelling over the thrilled audience like a trumpet call to arms"; and with an eye flashing unutterable fire, he exclaimed: "Give me liberty, or give me death!"

Would that at this present time more of this spirit of '76 could be seen in the actions of both private and public individuals! Then would the blind devotee of chance and the vacillating expectant of popular favor shrink abashed before the presence of the truly acting and thinking man. We have in this present day too many who proclaim more wise sayings than ever Socrates dreamed of; and yet how few ever mold these vain imaginings into the forms of sober, living realities. Whether we consider the characters of a Jay, Otis, Hamilton, Warren, Hancock, or an Adams at the bar, in the cabinet, or on the field, they were still the generous foes, the peerless knights, the bold representatives of noble principles *sans peur et sans reproche.* Wherever the strong arm was needed, or the gallant heart, or the eloquent tongue to smite down the oppressor or to raise up the fallen, the first names called upon for the redress of wrongs and the vindication of rights were these and others of like stamp. Lord Chatham in a speech delivered in the House of Lords thus speaks of the acts and official efforts of our great men: "When you consider their decency, firmness, and wisdom, you cannot but respect their cause and wish to make it your own. For myself, I must declare and avow that in all my reading—and it has been my favorite pursuit—that for solidity of reasoning, force of sagacity, and wisdom of conclusion, under all the circumstances, no nation or body of men can stand in preference to the general congress at Philadelphia." If this be the opinion of the distinguished English statesman, how should we emulate their examples and study deeply their acts and those pure motives which proved the controlling passions of their illustrious lives!

My subject for the senior stage is "Action in America." They tell me that I was one of the prominent candidates for the valedictory; yet this honor was awarded to Dr. Magie's son because of his higher grades and longer connection with the institution. There are several in our class who, I am persuaded, can do much better than he; yet let me in no manner detract from his honors.

Wrote Uncle Henry on Tuesday urging upon him a fulfillment of his promise "to see the boys in Princeton," and wishing him every success in the support of Democratic principles.

I am afraid I always tire by my long letters, and therefore will close, with best love to you, my dear mother, father, sister, aunts, cousin, uncle, and all friends. Brother unites.

Your own son,
Charles C. Jones, Jr.

P.S. Wrote Father on Wednesday and directed the letter to Charleston. During the meeting of the General Assembly we anxiously noticed every item of importance as presented by the Charleston *Standard*. It was thought by many that Father would be the successful candidate, yet I see he did not suffer his name to stand in nomination. Received a very interesting letter from him yesterday. The citizens of Charleston must have been very hospitable, and no doubt the impression formed upon the Northern delegates was highly agreeable. Such an effect is happy, and conduces much to the union of the various branches of the church. Dr. Maclean figured largely, and will doubtless return in a fine humor and "full of talk." The resolution with regard to Father's report must have been gratifying to him, and was in fact an unusually flattering compliment. Will write again soon.

Your affectionate son,
Charles C. Jones, Jr.

Respects to all friends.
Howdy for the servants.

MRS. MARY JONES *to* MR. CHARLES C. JONES, JR.[g]

Maybank, Friday, June 4th, 1852

My dear Son,

I must congratulate you upon the result of your final examination—honorable to yourself and satisfactory to your parents. Yes, my dear child, *your mother blesses you* for all your filial love and kindness, and that during the whole of your college course you have never caused one pang to her anxious bosom either by neglect of your studies, by extravagance, insubordination, dissipation, or immorality; but on the contrary she has rejoiced and rendered grateful thanks often to her Father in Heaven for preserving your footsteps in the paths of truth and honor.

One of the most interesting periods of your life has now passed—*beyond recall,* I was going to say, but I trust not. You have been gathering mental stores for the necessities of future years, and have, I hope, laid up the incorruptible treasures of true wisdom and knowledge. I have no doubt that you have formed many warm friendships, and in after life your college days will be linked with tender and interesting associations. From the classic walls of Old Nassau, from youthful associates and loved pursuits, you will very soon pass to the arena of life—no longer under "tutors and governors," directed and guarded by parental counsel and control, *but a man,* thrown upon your own responsibility, *rising or falling from your own principles and conduct, your character* as known and read of all men in your daily walk and conversation. My own dear Charles, one only grief—and that the greatest—fills my heart. You have never yet whispered to my longing ears: "Mother, *I love my Saviour*. I trust His Blood has cleansed away my sins. His grace renewed my heart. I will profess His name. I will devote myself to His service." God enable you, my child, from the heart to do this without delay! I know that He is a faithful covenant-keeping God. I believe His promises, and I wait for His salvation.

Your kind and affectionate letter to your afflicted aunt and cousin is highly prized by them—also your brother's—and your letter to your uncle and aunty. Such expressions of affection and sympathy from you both, who must now strive in some degree to fill the place of the departed, are very satisfactory to their sad hearts. Today the trunks and box arrived at the Bluff. All that they have *heard* must have seemed to be an idle tale compared to these memorials of the dead. Oh, how I dread myself to look again upon them!

Your dear father has had so much to do that he has had no time for rest or improvement. On Monday he goes up to Hinesville on the business of the *estate,* for which I copied for him today twelve pages of foolscap—which makes my hand so stiff that I write with difficulty tonight. . . .

Providence permitting, your aunt and cousin expect to leave the county with us on Tuesday the 15th for Philadelphia, that we may have ample time for reaching Princeton, if prospered, before commencement. Will write of our movements. The servants inquire constantly with great interest of your brother and yourself, and send many howdies. *Little Jack* is our waiting man. It is Saturday night, and I will leave the last page for your father on Monday. May you both, my dear children, be prepared for the rest of the holy Sabbath Day! With love from Father and Sister and that of

Your affectionate mother,
Mary Jones.

Mrs. Mary Jones *to* Messrs. Charles C. Jones, Jr., *and* Joseph Jones[g]

Maybank, *Thursday,* June 10th, 1852

My dear Sons,

Your father left so early Monday morning that the letter was forgotten. Your uncle called for him by five o'clock. They reached Hinesville at half-past ten o'clock, and he returned to the Island that night—a distance of fifty-two miles; your father remaining at Arcadia, where he held a meeting for the people, and the next night did the same at Montevideo.

It has been a great source of gratitude to our Heavenly Father that so many from Arcadia have within eighteen months professed religion and seem to be walking worthy of the Christian name—all connected with Midway Church. *Charles* joined the last Communion. My heart felt bursting with love and thankfulness as I saw the great man kneel as humbly as a child for baptism; a true change seems to have passed over him. Robert Mallard, the two Bakers, and young Cassels also came forward. *To me* it was one of the most touching and interesting occasions I ever witnessed: all in the bloom of youth and vigor of early manhood consecrating their bodies and their spirits to their gracious Saviour!

We are engaged to dine at Social Bluff. It is nearly one o'clock, and I must close. With the blessing of God upon us, we expect to take the stage at Midway Church on Tuesday, and hope to reach Philadelphia by the last of the week. Were it not for the prospect of *seeing my beloved sons* my heart would reluctantly leave these quiet shades, this happy home. All the servants send howdy for you. Father, Sister, and all friends unite in best love to you.

Ever, my dear sons, your affectionate mother,
Mary Jones.

MR. CHARLES C. JONES, JR., *to* REV. *and* MRS. C. C. JONES[g]

Princeton, *Monday,* June 14th, 1852

My dear Parents,

The hour draws near when we shall again meet, and my heart gladdens at the prospect. Locke speaks of "positive ideas from privative causes." This is clearly felt in the case of absent friends, for memory often presents the images of those far away in living characters, recalling all those endeared associations which are calculated to impart action to the scene and transform things past into things present. If there be one thought which more than all others gladdens the heart of the absent, it must be the assurance that they are not forgotten by "the loved ones at home." The poet in alluding to this feeling has beautifully remarked:

> 'Tis sweet to know there is an eye will mark
> Our coming, and look brighter when we come.

If the passion of love be so strong, enduring, and powerful on earth, where frail human nature is liable to so many sinister surmises and miserable weaknesses, what must be the exalted character and matchless purity of that affection which in heaven is known as love! Would that everyone could in reality unite with Wordsworth:

> Love
> Dependent as in part its blessings are
> Upon frail ties, dissolving or dissolved,
> On earth, will be revived, we trust, in heaven.

It seems to me that one of the chief enjoyments of heaven must consist in renewing the pleasant acquaintances once formed yet severed on earth, and in cherishing these with a sanctity of devotion and a purity of affection of which we can at the present time form but a faint yet delightful conception.

This feature of love and universal kindness is also the distinguishing characteristic of the Christian religion—one which composes a wide difference between the paradise of the Mahometan, with its houses and bowers of amaranth, or the Valhalla of Odin, and that "house not made with hands, eternal in the heavens." While in the former the warrior who had perished in battle received golden plumes for every wounded limb and heavenly wings, the poor and friendless dare not hope for those abodes or expect a kindly welcome from the beautiful virgins, the inmates of those fabled palaces. Yet the New Jerusalem has seats prepared for all; and the worthy aspirant needs not the abominable sacrifices or favorable auspices of the Roman, is subject to no vacillating diviners, depends not upon the power of wealth or the victories of a battlefield, but looks for a reward when he has humbly appropriated to himself that Blood of Jesus which "cleanses from all sin." How beautiful and how simple is the Christian dispensation, and how striking the contrast when its regulations are considered with reference to those false rules and standards which are the offspring of human invention and framed by designing imposters to meet the depraved state of man in a way that caters to his passions and allows an exercise of them under the garb of religious rites.

While I write, a funeral is passing. The hearse contains the body of a Mr. Olin, a young man and a graduate of this college. The Whig members are in attendance with their badges, he having formerly belonged to their hall. The universality and certainty of death are fearful truths, and come home with peculiar power to the hearts of those who have but lately felt in family the tread of the last enemy. That lesson was a fearful one, and I desire to carry a lively remembrance of it with me to my tomb. *Pallida mors aeque pede pulsat, pauperum tabernas, regumque turres. Vive memor lethi: fugit hora.*

Have just completed a perusal of Cooper's *Naval History*. The interest which an American reader takes in this book is that of no ordinary character. The history of our struggles both upon land and upon the sea possesses a charm which nothing can borrow, nothing counterfeit. When we recur to these scenes which tried the souls of our ancestors; when we read the burning eloquence of an Otis, or dwell with rapture upon the inspiration of a Henry; when we behold the standard of a Warren full high advanced, and the flag of a Lawrence, although tattered and gory with the blood of dying freemen, still floating freely above the shattered deck; while above all these the eye rests upon the Father of his Country, majestic in person, thought, and daring—then does the bosom swell with the proudest emotions, and we involuntarily exclaim with our honored statesman: "This—this is eloquence, or rather it is something more than all eloquence; it is action—noble, sublime, godlike action." Our entire history, although comparatively short, is still a recital of deeds of surpassing nobleness, of principles gallantly defended and wisely chosen, of an advancement and improvement rarely if ever equaled.

Uncle Henry spent a day with us in Princeton. It was a truly happy meeting, and many were the pleasant topics discussed. From him we learned a full account of all friends in Liberty. I am perfectly surprised and vexed at Mr. Peace's ridiculous and outrageous behavior. Surely he must be suffering from a softening of the brain. Yet my cousin has her guardians, and the "youth" shall be made to know his proper place. Uncle Henry is now in Saratoga. We paid him every attention, and hope that he was very much pleased with his visit.

Hoping to see you all soon, I remain, my dear parents, with warmest love to selves, Aunts Susan and Betsy, Cousin, Sister, Uncle, and all friends, in which Brother unites,

Your affectionate son,
Charles C. Jones, Jr.

Commencement occurs on the last day of June.

If Mr. Pierce is elected, I want to get the appointment of secretary of legation to some country of Europe. I expect to take the stump during the canvass.

Howdy for all the servants.

REV. C. C. JONES *to* MESSRS. CHARLES C. JONES, JR., *and* JOSEPH JONES[g]

Philadelphia, Saturday, June 19th, 1852

We arrived here, my dear sons, yesterday about one o'clock, thus by the new arrangement bringing us some twelve hours in advance of the old arrangement, and saving one whole night's riding—to which we had no objection. All well, but fatigued. Your Aunt Susan and Cousin Laura feel their return to the Markoe very much. Their affliction is great and permanent. Where they will spend the summer is not yet determined—chiefly here, perhaps.

Our visit home has been in many respects pleasant, and hope profitable in many ways. But I was too much occupied to recruit much, though I have, through God's blessing, improved some.

Your letters all reached us in Liberty, and afforded us great satisfaction. Nothing fills the hearts of your parents with more delight and gratitude than to hear of your health and prosperity, and above all of your good conduct and character. We are anticipating in prayer and faith the day when you will both embrace truly and heartily the Lord your Redeemer. We never can be at rest until we have good hope of your salvation.

All your relatives inquired most particularly after your welfare, and were glad to hear that you were doing well. And the people all sent howdy for you, and say you must make haste and come home. They are generally well, and appear to be doing well. County healthy. Crops of cotton tolerable: somewhat injured by cold in the spring. Corn crops very promising. The climate both at Montevideo and Maybank was delightful, and the quiet refreshing.

Dr. Maclean very politely invited me to come with my family to his house at commencement. We know how hospitable a man he is, and should not like to trespass upon his kindness, nor be in the way of friends who have a stronger and prior claim on him. I do not know exactly what to do. You can tell him delicately what I say, and let me have his answer. Your aunt and cousin, I think, will come up too; in that case we will have to make some

364

other arrangement perhaps—at least for a part of us. Are Mrs. Van Dyke's rooms taken? Could she accommodate us for a few days at commencement should your aunt and cousin conclude to be present?

Write us particularly next week. Your mother and sister and aunt and cousin all unite in sincere love to you. Hoping to see you soon, I remain, my dear sons,

Your ever affectionate father,
C. C. Jones.

P.S. Do you want any *money?* Let me know at once if you do.

Mr. CHARLES C. JONES, JR., *to* REV. *and* MRS. C. C. JONES[t]

Princeton, *Thursday,* June 24th, 1852

My dear Parents,

After bidding you farewell at the Markoe I reached the boat in due season en route for Princeton. One of the first passengers on whom my eye rested was our respected friend Dr. Maclean. He remarked that he had twice called at your office in order to see you, and I doubt not insist upon the acceptance of his kind offer to make his house your home at commencement. One of his first inquiries was: "Well, I hope your friends will all stay with me next week?" I informed him of your determination, upon which he expressed his pleasure. We conversed until the boat reached Tacony, when we parted, the doctor proceeding farther up the river to Bordentown. The cars arrived in Trenton at half-past four, and there I found a hack just starting for Princeton and of course secured a seat. After a pleasant ride of two hours we saw the shady streets of this little town. . . .

Today several mowers are in the campus, cutting the grass, which is now some two feet in length. It will appear quite prettily when you reach Princeton. We will try and have everything ready for your visit, and I hope you will not be disappointed in the performances.

The road from Trenton to this village is the same as that traveled by Mercer and his division during the Revolution, and you pass directly over the battlefield. The coachman was formerly a resident of Georgia, and drove a line of stages from Brunswick to Mobile. He was in Florida during the Indian War, and was communicative on the subject.

Hoping, my dear parents, to see you next week, I will close, as the mail is almost starting. With warmest love to you both, my dear aunt, cousin, and sister, I remain

Your devoted son,
Charles C. Jones, Jr.